PUERTO RICO

GRAND CUISINE OF THE CARIBBEAN

PUERTO RICO

GRAND CUISINE OF THE CARIBBEAN

JOSÉ L. DÍAZ DE VILLEGAS

PHOTOGRAPHY JOCHI MELERO MUÑOZ

DESIGN JOSÉ L. DÍAZ DE VILLEGAS FREYRE

TRANSLATED BY MADELEINE COLÓN

EDUPR

UNIVERSITY OF PUERTO RICO PRESS
SAN JUAN, PUERTO RICO

Puerto Rico, Grand Cuisine of the Caribbean, by José L. Díaz de Villegas

ISBN 0-8477-0415-7

Photography: Jochi Melero
Design: José L. Díaz de Villegas Freyre

LA EDITORIAL DE LA UNIVERSIDAD DE PUERTO RICO
P.O. Box 23322
San Juan, Puerto Rico 00931-3322
www.laeditorialupr.org

Printed in Italy

First printing

To Madame Villón, who has shared every moment.
J L D V

Dedicated to the light and the ancient fire and to those who have
guided me to its knowledge, Arturo Melero and Aida Muñoz,
patient magicians of the mysteries of photography and of cooking.
J M M

To my mother and father, Graziella and José Luis,
with eternal thanks.
J L D V F

Organic arugula in Dong Nguyen's farm, in Barranquitas.

CONTENTS

PROLOGUE I

ERIC RIPERT

EXECUTIVE CHEF AND PARTNER,
LE BERNARDIN, NEW YORK

In 1986, my dear friend Alfredo Ayala extended an invitation to me that I couldn't resist: to spend a month of vacation in San Juan. In exchange for Alfredo's hospitality, I organized Bastille Day dinner at his Ali-Oli Restaurant and gave a few classes. This was the beginning of my love affair with Puerto Rico, its people, and its culture.

I was very surprised to see so many beautiful and abundant fresh fruits and vegetables. I loved the folklore around the *kioskos*. In Piñones, I ate hundreds of *alcapurrias, bacalaitos* and *mofongos*. Alfredo and his friends guided me through *lechoneras*, as well as markets and small restaurants, educating me on the food culture of the island. I stayed in El Yunque and Dorado, visited Rincón, Aguadilla, Ponce…I even tried to dance salsa in every town.

After eighteen years of finding great excuses to return to Puerto Rico every year, whether it be for attending charity fundraisers, producing a chapter for my own cookbook, or visiting my friends and family (I married a Puerto Rican), I now consider myself a veteran of the island, especially when it comes to cuisine.

Typical island cuisine is always very good, of course, but generally it is not refined, since home-style recipes are dominant. Today, all over the world, regional cooking provides inspiration for chefs. Yet, many moons ago, continental cuisine dictated what chefs prepared for their guests, wherever they were cooking. It didn't matter if you were in San Juan,

Miami or London-food was uninspired. What a pity that all the wonderful local produce-all the roots of Caribbean, Latino and ethnic cuisine-were totally ignored and overlooked!

Nowadays many extremely creative and talented chefs draw inspiration from Puerto Rico's bounty, and they are reinventing their own cuisine. They select the best ingredients locally and import what they are missing to create an intelligent fusion between their own heritage and Eastern or Western influence. Cooking is lighter but flavors are still intense; presentations are important as well. Their cooking is a tribute not only to their own culture, ingredients, farmers and growers, but also to Mother Earth.

This beautiful compilation of recipes is the reflection of today's talented Puerto Rican chefs. Chef Alfredo Ayala, who pioneered this revolution, and José Luis Díaz de Villegas (Paco Villón), who defended and fostered this revolution through his articles in the press, should be proud.

This is the cuisine of Puerto Rico at its best.

PROLOGUE II

SANTI SANTAMARIA

COOK, CAN FABES,

SANT CELONI, BARCELONA

My friend, an admired writer and artist, Paco Villón has honored me by entrusting me with the prologue to a cookbook, a contemporary Puerto Rican book "cooked up" by the professional chefs who preside over the island's best restaurants. I am both pleased and grateful.

Puerto Rico, the Grand Cuisine of the Caribbean, is a book in which the cooks reveal their secrets; their voices identify and describe modern Caribbean cuisine of a certain moment. I am convinced that this is a seminal work. Furthermore, this book will acquaint people with a culinary reality that is still unknown to many gastronomes and globetrotters. Its splendid images are a beautiful reflection of a gastronomic reality of unstoppable vitality and enthusiasm. These lines are meant to share my passion for cooking with all those people that I have had the immense pleasure of meeting, and whose generosity has touched me. To me, Puerto Rico has seemed like a diamond in the rough. To the extent that it is possible for a visitor, we have been able to gain insight on the island with our friends and family, and to become impassioned by its character, which has infused us with the desire to partake of its life.

As often happens to those of us who are cooks, more than discovering a style of cooking, our true pleasure lies in savoring the work with all of our senses. I'll never forget that afternoon spent at the Luquillo kiosks, tasting fritters so pleasurable that I treasure the memory.

Today's modern cuisine is undergoing an authentic conceptual revolution, both aesthetic and practical, in which the artisans of the kitchen are being transformed into true creators. Just leafing through this cookbook, one can begin to understand this revolution in the culinary arts. The social recognition that a cook enjoys today was unthinkable decades ago. This progress is due first of all to the cooks' efforts, but it is also undoubtedly also due to the work of all of those who have contributed to disseminating those efforts. Writers, journalists, gastronomes, and editors have achieved a just recognition for cooking as one more of the arts.

In such a globalized world, it is difficult for the Puerto Rican kitchen to retain its personality, not only because powerful economies impose their norms of dietary behavior, but also because the professional world influences society with culinary styles that deviate from tradition. I could not imagine a Puerto Rico without enjoying its particular culinary art of pork. Your culture, dear friends, tastes of *chicharrón*. Whoever has not savored it at a roadside stand, has never really ever been on the island.

Much is said about fusion cooking, when the Puerto Rican kitchen is an authentic example of what fusion should be. Local cooks have had the spirit to strengthen their authentic cultural values, to delve deeply into them and cherish them.

Thus, ancient Taino cookery lives on in products of today's Puerto Rican kitchen, adapted to today's palates, with the inclusion of the *ñame*, of African origin, and the sweet patato (Ipomoea batata) and cassava (Manihot utilissima), of Caribbean origin, all prepared with techniques contributed by the Spanish colonists, such as the sofrito.

A stewed meat, with rice and beans, always transports us to *criollo* cooking. Culinary Puerto Rico has its traditions, its leitmotifs, and its delicious *sorullos* (corn fritters), that accompany the delicious fish served on the southern coasts. What wisdom in a *serenata*, some tomatoes, or a *yautía* (tanier)! The ecclesiastic calendar, as in Europe, has marked a very particular recipe group.

I write this prologue while enjoying a *longaniza* from my beloved Catalonia, during an insufferably hot evening, and if I close my eyes, I can imagine myself strolling through Old San Juan, savoring a rum, looking forward to a friend's party where we'll eat rice with pigeon-peas.

When I come to Puerto Rico, I make a point of visiting the Pablo Casals Museum. My devotion to the master is so great that I believe that all citizens of the world share a deep and close kinship with the land of Puerto Rico. Casals' music stimulates our complicity in an ode to freedom and plea for justice for all human beings. If we cooks, the men and women of the kitchen, could achieve through our dishes that other human beings create new "Cants dels ocells" that would warm the hard-hearted powerful, we would be far happier than we seem now.

The cooks of Puerto Rico, those featured in this magnificent book, as well as those whose work is yet to come, or the anonymous contributors to an unprejudiced style of cooking, with its own identity, in contrast to Inquisitorial censure, are an essential part of the culture of a people. We would be wise not to forget this vital cultural expression; it is not a question of ephemera as some assert; culinary culture is comparable to language. Culinary practice is a memory handed-down as a highly valued treasure, a part of the cultural heritage of humanity.

We celebrate the publication of this book for its affirmation of the right to be different and to demonstrate solidarity, for being what we are, for not ceasing to be like our Puerto Rican cooks, who share all their knowledge, feelings, and truths, whose work stimulate us to be happier.

My compliments to the chefs: Wilo Benet, Mark French, Mario Pagán, José Rey, José Santaella, Augusto Schreiner, Franco Seccarelli, Daniel Vasse, and Aaron Wratten.

ACKNOWLEDGEMENTS

THE MOST IMPORTANT HERITAGE

We would like to thank all the people and institutions that have helped this book become a reality. This project was born of a vision of Puerto Rico's place in the world culinary culture, and it was made possible thanks to the commitment of many people.

To the president of the University of Puerto Rico, Antonio García Padilla. To the Editorial Board of the Editorial de la Universidad de Puerto Rico, and its president, Ángel Collado Schwartz, for their vision and guidance. To Manuel Sandoval, executive director, and to the entire staff. To the editor Don Jesús Tomé.

Thanks to Santi Santamaria and Eric Ripert, who, in addition to being master chefs, demonstrated their literary skill in the prologues.

To Wilo Benet and Lorraine, Mark French and Melody, Mario Pagán, José Rey and Maximino Rey, José Santaella, Augusto Schreiner and Claudia, Franco Seccarelli and Sandra, Daniel Vasse, Lucette, Frank and Valerie, Aaron Wratten and Wilhem Sack. To the entire staff of the restaurants Pikayo, Mark's at the Meliá, Chayote, Compostela, Augusto's, Il Perugino, Chez Daniel, Horned Dorset Primavera, and Fine Cooking.

This book would not exist without Rosita María González. Her diligence and organization as editorial assistant kept us sane.

To the people that have contributed their recipes and the preparation of dishes: Ramón Carro, of Chef Ramón, in Salinas; Javier and Anina Rojo, of La Mallorquina; Carmen Aboy de Valldejuli, Adita Mattei, Emma Carrasquillo, Mayra Álvarez and Maggie Sáenz, from the Iglesia Bautista de Medianía Alta, Loíza; Doña Palmira Borrás; Doña Marina López; José Campo, general manager, and Mario Ferro, Executive Chef of the Caribe Hilton; Cristóbal Jiménez and his wife Yvonne; Deogracia Méndez and his family, of Millie's Place, in Sabana Seca; Melquiades and José Oscar Tirado Quiñones, of El Mesón de Melquiades, in Jájome; Jesús Pérez and his family, of La Casita Blanca; Don Manolo Ceide, owner, and Frank Cedeño, chef, El Mesón Gallego; Emil Graf, former executive chef of the Caribe Hilton, and Octavio Ravelo, of El Metropol.

To the institutions and persons who granted us permission to reproduce works of art: Instituto de Cultura Puertorriqueña, Museo de Arte de Puerto Rico, Museo de Arte de Ponce, Norman Rockwell Museum, San Diego Museum of Art, Corporación de las Artes Musicales, Familia Meduña-Ferré. To the artists who enthusiastically supported this project: Myrna Báez, Annex Burgos, Luis G. Cajigas, Antonio Martorell, Néstor Otero, Carmelo, and Manolo Sobrino. To Biblioteca Carnegie and Arquetipo for their cooperation.

To Santos Rivera for his executive production and to the staff of Paradiso Films, especially José Vázquez, Karolina Kohkemper, Juan Enrique Figueroa, Jesús Martínez, Ricky Alfaro, Jorge Sosa, Carlos García and Willy Montañez. To Mayna Magruder and Gerardo Calderón, for the art direction and styling of studio photography. To Willy Berríos and Frank Elías, for their beautifully executed additional photography.

To the editors and translators Madeleine Colón, Ann Chevako, Terry Chevako, Holly Wittman, Karen Paddock, Jessica Febles, Ann Jones, Amy Leah Fontenot, Olga González, Marissa Feanco, Lourdes Guerra, and Armindo Nuñez.

To Anthony Hall, for his patience and pre-press skill. And thanks for the laptop. To Ricardo Ávalo and Carlos Rivero for their indispensable help in the design of the book. To Ramón Pinto for his advice.

To Dong Nguyen for welcoming us to her farm in Barranquitas. To Luis Lavergne and his wife Joanne, for offering their country house in Cayey for the photos of José Santaella. To Graziella, Toya, Lourdes, Xaró, Lucas, Lucía and Adrían, for their patience and support.

José Luis Díaz de Villegas, Jochi Melero
y José Luis Díaz de Villegas Freyre

INTRODUCTION

A JOURNEY THROUGH FIVE CENTURIES OF FLAVORS

Calle Mercado, Luis G. Cajiga, 1953

Bodegón con Aguacates y Utensilios, Francisco Oller, 1890-91

Although restaurants – establishments that serve food that restores- have existed since the sixteenth century, it was not until 1782, when a Paris chef named Beauvilliers caused quite a commotion when he opened La Grande Taverne de Londres, considered to be the first true luxury restaurant in the world. The place had a menu, an elegant salon, trained chefs, uniformed waiters, and table linens.

That same year, Bishop Fray Iñigo Abbad y Lasierra, Puerto Rico's first historian, wrote a detailed description of the island and its people: "They use neither tablecloths, nor napkins, glasses or flatware, they generally eat seated on the ground; their victuals are merely a pot of rice, or white sweet potatoes, yams, pumpkins, or all of these together." He described their other eating habits as quite simple.

In a country such as this, with limited resources, where there was a numerous slave population and a high illiteracy rate, it would be logical to suppose that more than a century would elapse before the creation of anything remotely resembling a restaurant. Yet there are reports that Don Antonio Puig opened a café at 27 San Justo Street, in Old San Juan, La Mallorquina, which years later became a popular restaurant. In 1900 it was purchased by Don Rafael Fabián, whose descendants have preserved its original atmosphere for a century, claiming that it is the oldest restaurant in the Americas.

Apparently it was not unique, for in 1877, an advertisement in La Correspondencia informed that the Restaurante Nacional was moving to Luna Street, also publishing a menu. What food was eaten at a quality restaurant in San Juan at that time? French omelettes…German Beefsteak…Mignon à la Russe…Llombí à la façon de Napoléon…and so forth and so on…Not a single *criollo* dish, although llombí probably is *carrucho* —a mollusk called lambí in the French Caribbean, and conch in the Florida Keys.

In 1902, simultaneously with the political changes that followed the United States victory in the Spanish-American War, a café opened in Old San Juan, La Bombonera, which still exists and remains very popular. During the same period, a Neapolitan, Vicente Rinaldi, opened an Italian Restaurant, El Vesubio, on Fortaleza Street, of which there remain only memories.

When Puerto Rico became an American colony, our incipient gastronomical panorama didn't change much, and there were great economic fluctuations. The Depression of the 1930s followed a period of prosperity. These were the times when Rafael Hernández, a musical genius, composed the world renowned Lamento Borincano (Puerto Rican Lament), recounting the misery and economic straits that had befallen the island.

Don Edgar Galiñanes, whose family owned El Nilo, a popular restaurant until the 1960s, remembers that period: "In the 20s and 30s there wasn't a 'gourmet' restaurant in San Juan. The Hotel Palace had a good dining room…Prohibition was in effect; wine was prohibited, so there were limitations compared to later restaurants."

In good times or bad, there are always food lovers, people interested in eating well. In 1933, under the leadership of a young man named Rafael Alvarado, a group of young men founded El Club de los Comelones de San Juan (The Gourmands' Club of San Juan), as was evidenced by the old photos displayed at the *fonda* Don Alvarado, on Duffaut Street in Santurce. The first Puerto Rican gastronomical society? Could be.

A year earlier, F.D. Roosevelt had become President of the United States. Our economy did not undergo a dramatic change until Prohibition was repealed, Puerto Rican troops had fought in World War II and Korea, and Puerto Rico had become a commonwealth of the United States. In the 1950s, restaurants began to sprout up in San Juan, such as Cathay, La Gallega, Mago's, and others. None aspired to compare with Antoine's in New Orleans, or Delmonico's in New York. A cynic might say that our gastronomic map began to change when the economy improved, as the master of ceremonies in Cabaret sings: "Money makes the world go round, the world go round…" because, without clients to foot the hefty bill, there cannot be haute cuisine restaurants.

The clients arrived at the new hotels built on the San Juan coastline and beaches, extending from the Caribe Hilton which abutted the colonial Fortín San Jerónimo (Fort Saint Geronimo), all the way to Isla Verde, where the luxurious Hotel San Juan was built, near the airport that received plane-loads of tourists.

The hotels needed high quality chefs, and they arrived, mostly from Europe. Restaurants were opened, such as Trader Vic's and The Rôtisserrie El Castillo, at the Caribe Hilton; the Alhambra at the Sheraton; and the dining room at the Dorado Beach, and excellent European chefs such as Hans Moosberger, Walter Hünzinger, Rudy Demel, Emil Graf, Albert Kramer, and Alfred Fahndrich took charge of the hotel kitchens.

A benchmark on our gastronomical route was established in 1951, when two Swiss men, Pierre Lohner and Pierre Greber, who had come to Puerto Rico to work at the Hilton, opened the Swiss Chalet. A central European menu, good cooking and service contributed to the Swiss Chalet's reputation, which for years was considered one of the best restaurants in San Juan.

After 1960, Cuban exiles with experience in the field arrived in Puerto Rico, and one particular restaurant left its mark: La Zaragozana, which made a popular black bean soup. At the same time, an interesting character, Signor Rossicci, who had been King Farouk's butler in Egypt, opened a very different Italian restaurant, Italianissima, in Santurce. In the Condado area an elegant restaurant specialized in classic Spanish cuisine, El Hostal Castilla; several of its chefs went on to open their own good restaurants. At the end of the sixties, three French chefs, Raymond, Didier, and Michel, arrived via separate routes. They have since joined

Jíbaro Negro, Oscar Colón Delgado, 1941

forces at La Chaumière Restaurant, which has been in Old San Juan for 35 years.

In 1966, I was living in Miami, Florida when my brother, who lived in Puerto Rico, invited me and my wife, Graziella, to spend a week's vacation in San Juan.

Upon arrival I discovered a whole new gastronomic world, which contrasted deliciously with the 1960s scene in Miami. In the capital, a mosaic of eateries existed: there were restaurants offering *criollo* food and others claiming so-called "International" fare, as well as those which specialized in serving Spanish, Italian, Chinese and Cuban food, the latter, just recently arrived in Puerto Rico.

In the mountains and valleys of Puerto Rico, one was tantalized by the aroma of spit-roasted pig, the exotic flavor of *maví*, the delights of cod fritters which large black women of *cimarrón* or *liberto* descent prepared in huge cauldrons. The tropical setting, the common language, and the ambiance revealed our common roots, our Caribbean origins. I was reminded of my Cuba; yet at the same time, there was a difference.

Two years later, we had moved to Puerto Rico and I was practicing engineering. In 1970, my life took a sharp turn, and suddenly I found myself transformed into a newspaperman. Little did I know that an article that I wrote about Christmas and which was published by the fledgling newspaper, *El Nuevo Día*, would be the prologue to an increasingly important part of my career for 34 years, and that I would witness an incredible gastronomic transformation.

At the same time, French nouvelle cuisine boomed; soon the Basque Country rescued and modernized its cooking; the movement spread to innovation in Catalonia and Italy, rapidly reaching California, and, quite surprisingly, Puerto Rico, which began to experiment along these lines toward the end of the 1970s.

In 1957, *The New York Times* named a man to direct its food section, thus breaking with a long tradition of women food editors. He was Craig Claiborne, a graduate of the hotel school in Lausanne. He rapidly revolutionized restaurant criticism and became the world's most important newspaper food writer.

Claiborne visited Puerto Rico often, and in 1982, he named a small San Juan establishment, La Fragua, to a list of the world's best 20 restaurants. La Fragua's chef-owner, Cristóbal Jiménez, demonstrated that he could make Spanish food that did not belong in a tasca, while scrupulously avoiding the excesses of Escoffier's followers. Soon after, Claiborne agreed to participate in a Puerto Rico Tourism Company advertising campaign, in which he said that Puerto Rico was the gastronomic capital of the Caribbean. This was true, not only in 1982; but, with time became more evident, bearing up all through the 1990s, and it is still true today.

A California friend often travels to Puerto Rico, and not long ago I asked him what he thought of our restaurants. "Puerto Rico has very good restaurants; and those among its best compare well to the best restaurants in San Francisco." My friend is Emmanuel Kemiji, who until recently was master sommelier at the San Francisco Ritz Carlton.

In 1979, almost a contemporary of Cristóbal Jiménez, Alfredo Ayala, a culinary genius, had opened a small restaurant, Ali-Oli, which offered modern food and used local ingredients in innovative dishes. Each, in his own style, established landmarks in a new era.

A decade earlier, hotels had begun to offer gastronomic gala dinners. Food and wine societies were founded, such as the International Food and Wine Society and the Lucullus Circle. Thus, after dinner, the hotel chefs would emerge from their kitchens, immaculately turned out in white, decked out in their

Sandía, Carmelo Sobrino, 1997

Diálogo con objetos cotidianos, artists' book, Néstor Otero and Annex Burgos, 2001

medals, to the applause of the gathering.

Slowly, following in the footsteps of their precursors Jiménez and Ayala, other chefs established their own restaurants, and as in Europe and the United States, became true stars. Their faces, recipes and activities appeared in newspapers and magazines. Many young people began to consider the lucrative and desirable aspects of a culinary career, similar to those of any other profession. The nineties witnessed the growing ranks of a large group of young, talented, well-trained Puerto Rican chefs, as well as several Europeans possessed of contemporary

ideas, all of whom have molded the character of today's restaurants in Puerto Rico.

Let's take a break in our story to take a look backwards. Puerto Rico has forged a cultural identity over the last 500 years, wrought throughout periods of penury and of prosperity, achieved despite absolutist colonial governments. All the arts flourished including: painting and literature, and culinary tastes became more refined. In 1859 the Impresora Acosta (Acosta Printers) published the *Cocinero Puerto-Riqueño* (The Puerto Rican Cook), containing hundreds of recipes, and which was an adaptation for Puerto Rico of the *Manual del Cocinero Cubano* (The

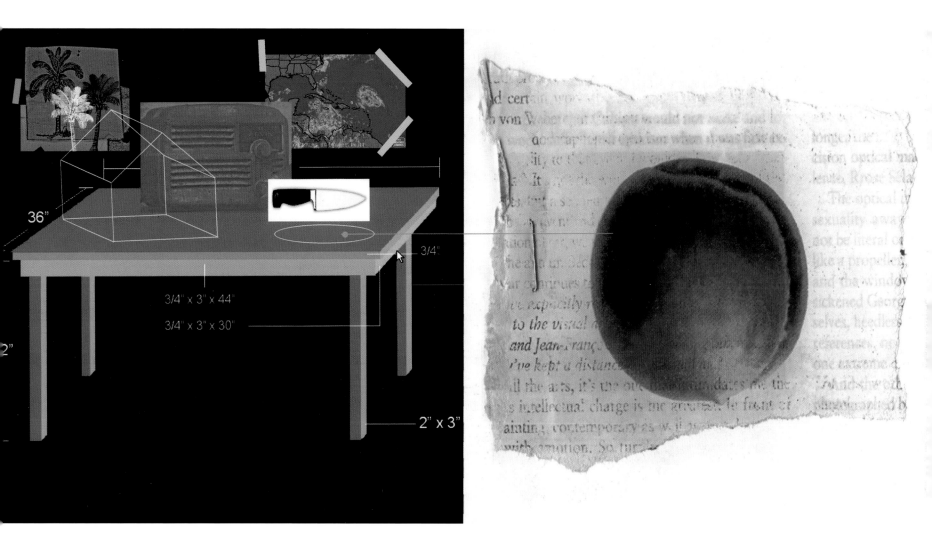

Cuban Cook's Manual), edited in Havana in 1857.

For the rest of the nineteenth century and the first half of the twentieth century, the only significant book published on the subject of Puerto Rican cooking was apparently the one written by Elizabeth B. K. Dooley, *The Puerto Rican Cookbook*, published in 1948.

Two years later, the University of Puerto Rico Press made a great contribution to our culture when it published *Cocine a Gusto* (Cooking to Own's Taste), written by the Home Economics professors, Berta Cabanillas and Carmen Ginorio. Their prologue states: "A sense of historical responsibility has inspired us to publish this book: to leave a permanent written record of recipes that have been passed down from generation to generation as part of our oral traditions: to help consecrate our regional cooking…"

In 1954, Carmen Aboy Valldejuli published *Cocina Criolla* (Criollo Cooking) which became the culinary bible for Puerto Rican brides. Later, in 1970, Dora Romano published *Cocine Conmigo* (Cook with Me), which completed a trilogy of traditional Puerto Rican cooking. Later works on certain aspects of our cuisine have been published, but very few have had mass market distribution such as the books written by U.S. chefs which have reached bestseller lists.

Many factors, both local and worldwide, have contributed to the last five decades' development of our gastronomy. The proliferation of books and magazines on cooking, food and wine sections, wine reviews, and restaurant reviews in local newspapers, the ease of air-cargo food delivery, the greater variety of local ingredients, and cooking classes for aficionados, such as those offered at The Kitchen Shop for nearly twenty years, have exposed the public to the experience and cuisine of great international chefs.

Twenty-first century Puerto Rico can be proud to offer, to both traveler and resident, a culinary spectrum unrivaled in the rest of the Caribbean, transcending mere 'home cooking' without losing its roots. The presence of good *fondas* — which fight for subsistence against the worldwide invasion of fast foods — complements the supply of excellent restaurants, preservers of the heritage of the *Arawaks*, of our Caribbean neighbors, of the African slaves, of the Spanish immigrants, and even of the Americans.

Our music is polyrhythmic, with origins in Dahomey and Arab Spain, in Cuba, Santo Domingo, and the southern United States. So is our cooking. This enriches us because we have managed to maintain an individuality of our particular rhythms and flavors, suffused with Puerto Rican character. Art, music, literature, and cooking are all aspects of a single culture. It is the transformation of a particular cuisine, which has much more Spanish influence and much less French influence than is the case in other Caribbean islands, into first tier haute cuisine, that is a gastronomic miracle.

Today's educated Puerto Rican will equally enjoy a *lengua estofada* (stewed tongue) with *mofongo* and a cold beer at the *plaza del mercado* as he will a *foie-gras* in a tropical fruit sauce at one of San Juan's luxury restaurants, accompanied by fine wine. Unlike 1940, today one can eat at Italian restaurants that compare favorably with many of their counterparts in Italy — as an important Tuscan winemaker recently confessed to me- one can enjoy the contemporary taste of Spain without going to the Paseo de la Castellana; one can savor first rate Chinese food, or a cassoulet reminiscent of Toulouse, while also fully appreciating our chefs' contemporary tropical creations.

In 1950, the publication of the Cabanillas-Ginorio book constituted a benchmark in cultural history for the University of Puerto Rico Press. Now, at the beginning of the third millennium, the Press's decision to publish two new books, *Cocina Artesanal* (Artisanal Cooking) by Doña Emma Duprey, and this volume, *Puerto Rico: la gran cocina del Caribe* (Puerto Rico: Grand Cuisine of the Caribbean) has arrived at precisely the right moment to bookend the work which began over five decades ago.

This book aspires to recognize our heritage; to delve into our culinary roots and traditions and to nurture them; to keep alive kitchen work; and to give homage, through the histories of a representative group of chefs, to all the men and women, who, while they labor over a hot stove, contribute richly — with *sabor* — to our culture.

Service Compris, Antonio Martorell, 2003

El Pique de las Siete Lunas, José L. Díaz de Villegas y D'Estrampes, 2001

One day in 1981, Jochi Melero invited us to dinner at Ali-Oli, a recently opened restaurant on Roberto Clemente Avenue, way out on the very edge of San Juan. Melero brimmed with enthusiasm and said that it was the only completely different spot in all of Puerto Rico. We arrived to find a young Puerto Rican chef at work: Alfredo Ayala, who cooked for and tended to his clients in an improvised dining room, set up in his brother's carport. To me it was a revelation to discover this industrial engineer-turned-chef, developing a cuisine never seen before in Puerto Rico.

Alfredo, who had recently arrived from California, had spent 6 months working at a restaurant not far from Chez Panisse, where Alice Waters was revolutionizing the American kitchen. Following three years of engineering in Africa, traveling throughout Europe, and then returning to Puerto Rico, Ayala decided to concentrate on cooking, and at Ali-Oli, he had a modern menu, rooted in Puerto Rican traditions.

In 1981, Carlos Castañeda, the director of the daily newspaper *El Nuevo Día* entrusted me with organizing a panel to select the best restaurants in San Juan, and in May of 1982, the first jury of the Certamen del Buen Comer (Fine Dining Awards) honored La Rôtisserie at the Caribe Hilton with a Gold Fork, a distinction accepted by the Rôtisserie's talented chef, Augusto Schreiner. Five Silver Forks were awarded; one silver fork went to Ali-Oli, which had only been open for 6 months. Ali-Oli was a success.

The prominent entrepreneur don René Aponte and his wife, Elsa (both of whom have since died), were two regular clients of Ali-Oli and two of the most influential people in the development of gastronomy in Puerto Rico. The Apontes were consummate travelers, intimately acquainted with the best restaurants in Europe and owned a remarkable collection of Bordeaux. Above all, they recognized talent when they saw it. With the help and encouragement of the Apontes, Ayala moved to new premises on the ground floor of the Excelsior Hotel, in Miramar.

The new Ali-Oli, designed by the architect Cheo Ramirez, who later co-owned Amadeus restaurant, was an intimate and elegant salon which included, for the first time in Puerto Rico, an excellent wine list and refrigerated wine cellaar. Ayala inaugurated it in 1984, and during the four years that he owned it, Ali-Oli won four consecutive Gold Forks and changed the physiognomy of eating in Puerto Rico. Ayala is a culinary genius who has never forgotten his roots in Barranquitas (a town in the mountains), and who has never ventured into a culinary school, having spent only one week at a *stage* in the restaurant Jamin, in Paris, in 1986.

On August 1, 1986, at the height of Ali-Oli's success, I interviewed Ayala on his thoughts about the new Puerto Rican cooking on the occasion of an historic gala dinner for 60 people he was preparing: "Yes, you can take the tastes of the *fondas* into the most sophisticated kitchen...It has been proven that it can be done well at that level...this is the first time that it will be done, maintaining the purity of the Puerto Rican menu." Two days later, Ayala served six dishes, each inspired by traditional Puerto Rican food, and each was accompanied by a tropical fruit in season.

Ayala's kitchen did not develop in a vacuum, and he recognized people who had made significant contributions to fine dining in Puerto Rico. Among them, he named Paula Paley, who, at her tiny shop, sold food prepared in a special way, food inspired by autochthonous products. Others were doña Elsa Aponte, Dolly Colón, Augusto Schreiner, the writer Ellen Hawes, Jacqueline Kleis, and doña Alice Huyke, the latter, a wonderful cooking teacher. Her daughter, Giovanna, learned from her and became sous-chef for awhile at Ali-Oli. A young chef, Manuel Martínez, had been Ayala's right-hand man for many years and at present is the chef at Ayala's restaurant, Las Vegas, on the road to El Yunque.

Between 1981 and 2004, Alfredo Ayala has created a body of work that clearly demonstrates that it was he who initiated the culinary transformation in Puerto Rico at Ali-Oli; at Yuquiyú, at Sea Grapes, at Chayote, at Su Casa and at Las Vegas.

It has indeed been my privilege to witness the years of the genesis of a new cuisine.

THE FRUIT OF MY LAND

PAPAYA (Carica papaya)

Also known as *lechosa*, it is indigenous to the Caribbean, and it grows wild in Puerto Rico. It can be eaten ripe as a fruit or green in salads; it can also be cooked in a sugar syrup as a dessert or preserve. Some have yellow pulp and some red, which is more succulent. The tree is not tall and the fruit can vary in size: some are small as avocadoes, others are much larger. It contains an enzyme, papain, which is a digestive aid.

MAMMEE APPLE (Mammea americana)

Also called yellow mammee, it is often used to make syrup-based preserves and desserts, although, when very ripe, it is also eaten raw. It is indigenous to America and was already acclimated to Puerto Rico at the time of Christopher Columbus' arrival.

MANGO; MAMMEE ZAPOTE, TAMARIND (Mangifera indica, Pouteris zapota, Tamarindus indica)

The mango, at left, is from India and it did not reach Puerto Rico until the mid-nineteenth century. At present, it grows wild; there is also large scale commercial cultivation, which supplies both the export market and local demand. It is eaten as a fruit, used in chutneys and in marmalades, sorbets and desserts. The tamarind, at center, is acid and sour, and its pulp is sold mixed with sugar. It may be used in sauces and desserts. The mammee zapote, at right, was almost extinct; until recently when it began to be cultivated again. It is very popular among the Cubans and Dominicans who live in Puerto Rico. Its pulp is vermilion-colored and it is excellent for use in juices and ice creams.

PLANTAINS AND BANANAS (Musa paradisiaca, Musa sapientum)

At top left the plantain, whether ripe or grren, is not eaten as a fruit, but as a vegetable. It is Asian in origin and reached the Caribbean via Africa. It was for centuries the main foodstuff in Puerto Rico. Bananas are smaller and are eaten as vegetables when green; as fruit when ripe.

GREEN PEPPERS, HOT PEPPERS, AJÍES DULCES (Capsicum frutensis)

The green peppers, above, are sweet and primarily used to make *sofrito*. Below; the hot peppers are used to make condiments, which are bottled and sold. Puerto Rico's food is not spicy, but hot sauce (pique), see painting on page 12, is usually offered as an option. The small round peppers at right are not hot; they are used in *sofrito*.

CONDIMENTS

At left, culantro is stronger in both aroma and taste than is cilantro (at right). Annatto (Bixa orellana), or *achiote*, in the bowl above, is used primarily to color foods, by frying it in lard or vegetable oil; ginger is used in chutneys and desserts.

BREADFRUIT, OKRA, CHAYOTE (Artocarpus arcilis, Hibiscus esculentus, Sechium edule, Persea americana)
Breadfruit, above, was brought to the Caribbean by Captain Bligh, he of the HMS Bounty; it is eaten boiled, fried; and even in desserts. The *chayote*, also called Christophine and mirliton, comes from Mexico and is also quite versatile. Okra arrived from Africa and is eaten stewed as well as in soups and in salads. The avocado, which grows practically wild, is commonly consumed in salads.

TUBERS

Cassava, upper left, was the Caribbean Indians' principal sustenance. They also ate *yautía* (tanier or taro root), upper right. Below, at center, are sweet potato or *aje*. At lower left, *ñames* of African provenance. At extreme right, celery root, similar to celeriac.

BEANS

The *gandules*, pigeon peas (top right), came from Africa; but the red kidney beans are Caribbean and Mexican in origin. Both are part of the Puerto Rican daily diet.

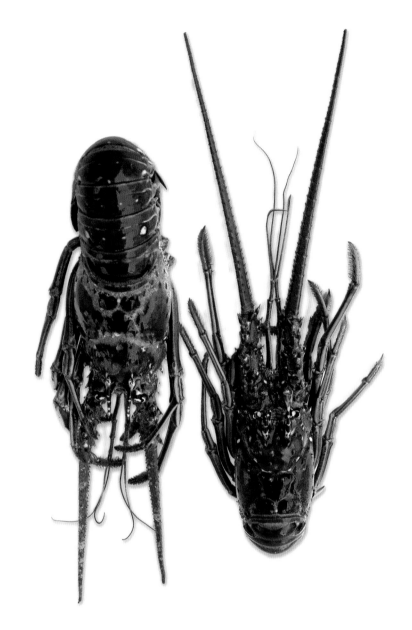

FISH

Puerto Rico's waters have never been extensively fished (there was a time when fishermen didn't go out to the sea because they were afraid of the pirates), although the seas abound with delicious varieties of fish. Above, the *chapín*, a kind of trunkfish, is ugly but much enjoyed in fried *empanadillas* (turnovers). At center, *arrayaos*, are wonderful fried whole, served with *Mojo Isleño*. Below, shallow-water small fish that are delicious.

SPINY LOBSTER

The Caribbean spiny lobster and cold water Maine lobster are very different. Spiny lobster is cooked in any of the ways that Maine lobster is, but spiny lobster has more flavor.

SNAIL AND CONCH

The *bulgao*, at left, although smaller than abalone, is similar to it and is served cooked, as well as raw. Conch or lambi, even when used in salads, must be boiled first.

Lamb Pionono. Page 40

WILO BENET

A CHEF AT THE MUSEUM
AND BEYOND

The Palace of Santa Catalina, better known as La Fortaleza or The Fortress, was built between 1533 and 1540 as part of the defenses for the city of San Juan. It soon was found obsolete and was converted into the Puerto Rican governor's residence. It is the oldest building in the Western Hemisphere which has been in continuous use as an executive mansion.

An afternoon in November of 1989, my wife and I went to a gathering which promised to be extremely interesting. Palmira and Pellín Borrás, who are our partners in El Colegio del Vino (The Wine Academy) had invited a young chef, Wilo Benet, and his fiancé, Lorraine, to their Guaynabo home to give a cooking demonstration in the Borrás family's spacious kitchen. The governor, Rafael Hernández Colón and his First Lady, doña Lila Mayoral, had contracted Benet as executive chef at la Fortaleza, where Lorraine was Assistant Director of Internal Affairs.

Years earlier, young Benet had left behind a career as a photographer at the Florida Institute of Technology when he abandoned his studies, and went to work at a restaurant, washing dishes. That job motivated him to want to dedicate himself to cooking and he returned to Puerto Rico, where he worked for an entire year, without pay, as a kitchen assistant to chef Augusto Schreiner at the Caribe Hilton. His interest in the culinary arts continued and he applied and was admitted, in the mid-eighties, to the prestigious Culinary Institute of America (CIA), in upstate New York.

As a graduation requirement, he did his apprenticeship as chef's assistant at The Top of the Hub in Boston, but as soon as he graduated, he obtained his first job as chef at a restaurant on Fifth Avenue and 9th Street, in Greenwich Village, in New York. He soon went on to better known restaurants such as Le Bernardin, a restaurant which Gilbert and Maguy Le Coze had successfully moved from Paris to midtown Manhattan.

As the song says: If you make it in New York, you make it anywhere, and so the young chef strived to get ahead. "In the morning, I worked at Le Bernardin as assistant to the pastry chef and in the evening I worked at the Water Club as chef poissonier. I worked 14 to 16 hours a day, 6 days a week." At Le Bernardin,

Wilo had the opportunity to get to know how an haute cuisine French restaurant functions, and at the Water Club, he accumulated experience at a high volume restaurant, which served 500 covers per night.

A short time later, a great chef, Christian Delouvrier, who had been chef de cuisine with Alain Senderens in Paris, took charge of the restaurant Maurice at the Parker-Meridien Hotel, and Benet found work with him. That experience, as well as the others he accumulated in New York, gave him the rigorous discipline of French tradition which, nuanced by the creativity of nouvelle cuisine, would later serve him well.

He was in New York when he received the offer from La Fortaleza and he decided to return to Puerto Rico. His great opportunity seemed to have arrived. "An apprentice chef's true schooling lies in the work done at top-notch restaurants, that is where one is put to the test; one faces the challenge of using the skills acquired at culinary school," he confided to Maite Ribas, a reporter at San Juan's *El Nuevo Día* newspaper, as he recalled his years in New York.

That afternoon at the Borrás', the demonstratiaon menu was simple, but interesting. It was a sample of his offerings made for the First Lady, and served at state dinners at La Fortaleza. That day, he demonstrated how to make four dishes: Tuna Carpaccio with Pimento Jelly, Octopus Squid Risotto, Venison with Caper Sauce, and a classic Crème Brûlée. My tasting notes from that afternoon, indicate that the venison was excellent and that the chef told us that the sauce for the octopus was improvised at the Governor's home in Ponce, using red wine, capers, cream and butter. For the first time, I also witnessed a tuna carpaccio prepared according to the technique he had learned at Le Bernardin, accompanied by a very personal touch: red and yellow pimento jelly, his own idea.

Recipes with rum

Rums of Puerto Rico, published a promotional book in 2004, with recipes that use Puerto Rican rum, specially created by Wilo Benet.

Sea Bass and Celery Root Brandade with Scallion Emulsion. Page 37

Fried Whole Red Snapper in 'Criollo' Sauce. Page 36

I thus perceived, on that first day of our acquaintance, the indications of the creative capacity that Wilo would fully develop during his career as chef and restaurateur. And he had news for us: He and Lorraine, who had studied hotel and restaurant management in Puerto Rico and had gone to further studies in Barcelona, were opening a small restaurant in Old San Juan, which would be the first link in a career of uninterrupted success.

The year 1990 brought a new restaurant, Pikayo, to Puerto Rico. "Why Pikayo?" I recall asking Wilo that Sunday. "We plan to serve Cajun-inspired dishes and the New Orleans kitchen reminded me of 'picayune'…the most important New Orleans newspaper is the Times-Picayune." I doubt that Wilo was aware at the time of the etymology of the noun 'picayune': derived from an antique southern United States coin valued at one half of one Real.

Wilo's style of cooking, coupled with Lorraine's direction of the long and narrow dining room, soon made that first Pikayo popular among food lovers. It was Puerto Rico's first restaurant to serve dishes from the modern New Orleans Cajun kitchen, such as Paul Proudhomme's 'blackened redfish', a favorite on Pikayo's menu. A year later, chef Jean Vigato came to Puerto Rico. He was chef-owner of Apicius, a two-star restaurant which was causing a sensation in Paris, and he was in San Juan to cook an important and successful dinner with Wilo and his kitchen brigade at Pikayo.

The couple outgrew the intimate space of the Old San Juan restaurant and Pikayo moved to a Condado hotel, located in a tourist zone bordering the picturesque Condado Lagoon, and thus began a new stage. Wilo's kitchen had left behind its Cajun phase and had sought new horizons with a menu incorporating far more characteristics of the new *criollo* creative cuisine. At this point, international food and wine publications began to keep an eye on the new culinary star that had appeared in Puerto Rico.

Wilo had demonstrated his organizational skills early in his career and thus, he received an offer to take charge of the restaurant and the administration of a new resort located on the south coast of Puerto Rico, Copamarina, on Guánica beach. He worked in this capacity for two or three years, but he reached the point of exhaustion. Pikayo, in the Condado, continued its ascending trajectory under Wilo's direction as he simultaneously served as administrator of the Guánica hotel.

Wilo had continued participating in charity dinners and international culinary activities, such as the Aspen Food and Wine Classic organized by Food and Wine Magazine, where he represented Puerto Rico, teaming with Augusto Schreiner and Alfredo Ayala. In 1994 and 1995 he captained Puerto Rico's Culinary Team, winning gold and silver medals at the culinary competition Taste of the Caribbean.

Something extremely important occurred along the way. The University of Puerto Rico and the Culinary Institute of America, as part of a continuing education program, decided to experiment with establishing a branch campus of CIA in San Juan. Wouldn't a distinguished alumnus be the most logical choice to organize and direct the courses? And wasn't Wilo Benet the most obvious choice? The programmed course of study was successfully completed, from which several young Puerto Ricans benefited, but which for financial reasons was never repeated.

By the end of the nineties, the spectacular Puerto Rico Art Museum was under construction, incorporating a remodeled hospital located in a central area of San Juan. The plans included an haute cuisine restaurant. Proposals were requested from three chefs: Augusto Schreiner, Mark French, and Wilo Benet. The Museum chose Benet's proposal and Wilo's career entered a new period, for the offer included taking charge of food service at a great many of the activities held at the Museum itself.

Wilo and Luis Gutiérrez Architects spent months planning the new restaurant, and he and his assistant chefs worked equally long hours organizing a

Green Tomato Flower, Wilo Benet

Above, preparing red snapper for frying. Left, the finished dish. Page 36

new menu. The results were spectacular in both aspects, as the restaurant is one of the most beautiful in America, and this last incarnation of Pikayo has achieved culinary maturity demonstrating a creative kitchen grounded in the tradition of popular Puerto Rican cooking, yet thoroughly sophisticated in character, as can be appreciated by the recipes in this chapter. The restaurant's small terrace, which faces the Museum's beautiful garden, turns lunch into a unique gastronomic experience.

At lunchtime at Payá, Wilo Benet's new restaurant, he and I sat and talked about his early years as chef at La Fortaleza. "When I tested for the position with Hernandez Colón at the Executive Mansion, I prepared a sample dish, a simple salmon with Vermont mustard. I have evolved a great deal since then."

At the first Pikayo, his style of cooking became more personal, as Wilo was no longer governed by Hernandez Colón's particular needs and tastes. Yet, he says, "The underlying principles of my cooking remain the same: first rate ingredients and simplicity, although one eventually realizes that some recipes can be simplified while others cannot. At the first Pikayo, I felt that I had not gone to the Culinary Institute of America to return to San Juan, to fry tostones (fried green plantains) and to stew beans, but, without realizing it, I have become an exponent of Puerto Rican cooking."

Where has your evolution taken you? "I have evolved in that I have learned to teach, to delegate, to train…one cannot do everything. I have followed the steps of others who have succeeded in this field. My assistant, Alex, my chef de cuisine at Pikayo, has been with me for a long time – and I have trained him for nine years – and now I can delegate a great deal to him. I understand that the person who goes to the restaurant feels better when it is the owner who cooks, but I always keep my eye on everything. I wouldn't compare myself to Emeril Lagasse, but instead to a Jean-Georges Vongerichten." Lagasse is an American chef who owns several restaurants and who has become a popular star of a television cooking show. Vongerichten, a great chef, who also owns several restaurants in New York, Las Vegas, and other cities, and has throughout maintained a signature style of cooking: French with oriental influence and has also preserved a more formal style than Lagasse.

Benet owns two restaurants, a catering business, has just finished writing a book and has another in the works and I comment about the stress of having so many responsibilities.

"No, I don't feel stressed. I've divided my itinerary so that I enjoy leisure and work equally. Lorraine knows that my great passion is cooking, but I am always there for my family."

Since the outset of his career, Wilo has been an exceptional witness to the development of gastronomy in Puerto Rico and his comments on this subject are interesting. "Gastronomy has changed in Puerto Rico. Today's availability to the public is enormous. There has been development and planning. We have positioned the food and beverage industry in relation to tourism. The food and beverage industry is enormous. I have seen sensational growth in the consumer public, who today is knowledgeable about food and wine. People are surprised by the fine wines available in Puerto Rico."

This subject leads to a question: Is there a new Puerto Rican cuisine?

"Yes, there is a new Puerto Rican kitchen. But, it has gone through stages: first came Alfredo Ayala, influenced by the French, followed, later, by the fruit sauces made by Giovanna Huyke; then, me, influenced by the Oriental. We have achieved a lot of things, we have been doing many things, things with character. I think we will continue "fusion" with the oriental kitchen, there are young people, with impetus: Alex Sánchez of Chef Alex in Cayey, Mario Pagán at Chayote. There are young people willing to brave the waters."

Benet belongs to the group of chefs who, since the beginnings of their careers in Puerto Rico, have tried to stimulate local production of quality products to supply top restaurants. "Although we have made progress and have developed small farmers with specialized produce, we still need to further develop our agriculture. The gastronomic development is tied to agricultural development."

At present Puerto Rico has several culinary schools which graduate each year a certain number of young men and women who aspire to be the new Wilo Benet, and others who aspire to study in the United States, whether at CIA, Johnson & Wales, or elsewhere. There are those who feel that CIA is too classic, that it has overly emphasized North American cooking and hotel cuisine. "The school is now offering courses that are more contemporary, more in tune with the times. Here, culinary education has been improving slowly. The programs are deeper and more complex, with better facilities."

I observe Payá's innovative menu, its operation, and Wilo invites me to visit the ultra modern kitchens. "It is a larger restaurant and its price point is much more economical. Kenny Medina, my old chef de cuisine is in charge, but I can see the kitchen via closed circuit, whether I'm at Pikayo or at my office, and I am always in touch via Internet. The new technology permits managing greater volume without sacrificing quality. That has been the key." To manage his multiple food businesses, he has established an office with ten employees. Wilo has returned, over time, to an old love, photography. The art hanging in his office is photographic: digital alterations of photographs he has taken of different foods and ingredients. An example of this work appears in this chapter. Wilo has other hobbies, among which, believe it or not, is cooking. Many a Sunday our chef will put on his shorts, light his barbecue and cook for family and friends. What do you make? We ask. "Hot dogs and Kobe Beef steaks! I'm a hot dog fanatic, and I love steaks!"

Pikayo Caesar Salad

Serves 8

The croutons

1 green plantain, diced
Vegetable oil

The dressing

1 cup olive oil
1 cup canola oil
½ cup water
½ cup lemon juice
6 egg yolks
7 ounces anchovy fillets
1 ounce Parmigiano Reggiano, grated
Salt and pepper to taste

The salad

2 cucumbers, sliced lengthwise, into very thin
**   slices, approximately ⅟₃₂" thick**
4 hearts romaine lettuce, cut into slices
approximately 6" long

Presentation

1 cup miniature tomatoes
'Parmigiano reggiano', grated
1 tablespoon scallions, julienned
Micro chives, or regular chives or scallions,
**   minced**

Caesar salad originated in Tijuana, México. This version adds cucumbers and miniature tomatoes. If micro chives are not available, then finely minced scallions or regular chives may be used. The sauce is similar to the original.

The croutons

Using a skillet, fry the green plantains in very hot oil. Drain well, and reserve.

The dressing

Using a hand-held blender, emulsify all the ingredients for the dressing in a bowl. Season with salt and pepper.

The Salad

Shape cucumbers into a ring. Wrap and tie the lettuce leaves with the cucumber slices, so that the cucumber serves as a ring and the romaine stands upright on the plate.

Presentation

Place the lettuce, tied by the cucumber, in the center of the plate. Pour dressing over lettuce, starting at the top so that it will settle into the center of the lettuce. Spill dressing on the outside of the bunched lettuce. Sprinkle with Parmigiano Reggiano and plantain croutons. Place four miniature tomatoes around the lettuce, and lightly scatter around with scallions.

Beet and Goat Cheese Salad

Serves 6

The vinaigrette

4 ounces olive oil
½ cup hazelnut oil
1 ounce rice vinegar
1 tablespoon sugar
2 shallots, minced
Salt and pepper to taste

The salad

1 pound goat cheese, softened
3 beets, cooked and cut into disks 1 ½"
diameter and ¼" thick

Presentation

1 bunch arugula
3 tablespoons toasted hazelnuts, minced

The use of hazelnut oil and toasted hazelnuts gives this dish a particular aromatic touch. The goat cheese is essential.

The vinaigrette

In a bowl, whisk together the olive oil, hazelnut oil, rice vinegar, sugar, and shallots. Season with salt and pepper.

The salad

Fill a pastry bag fitted with a ⅜" tip with softened cheese. Place seven beet slices on the work surface. Pipe enough cheese onto beets to cover each of 6 slices. To assemble, build a tower. Crown with the last beet slice which has no cheese covering. Repeat assembly process with the five remaining portions.

Presentation

Place a beet-and-cheese-tower in the center of each dish, drizzled with vinaigrette. Top tower with a few arugula leaves. Sprinkle a few toasted hazelnuts around tower. Serve cold.

Fried Whole Red Snapper with Criollo Sauce

Serves 5

5 whole red snappers, 1 ¾ to 2 pounds each

The marinade
1 ½ cups olive oil
3 ounces of criollo seasoning (adobo)
1 ½ onions, thinly sliced

The criollo sauce
1 cup olive oil
2 ½ onions, minced
1 red pepper, minced
1 yellow pepper, minced
1 green criollo pepper, minced
60 ounces tomato sauce
4 ounces capers
4 ounces white vinegar
½ cup of water
8 ounces sugar
1 bunch cilantro, minced
¼ cup whole garlic cloves, sliced after measuring
Salt and pepper to taste

The taro root puree
1 ½ cups taro root, peeled and cut into 3 or 4
  pieces
2 tablespoons softened butter
Salt

The fish
All-purpose flour

Presentation
20 to 25 fresh green beans, boiled or steamed
Lime juice

Known as 'chillo' in Puerto Rico and 'pargo' in Cuba, it is also known as red snapper in the Florida Keys. This method is perfect for achieving a crispy fish, but use the maximum size recommended by the chef. Yellowtail or mangrove snapper may also be used.

Carefully clean the snapper, taking care to gut well and eliminate gills. Wash well to remove residual blood.

The marinade
In a bowl, mix the olive oil, the *criollo* seasoning, and the onions.

Score the snapper on both sides. Place the snapper in a large glass or stainless steel baking dish. Cover with sufficient marinade mixture. Refrigerate, covered, for 24 hours.

The 'criollo' sauce
Place the oil in a large saucepan over medium heat. Fry the onions and the peppers until softened. Add the rest of the ingredients and cook until incorporated. Reduce heat and continue cooking until sauce has thickened and taste is concentrated. Correct seasoning.

The taro root puree
In a saucepan, boil the taro root in water until tender. Drain well and transfer to a bowl. Add the butter and mash well. Season with salt.

The fish
Remove the snappers from the marinade, and wipe off excess oil. Pour flour onto a baking dish and, one by one, lightly flour the fish. Take the fish by the tail and shake to remove excess flour.

Lay the fish on the work surface. Skewer the fish with a wooden skewer, through the tail and at the point where the head joins the rest of the body, making it ring-shaped. This will allow fish to maintain a shape which permits presentation that is crispy and golden on both sides.

Using a deep fryer or a large cauldron, heat vegetable oil to 350°F. Submerge the entire fish in the oil until golden and crispy. Drain on paper towel, and repeat the operation with the rest of the fish.

Place some taro root puree in the center of a plate and surround with a little of the *criollo* sauce. Place the fish atop the taro purée, so that it appears as though it is swimming upstream. Decorate with 3 to 5 green beans. Squeeze a few drops of lime juice over the fish. Accompany with *criollo* sauce and *tostones*.

Sea Bass and Celery Root Brandade with Scallion Emulsion

Serves 5

This modern version of this French Provençal dish substitutes a purée of celery root (a very popular tuber in Puerto Rico) for the more traditional potato.

The purée

2 ½ celery roots, peeled

½ pound salt cod; boned, skinned, desalted, and shredded

4 ounces butter

3 tablespoons olive oil

Salt and pepper to taste

The purée

Place celery root in a large saucepan filled with salted water, and boil until tender. Remove from pot and drain well. Mash well in a large bowl, incorporating the shredded salt cod. Add butter and olive oil, and mix well. Correct seasoning. Reserve.

The emulsion

2 cups milk

½ cup water

1 onion, minced

1 potato, diced

6 ounces scallions

4 ounces extra-virgin olive oil

Salt and pepper to taste

The emulsion

Place the milk, water, onion, potato, and scallions in a saucepan, and cook over high heat until the potato is well-cooked. Remove from heat, and with an immersion beater, emulsify with the olive oil. Correct seasoning. Reserve.

The fish

2 ½ pounds sea bass fillet, in 8-ounce portions

Butter

The fish

Preheat oven to 350°F. Butter both sides of the fish. Using a grill or griddle, sear on both sides. Finish cooking in the oven, taking great care to save the fish's natural juices.

The presentation

Place a portion of celery root in the center of a plate. Place the fish exactly on top of the purée. Surround with emulsion, and serve immediately.

Tenderloin with Caramelized Onions

Serves 8

16 beef tenderloin medallions, 4 ounces each

Marinade
1 cup garlic cloves, ground
4 cups olive oil
4 tablespoons criollo seasoning (adobo)

Potatoes
8 Idaho potatoes, cut into matchsticks
Vegetable oil
Salt

Tenderloin preparation
7 onions, thinly sliced
2 ounces white vinegar
1 quart chicken broth
10 ounces butter
Salt and pepper to taste
Olive oil

This is an elegant version of a dish adapted from the popular kitchen; it substitutes beef tenderloin for a cheaper cut of meat. Benet says that this is the most popular dish on his menu.

Marinade

Gently pound each beef medallion with a mallet, until each piece is ¼" thick. In a large bowl, mix all the marinade ingredients. Place the steaks in a glass baking dish. Pour marinade over the medallions. Cover and refrigerate for 24 hours.

Potatoes

When close to serving time, fill a skillet or deep fryer with oil. Place over medium high heat. When oil is quite hot, fry the potatoes until crispy but still flexible. Remove potatoes and set them aside, keeping them hot. Sprinkle with salt.

Tenderloin preparation

In another very hot skillet, add a little olive oil, and place over medium high heat. Sear the marinated medallions, turning them rapidly; do not overcook. Move to a dish.
In the same skillet, sauté the onions in olive oil over medium heat, trying to caramelize as much as possible. Add vinegar and scrape skillet to remove onions stuck on the bottom. Add enough chicken broth to thicken the sauce slightly. Whip in butter. Correct seasoning.

Presentation

To serve, place alternating layers of tenderloin and onions on a plate. Pour a little sauce over the layers and crown with fried potatoes. Serve very hot, alone or accompanied by rice and *tostones*.

Lamb Piononos

Serves 6

The piononos

6 ripe plantains, sliced lengthwise

Vegetable oil

Olive oil

½ onion, finely chopped

½ red pepper, finely chopped

½ green pepper, minced

½ tablespoon ground garlic

1 ½ pounds ground lamb

2 tablespoons chicken broth

1 cup Spanish tomato sauce

1 ½ tablespoons cumin

6 eggs, beaten

Salt and pepper

The sauce

3 tablespoons olive oil

1 ½ carrots, cut into small cubes

3 celery stalks, minced

1 onion, minced

5 garlic cloves, minced

1 bottle dry white wine

2 tablespoons black peppercorn

2 bay leaves

2 tablespoons thyme leaves

2 cups demi-glace

2 tablespoons cornstarch dissolved in 1

tablespoon water (optional)

Salt and pepper to taste

Presentation

Asparagus or other green vegetable, cooked

Another elegant version of a popular Puerto Rican dish, 'piononos' are ripe plantain strips, ring-shaped and filled with beef. This dish preparation calls for lamb and is served with a sauce made from a veal-based reduction (demi-glace).

The piononos

Fry the plantains in a skillet (or a deep fryer) in vegetable oil until golden. Remove from oil and drain on paper towels.

Heat a little olive oil in another skillet, and fry the onion, green pepper, and garlic. When these become translucent, add the lamb and mix, incorporating the chicken broth and the tomato sauce. Cook until reduced. Season with cumin, salt, and pepper. Reserve.

Preheat oven to 350°F. Using a little olive oil, grease 6 ovenproof molds and cover the bottoms with parchment paper. Arrange the plantain slices in the molds, covering bottoms and sides. Press well against the sides so that walls are firm. Slice the extra plantain slices into quarters, and fill in any empty spaces.

Fill the cavity with the ground meat. Pour the beaten eggs over the *pionono*. Bake for 20 minutes.

The sauce

Meanwhile, heat olive oil in a saucepan, and sauté carrots, celery, onions, and garlic. When the vegetables are translucent, add the wine. Add peppercorn, bay leaves, and thyme. Reduce to one half, and add *demi-glace*. Reduce further by one third. If necessary, thicken with cornstarch and water. Correct seasoning with salt and pepper. Strain and reserve, keeping it hot.

Presentation

On a plate, place a layer of asparagus or any green vegetable; remove the *pionono* from the mold and place it in the center of the plate over the vegetables. If the paper has adhered to the bottom, remove it to expose the bottom. Surround the *pionono* with a ring of the sauce.

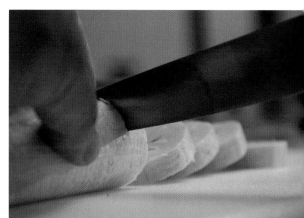
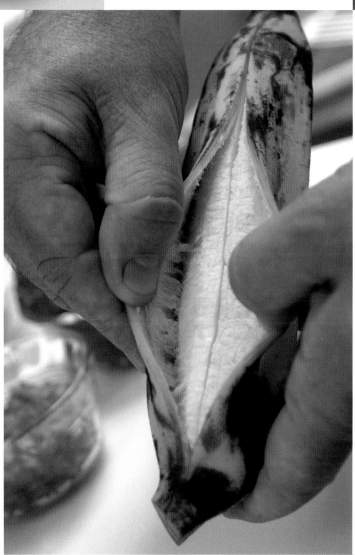

Dulce de Papaya

Serves 10

3 large green papayas
2 quarts water
8 cups sugar
1 ½ cinnamon sticks
1 tablespoon whole cloves
Puerto Rican white cheese

The chef's childhood certainly was the inspiration for this dish. Coupled with the ideal cheese, Puerto Rican white cheese (a specialty of several mountain towns, such as Naranjito, Barranquitas, Ciales, and Lares), this dessert is a Puerto Rican favorite.

Peel the papayas and discard seeds. Cut into 1 ¼" slices.

Place the following into a large saucepan: *papaya*, water, sugar, cinnamon, and cloves. Boil over medium high heat until the liquid acquires a syrupy consistency and the papayas are both tender and firm.

Refrigerate overnight before serving.

Serve with white Puerto Rican cheese.

Cheese Soufflé

Serves 10

The guava sauce

3 cups guava paste

1 cup water

Sugar (optional)

The Soufflé

1 ½ pounds cream cheese, softened

½ pound Manchego cheese, freshly grated

½ pound Parmesan cheese, freshly grated

2 eggs

½ cup sugar

½ cup flour

1 cup egg whites

Super fine sugar

Butter

The fusion of Manchego, a Spanish cheese made from sheep's milk, with Parmesan imparts a very different taste to this soufflé. The very original idea of accompanying the dish with a sauce made from guava, an autochthonous Puerto Rican fruit, lends a new twist to a traditional dessert.

The guava sauce

In a bowl, dissolve the guava paste in one cup of hot water, and add sugar if necessary. If too thick, add a little more water until sauce reaches a thick consistency, but make sure it's still fluid.

The soufflé

Preheat oven to 350°F.

Mix all ingredients for the soufflé in a bowl, except for the egg whites.

In another large bowl, beat egg whites soft peak stage is reached. Carefully fold in all the ingredients from the other bowl, using a rubber spatula, so that egg whites maintain maximum volume.

Butter the individual soufflé dishes, and cover the butter with granulated sugar. Pour the soufflé mixture into the molds, filling ¾ of each dish. Bake for 20 minutes; the soufflé should rise at least 3" above the dish's rim. Remove from oven and dust lightly with super fine sugar.

Serve with guava sauce.

Smoked Salmon and Caramelized Mango with Avocado Tomato Relish. Page 54

MARK FRENCH

GOURMET LIONS

Mark and Melody French have made their home in the city of Ponce, following a journey of arduous training and tours of duty at hotels which took them through Kansas City, Toronto, and San Juan

Ponce, situated on the south coast of Puerto Rico, is the island's second largest city, named in honor of Juan Ponce de León, the first governor of the island. In 1519 he died in Cuba from injuries inflicted while fighting the indigenous people of Florida. Thus Ponce was not founded by Juan Ponce de León, but by his great-grandson, Juan Ponce de León y Loaiza, a century la-

ter. Ponce is known as the City of the Lions, according to *ponceño* lore, in reference to the first Ponce de León. Who knows whether or not the legend is true or false? Two golden lions stand guard on the bridge that marks the entrance to the old city, and the Fountain of Lions attracts attention at the Plaza de Las Delicias, located in the heart of the old city.

Ponceños are proud to have given Puerto Rico great political figures, the rum called Don Q, and one of the island's most extraordinary popular musicians, the legendary *plenero* Bun-Bún. The old city situated nearby this plaza, has been restored and rebuilt recently. The cathedral and the firehouse are located on this plaza; a picturesque structure, known as the parque de Bombas, built in 1882, is a red and black-striped wooden building.

The Hotel Meliá, filled with memories and old photographs of the city is located about 50 yards from the firehouse, on Calle Cristina. Its ground floor houses, in the opinion of

Lamb Chops with Goat Cheese Crust. Page 61

Plena and the pleneros

Although Ponce claims to be the birthplace of the most danceable popular music in Puerto Rico, which, until displaced by *salsa* and *merengue*, was the *plena*, its origins are in doubt. The composer and historian, Rafael Aponte Ledée, believes that the *plena* has both influence from Africa and from the English-speaking islands of the Lesser Antilles. The *plena* was extremely popular during the 1930s and 1940s, particularly in the *barrio* San Antón in Ponce. Its lyrics chronicled events in the *barrio*, the city, and the country, and made several *pleneros* from San Antón famous.

many, the best restaurant in Ponce, where its chef-owner offers his clients a menu that features first rate-contemporary Caribbean cooking.

That dining room is frequently filled with well-known people, *ponceños* and professionals who have made important contributions to that enticing city. Until shortly before his death, Don Luis Ferré, former governor of Puerto Rico, could be seen, always occupying the same table. He was a visionary benefactor of the arts who gave Ponce one of the best art museums in Latin America.

Destiny has placed Mark French in Ponce. No one, neither he, nor the *ponceños* could ever have predicted his settling in the city. Mark is from Baltimore, where he grew up with his mother and seven siblings following his parents' separation. The family was of modest means, so Mark went to work when he was still very young, he had to help his family. And he worked while studying in school. He and a brother baked bread during their free time, which they sold in the neighborhood, and when he was older, he left high school to wash dishes and help out in the kitchen of a nearby restaurant. "I had friends who were chefs, and I learned by hanging around them." Later, he found steady work with a German chef at a country club, where he remained for 5 years. "He'd pick me up in the afternoon, to take me to the club. He'd give me a ride in order to make sure that I got to work, because I had a day job working at a bakery." Mark learned a lot from the baker, particularly about pastry making, "I still make all the desserts served at my restaurant." The chef, Albert Kirchmeyer, went to culinary competitions in New York, and he took young Mark with him as his assistant. Mark absorbed everything, learning among other things to make ice sculpture, a skill that he later put to good use in his hotel work.

One day he received an offer from another country club located in Kansas City. "I accepted immediately, my dad lived in that city, and it was a great opportunity to move to be closer. But that country club was terrible, everything was awful there." The net result was that he stayed in Kansas City, but left his job. "I quit that job. It was the first time that I had ever quit a job, but I stayed in Kansas City because I was contracted by a hotel." He found hard work at the hotel where something else awaited him as well.

Mark soon met a young woman, blonde and blue-eyed, who worked as a waitress in the hotel barroom. Her name was Melody and a romance began in Kansas City that has taken them through the kitchens and restaurants of several hotels, reaching Ponce, where it endures to this day.

I thought Mark was Canadian and had thought so for years. Obviously, I was mistaken altough I was on the right track, Mark arrived in Puerto Rico via Canada. The Vista Hilton bought the Kansas City hotel and Mark was transferred to Toronto. "I asked Melody to go with me, but we couldn't get a work visa for her, so she had to stay behind in Kansas City for two years."

Sometimes, time puts things into perspective; what at the moment is irritating later seems amusing. "The executive chef at the Toronto Airport Hilton was Swiss and was convinced no Americans could cook. When I arrived, he assigned me to the task of opening the restaurants in the morning, and of taking care of breakfast and banquets. My Kansas City assistant had gone with me to Toronto. Upon our arrival, the Swiss chef named him sous-chef, because he was German and his name was Martin Woltner. Now he works with Wolfgang Puck; he is a very good chef."

Two years later, Hilton presented Mark with another opportunity; again he was offered a transfer – this time with the choice of Puerto Rico or Guam. Melody went to Canada on vacation and the couple decided to marry wherever his transfer took them. They sat down to plan their next steps. Obvious result: Puerto Rico, because the position payed $1,000 more.

The couple arrived in Puerto Rico to find the Caribe Hilton in the midst of change: it was July, 1989 and the executive chef, Augusto Schreiner, had re-signed to open his own restaurant and Mario Ferro, a Colombian chef, took charge. Today he is still executive chef. Mark knew Ferro from Kansas City and Ferro named Mark his executive sous-chef.

It was hurricane season. The media urgently announced an approaching hurricane named Hugo. Mark and Melody had been on the island two months. Kansas City was sometimes hit by tornados, but Mark and Melody had never seen a hurricane, and they only knew what they heard from the *boricuas* in the kitchen: "No way. Puerto Rico hasn't had a hurricane since Santa Clara, in 1956."

On September 18, 1989, the winds of Hugo hit the coast of San Juan, baptizing the young couple with sea foam, salt spray, and sand. Precisely then, Mark and Melody were in the process of moving into an oceanfront apartment. At the hotel, hurricane winds and heavy rain slammed into the building. Guests and hotel staff pitched in to do the best they could by propping up storm protection, improvising meals, and trying to find out what was happening, because supposedly hurricanes no longer hit Puerto Rico.

Melody and Mark chose a full-dress military wedding – with a difference: their wedding took place, not at a military chapel or a military facility, but at the Caribe Hilton, in a quaint old spot that had once been a restaurant. They were surrounded by cooks, who formed a two column honor guard for the ceremonial "arch of sabers": they raised saucepans and skillets, sieves, ladles, and huge spoons, forming an archway through which Melody and Mark passed…not crossed sabers, but cooking utensils…

They spent their honeymoon in the Lesser Antilles, in Barbados, at the Barbados Hilton. Who was the hotel manager at the time? Gunther Mainka, the chef from whom Augusto Schreiner had first heard of the Caribbean, when both worked at the Düsseldorf Hilton.

Melody French with a customer in the dining room.

Chocolate sauce is poured on a cake, for the Chocolate Symphony with Banana Ice Cream. Page 64

"We didn't know Gunther, but he went overboard with attention and even gave us his car keys so that we could sightsee. I hadn't ever driven a car with the steering wheel on the right, because in Barbados, you drive on the left, English style."

The newlyweds settled into a routine, she working at the Chart House Restaurant, in the Condado section of the city, near the Hilton. Mark, on the other hand, doing a thousand things required of an executive sous-chef at a large hotel.

At the time, Hilton had two hotels in Puerto Rico: the Caribe Hilton in San Juan and the Mayagüez Hilton, located in an important city on the west coast of the island. Suddenly, the general manager and the food and beverage manager quit, without explanation. The management brought in Gunther Mainka from Barbados to take charge temporarily. Mainka arrived to find a surprise: the Chaîne des Rôtisseurs, a gastronomic society, had scheduled a gala dinner at the Mayagüez Hilton. But Mainka had no chef, so he sent San Juan an SOS. Mario Ferro, executive chef in San Juan, couldn't get away, so he recruited Mark French. "I'll go, if you fly me to and from Mayagüez, and I'll need to take my assistant."

The chef in Mayagüez had planned a menu approved by the Chaîne des Rôtisseurs, and the ingredients for the dinner were already on hand. So Mark and his assistant arrived in Mayagüez and cooked for the entire event, which ended with a round of applause. "We were dead tired, but there was wine left over, and we were hungry. We sat down to eat and drink wine…after which we collapsed from exhaustion."

When Hilton built a new hotel in Ponce, Mainka was named manager, and he called Mark to be executive chef. "Ponce had never had a hotel like that. Prior to opening, we worked for six months without taking a day off." When the hotel opened, Mainka asked Melody to train the dining room staff, but instead he made her manager of the two hotel restaurants. Mark and Melody were key to helping put the Ponce Hilton on the gastronomic map with the restaurant, La Cava del Ponce Hilton.

Most chefs aspire to owning their own restaurant. Mark and Melody were no exception. In July,

1997, Mark and Melody inaugurated their restaurant at the Hotel Meliá much to the delight of the *ponceños*. "It was very different from my hotel experience. I had to prepare a menu, create dishes, work on a small scale…and we did everything ourselves…Melody had to train the staff as well as participating in the interior design and organization of the dining room."

They have been developing a cuisine that increasingly includes more of the tastes of Puerto Rico. "We can find more ingredients locally; it's incredible how the vegetable supply has changed over the last 10 years. There is a man whom I helped financially to produce bean sprouts, now everyone in Ponce buys from him." The *plaza del mercado* (marketplace) supplies a lot of Mark's kitchen needs.

Has it been difficult for a Baltimore bread maker, transplanted to Ponce, to acquire a clientele? "Slowly, the *ponceños* have accepted me into the community. I have very faithful clients, who come once or twice a week." Mark points out that before, his clients had to go to San Juan to eat well and that's no longer the case. "They've been learning, and I've been learning. They won't let me remove certain dishes from the menu. The area also has new restaurants with young chefs. Promising young *boricuas* spend time in my kitchen."

Looking back to the day when they chose Puerto Rico over Guam — are they satisfied? Mark bursts into laughter and answers with a twinkle in his eyes: "I can't complain." Melody, who is still the maître d' joins the conversation. "At first, clients arrived without reservations and found the restaurant nearly full. I'd say, 'You don't have a reservation? I regret that we don't have a table, if only you'd called me for a reservation.' They looked at me in surprise and said, 'In Ponce?' and I'd answer, 'Yes, in Ponce…Now, everyone knows that on our busiest days, reservations are necessary."

Pan Fried Swordfish with Parmesan Cheese Funche. Page 60

Morgan and Noah

During early summer of 2004, the sommelier Marcos Mercado and I were serving wine at a charity event at the Ponce Museum, when an angelical vision appeared: a young girl with large blue eyes, dressed in a white chef's jacket and an apron that almost reached the floor. She wore an enormous smile, and she carried two platefuls of finger food which her father had sent in from another station. She was Morgan, Mark and Melody's daughter, who was her father's assistant that evening. The regulars at Mark's at the Meliá are Morgan's good friends – and her brother, Noah's, as well. They both often go to the restaurant with their mother, sometimes spending their Sundays there. Who knows, they just might follow in their mother's and father's footsteps.

Smoked Salmon and Caramelized Mango with Avocado Tomato Relish

Serves 4

Relish

¼ cup tomato, diced

¼ cup purple onion, minced

¼ cup cucumber, diced

2 scallions, minced

2 tablespoons cilantro, minced

Juice from ½ lime

Juice from ½ orange

2 tablespoons extra-virgin olive oil

2 tablespoons white vinegar

¼ cup avocado, diced

Salt and pepper

Parosley Oil

1 tablespoon parsley leaves

½ cup olive oil

Juice from ½ lime

Tabasco sauce to taste

Salt and pepper to taste

Salmon and Caramelized Mango

2 ounces smoked salmon, 4 portions

4 thin slices mango, cut lengthwise

Presentation

Radicchio leaves

Lettuce leaves

4 miniature tomatoes, halved

When Mark French created these recipes, we were at the height of Puerto Rico's mango season, which Mark uses to his advantage by featuring this rich tropical fruit in several recipes. Here, he used mango as an ingredient with the salmon and an interesting combination for the relish.

Relish

Mix all ingredients thoroughly in a bowl. Reserve.

Parsley Oil

Place all ingredients into a blender and blend until puréed.

Salmon and Caramelized Mango

Dust a warm skillet with a tablespoon of sugar. Add a portion each of salmon and mango. Sauté for a minute and a half on each side until caramelized. Remove from skillet and keep warm. Clean the skillet and repeat the procedure with the remaining portions.

Presentation

Place a few lettuce leaves in a deep dish. Place a few radicchio leaves next to the lettuce and two tomato halves. Arrange a slice of mango and top with one salmon slice. Pour sauce over the salmon. Decorate the plate with a few drops parsley oil.

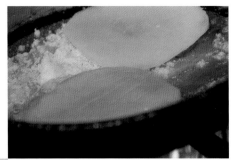

Sofrito criollo

The Puerto Rican sofrito is different from the Spanish sofrito, as it is ground in a blender in a large ammount and is kept in the refrigerator until needed, when it is used in small portions. Sometimes it is sautéed.

In a blender, combine 1, seeded and chopped tomato, 1 seeded and chopped green pepper, ½ chopped onion, 1 tablespoon olive oil, 3 chopped ajíes criollos, 2 chopped long cilantro leaves, 3 small cilantro leaves, ¼ teaspoon oregano. Blend until the mixture becomes a paste. Keep tightly covered in the refrigerator until needed.

Vianda and Chicken Soup al Cilantro

Serves 10

Chicken Broth

1 small chicken, cut into 8 pieces

2 carrots, sliced

2 small onions, sliced

3 celery stalks, sliced

2 bay leaves

2 tablespoons peppercorns

Water to cover

Soup

1 cup onion, diced

1 cup red bell pepper, minced

2 or 3 small, round green peppers, minced

6 garlic cloves, sliced

1 cup sofrito criollo

3 pounds mixed viandas or tubers (malanga, taro root, sweet potato, pumpkin and other available Puerto Rican tubers), peeled and cut into 2" slices

2 tomatoes, diced

1 sprig cilantro

2 small envelopes annatto powder (optional)

Olive oil

Salt and pepper

Tuber Chips

Mixed tubers (cassava, sweet potato, igname, etc.), very thinly sliced

Vegetable oil for frying

To serve

Parsley oil (see Smoked Salmon and Caramelized Mango with Avocado Tomato Relish recipe)

This vianda or tuber soup is a variant of the popular sancocho de gallina which is eaten in several areas of the Caribbean. 'Guinea' could be used in lieu of chicken.

Chicken Broth

Place all the ingredients into a stockpot. Simmer over low heat for one and one half hours. Remove the chicken and cool. Skin and bone the chicken. Strain the broth. Correct seasoning. Shred the chicken meat and reserve for later.

Soup

Heat the olive oil in a stockpot. Sauté onion, peppers, *ajíes* and garlic until translucent. Add the *sofrito* and the tubers and season with salt and pepper. Cover with the chicken broth and simmer over low heat for an hour, until the vegetables are tender.

Pour the soup into a blender, in two or three parts, so it doesn't spill. Process at high speed until puréed. Transfer to a saucepan. Add the diced tomato, the boned chicken and the annatto powder (optional) and mix well. Correct the seasoning and heat, if necessary.

Tuber Chips

Heat the oil over high heat in a deep skillet or deep fryer. Fry the sliced tubers until crisp. Remove with a slotted spoon and drain on paper towel.

To serve

Pour soup into soup bowls and garnish with parsley oil and fresh cilantro leaves. Place several tuber chips on the rim of the saucers.

Duck in Tamarind with Cassava Mojo and Avocado

Serves 10

Duck

10 duck breasts, skinned and tendon removed
1 cup onion, chopped, diced, minced
4 tablespoons garlic, mashed
2 cups tamarind syrup
2 cups white wine vinegar
1 cup olive oil
4 ounces brown sugar
2 cups ketchup
5 bay leaves
Salt and pepper

Cassava Mojo

2 large cassavas, peeled and cut into chunks
Vegetable oil for frying
1 onion, julienned
1 green bell pepper, julienned
1 red bell pepper, julienned
8 sweet ajíes
2 garlic cloves, sliced
1 cup white wine vinegar
1 cup cilantro leaves
All-purpose flour
Salt and pepper

Parsley Oil

1 bunch parsley, chopped
Juice of two green limes
1 cup extra-virgin olive oil
Tabasco sauce, to taste
Salt

Duck takes well to things sweet, thus, the caramelized crust. The Caribbean has an abundance of tamarind and in Puerto Rico, one can find the fruit, or already processed with sugar and in a concentrated form. 'Mojo' is a sauce or condiment.

Duck

Remove the hard tendon that runs under the breast of the duck. Take a very sharp knife to score the skin making a grid pattern, without cutting into the meat.

Heat butter in a saucepan. Sauté the onion and garlic until translucent. Add the syrup, the vinegar, the sugar, the ketchup, and the bay leaves. Cook until mixture reduces, without thickening much.

Preheat oven to 350°F. Season the duck breasts with salt and pepper. Add the breasts to the caramel syrup; they should be well covered. Heat a skillet over medium-high heat. Seal the breasts, skin side down (Extra fat is not necessary as the duck releases a lot of fat). Turn and seal the other side and cook for a minute. Place the breasts in a baking dish. Roast for 10 minutes.

Cassava Mojo

Boil the cassava in a saucepan filled with salted water. Cook until tender. Remove, drain and let cool. Cut the cassava in long batons. Dredge lightly with flour. Fry the cassava in a skillet filled with oil, over medium-high heat, until crisp. Remove with a slotted spoon and drain on paper towels.

Heat some oil in a saucepan and sauté the onions and the peppers, the ajíes and the garlic. When they are translucent, add the rest of the oil, the vinegar, the cassava and the cilantro. Season with salt and pepper.

Parsley Oil

Process at high speed the parsley leaves, the olive oil and the limejuice, until puréed. Pour into a bowl and season to taste with salt and Tabasco sauce.

Avocado and Tomato Sauce

Pour the vinegar into a small bowl. Slowly pour in the olive oil while beating with a wire whisk, until emulsified. Add the avocado and tomato and mix well, but carefully: the avocado must not be crushed. Reserve.

Piña Colada

All of the ingredients in this world famous cocktail are from the Caribbean; pineapple was given to Columbus' crew by the indigenous people of Guadalupe and coconut has been around since time immemorial; rum, of course, could not be more Caribbean.

Although La Barrachina Restaurant in San Juan claims to be the creator of the *piña colada*, friends of mine, who worked at the Caribe Hilton during the seventies, tell a charming story.

"While Monchito Marrero was the bartender at the Pool Terrace Bar, the owner of Coco López took him several cans as promotional materials. Marrero made a test batch: he poured 3 ounces of Coco López into a blender, 6 ounces of pineapple juice, and 1 ½ ounces of white rum. He added crushed ice to the blender, blended all the ingredients, and served the drink as a frappé in two tall glasses, garnished with a pineapple slice; he named his creation Piña Colada." And so, according to them, without further ado, that renowned cocktail became a celebrity.

A national kitchen is far more than the mere origins of the ingredients used in a country. Could one imagine Italian cooking without tomatoes, polenta, and pasta? Yet after the Discovery, tomatoes and corn reached Italy from Mexico, and pasta possibly came from China with Marco Polo.

A regional or national kitchen is the compendium of dishes which constitute the eating habits or customs of a particular area; it is the practical and everyday food consumed by the majority of the inhabitants of a region or country, in their homes and in their restaurants, which distinguishes it from what is cooked in other regions and countries. It may include native and foreign ingredients, as well as dishes and techniques borrowed from other kitchens. It may even include remote influences, but there will always be a core group of distinctive dishes, ingredients, and procedures which sets it apart, although it may share common elements with other regions.

Look at Spain. The Basques cook differently from the Catalonians, and both have renewed their regional cuisine through French influence, while striving to maintain the character of their ingredients and cultures. Yet, they still remain within the Spanish cooking canon. Each of the three Caribbean Spanish speaking countries; Cuba, the Dominican Republic, and Puerto Rico, have their own particular cuisine, even though they are 'first cousins'. *Cilantro*, which is very popular in Puerto Rico, isn't used much in Cuba, where parsley predominates. The shallot is omnipresent in the Dominican Republic, yet in Puerto Rico it is rarely used. In Puerto Rico, plantains are used to make *pasteles* and *mofongo*, whereas in Santo Domingo, they are used for *mangú*. The plantains are mashed and boiled for *paste* les, while they are fried for *mofongo*. *Mangú*, in contrast, is made by boiling the plantain, then pureeing it with oil. Just as in France, Spain, or Italy, the people of Puerto Rico have conserved popular cooking both at home as well as in restaurants. The globalization of agriculture, fishing, and fast foods threaten the subsistence of this popular kitchen. But at present, the cuisine of the best restaurants is perhaps not so distant from the tastes of popular cooking 50 years ago.

Puerto Rico is the only country in the Antilles which suddenly made a huge leap and transcended popular Puerto Rican cooking by creating a haute cuisine without losing its roots; quite the contrary, it consolidates its origins more and more each day.

Many of the chefs' recipes featured on the pages of this book clearly reveal the heritage of those original inhabitants, and illustrate how they have integrated traditional ingredients into their highly imaginative cuisine.

To cite two examples, chef Mario Pagán's recipe for *Frituras de yautía con ensalada de bacalao* (*Yautia* fritters with codfish salad) uses the same *yautía* that was used by the Taínos, cooking it as a fritter and accompanying it with a variation of the traditional *serenata de bacalao*, a salt cod salad with tubers and avocado. The avocado arrived from Mexico, but don't say that out loud, because it is so abundant on the island that no one would believe you. In Ponce, chef Mark French, an American, incorporates various Puerto Rican elements in many of his dishes. His recipe for *Pechuga de pato al tamarindo con mojo de yuca y aguacate* (Duck breast with tamarind and a sauce made with cassava and avocado) reminds us that the *Taínos* hunted migratory ducks which visit our lagoons; the tamarind used in his sauces is the fruit of a tree that was naturalized here centuries ago. The *mojo* reflects the emigration from the Canary Islands, mellowed by the tropics, and cassava could not be more *Taíno*.

An obvious theme we have hardly touched is the African influence that has contributed to all aspects of our culture, including cooking. But this is not an oversight; turn a few pages to find Interlude III, where you can read about Africa's contribution.

Borinquen Fondas

In San Juan and in the rest of the island, one finds *fondas* which are true treasures of popular Puerto Rican food. This is a small list of some of the authors favorite *fondas* and *lechoneras*.

San Juan

LA CASITA BLANCA
Calle Tapia, in Villa Palmeras
Specialty: kidney beans with pigs' feet

CAFETERIA DE LA FUNERARIA BUXEDA
Calle César González, Hato Rey
Specialty: chicken broth and mofongo

Loíza

EL BURÉN DE LULA
Specialty: Cassava fritters, 'cazuela de batata y calabaza'

Sabana Seca

MILLIE'S PLACE
At the corner by the ballpark
Specialty: Landcrab stew

Cayey

EL CUÑAO
Cayey exit from expressway #52, toward Aibonito
Specialty: spit- roasted pig and *gandinga*

Toa Baja

GUACARO
Specialty: tripe

Santa Isabel

LA FONDA DE ÁNGELO
A block from the Plaza de Recreo
Specialty: fried *Arrayaos*

Salinas

CHEF RAMÓN
La Playita de Salinas
Specialty: Fresh fish from the south coast

Rincón

EL CURVÓN
Carretera 115
Specialty: Rincón lobster salad

Borinquen

The island measures approximately 160 km by 53 (111 miles by 35.5). It has a population of 4 million – plus another two million scattered throughout the United States. Though the island has few natural resources, there is a good infrastructure for agriculture, commerce, finance, marketing, higher education, and communications.

Surprisingly, the island has given us four Miss Universe titleholders, several opera singers and world-class musicians, a dozen boxing champions, several extraordinary baseball players, a candidate for the Nobel Prize for literature, several internationally renowned scientists, and some of the best cooks and restaurants in the Americas.

Although Borinquen is commonly used in Puerto Rico, the Taíno name for the island seems to have been Boriquén.

Lunch at La Casita Blanca: avocado salad, pig's feet with chickpeas, white rice, and stewed saltcod. At the back, bottles of 'pique', or hot sauce. In the glass, 'maviada', made with 'mavi' root and rum from a secret recipe.

Top, La Casita Blanca in San Juan. Lower right, the terrace at Chef Ramón, in Salinas.

Traditional Salinas Mojo Isleño

In a small, heavy pot heat ½ olive oil, a sliced onion, a chopped tomato, and 5 whole garlic cloves until the onion softens. Add 5 bay leaves, ½ cup vinegar, black peppercorns, salt, 1 teaspoon sugar, ½ mid-size can of red peppers, ½ cup mixed olives and capers, rinsed, and a little water. Cook on low heat until thick.

Ramón Carro's Cocktail Sauce for Oysters

Yields 2 cups

1 cup tomato sauce

1 cup ketchup

2 tablespoons horseradish

Juice of ½ lime

1 tablespoon shallots, diced

Salt and pepper to taste

Wherever there is both an ocean and oysters, there will be cooks with their own versions of sauces for the oysters. My mother, who was from New Orleans, and who praised that city's oysters, had three axioms: that one should only add lemon, that unless the oyster twitched, it wasnot fresh, and that oysters are to be eaten only during the months that end in the letter 'R'. This delicious formula is Ramón Carro's, owner and chef at Chef Ramón, in Salinas, on the island's south coast, where the oysters used are the tiny ones that grow in the mangroves. Use just a little sauce, so as not to overwhelm the oysters' taste. The sauce can be kept in the fridge. Oysters were an important food for the early Amerindian Arawak who populated the Antilles.

Mix all ingredients in a bowl, using a wire whisk. Transfer to a glass or porcelain container, cover, and refrigerate.

La Casita Blanca's Red Kidney Beans

Serves 4

Sofrito

Culantro (large leaf)

Cilantro

2 ajíes dulces, seeded

1 green pepper, chopped

½ onion, chopped

2 garlic cloves, peeled

Red Kidney Beans

1 pound Red kidney beans

¼ pound ham, chopped

2 pigs' feet, desalted, cooked in water and chopped

2 tablespoons tomato paste

1 tablespoon olive oil

3 potatoes, peeled and chopped

½ pound pumpkin, peeled and chopped

Salt to taste

Red kidney beans served with white rice could be called the Puerto Rico's national dish. Every cook has his or her own recipe, and this one comes from La Casita Blanca, a well-known 'fonda' in San Juan that has been mentioned in many international food and wine magazines. Jesús Pérez, the owner, inherited the restaurant from his mother, Doña Aurora, and this is her recipe, which includes cooking ham and salt pigs' feet. The rule on seasoning: season to taste. Pérez and his wife are patrons of several community projects which they have established, one of which is a library in Villa Palmeras.

Fill a large pot with water, add the kidney beans. Let soften overnight.

Sofrito

Put all the ingredients into a blender and process, until thoroughly chopped up. Transfer to a bowl and reserve covered until needed.

Red Kidney Beans

Boil the beans for an hour in a cookpot placed over medium heat. Draw off some water, if necessary. Add the ham, the pigs' feet, the *sofrito*, the tomato paste and the olive oil.

When the beans are tender and the stew has almost thickened, add the potatoes and the pumpkin. Cook over low heat, until the potatoes and pumpkin soften. Serve with white rice or stewed rice.

Vieques-Style Arepas

Yields 10-12 arepas

2 tablespoons butter

2 tablespoons cold lard

2 cups all-purpose flour

1 tablespoon baking powder

Salt

1 cup cold water

Vegetable oil to fry arepas

Place all ingredients in a bowl with the exception of the water. Using two spoons, cut the butter and the lard into the flour and the other dry ingredients, until well mixed. Add the water and continue mixing thoroughly. Continue kneading the dough on the work surface, until well mixed.

Shape 10 to 12 small rolls (or more, according to the size). Let rest for 35 minutes. Place the rolls on the work surface and flatten them into ¼" thick disks, using a rolling pin. Fold the disks like handkerchiefs.

In a large pot, fry the arepas in very hot vegetable oil until they are golden. Remove from oil with a slotted spoon and drain on a paper towel.

Preparing 'arepas', 'empanadas de jueyes', and 'tortillas dulces' at Mediania Alta Baptist Church in Loíza.

Rock Cornish Hen Stuffed with Congrí from El Metropol

To stuff 4 hens

Congrí

4 ounces bacon, chopped into small bits

8 ounces cooking ham or chicharrón,
  chopped in small bits

1 tablespoon vegetable oil

1 medium onion, minced

1 green criollo pepper, medium sized,
  minced

2 garlic cloves, mashed

Oregano, to taste

1 cup black beans, cooked Cuban style

Salt, to taste

1 bay leaf

1 ½ to 2 cups water

1 cup medium grain rice

Adobo, or Marinade, for the Hens

4 Rock Cornish Hens

2 garlic cloves, mashed

2 Seville oranges

Oregano, to taste

Salt and pepper to taste

Basting Sauce

1 cup beer

¼ cup sherry

3 tablespoons tomato sauce

Oregano to taste

2 garlic cloves, mashed

Olive oil

Paprika, to taste

Don Pepe Canosa, a Cuban exile, came to Puerto Rico in the mid-sixties after having been imprisoned in Cuba following the 1961 Bay of Pigs landing. Shortly after arriving, he and his wife opened a restaurant that served Cuban food and named it Metropol. This stuffed Rock Cornish hen has been on the menu since the restaurant's beginnings, and for 40 years has remained the most popular dish at the Canosa family's restaurant, all of which are called Metropol.

This recipe is courtesy of Octavio Ravelo, Canosa's son-in-law and the owner of one of the Metropol restaurants.. Although Metropol makes 'congrí' with black beans, the original recipe from eastern Cuba, calls for small red kidney beans. I suggest the seasoning described below to marinate the hens, but you may use any marinade you prefer.

Congrí

In a saucepan, brown the bacon with the ham or chicharrón in oil. Cook over medium heat, until the bacon is browned and has lost its fat. If it is very greasy, dispose of excess. Add the onion, the green pepper, the garlic, and the oregano. Stir-fry until the onion and the pepper have softened. Add the black beans with their liquid, then add the salt, the bay leaf, the water, and the rice. Cook for 18 to 20 minutes until ready.

Adobo or marinade for the hens

Season the hens with the garlic, the Seville oranges, the oregano, salt and pepper. Place in a baking dish and refrigerate, covered, for 3 hours. Remove hens from the refrigerator and let sit at room temperature for ½ hour. Preheat oven to 350°F.

Basting sauce for the Hens

In a bowl, combine the beer, the sherry, the tomato sauce, the oregano, the garlic, and the olive oil. Stir, making a thick red mixture.

Preheat oven to 375°F. Season the hens with salt and pepper inside and out. Stuff with the congrí and close the stuffed cavity. Truss the hens and place on a baking sheet, with the breast side up. Pour half the sauce over the hens. Dot with olive oil and dust with paprika. Roast ½ hour. Turn the hens, baste with sauce and roast ½ hour. Turn the hens again, so that breast side is up. Baste with sauce and roast ½ hour more or until browned, adding the remaining sauce.

Editor's Note: 1 cup of canned beans may be used. Rock Cornish hens may be substituted by small chickens or partridges.

Frank Cedeño's Goat Kid Fricassee

Serves 8

6 pounds goat kid, chopped and cleaned

Adobo for seasoning kid

4 garlic cloves, crushed

2 bay leaves

5 tablespoons dried oregano

Salt and pepper

3 tablespoons vegetable oil

Fricassee

2 onions, minced

2 green peppers, minced

2 celery stalks, minced

½ cup white wine

3 red potatoes, chopped

2 carrots, chopped

Extra-virgin olive oil

In 2002, when I did a series of 12 programs for WIPR-TV of Puerto Rico, I dedicated a program to Dominican cookery. Chef José Abreu, chef and co-owner of the well-known restaurant José-José in San Juan, cooked a goat kid Dominican-style at his farm in Aibonito. Nobody makes a kid fricassee as well as the Dominicans, and today, it is Frank Cedeño's turn. He is chef at El Mesón Gallego, a restaurant, which despite its Spanish name, serves several 'criollo' dishes. The Puerto Rican cooking industry has undergone enormous Dominican influence, both in private homes and in many restaurants whose chefs are Dominican.

Adobo for Seasoning the Kid

Place the kid in a baking dish. Season with the garlic, the bay leaves, the oregano, and salt and pepper. Cover and refrigerate overnight.

Fricassee

The following day, pour vegetable oil into a stew pot or caldero. Add and fry the onion, the peppers and the celery stalk until tender and well mixed. Add the meat and its adobo, stir and cook 5 minutes. Add the wine, mix and simmer, half-covered, for 2 hours. Add the potatoes and carrots and cook for half an hour, or until tender.

Serve with white rice.

MARIO PAGÁN

HEARTH AS
INHERITANCE

Red Snapper with Avocado and Tangerine Salad, and Pumpkin Fritters. Page 99

Not all great chefs find their vocation at an early age, as did Augusto Schreiner. For some it is a roundabout route, and Mario Pagán belongs to this latter group.

Younger – and lighter by more than a few pounds – Mario was an equestrian, accomplished in the rarified and elegant world of the Paso Fino, a world he still enjoys, breeding and exhibiting at the well-attended fairs in Puerto Rico.

During those years of his adolescence and school in San Juan, Mario's learnings never seemed to be directed toward the kitchen; the only thing he knew about cooking was watching the woman who worked as a cook at his house. But it seems that although he didn't know it, he carried the culinary genes of his mother, a good cook with a fine palate, and of his grandmother, who was famous for the cakes she baked as a hobby.

She even put together wedding cakes, which another lady would decorate before they were given as gifts. "She made a carrot cake that was so good that a friend of mine wanted to market it." The grandmother was not so skilled at traditional cooking, but she would experiment and prepare dishes with different flavors. "She did have a specialty which she made on Good Friday, an oriental fried rice with lobster, which was spectacular…We grandchildren waited all year for the Good Friday family get-together."

One day, after seeing and tasting so much, Mario went ahead and made his grandmother's carrot cake one Christmas. Quite a while would go by before he would come near a kitchen again, except to heat up coffee.

The career young Mario Pagán finally chose was architecture, and as soon as he finished high school he was admitted to a school of architecture at a New Jersey university. "But winters were cold in New Jersey and I applied to a school in Miami." So Mario went down to Miami looking for a climate more like that of his native Puerto Rico.

"When I went to study architecture at Miami Dade Junior College, I found a part-time job as a draftsman, until one day a friend, Harold Fournier, found me a job at Chili's, earning $12 an hour as a grill cook."

For our young apprentice chef, that job was a great experience. "It was a good foundation; lots of work, long hours at night…None of the glamour of those chefs you see on TV." Little by little, architecture was left behind and Mario decided to take a break from college, joining Pan American Airways as a flight attendant, which he followed with three years at Iberia, the Spanish airline. "My route took me to Central and South America, but we could ride to any country where Iberia flew." Thus, Mario traveled throughout Europe, discovering the world of gastronomy, beyond Chili's, hot dogs and hamburgers.

"I couldn't go to expensive restaurants, but I remember a small family–owned and run hotel in Prague…The owner cooked, and I could smell the delicious aroma of truffles in my room. Every afternoon he set out five tables in a small courtyard, and there he served a

Cooking never interested Mario Pagán, although he enjoyed watching his grandmother

bake. Yet, he discovered the art of cooking, and found himself at culinary school

Taro Root Fritters with Codfish and Ali-oli Sauce. Page 94

tasting menu that changed daily…He did it as a hobby… That's what I call a passion for cooking!" Mario Pagán was even more impressed by the abundance of similar places throughout Europe.

And on one those trips, he also discovered Middle Eastern and Asian cuisine. "The cooking styles that I most like are Arab and Oriental. I could spend years taking recipes from these styles and adapting them to our tastes."

Finally, Mario stopped flying and returned to a kitchen, this time to an Italian restaurant in Coral Gables, Bugatti, a very old establishment owned by a German family where Northern Italian cooking attracted a very loyal clientele. Later he found work in an even more formal kitchen with a hierarchy and designated work stations. At the Grand Bay Hotel in Coconut Grove, the executive chef was Pascal Oudin, a Frenchman who is now chef-owner of the excellent Pascal's on Ponce in Coral Gables; Mario discovered another world. "I worked for room service, the midnight shift. This was my first experience in a real kitchen." He not only worked hard and long hours, he also received wise advice: "There was a sous chef who told me: 'Anything one cooks must be prepared with love, even if it's a hamburger, because everything tastes different when it is cooked with love.'"

Then one day, Carlos Álvarez, his fiancée's father, told him that if he was serious about making cooking his career he should study seriously, and that he should take advantage of the fact that Johnson and Wales University, a Rhode Island institution, with a prestigious culinary school, was establishing a North Miami campus. Mario was soon enrolled. "I already knew a lot, but in any case, I learned a lot there…and anyway, a diploma is always a good thing to have."

At night he worked at Tamarind, trendy restaurant at that time, whose executive chef was Carmencita González, the talented and experienced Puerto Rican chef…"I was the sous chef…" Carmen is now chef-owner of Carmen, The Restaurant, in Coral Gables.

In order to graduate, Mario was required to prepare a thesis with three other students in which they designed a restaurant, which they named Cilantro. Drawing upon his architectural studies, "I made a scale model which caused a sensation. We took first place."

In the early 1900s, Norman Van Aken, who had made a name in Key West, opened Norman's, in Coral Gables, which soon became the place to be. Mario Pagán was by then a graduated chef with experience and he went to work at Norman's. "Norman was like a movie star. A TV or Hollywood personality would contract him to cook for an event, and Norman would steal the show. He was not even accessible to us, his kitchen staff." Mario was at Norman's when he received a call for help from Alfredo Ayala, who needed an assistant at Chayote, his restaurant in Miramar in San Juan.

It was at Chayote that Mario perfected his career as a chef. When Ayala decided to sell Chayote, and open a simpler country restaurant en route to El Yunque rainforest, Mario was almost ready to be his own boss, a chef-owner. Working with an artist like Ayala had given him what he needed.

"Alfredo is amazing, I've seen him pull tricks out of his sleeves, and I ask myself, where did he get that? I am a faithful follower of his culinary style and technique, but one of the most important things that Alfredo taught me is that the creative moment in a kitchen is best when you're performing under pressure. I love that rush…I lose my appetite…I love the anxiety I feel." Only someone who has been in a restaurant kitchen with a full house or at a banquet at the moment when the meal is to be served can understand Mario's words: "I compare cooking to a battle: there are shouts, tension, blood, heat, fire, fights…and there has to be discipline, as though you were in an army."

That young man who spent several years studying a demanding career like architecture has become a creator who continues to develop and learn every day. "Once I heard the great chef, Gilles Epié, one of the 50 master chefs in the United States, state: 'Pride is a creator's greatest enemy. When pride rears its head, you must hammer a nail into the wall, and hang pride from that nail.' "

Mario continues to ride his Paso Finos in his free time. His other passion is car racing, but he devotes a lot of his time to his popular restaurant, Chayote, and another project that keeps him fired up: a new restaurant with a tropical-oriental flavor at the Caribe Hilton in San Juan.

What would this chef, who at 36 has traveled the world and achieved success, advise young people beginning their culinary careers?

"First, be honest in what you cook. If it is Arab, then it must be Arab; if Chinese, then Chinese…I would tell them to seek work where the hours are long, and to understand that a chef is truly an artist who must be in love with his work. For me, taking apart a stove, cleaning it, and then, putting it back together, is not work, it is a pastime."

The chef prepares the Salmon Tartare. Page 93

Good Friday in Puerto Rico

The Catholic religion continues to predominate in Puerto Rico. Many people who do not practice during the year feel devout during Holy Week, and there are customs related to abstinence and fasting that are not only what the Church would mandate. For example, one of these customs dictates that one must eat fish on Good Friday. It is not that one must fast or abstain from eating meat; it is virtually an obligation to eat fish or shellfish. So in many homes, Holy Thursday and Good Friday are treated as a family occasion by those who do not attend services, and even by those who do.

The Paso Fino Horse

Juan Ponce de León, as part of his quest for the Fountain of Youth, imported horses from Spain. Those horses were ancestors of today's Paso Fino, whose bloodlines are zealously protected by various associations, as well as the government. The equine is not large, but its gait is extraordinarily elegant, and the Puerto Rican Paso Fino has a graceful side-step, even as a foal. A good Paso Fino may cost many thousands of dollars; its care, handling and riding is extremely specialized.

Salmon Tartare with Sesame Seeds and Green Plantain Tostones

Serves 4

The salmon tartare

4 ounces fresh salmon, finely chopped

2 ounces smoked salmon, finely chopped

1 teaspoon shallots, finely chopped

1 ounce black sesame seeds, toasted

2 ounces sesame oil

½ cup mayonnaise

½ teaspoon Ali-oli sauce (see Codfish
   Fritters recipe, page 94)

3 scallions, finely chopped

1 teaspoon fresh ginger, grated

Salt and pepper

The tostones

2 green plantains

Canola or soybean oil for frying

Nori nests

3 sheets of edible sushi paper (nori) cut in
   thin slices

Canola or soy bean oil for frying

To serve

½ teaspoon Ali-oli sauce

A dish with ingredients from different latitudes; the salmon is from cold northern — or southern — waters, but the combination with the 'tostones' is simply delicious.

The salmon tartare

Mix fresh salmon, smoked salmon, shallots, sesame seeds and scallions in a mixing bowl. Squeeze the ginger and let the juice fall on the salmon mixture. Add the sesame oil and the mayonnaise and mix well. Season with salt and pepper and mix again. Set aside in a cool place.

The tostones

Peel the plantains and slice in 1" thick pieces.

In a heavy skillet or frying pan, heat the oil. Fry the plantain slices a few at a time, until they start to brown, but are still tender. Remove with a slotted spoon, drain on paper towels and let cool to room temperature. Repeat until all slices are fried. Place the slices, one by one, between brown paper sheets and pound flat with the palm of your hand, or the flat side of a cleaver. Heat the same oil you were using and fry the *tostones* again until golden brown. Remove with a slotted spoon and drain on paper towels.

The nori nests

Make small nests with the nori paper slices. Heat oil in a skillet and fry over high heat. Remove with a slotted spoon and drain on paper towels.

To serve

Place *tostones* on a serving tray, leaving a ½" separation between them. Spoon salmon tartare on top and crown with nori nests. Spoon some Ali-oli sauce between the *tostones*.

Taro Root Fritters with Codfish and Ali-oli Sauce

Serves 4

The codfish salad

½ pound codfish, desalted, skin and bones
   removed

1 tablespoon vinegar

1 bunch scallions finely sliced

1 tablespoons extra virgin olive oil

½ piece ripe avocado peeled and finely diced

Juice of one lemon

The fritters

1 pound taro root, grated

1 egg

1 teaspoon baking powder

Salt and pepper to taste

Vegetable oil for frying

Ali-oli sauce

2 egg yolks

3 garlic cloves

Juice of one lemon

1 cup extra virgin olive oil

Salt

The Caribbean custom of combining tubers with codfish works fine with this recipe. The addition of vinegar and olive oil to the codfish is also akin to a popular Puerto Rican dish, 'Serenata de Bacalao'

The codfish salad

In a bowl, flake the codfish with your hands. Add the olive oil, chopped scallions, diced avocado, lemon juice and vinegar. Carefully mix all the ingredients. Cover and refrigerate.

The Ali-oli sauce

In a food processor, fitted with the steel blade, mix the egg yolks, garlic, lemon juice and salt. Turn the machine on and off a few times. With the motor running, pour the olive oil through the feed tube in a thin stream, until the sauce thickens.

The fritters

Combine the egg and the grated taro root in a mixing bowl and mix well. Add the baking powder, salt and pepper and finish mixing. With your hands, make four round patties. Heat the oil in a skillet. Fry the fritters over high heat, until golden brown on both sides. Remove the fritters with a slotted spoon and drain on paper towels.

To serve

Take out the cod salad from the refrigerator. Cut each fritter in two and place some codfish salad over each half. Add a spoonful of Ali-oli sauce on top of the fritters.

A tip from the chef: Fritters can be made small to serve as appetizers or bigger as a main course.

Crayfish Risotto with Celery Root and Watercress

Serves 4

The crayfish risotto

12 crayfishes, with their heads on

½ cup watercress leaves

**4 ounces celery root, peeled, boiled and
  diced**

4 cups crayfish stock (see below)

½ teaspoon grated shallots

½ cup whipping cream

A pinch of saffron

2 tablespoons butter

1 tablespoon mashed garlic

1 cup arborio rice, washed

¼ cup dry white wine

Salt and pepper

Crayfish stock

6 cups water

2 cups white wine

1 teaspoon black peppercorns

1 onion, chopped coarsely

2 carrots chopped coarsely

2 celery stalks, finely chopped

To serve

Watercress leaves

The use of celery root gives this dish a different personality.

Crayfish stock

In a large saucepan, combine onions, carrots, celery stalk, peppercorns, crayfish shells and heads, wine and water. Bring to a boil over medium-high heat. Turn the heat to low and cook until stock has reduced to half. Strain and set aside.

The crayfish risotto

Heat butter in a large skillet and sauté garlic, shallots, saffron and crayfishes, but without heads and 4 with their heads, until crayfishes are red all over. Remove the crayfishes with tongs and set aside. Add the rice and mix well. Add the stock and cook, stirring constantly for 20 minutes. Stock should be added, ½ a cup at a time, stirring constantly and adding the stock as it dries. When it is almost done, add cream and wine. Season with salt and pepper and mix well. Add celery root and watercress and mix.

To serve

Place a portion of risotto on center of plate and acrayfish head in the middle. Decorate with watercress leaves.

Curried Cassava and Crab Pasteles with Piquillo Red Pepper Sauce with Papaya and Mango Chutney

Serves 4

The pasteles

1 cup crab meat, frozen or canned

¼ pound cassava, peeled, boiled and grated or ground

1 green pepper, finely chopped

1 garlic clove, finely chopped

¼ tablespoon curry powder

2 tablespoons lemon juice

6 tablespoons mayonnaise

⅛ cup all purpose flour

¾ cup breadcrumbs

1 egg, beaten

6 tablespoons mayonnaise

Peanut oil for frying

Red pimiento sauce

2 ounces Spanish pimientos, finely chopped

4 ounces mayonnaise

The chutney

½ cup mango pulp, finely chopped

½ cup papaya, finely chopped

1 teaspoon honey

½ teaspoon white vinegar

Tabasco sauce, to taste

To serve

Assorted salad greens, like arugula, romaine, and Boston lettuce, shredded

Rosemary sprig

Although pasteles translate as pies, these are really small rectangular crab cakes, fried and baked. The British Antilles has a great Indian influence and from these islands we have inherited the curry and the chutney that add flavors to this dish.

The pasteles

Combine crabmeat, cassava, green pepper and garlic, in a mixing bowl. Mix well. Add lemon juice, mayonnaise and curry. Season with salt and pepper.

Have ready a dish with flour, a bowl with the beaten eggs and another tray with the breadcrumbs. With your hands, form 4 rectangular cakes or *pasteles*.

Coat the *pasteles* with flour; dip in the beaten eggs and coat with breadcrumbs. Refrigerate, covered, for one hour.

Preheat oven to 325°F. Fry the *pasteles* in peanut oil in a deep skillet or frying pan, over high heat, until golden on both sides. Remove carefully with a slotted spatula and drain on paper towels. Place the *pasteles* in a baking dish and bake for 6 minutes. Keep warm.

Red pimiento sauce

Mix the chopped *pimientos* and the mayonnaise well in a mixing bowl.

The chutney

Mix all the ingredients well in a mixing bowl.

To serve

In the center of serving plates, place about half a cup assorted salad greens. Add one *pastel* on top and top with chutney. Pour *pimiento* sauce on the plate, around the pastel. Decorate with a rosemary sprig.

Dolphin Filets with Chickpea Croquettes and Fresh Tomato Sauce

Serves 4

The Tomato sauce

10 tomatoes, peeled, seeded and chopped

3 ounces onion, finely chopped

4 ounces butter

Salt and pepper

The chick pea croquettes

10 ounces dried or canned water packed chickpeas

3 ounces finely chopped onion

2 ounces all purpose flour

1 egg, lightly beaten

4 ounces breadcrumbs

Salt and pepper to taste

Vegetable oil for frying

The fish

4 eight onces dolphin filets

Olive oil

4 tablespoons butter

To serve

Parsley leaves

Dorado is called dolphin or mahi-mahi in English; it is a fish, not the sea mammal of the same name. It is delicious and is fished in the waters around Puerto Rico when in season.

The tomato sauce

In a casserole, place the tomatoes, half the onion and the of butter, cook over low heat. Continue cooking until very tender and thick. Season with salt and pepper. Transfer to a food processor or blender. Process until you have a thick sauce. Drain through a chinois or a fine sieve.

The chickpea croquettes

If you are using fresh dried chickpeas, cook in salted water in a saucepan until they are tender. If using canned chickpeas, just drain. Purée the chickpeas in a food processor or blender.

Mix the purée with the onion and the egg in a mixing bowl. Season with salt and pepper. Form this dough into round croquettes. Lightly flour the croquettes, dip into the beaten egg and run through the bread crumbs. Fry in vegetable oil in a large skillet or frying pan over medium-high heat, until golden brown and crisp. Remove from pan with a slotted spoon and drain on paper towels. Keep warm.

The fish

Preheat the oven to 375°F. Season the *dorado* filets with salt and pepper on both sides. Sear the *dorado* in butter in a heavy skillet, over medium heat, on both sides. Remove carefully with a slotted spatula. Drain on paper towels and transfer to a buttered baking pan. Bake 6 to 8 minutes, until crisp and tender, but not overcooked, because they will be too dry. Keep warm.

To serve

Cover serving plates with a thin layer of tomato sauce. Place a *dorado* filet in the middle of the plate. Top with a chickpea croquette. Garnish with a parsley sprig.

Serves 4

Puerto Rican avocados are meaty and flavorful, but they don't grow all year round. Pick a pumpkin that is meaty, but not watery, to have a perfect dough.

The avocado salad

2 avocados, peeled and finely diced

½ bunch scallions, finely chopped

¼ cup honey

2 tangerines, peeled and cut in segments

½ red onion, minced

Sal and pepper

The avocado salad

Combine the avocados, scallions, honey, tangerine segments and onion in a mixing bowl. Season with salt and pepper. Set aside

The sauce

½ onion, finely chopped

3 garlic cloves, minced

10 tangerines, peeled, seeded
   and cut in segments

2 cups fish stock (see recipe for Crayfish risotto,
   page 95, and substitute fish for crayfish)

½ cup whipping cream

The juice from three lemons

Salt and pepper to taste

The sauce

Heat olive oil in a large skillet. Sauté the onion and garlic over medium heat. Add the tangeries segments and mix well. Add the fish stock, whipping cream and lemon juice, mix well and cook over low heat. Beat with a wire whisk to obtain a creamy sauce. Season with salt and pepper.

The pumpkin fritters

1 pound pumpkin, peeled, boiled, strained and
   drained

1 teaspoon ground cinamon

½ cup brown sugar

1 egg

½ cup breadcrumbs

Canola oil for frying

The fritters

In a large mixing bowl, mash well the cooked pumpkin. Add cinnamon, brown sugar, egg and breadcrumbs. Mix well and, with two soupspoons, shape the fritters.

In a deep skillet or frying pan, fry the fritters in canola oil over medium-high heat, until golden. Remove with a slotted spoon and drain on paper towels.

The fish

4 red snapper filets, 8 ounces each, deboned
   but with skin on

All purpose flour for coating

Salt and pepper

Extra virgin olive oil

The red snapper

Season the snapper filets on both sides with salt and pepper. Coat lightly with flour. Sauté in olive oil in a large skillet over medium-high heat. Brown the skin side first, until crispy. Turn over and cook the other side for one minute.

To serve

Thyme sprig

To serve

Coat the serving plates with the sauce. In the center of the plates, place one fourth of the avocado salad. Top with red snapper filet and garnish with a thyme sprig. On one side of the snapper filet, place 2 or 3 pumpkin fritters and sprinkle with minced chives.

Coconut Crème Brûlée

Serves 4

1 ½ cups whipping cream

4 egg yolks

2 teaspoons rum or coconut liqueur

2 vanilla beans or ½ teaspoon vanilla
  extract

2 tablespoons brown sugar

2 tablespoons grated coconut

To serve

Grated coconut

Toasted grated coconut

8 Strawberries

Hierbabuena (mint) sprigs

The Crème Brûlée is a classic French dessert that here, with the addition of coconut and 'hierbabuena' (mint), takes on a tropical personality.

Preheat oven to 275°F. In a mixing bowl, mix the egg yolks, cream, rum or coconut liqueur, brown sugar and grated coconut. Slit the vanilla beans and scrape the inside into the batter. Mix thoroughly with a wire whisk and pour into individual ramekins or ceramic molds.

Place ramekins in a baking pan with one inch of water and bake in a bain-marie (double boiler) until the custards are set (about 45 minutes). Take the ramekins from the oven. Let cool in the water. Refrigerate until very cold. Preheat the broiler in the oven. Take out ramekins from the refrigerator; sprinkle brown sugar over the custard. Remove excess sugar. Place the ramekins on a baking pan and caramelize under the broiler, being very careful not to burn them.

To serve

Sprinkle grated and toasted coconut over the custards.

Place the ramekins in the center of serving plates. Garnish with two strawberries on one side of the ramekins and a pluche of mint over the custard.

Grandmother's Carrot Cake ~ Traditional Recipe

Yields one cake

1 pound carrots, unpeeled
4 eggs
2 cups sugar
2 cups all purpose flour, sifted
1 ½ teaspoons baking powder
1 ½ teaspoons baking soda
½ cup hazelnuts
½ cup raisins
1 ½ cups vegetable oil
1 teaspoon salt
Butter

"Since I was a child I saw my grandmother bake this carrot cake and it still is one my favorite dishes". Mario Pagán.

Preheat oven to 275°F.
Place the carrots in a large saucepan and fill with water to cover by 2 inches. Bring to a boil and cook until carrots are tender. Peel and chop the carrots. Reserve.

Beat the eggs and sugar in a bowl until thick and creamy. Add the flour, the baking powder and the baking soda and mix well with a wire whisk.

Coat the carrots, raisins and hazelnuts with all purpose flour to have them float in the batter and not sink to the bottom. Add to the batter with the oil and salt. Carefully mix well these ingredients into the batter, stirring just once.

Butter the sides and bottom of a baking pan. Pour the batter into the pan and bake for about 55 minutes, or until a toothpick inserted in the cake comes out clean.

JOSÉ REY

A LONG JOURNEY
FROM FILLOAS TO FOIE GRAS

Guinea Hen Breast Stuffed with Chanterelle Mushrooms. Page **124**

Compostela, long one of San Juan's great restaurants, has a bar at its entrance – several barstools and a small rectangular table. Nightly, after 11:00 p.m., three people dine regularly at that table; occasionally one or another newcomer will join the two. Any given evening, in the main dining room, a table of diners may linger, enjoying a Quinta do Noval 1963, a Hennessy XO or an *orujo* while the kitchen hands finish washing up, the cooks change into jeans and party shirts and the waiters, still in the dining room, discreetly set the tables for the following day. At last, the party of stragglers rises, and passes the threesome in the bar, who rise to bid good-night to their clients; well groomed and elegant men and women who return the farewells, taking in, with a touch of envy, the appealing food and the good bottles of wine laid out on the table.

Perhaps sometimes, one may see José Rey, Maximino Rey and Ignacio Pérez – the chef, the director and the head waiter of the dining room, sharing their table with a new face: a David Bosch, a great sommelier from Spain, a Santi Santamaria, the Michelin three star chef from Barcelona, or a Pepe Rodríguez, the celebrated winemaker from the Galician Rías Baixas. Or, maybe luck will allow you to share one of these intimate late night dinners and you will be graced with one of the highest privileges: dining at the small chef's table, which, although not physically in the kitchen, represents acceptance into that group: the ultimate accolade for serious food lovers.

A gilt frame, holding labels from several wine bottles and bearing a small engraved plaque, hangs on our walls at home. The labels are a Veuve Clicquot 1989, a Château de Chamirey, a B.V. Réserve Georges de Latour 1979 and a stellar Vega Sicilia Único 1968…a souvenir from one of those rare nights. The small plaque reads "A pleasure to have shared your 47th wedding anniversary…Ufff! That's many years! Rey and José", bearing witness to history.

José and Maximino make plans, taste new wines to buy for the restaurant or for distribution, gossip about politics, stock market fluctuations, the feats of the soccer teams Barça and the Atlético de Madrid and dream of possible vacation destinations – if they manage to get away. This is their intimate moment; an escape from the stress following a long day that begins at nine in the morning. It is a small reward that they allow themselves nightly, a small prize, earned by maintaining one of the best restaurants in the Caribbean…and in America.

José and Maximino are almost the same age, they bear the same last name, and although they both come from the same town, La Estrada, in the province of Pontevedra in Galicia, they are unrelated and were barely acquainted. After traveling the world, seeking their fortune, chance led these two *gallegos* to meet far from home, still in search of a decent living. Joined by destiny, they would launch a never imagined partnership and enterprise.

José recalls: "We actually met at driving school. There, Maximino, who had returned from several months in France where he had worked as a bricklayer, told me he was leaving for San Juan, Puerto Rico where an uncle who owned several shoe stores had offered him work. He left; I stayed behind. My father died and I, a youth not yet 20, was forced to help support my mother."

The young man finally found work aboard the German cruise ship, Bohème, which toured the Caribbean. José flew to Miami from Madrid, where the ship's tour manager met him: Samuel Zequeira Celas, a fellow Spaniard, greeted him with the surprising news that the Bohème was in dry dock where it would remain for awhile. But Lady Luck intervened when Zequeira Celas and his lady friend adopted the youth, taking him to visit St. Augustine, the oldest city in the U.S. and to Walt Disney World in Orlando. "I could not believe my eyes, everything amazed me…And the food!

Americans didn't know how to eat. Mother never cooked putting stuff on chicken the way they do at Kentucky Fried Chicken! And who ever heard of smearing French fries with ketchup?"

When they finally sailed on the Bohème, José found himself wearing a

Duck Liver with Caramelized Apple-Bananas. Page 126

A young Galician with a different taste

The *horreos* of Galicia, the chestnuts, the octopus, his mother's *caldo gallego*, *empanadas de atun* and his sister's *filloas* left their imprints on José Rey. When he went to work aboard the Bohème and found no familiar comfort food, nostalgia – and then hunger-consumed him. For a long time, the thin young man, not yet 20, ate only prosciutto and cheese sandwiches. Yet, he soon found enormous gastronomical pleasure in the soup the Korean kitchen crew made for themselves. "I had never eaten Asian food before, ever since, I have been a fanatic. The soup was very hot and spicy and made me cry, but I like it 'picante'." A Dominican waiter, José Garden, managed to supply him with the prosciutto sandwiches. Years later, Garden came to live in Puerto Rico and was captain at Compostela. Now he is co-owner of José-José, one of the good restaurants in San Juan.

white jacket, working as a busboy, ready to discover new worlds, such as the city of San Juan, Puerto Rico, one of the ports of call. Every Wednesday the ship docked in San Juan, and José would remember that his fellow countryman Maximino lived in that city, but he had no way to locate him. By chance, one day Maximino's meanderings crossed Jose's at a San Juan discotheque. "Just like today's ship crews, back then, we'd reach land and go party.

One night in the Condado, I heard a familiar Galician accented voice and, lo and behold, Maximino."

Maximino had never taken the job at his uncle's shops. He had instead gone to Café Valencia as a waiter. José remained aboard the Bohème and the two friends saw each other whenever the Bohème docked in San Juan. Again fate intervened; a fellow Spaniard who had made and then lost a fortune in Cuba, now an exile in San Juan and an accountant at Café Valencia, gave José advice: "The ships are great but it's time to consider settling down on land."

José took his advice, managing to stay in San Juan while Maximino arranged work for him at the restaurant, and the two became roommates, taking a small apartment.

Maximino soon moved on to a new, flashy and expensive restaurant, Don Pepe. Then he accepted an offer as maître d'hôtel at La Fragua Restaurant, which had recently opened to rave reviews. By this time, the two friends had been entertaining a dream and adventure: that of their own restaurant.

This was a beautiful, ambitious dream, but the reality was another: "The two of us are waiters, we cannot survive without a good cook". La Fragua had an old Spanish chef, Fructuoso Pascual, who had trained in the classical tradition in Spain. José says of him: "I have never seen anyone so professional, nor anyone who could handle a knife as well as Pascual." Maximino considered matters and spoke to Cristóbal Jiménez, the owner of La Fragua, who

Center, standing, Maximino Rey, partner and Maitre d'Hotel.

agreed to cede Pascual to the young men.

Soon Maximino and José were hammering nails and sawing wood, preparing for the opening of a restaurant at a crossroads in the heart of San Juan – where Santurce and the Condado merge. They named the restaurant Compostela in honor of the city of Santiago de Compostela, which is reputed to house the remains of Saint James the Apostle, the patron saint of Spain.

As the day of the opening approached, José asked Maximino: "Have you considered what the consequences would be if our chef quits or gets sick? We'd have no restaurant. I enjoy cooking and I believe I have what it takes, so if you don't mind, instead of working in the dining room with you, I think I'd better get into the kitchen and learn from Pascual."

And learn he did, blow by blow: "He was very tough. I started as a kitchen helper, but he lovingly taught me absolutely everything; he was a strict disciplinarian to boot. He could make all the classic sauces and was a master of the practical techniques in use by Spanish hotels fifty years ago. Pascual would say: 'The most important thing to know about cooking is how to chop parsley and onions.' He taught a lot, but, oh was he pushy (*jode, que jode, que jode*)."

One day, Luis Bosch, a Catalonian hotelier who contributed much to Puerto Rican gastronomy, took aside the apprentice chef. Bosch had noticed the young man's talent and determination and asked why José didn't go to see what the new Basque chefs were doing. And so, José Rey went off to seek a new culinary world, while Maximino, carrying his own weight, broadened and deepened his studies of wine. "Bosch called Juan Mari Arzak, pioneer of the New Basque Cuisine, who accepted me into his kitchen in San Sebastián for a couple of weeks, and Pedro Subijana invited me to work at Akelarre. It was a unique experience and I learned a great deal."

This marked the beginning of José Rey's signature cooking. He began to develop his Galician roots; the tastes of his childhood in Galicia mixed with the tendencies of today's cooking. He went into the kitchen of Santi Santamaria's El Racó de Can Fabes, in Sant Celoni, half an hour from Barcelona. He continued, going to Charlie Trotter in Chicago and Jean Louis Palladin at Jean Louis at the Watergate in Washington, DC. Gradually, José Rey, who had never gone to a cooking school, acquired something very important to a chef: culinary culture.

He learned from everyone. "I learned by watching, reading, and listening." And I'd add: by eating… and tasting. It is quite an experience to eat with José Rey at a restaurant, because his perception is

Salt Cod Serenata Terrine. Page 118

Twelve years

In 1994, when Compostela decided to close on Sundays, Maximino Rey confided in me saying, "When you are in this business, you reach the point of total exhaustion. It's been 12 years since we've had a day off. That's something!"

remarkable and he discovers aromas and tastes that are not easily perceptible. Recently, while conversing with him, I said: "José, you have certain qualities that distinguish you from other chefs: first, a sense of proportion, second, a fine palate, you perceive tastes, something not all chefs are able to do. And third, you possess imagination."

Europe taught the two Reys another lesson: style. The restaurant moved to a building across the street in the early 90s ratcheting up Compostela's style. The menu changed, the wine cellar expanded, additional waiters and cooks joined the team, and when Compostela opened its doors, it revealed elegant and refined interiors, with paintings by contemporary Puerto Rican artists.

In the fall of 1993, Yves Fourault, from Louis Roederer Champagne, presided over a gala dinner, "The Three Emperors", held by Los Amigos de la Buena Mesa, a gastronomic society. Compostela's attractive dining room filled with beautifully turned out women and elegant men in formal dress. Compostela had

come of age, and demanded entry into the ranks of the great restaurants of America. A year earlier, it had won Puerto Rico's most important gastronomic award, an honor shared with another of the greats — Augusto's, owned by José's friend, Augusto Schreiner.

Twenty two years have gone by since Compostela opened. Many consider it one of the best, if not the best, Spanish restaurant in the United States. Compostela has its own personality; it is not a Spanish restaurant in the French style; nor does it pretend to be Basque or Catalonian. No doubt José Rey's kitchen is influenced — more than in technique than in spirit — by the great Basque and Catalonian masters. Basically, it is Galician cuisine, with a touch of the Caribbean, and taken to a higher level by its creator's very personal imagination. This, at a time where the majority of young Spanish chefs seem to have been cloned in Ferrán Adrià's laboratory (if not Xeroxed copies).

"I try to do what Santi Santamaria says: 'based on our mothers' kitchen, but with refinement'. I try to rescue our mothers' tastes and to bring them to the tables at my restaurant. I discovered a whole new world of tastes in Puerto Rico, which had been totally unknown to me, and these tastes pervade and influence my cooking. I do not believe that Puerto Rico yet possesses the unity or movement that could represent a new cuisine for the Caribbean or for this island. I think there are various people experimenting, at their hearths, in search of new horizons. Perhaps that's what makes things so interesting."

Salt Cod Terrine

Serves 24

Terrine

4 pounds fillet of salt cod, loin only

2 red peppers

1 celery root, medium sized, peeled and chopped

1 taro root (yautía), peeled and chopped

1 white malanga, peeled and chopped

12 green asparagus, fresh, large, tough end of stalk peeled and sliced

Salt and pepper

Pil-pil sauce

4 garlic cloves

½ to 1 cup extra virgin olive oil

Skin and bones from the salt cod

The pickled green bananas (escabeche)

1 cup extra virgin olive oil

1 onion, finely sliced

3 garlic cloves, minced

4 tablespoons vinegar

Black peppercorns

Cilantro, minced

Salt

2 small green bananas, peeled and cut in small slices

Presentation

10 black olives, marinated in olive oil, pitted and chopped

Caribbean edible tubers can usually be found in Latin American markets. Substitutions are difficult for taro root and malanga, but you can try using mashed potatoes.

Terrine

Desalt the cod for 24 hours. Change water several times.

Fill a large saucepan with water and bring to a boil over medium heat. Add the salt cod and cook for 3 minutes. Remove. Immerse in iced water to stop cooking process. Drain on paper towel.

Skin salt cod and bone, reserve for the pil-pil sauce. Carefully separate the fish into thin sheets.

Preheat the oven to 400°F. Roast the peppers, turning occasionally, until skin has blackened. Remove and place inside a paper bag for 15 minutes. Remove from the bag, peel, seed, and core, discarding all. (You can also roast and blacken them over an open flame.)

Halve lengthwise, stretch and size to interior of the terrine or baking pan.

Bring water to a boil in large saucepan and place the three tubers. Cook until tender.

In separate bowls, mash each tuber and make three separate purées. Set aside.

In a deep skillet, gently boil the asparagus in salted water until al dente. Plunge the asparagus into ice water to stop the cooking. Slice in two, lengthwise.

Pil-pil sauce

In a large saucepan, add the whole garlic cloves and gently fry in the olive oil until golden. Add the codfish skin and bones and fry, stirring vigorously with a metal spoon or wire whisk. Add olive oil if necessary, and a little hot water, while stirring constantly. The sauce will emulsify, turning creamy. When ready, strain through a large chinois. If it is too thick, add hot water.

Terrine assembly

Using a terrine or baking pan, 12 x 3 ¼ x 3, brush the inside with olive oil and cover with plastic wrap (cling wrap). Arrange the bottom of the pan with a layer of asparagus with the flat side up.

Use a spatula to cover with some of the pil-pil sauce, followed by a layer of cod. Cover with red peppers and spread with pil-pil sauce. Layer with cod and cover with celery root purée, followed by a layer of cod and pil-pil sauce. Continue layering with taro root purée, cod, and malanga purée. Finish with asparagus, flat side down. Cover with plastic wrap, overlapping the pan. Cut strong cardboard sized to the interior of the terrine and cover with plastic wrap. Cover the terrine with the cardboard. Put some weight on top of the cardboard (some unopened soup cans will do) and refrigerate 24 hours.

The pickled green bananas

In a frying pan or skillet with olive oil sauté the onions and garlic, until tender. Add vinegar and cook for 10 minutes. Add the peppercorns and cilantro. Season with salt. Set aside.

In a stockpot over medium heat, boil the green bananas until tender, but not too soft. Strain and cool. Add the bananas to the frying pan. Mix well with the onions and garlic and transfer to a glass container. Refrigerate for several days. Take out of the refrigerator one or two hours before serving.

Presentation

Place a salt-cod terrine slice in the center of a plate, garnish with olives and pil-pil sauce. Top the slice with a portion of pickled green bananas.

Serves 4

A contemporary way of making lasagna that is delicious, either with Maine or spiny lobster.

Egg Pasta

2 cups semolina flour

Olive oil

3 eggs

2 tablespoons butter

Salt

Egg Pasta

Mix semolina flour with the olive oil, eggs and butter in a large bowl. Season with a pinch of salt. Knead the dough using the palm of your hands, pressing against the working surface, until no traces of flour are seen. Wrap up in plastic foil and refrigerate for two hours.

Take dough out of the refrigerator. Flatten the dough into a ¼" thick rectangle with the palm of your hand. Pass several times through the different numbers of the pasta machine until it reaches desired thickness.

In a stock pot, bring water with a little salt to a strong boil. Cook lasagna sheets for 4 or 5 minutes, until al dente. Drain well and dip into iced water. When cool, drain again and cut into 4" squares. Reserve, wrapped in kitchen towels.

Maine lobster

2 Maine lobsters, live, 2 pounds each or 2 Caribbean spiny lobsters, live, 2 pounds each

Butter

1 tablespoon shallots, minced

Salt and pepper

2 cups all purpose flour

Oregano, fresh leaves plucked from sprig

2 cups heavy cream

1 cup chives, minced

1 cup parmigiano reggiano, freshly grated

Maine lobster

Quickly chop through lobsters, 1 inch behind the eyes, using a sharp chef's knife. Then shell the lobsters, and twist and sever the tail. Carefully remove lobsters' coral tomalley and reserve. Yank off claws. Clean grit from head and discard. Insert a skewer into the tail to prevent curling as it cooks.

Place the head, tail and claws on a baking sheet. Steam bake until they turn red; or, boil in large pot of salted water for 12 minutes. Remove meat from lobster tail and cut into small medallions. Break the claws' shell with a mallet and carefully remove meat.

Heat butter in a skillet. Do not burn. Add shallots, and when tender, add lobster meat. Season with salt and pepper. Add flour and oregano while mixing. Add approximately 1 ¾ cup cream, just until the sauce thickens slightly and becomes creamy (adjust as necessary). Add some chives and part of the parmigiano reggiano. Mix well. Simmer gently for 2 minutes. Allow to rest.

Assembly

Cook the lobsters' corals in a small skillet, half filled with water, until red. Do not break the membrane encasing the coral. The coral is lobster roe, when the coral pouch is opened, it is sandy and red. Reserve.

Whip the rest of the cream and very carefully fold in the parmigiano reggiano. Heat in a double boiler, so that the sauce does not separate.

Cover a baking sheet with parchment or wax paper. Place 4 squares of pasta on the sheet, cover with lobster, then cover with another pasta square. Pour cream sauce over pasta. Dust with the remaining parmesan and the chives. Place under salamander or broiler and brown until golden.

Pour hot cream sauce onto plates. Serve lasagna in the center of the plate and sprinkle with coral.

Editor's Note: It is best to broil, served on heat-proof plates.

Corn Cream Soup with Wild Mushrooms

Serves 4

The combination of the corn soup with the wild mushrooms roll is delicious. Use whatever wild mushrooms are in season.

4 ounces sliced smoked bacon
1 onion, minced
1 tarragon sprig
12 tender ears of corn, kernels sliced off
4 cups chicken broth
4 cups heavy cream
Salt and pepper

Place bacon slices in a skillet, along with the minced onion and tarragon. Fry for two minutes. Add corn kernels and cook over medium heat for a few minutes. Add chicken broth and cream and cook for 20 minutes. Remove bacon and tarragon. Put soup in blender; blend until liquefied. Strain through a chinois or a fine-meshed strainer. Season with salt and pepper. Reserve.

The mushrooms

1 pound wild mushrooms, minced
4 ounces smoked bacon, julienned
3 ounces butter

The mushrooms

Place julienned bacon in a small skillet and fry until crisp. Remove from skillet and drain on paper towel. Sauté mushrooms in same skillet. Season with salt and pepper. Place mushrooms in plastic wrap. Roll tightly, as if making a sausage. Chill in refrigerator until firm enough to slice.

To serve

½ teaspoon curry powder

To Serve

Remove mushrooms and slice into 2" cylinders without removing plastic wrap. Place mushroom cylinders in center of soup bowls. Carefully peel off plastic wrap from mushroom roll. Heat soup well, and pour around mushroom rolls. Garnish with crisp bacon and curry powder.

Salt Cod in Tempura

Serves 4

1 pound codfish fillet, extra thick and desalted

Tempura
2 cups all purpose flour
12 ounces of beer
1 tablespoon yeast
2 tablespoons rice vinegar
2 tablespoons cilantro, minced
All purpose flour, to dust the cod
Salt and pepper
Olive oil

Presentation
Pil-pil sauce (see Salt Cod Terrine for recipe,
  page 118)

Fresh cod, sea bass, striped bass or halibut can be used with excellent results. Don't miss this great appetizer; you'll be a success with your guests.

The tempura
Pour the flour into a bowl and add the beer, the yeast and the rice vinegar. Beat the ingredients with a wire whisk, until well mixed. Cover with a cloth. Allow to rest.

Place the codfish into a saucepan and cover with water. Bring to a boil over medium heat. Retire from stove. Drain the codfish. Let it cool.

Debone the codfish by hand. Carefully separate 12 pieces of cod (it will come off as large flakes) and place on a plate (if there is codfish leftover, reserve for another recipe). Dust with cilantro and flour, press lightly with fingers. Repeat operation on the opposite side. If using fresh fish, instead of salted fish, add salt and pepper now.

Heat oil in a skillet over medium high. Dip the cod fish in tempura batter, and fry until golden on both sides. Remove with slotted spoon and drain on paper towels.

Serve with Pil-pil sauce.

Serves 4

1 pound red tuna fillet, sashimi grade

2 handfuls mesclun

½ tablespoon white vinegar

4 one-ounce cuttlefish

3 tablespoons olive oil

½ tablespoon Dijon mustard

2 tablespoons soy sauce

2 tablespoons rice vinegar

1 tablespoon sesame oil

½ cup toasted pine nuts

Salt and pepper

This is a very simple dish; the only thing is to be sure to use the very best tuna available. Everything can be ready in advance and assembled when ready to serve.

Shape tuna into a cylinder 1 ½" high x 3" wide. Wrap tightly in plastic wrap. Refrigerate 24 hours.

Wash the mesclun in iced water and white wine vinegar solution. Spin dry well in a salad spinner or blot dry on paper towel. Wrap in a clean damp dish-towel; place in a bowl. Refrigerate until needed.

Season the cuttlefish. Heat a small skillet and sauté the cuttlefish in olive oil until slightly golden.

Place mustard and soy sauce in a bowl and whisk well. Add rice vinegar and whisk vigorously. Add sesame oil and olive oil. Whisk until emulsified.

Remove tuna and mesclun from refrigerator. Slice tuna into thin medallions, without removing plastic wrap.

To Serve

Center handful of mesclun on each plate. Peel off the plastic wrap and arrange 4 slices of tuna, forming a cross. Place 3 cuttlefish in the center. Top with pine nuts, scattered over mesclun. Sauce mesclun and tuna.

Serves 4

2 guinea hens

Guinea Hen Broth

4 ounces smoked bacon, sliced

Olive oil

1 onion, chopped

1 carrot, sliced

2 garlic cloves, halved lengthwise

1 thyme sprig

1 cup red wine

1 cup beef broth

Stuffing

2 ounces butter

2 pounds chanterelles, minced

Salt and pepper

Olive oil

4 ounces smoked bacon, diced

4 shallots, minced

¼ teaspoon saffron threads

Garnish

Butter

4 carrots, small, with stem on

12 green beans, blanched and cooled in iced water

Guinea hens are very flavorful and very popular in Puerto Rico. Instead of chanterelles, you can use tender shiitake mushrooms.

Quarter the guinea hens, separating the breasts, legs and thighs. Skin and bone legs and thighs. Dice meat. Reserve. Reserve all bones.

Guinea Hen Broth

Brown the guinea hen bones and smoked bacon in olive oil. Add onion, carrot, garlic and thyme. Stir and cook for a few minutes. Add red wine, beef broth and water to cover. Simmer half an hour. Strain through a chinois, pressing bones and vegetables.

Stuffing and Sauce

Heat butter in a skillet. Don't let it burn. Fry half of mushrooms and the diced guinea hen meat. Season with salt and pepper.

Use a sharp knife to slit breasts lengthwise, on the side, making a pocket. Season with salt and pepper inside and out and fill with stuffing. Tie with string.

Preheat oven to 350°F. Heat olive oil in oven-proof skillet. Sauté the diced bacon until fat is rendered. Fry shallots over medium heat. Raise heat. Add breasts. Brown skin side, turn and brown opposite side.

Place the skillet in oven for 10 minutes. Remove from oven. Remove breasts from skillet. Reserve. Pour broth into skillet. Return skillet to stovetop. Add saffron thread and reduce sauce to one half over medium high heat. Correct seasoning.

To Serve

Heat butter. Sauté baby carrots and green beans.

Place breasts in center of plate, one on top of the other. Garnish with vegetables. Top with sauce.

Red Mullet Confit in Sherry Vinaigrette

Serves 4

4 red mullet, scaled, cleaned and filleted

Tomato Confit

1 cup extra virgin olive oil
4 garlic cloves, peeled
1 sprig thyme
2 tomatoes, medium sized, seeded
Salt and pepper

Sauce

1 tablespoon sherry vinegar
tomato oil

Presentation

Handful arugula leaves

Salmonetes, or red mullets are abundant in Puerto Rico's southeastern shore. Any small, white fleshed fish can be used as substitute.

Tomato confit

Preheat oven to 350°F. Heat ½ cup olive oil in a large oven-proof skillet placed over medium heat. Fry garlic and thyme until slightly golden. Place tomatoes in the skillet and roast for 45 minutes. Turn the tomatoes.

Remove tomatoes and reserve; do not cool. Reserve the tomatoes' cooking oil and the garlic cloves.

Salmonetes-Red Mullet

Heat the remaining olive oil in a nonstick skillet. Add fish, skin side down. Cook until crispy. Turn and cook 1 minute. Remove fish; do not cool.

Sauce

Place the tomato oil and garlic into the same skillet in which the fish was cooked. Add vinegar. Reduce slightly over low heat. Discard garlic.

Presentation

Place one of the tomatoes confit on a plate. Cover with two mullet fillets, forming a teepee. Drizzle with a little sauce. Place an arugula nest and sauce with the rest of the vinaigrette.

Duck Liver with Caramelized Apple-Bananas

Serves 4

1 Seville orange
1 duck liver, grade B (14 ounces)
Kosher salt
Pepper
1 ounce butter
4 apple-bananas (guineo manzano), peeled and halved lengthwise
1 tablespoon brown sugar
2 cups Port wine

The secret of this duck foiegras is to cook the liver over high heat in the stove, until both sides are caramelized, and then, finish briefly in the oven.

Pare orange zest with a vegetable peeler, work carefully to remove only the colored rind.

Dip a slicer in hot water and cut duck liver into 4 crosswise slices, ¾" thick. Reserve any leftovers, wrap in plastic wrap and save for another occasion. (It may be frozen, although not recommended). Season with salt and pepper. Refrigerate one hour.

Heat butter in a non-stick skillet. Briefly fry the bananas over medium heat. Dust with sugar, add orange zest. Stir and brown until golden and caramelized. Reserve.

Preheat oven to 350°F. Heat a non-stick skillet over medium heat. Butter the skillet. Place a slice of duck liver into the skillet. Press gently with a finger. When well browned, turn and brown the other side. Place skillet in oven. Cook for 2 minutes. Remove from oven, and save warm on paper towel.

At the same time, reduce Port by one half in a small saucepan. Pour the reduced Port into the duck liver skillet and deglaze.

To Serve

Place 2 slices of banana on the center of a plate and top with duck liver. Pour sauce over duck liver.

Serves 4

2 pounds ox tail

Salt and pepper

Olive oil

1 onion, sliced

1 carrot, large, sliced

3 garlic cloves, minced

Thyme sprigs

1 bottle red wine

1 ½ cup Port

2 tablespoons unsalted butter

1 cabbage

The secret of cooking ox tail is simply to let it simmer for many hours until the flesh separates from the bone. The cabbage leaves are best if steamed, but can be boiled.

Season the ox tail with salt and pepper, and brown in olive oil. Add onion, carrot, garlic and thyme and fry until softened. Add red wine and simmer over low heat for 6 hours. Check occasionally, if over reduced, add wine or water. Correct seasoning. Remove pieces of ox tail and debone. Reserve meat.

Return bones to sauce and cook 30 minutes. Strain and reserve.

Reduce Port by one half. Add to sauce and reduce by one third. Correct seasoning. To serve, whip butter into sauce.

Select 4 cabbage leaves from its center. Bring water to a rolling boil in a saucepan. Add cabbage leaves and blanche for 3 minutes (alternate method: steam leaves). Drain and place in a large bowl filled with iced water. Blot dry with paper towel. Place leaves on work surface. Flatten each leaf with palm of hand, central nerve in particular. Cut leaves into approximate squares.

Preheat oven to 325°F. Place a portion of ox tail on center of each leaf. Make a bundle by closing leave as an envelope, then turn. Place the roulades on a baking sheet and bake for 20 minutes.

To Serve

Place a roulade in the center of each plate. Top with sauce. Paint plate close to edge with sauce.

INTERLUDE
(2)

Quince, Cabbage, Melon and Cucumber, Juan Sánchez Cotán, c 1602

THE ALFAJOR THAT LOST ITS ALMONDS

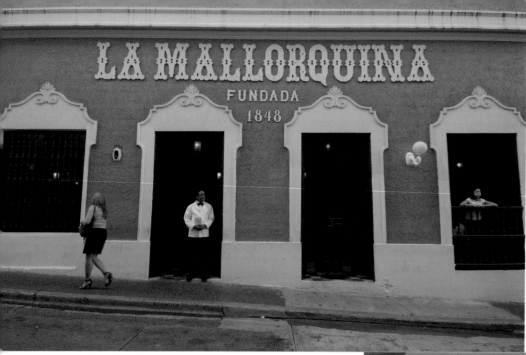

The Spanish influence on Puerto Rican cooking goes back to the earliest days of the colonization and is still manifest in our way of eating, as well as in the existence of grand restaurants in the Spanish style

La Mallorquina, in Old San Juan, founded in 1848, claims to be the oldest restaurant in continuous operation in the Americas.

Why has someone who writes about food and talks about wine become caught up in the labyrinth of history — events that took place 500 years ago? That is a question you may well be asking yourselves. I assure you, I dislike poking around where I'm not bidden, least of all when politics, religion, and cook pots are concerned. But, if I don't go into Al Andalus, I would skew my overview of how the inhabitants of a small island in the Antilles, Puerto Rico, cook what they cook.

Al Andalus is the name given to the Iberian Peninsula kingdoms occupied by the Moors for eight centuries. The Christians who expelled them from their last remaining bastion, the Sultanate of Granada, destroyed along the way the most important repository of cultural, artistic, scientific and perhaps culinary knowledge in Medieval Europe. This occurred simultaneously with Columbus' Discovery, whereby my concern.

The Moors, despite religious dietary restrictions, gave Spain a more refined kitchen, nuanced by the culinary wisdom of the Middle East. They made many kinds of bread; introduced sugar cane and sugar to Spain, distilled eau de vie, made sugar syrup, brought citrus fruits, dry fruits, rices, eggplant, spices, developed the techniques of sweet and sour cooking, fished for tuna with net-traps, made fried and charcoal grilled foods, meatballs, and fillings or stuffings. The vast Moorish culinary heritage could have remained in Spain, yet it perished, if not on the pyre of intolerance, on that of oblivion, because the Catholics who expulsed the Moors and the Jews from Spain were not at all "gourmets" and were little interested in cooking. Thanks to Allah that the Moorish art of pas-

try making has been preserved in Andalusia where it is still treasured today. But Spain, which was entering the Renaissance, retroceded to the Middle Ages in culinary matters.

Among the adventurers who reached the Antilles with Columbus were olive skinned Andalusians, Castilians, and natives of Extremadura. As we noted in earlier chapters, the seamen who disembarked in the Bahamas had endured days and days of the same dish, found the pacific Taínos, who didn't know much about cooking, but who had both food and women. During the early days, as to be expected, a mestization occurred, both in human and culinary terms, which was to continue with the arrival of the African slaves.

While all this took place in America, Spain maintained its course and the sixteenth century progressed. The court kitchen could have been from another planet. Abundance to the point of gluttony, ostentation, battalions of people in the kitchens, but light years away from the culinary fineness and complexity of the Italians and the French. The popular kitchen was far simpler, far more boring and far poorer, although it did find itself enriched by the new foods that were arriving from America: corn, tomatoes, hot (chili) peppers, sweet peppers, beans, vanilla and chocolate (which during a century, was drunk only by the court), potatoes and garden produce. Dishes that are considered very Spanish such as pisto (a vegetable stew), the Spanish omelet and chorizo (a spicy sausage) could not have existed had Columbus not reached America.

This new cookery, as these new products that slowly began to enter the Spanish mainstream, was still essentially rustic. It reached Puerto Rico after great delays and it took some time to become assimilated. Some of those ingredients which had traveled from America to Spain, slowly began the return over a period of three centuries. They returned with a Castilian accent, and proceeded to be integrated into our housewives' humble recipes. The Boricua taste displayed by the criolla and African cooks turned countrified dishes of Spanish ancestry into local dishes prepared by Black and mestizo hands, dishes which incorporated products from Borinquen's countryside. While Spain lagged behind France, in terms of sauces and stews, our kitchen slowly developed. At

Genara Méndez's Land Crab Stew. Page 138

The indispensable pernil de cerdo
At Christmastime there is no home in Puerto Rico that goes without pernil de cerdo, roast pork leg. This recipe is quite simple and very tasty, although there is no substitute for the crisp and crunchy pork rind of spit-roasted pig.

Lightly score the fatty side of fresh ham in a diamond pattern. Marinate in bitter orange juice, salt, pepper, garlic, oregano, and olive oil overnight in the refrigerator. Roast at 350°F, occasionally basting with its own juices. Roast is done when the meat thermometer reads 165°F (20 to 25 minutes a pound).

La Mallorquina's Seafood Asopao. Page 138

some point during our culinary history, *paella valenciana* turned into *asopao*; suckling pig, which is still roasted in Castile seasoned only with salt, in our version is a larger pig, seasoned with garlic and oregano and spit-roasted. The *esqueixada catalana*, a salt cod salad with tomato, pimentos and onion, turned *criollo*, becoming a *serenata* accompanied by *viandas* or boiled tubers. *Pote gallego* and *fabada asturiana* were transformed into stewed red kidney beans; *bacalaíto* is a Puerto Rican version of the shrimp *tortilla* of Andalusia. The *alfajores* of Granada lost their almonds in exchange for grated cassava and the *almojábanas* turned salty.

By the end of the eighteenth century and the early nineteenth, Puerto Rico saw the immigration of Catalonians, *isleños* from the Canaries, Majorcans, Venezuelans, and Corsicans, the production of sugar and coffee increased, and a rural social class emerged which possessed greater economic resources. At mid-century there were 50,000 slaves; in 1869 the island had 600,000 inhabitants.

Puerto Rico was self-sufficient in that it could feed itself frugally and its dependence on Spain and the United States existed for a supply of products that could only be consumed by a small fraction of the population. But this small nucleus was shaping and defining our country-bourgeois kitchen, substantial, tasty, and free of extravagance.

By then the French influence had refined Spanish cuisine. Following the ascent of the Bourbons to the Spanish throne and Spain's occupation by Napoleon, Spanish cuisine became more refined by this influence. During that period, cookbooks on regional cooking were published, some of which were quite good. Something similar occurred between 1857 and 1859, which pertains to our story.

In 1857, Don Eugenio de Coloma y Garcés published The Cuban Cook's Manual (Manual del Cocinero Cubano), a book of more than 600 recipes, which claimed to include Spanish, American, and International cooking adapted to "uso, costumbres y temperamento de la isla de Cuba" or the usage, customs, and temperament of the Island of Cuba. The New York City Public Library has three copies and the National Library of Cuba, I believe, has four.

But the story does not end there. In 1859, the Imprenta Acosta of Puerto Rico published the Manual del Cocinero Puerto-Riqueño (The Puerto Rican Cook Manual). This book was not to be found anywhere, but fortunately, in 1971, the Editorial Coquí of San Juan, published a fourth edition of this book, which, as the publishers explain in the prologue, is based on a 1890 edition, also published by the Imprenta Acosta, which had been preserved somewhere.

One day, as I compared El Cocinero Puerto-Riqueño with the Manual del Cocinero Cubano (I have a photocopy of it), I found both books to be almost identical. A few recipes had different names; others had been added in the Puerto Rican book, possibly to make it more local. At the same time, the Cuban book produced two offspring: Nuevo Manual de la Cocinera Catalana y Cubana…Compiled by Juan Cabrisas in 1858 and El Cocinero de los Enfermos, Convalecientes y Desganados, Manual de Cocina Cubana in 1862. The two seem to be compendiums and adaptations of El Manual del Cocinero Cubano.

These historic books are very important, because in the mid-nineteenth century the existence of a true Cuban kitchen and a true Puerto Rican kitchen was recognized. Half the recipes were really *criollo* and many are still in use. Others compile much of what was eaten in Cuba and Puerto Rico at that time, although, if one analyses the future direction taken by both kitchens - the Cuban and the Puerto Rican - one sees, that despite having common roots and many similar elements, each later pursued a separate or diverging route. There is a point however that intrigues me: the Puerto Rican book features recipes which use parsley, and cilantro as a condiment is absent, which usage, unless I am mistaken, antecedes by far the book's publication.

El Cocinero Puerto-Riqueño was obviously meant for the small percentage of the population of Puerto Rico (upscale market, as we say now), which could, first of all, purchase the book, and, secondly, read it, because that period was one of a very high rate of illiteracy. As frequently seen in those cookbooks, the recipe grouping is erratic, the quantities for ingredients

From left to right, the popular 'mallorcas' at La Bombonera, in Old San Juan; a waiter operates the old Cuban coffee-making machine; the customers enjoy the fare.

is generally either approximate or not given, the instructions are for people who already cook and thus, sometimes appear to be written in code. This book indicates that in the mid-nineteenth century, the island's predominant culinary influence was Spanish; and it has remained so to this day.

Let's take a look at some dishes from our kitchens which appear in any more modern and recent book. What could be more Puerto Rican than *salmorejo*? Yet, the origins of that name are lost in the depths of Andalusian history. Salt cod and rice —daily fare in many parts of Spain- were, during centuries, staples for everyone, rich or poor, because they could be stored without refrigeration, as could herring. Where did our oranges and lemons come from? Tripe, in different preparations, pigs' feet with chickpeas? Desserts in sugar syrup? Look at the supermarket shelves replete with olive oil and what desserts do we eat at Christmas? *Turrón* from Alicante and Gijón…and *membrillo*, quince paste. All of these are as Spanish as the clicking of castanets, but in Puerto Rico, the castanets resonate in the rhythms of *bomba* and *plena* drums.

There is something that cannot be overlooked. In recent years, for the first time in culinary history, Spain has been upstaging the French with chefs like Ferrán Adrià, Juan Mari Arzak, Santi Santamaría, Martin Berasategui, and others. The entire world is focused on Cala Montjuic, Sant Celoni, and San Sebastián, and the wines of Rioja, Priorat, and Ribera del Duero, need bow to none.

Today, many of our restaurants clearly exhibit modern Spanish influence, despite the Caribbean trend to include autochthonous ingredients. Further, the outstanding Spanish chefs have maintained an interesting equilibrium, balancing several styles of cooking: the traditional Spanish, modern Spanish, Caribbean, and, sans doute, French.

José Rey, a Galician, who has spent stages in Basque country and Catalonian kitchens, combines different styles in his recipe for the Salt Cod *Serenata* Terrine: the austerity of the *viandas criollas*, the richness of the Pil-pil sauce, which is egg, garlic and olive oil, and he uses the French technique of making a

terrine. On the other hand, an American chef gone native, Aaron Wratten, presents us with one of his favorite dishes, a curious version of gazpacho, and Augusto Schreiner, in his rice with squid and saffron, suffuses the dish with the aromas of Spain.

In Puerto Rico, it is not possible to evade the influence of Spanish cooking, whether at a Saturday lunch at El Teide restaurant, where Manuel Piqueres, from Santander, prepares "a stew, a roast, and a glass of wine"; or El Pescador's rice with squid, made by Antonio Núñez, a former toreador; the pimentos stuffed with crabmeat by the chef José Abreu at José-José, the tapas eaten at El Chotís while one watches the Real Madrid or el Barça soccer matches and the ubiquitous *caldos gallegos* and *empanadas* at Spanish bakeries in San Juan, such as La Ceiba and Kasalta; the successful dinners that chef Jesús Ramiro organizes several times a year at his restaurant, Ramiro's, which feature great chefs and gastronomic celebrities from Spain. Ferrán Adrià cooked at Ramiro's (then called Reina de España) for one week, years ago, when he was very young, early in his career at El Bulli.

Spanish *panaderías* or bakeries have flourished, primarily in San Juan, in the last three decades. They are far more than *panaderías*; they serve strictly Spanish food, such as lunch with *Caldo Gallego* and *pan de la abuela* at La Ceiba or a breakfast with *Pulpo a la gallega*, as I recently had with Jessica Harris, the insatiable historian of the African influence on the food of the Americas. And let's not mention wine. Which are the best selling wines on the island? The Riojas and the Ribera del Duero.

One could therefore ask: could this be Admiral Cervera's revenge for his defeat by the United States Navy in Santiago de Cuba? Well, *piano, piano*. One hundred and eight years of North American presence have left us another culinary heritage, perhaps less sophisticated and much younger, but nevertheless, very important, because its penetration is many pronged: through supermarkets, television, the media industry, and fast foods.

Capitán al Corto Caldo
Capitán in Court Bouillon

Serves 2

**2 eight-ounce portions capitán (a fish,
similar to red snapper), very fresh**

3 ounces leeks, julienned

3 ounces carrots, julienned

2 ounces celery stalks, julienned

1 tablespoon parsley, minced

2 bay leaves

1 sprig fresh rosemary

¼ quart light fish broth

3 tablespoons garlic, minced

½ cup Fino sherry

2 ounces extra-virgin olive oil

6 saffron threads

Salt to taste

Sweet paprika

Garnish

1 tomato

Bay leaves

Parsley leaves

Craig Claiborne (see Introduction) wrote a story in the New York Times about Chef Cristóbal Jiménez, from Salamanca, and he published this recipe along with his article. Claiborne also included La Fragua among his choice of the best 20 restaurants in the world. At present, Cristóbal cooks only on weekends and only for his wife and friends. His business as an importer of fish and his three restaurants keep him busy. His cooking, with fresh ingredients and sauces made to perfection, pioneered the new Spanish cooking in Puerto Rico, and he has been one of the most important contributors in making Puerto Rico the gastronomic capital of the Caribbean.

Place the fish in a saucepan. Add the leeks, the carrots, the celery stalk, the parsley, the bay leaves, the rosemary, the fish broth, the minced garlic, the sherry, the oil, the saffron and a sprinkle of salt. Cover and simmer over low heat for 10 minutes.

To serve

Remove the fish from the saucepan. Place two spoonfuls of vegetables in the center of a soup plate and place the fish on the bed of vegetables. Pour broth over the fish and scatter with vegetables. Dust with paprika and, if desired, a few additional saffron threads.

With a small and very sharp knife, cut long strips of tomato ½" wide and shape the strips into roses. Decorate each plate with a tomato, 2 bay leaves and a parsley sprig.

Editor's Note: Capitán (Lachnolaimus maximus) is a fish found in our waters, similar to red snapper. If capitán is not available, you may substitute with red snapper.

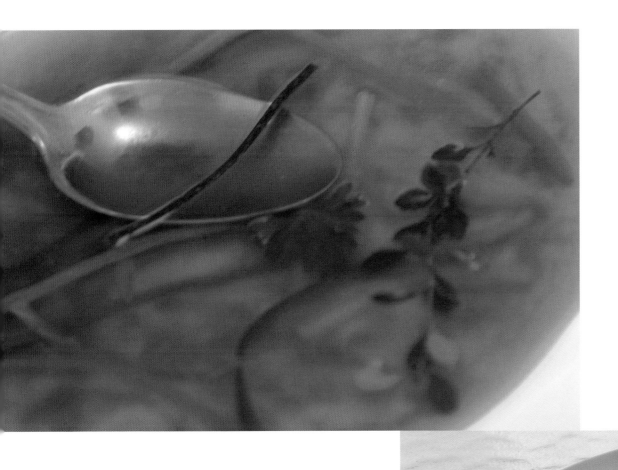

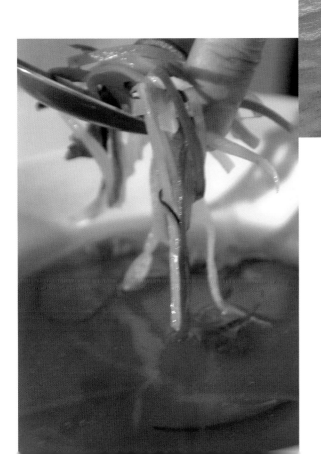

El Salmorejo de Jueyes de Genara Méndez
Genara Méndez Land Crab Stew

Serves 8

4 tablespoons garlic, mashed

½ small onion, finely chopped

2 small round green peppers, finely
   chopped, minced

2 olives, minced

½ green pepper, finely chopped

¼ red pepper, finely chopped

1 ounce corn oil

6 tablespoons tomato sauce

½ cup water

2 pounds crabmeat (land crab)

Deogracia Méndez grew up near to what today is Levittown, a suburb across the bay from San Juan. Since childhood, he caught landcrabs on the beaches and in the mangroves. Now, he and his wife Genara, and their daughters Millie and Evelyn have Millie's Place Restaurant, located in the town of Sabana Seca, west of San Juan. Doña Genara's Salmorejos de Jueyes is authentically criollo and is justly famous throughout Puerto Rico. Deogracia no longer traps land crabs; he chooses them, purchases them while they are still small and then fattens them with fruits and vegetables in the cement pens behind his restaurant. His land crabs have been served at El Gran Cocinamiento del Banker's Club, a longtime event at that exclusive club. The Puerto Rican Salmorejo seems to be a local version of the ancient Andalusian sauce which bears the same name and is made in a mortar, cooked for a bit, and usually served with poultry and game. The salmorejo made in Córdoba is like a thick gazpacho and does not remotely resemble this other formula.

Pour oil in a skillet, and fry all the ingredients over medium heat, until tender. Add the crabmeat, stir well and cook covered, over low heat, for 15 minutes.

To serve, pour into a small bowl placed on a saucer.

Asopao de Mariscos de la Mallorquina
La Mallorquina's Seafood Asopao

Serves 4

8 cups water

Salt

1 cup tomato purée

6 tablespoons sofrito puertorriqueño

½ pound shrimp, shelled

½ pound octopus, sliced

½ pound squid rings

4 large prawns, shell on

4 mussels

2 cups medium grain rice

1 cup dry sherry (Tío Pepe)

1 cup small green peas

Red pimentos, cut in ¼" strips

La Mallorquina in Old San Juan, founded in 1848, claims to be the oldest restaurant in the Americas in continuous operation (see Introduction). The Asopao, a typical, popular Puerto Rican dish is a direct descendant of the 'Paella de Mariscos' (Seafood Paella), although there is also 'Asopao de Pollo'. Take note that Puerto Rican sofrito is used, which is either crushed in a mortar or ground in a blender; classic Spanish sofrito uses minced ingredients and is sautéed. If an herb is used, it should be cilantro rather than parsley.

In a casserole, add the water, salt, tomato purée, sofrito, octopus, squid, the large prawns and the mussels. Bring to a boil. Add the rice and cook for 15 minutes. Add the sherry and stir.

Serve in soup bowls, decorate with the green peas, *pimientos morrones*, and the asparagus.

Olla del campesino

This dish, a precursor of the popular 'sancocho', appears in various books from around 1857. La Olla del Campesino, from 'El Cocinero Puerto-Riqueño', is the same as Ajiaco de Monte, published in the 'Manual del Cocinero Cubano'. Both, evidently, are either a hispanicized version of the Taíno 'ajiaco', or a Caribbean version of 'Cocido Español', however you prefer to see it. We reproduce the recipe with its original punctuation and spelling found in the Spanish edition.

"In a very large stock pot, half-filled with rainwater, add three pounds jerked smoked pork, a chicken, or half a hen, an onion, quartered, and four mashed garlic cloves. Boil for one hour and then skim the surface, and then add the following tubers, peeled and washed with lemon: tender green plantains, *ñame, malanga, boniatos, calabaza, yuca, chayote,* and tender corn; let all of this boil for one more hour; then grind in a mortar these spices and herbs: cilantro, cumin, black pepper and some saffron. After all these are mashed, take a piece of the boiled *malanga,* put it into the mortar, mash it with the spices and then thin with some *ajiaco* broth, mix well and then return the mortar's contents to the pot. Add some lemon juice, taste and correct the seasoning: a sour flavor should predominate. Boil an additional half hour, being careful to stir it occasionally so that the tubers don't stick to the bottom, and at the end of which time, the soup is ready to serve."

Left, the ingredients for the 'Olla del campesino' (pumpkin, 'yautía', 'name', 'chayote', jerk beef, chicken, beef chunks, corn, onions, lime, cassava, garlic, and green plantains); right, the ingredients for the Cocido madrileño (onions, noodles, potatoes, chick peas, cabbage, ham, blood sausage, chorizo, chicken, beef chunks, and garlic cloves).

The cookies

8 ounces flour

4 ounces butter or lard

4 tablespoons sugar

1 beaten egg

Lemon zest

1 egg beaten with 1 tablespoon water

Filling

1 pound sugar

Water

Lemon rind

1 small cinnamon stick

1 pound almonds, ground to a paste

These are round cookies that have been filled with 'dulce de leche' (caramel) or almond paste. There are different versions; this recipe is an adaptation of an ancient formula from time immemorial.

Cookies

On a work surface, shape the flour into a ring. Add butter or lard, sugar and egg in the center of the ring. Push the flour inward to the center with a fork. Mix well and knead, until a ball is formed.

Preheat the oven to 375°F. Roll out the dough with a rolling pin, until it is ⅛" thick. With a 2" cookie cutter, cut into disks. Brush with beaten egg and place on baking sheet covered with a silpat liner or with parchment paper.

Filling

Make a sugar syrup in a sauce pan, with the water, sugar, cinnamon stick and lemon rind. Cook until the syrup reaches the thread stage. Add the almond paste, mix well and cook over medium heat until you have a homogenous paste. Let cool.

Assembly

Spread the almond paste-syrup over half the cookies. Cover the first half by placing the remaining half atop the first.

Editor's Note: An almond or almond slivers may be centered of top of each Alfajor when baking.

Alfajores criollos

1 ½ cups ground cassava or manioc meal

1 egg, slightly beaten

1 tablespoon butter

½ teaspoon milk

Pinch powdered cinnamon

Pinch ground cloves

¼ teaspoon grated ginger

Salt to taste

Sugar to taste

Butter, to grease pan

Alfajores are an Arab legacy and are a very popular dessert in Andalusia, whence they propagated to America, where they are prepared in various ways in different countries. In Puerto Rico, they underwent creolization, lost their almonds and gained ground cassava. They can take varying amounts of sugar and spices. It's possible that Puerto Rico's most common version of this dessert reached us from Venezuela, but the opposite is also a possibility.

In a bowl, knead the ground cassava with the egg, butter, milk, powdered cinnamon, ground cloves, grated ginger, salt and the sugar.

Preheat the oven to 350°F. Grease a small baking dish with butter. Spread the dough on the baking dish. Cook until done: a toothpick inserted into the center will come out clean.

On the left, casabe flatbread; on the right 'Alfajores Criollos'.

Right, Rice with Kumquats and Cilantro. Page 158
Extreme right, Lamb Tartare with Pigeon Pea Fritters. Page 160

JOSÉ SANTAELLA

A TRAVELER IN SEARCH OF
THE PERFECT TASTE

What could be a better spot to interview a chef: a big old building painted green and pink, on Canals Street facing the Stop 19 Plaza, as San Juaneros fondly call the Santurce marketplace

At the greengrocers, and the poultry markets, the fruit juice and fruit shake stands, and at the botánica, every one is a friend of José Santaella's. The moment he sets foot into the market, which he does almost daily, his progress is delayed by greeting everyone by name: "Hola, Tito. How are you Carmen? Pancho, have the avocados arrived? Let me see the passion fruit." The marketplace is familiar ground, near the neighborhood where José has lived since childhood.

His father, Don José Antonio Santaella, owned several food businesses, among them a cafeteria and a Mexican restaurant, at the corner of De Diego and Ashford Avenues, the site of an earlier landmark: Under the Trees, a popular Condado eatery. So José grew up near that corner and eating at family restaurants.

Seated in the small office of his catering business, José effusively converses with me on the subject about which he feels most passionate: cooking. He is electric, exuding good humor and savoir faire. We giddily jump from one subject to another with dizzying speed, only to come back to where we started. "I think we must both have ADD." I tell him, and he bursts out laughing.

"At home everyone cooks well. Mami is a terrific cook…she makes stewed tongue, pigs' feet, *rabo encendido*, salt cod *serenata*…"

José does not hide his taste and love for *criollo* food and proudly recounts that he is the fifth or sixth generation of his Puerto Rican family. "My parents are from Trujillo Alto and Mayagüez, one of my grandfathers is from there, his wife was from Hormigueros and the other grandparents were also from Trujillo Alto, all four are *Boricua*. One of my grandfathers ate very simply: a clear chicken broth with noodles. But he always had dessert, which could be *almojábanas* or a bread pudding – with or without raisins.

And which are you favorites of your mother's cooking? "Mami makes a meat dish which was an accidental success - she herself says that she was never satisfied with how her *carne guisada* turned out – after stewing it, she shreds it by hand and finishes cooking it with Pumpkin Pie Spices. I love it, but I always ask her to make *arroz con pollo* (rice with chicken)… Hers is spectacular."

Surrounded by sweets, going in and out of family kitchens where everyone cooked well and enjoyed eating well, José is right in saying "My culture is totally about food, I spent my childhood eating with my family at the best restaurants of San Juan, the cuisine of San Juan. Restaurants thirty years ago were very Spanish, but there were other restaurants, such as the Rôtisserie at the Caribe Hilton which fascinated me…all those flambés…I was ten years old when I went into the kitchen and made Cherries Jubilee, which I had seen the waiters make at our table. Nostalgia is evidently a strong stimulus: At age 36,

Chef Santaella at the 'Plaza del Mercado' in Santurce.

Risotto and Bacon Patties with Osetra Caviar in a Champagne Sauce. Page 156

today, José's catering menu includes a dessert called 'Fruit Jubilee', inspired by the classic dessert. Brought up in this manner, the logical consequence would have appeared to José to go straight into culinary school, to continue his family tradition. But José detoured, making a few stops along the way, before arriving at his ultimate goal, which was also his origin.

José studied advertising at Barry University in Miami ("I had to study something"), returning to Puerto Rico and graduating from Sagrado Corazón University with a major in communications.

"At Sagrado Corazón I made patés which I took to professors as gifts; in Miami, I cooked for all of my friends. I always cooked, I cooked a lot." One day, he left his apartment kitchen and took a job in a restaurant kitchen. After class, he worked as a chef's helper at a small Coconut Grove restaurant, with an Italian-American kitchen. Advertising and Communications soon fell behind, receding into the background, only to reappear when needed as tools useful for José's catering business.

Didn't you ever consider going to culinary school? "From day one, I didn't ever want to go to culinary school…I wanted to go to restaurants, to learn the hard way…blow by blow…" Soon he found the opportunity to do just this.

He returned to Puerto Rico and met the chef Alfredo Ayala, who offered him work in his kitchen and with whom he has maintained friendship ever since. "I learned a lot, because I had to do everything." Ayala sold his restaurant to Augusto Schreiner in 1988, and Santaella stayed on. "I worked for Alfredo for a year and a half, but I spent much less time with Augusto, who also taught me a great deal."

José Santaella is an incorrigible globetrotter, so, again, he found just the right opportunity to continue his work-travels; taking advantage of having met a young French chef, also a friend of Ayala's, who had just joined Gilbert La Coze at Le Bernardin, already one of New York's top restaurants. Eric Ripert, the young and already proven chef, had been sous-chef to Joel Robuchon in Paris, now gave Santaella a job in his kitchen and that experience left its mark on Santaella's culinary career. "I spent a summer with Eric…it was such a great experience, so extraordinary…He put me to work with François Paillard, one of the great pastry makers of the United States, who is now the owner of Paillard Pâtisserie in New York…what a university that was…four months with those giants!"

By then, José was almost ready to go off on his own, but first he taught cooking at The Kitchen Shop, where many great chefs had taught: Jean Pierre Vigato, Arianne Daguin, Mark Militello, Eric Ripert, and many more, until, in the early 1990s, it closed.

José established his own catering business in 1992. His apprenticeship continued, new horizons and new opportunities opening the doors to new experiences. A friend knew one of the original chef-pioneers of the new Californian cuisine, Jeremiah Towers, owner of Stars in San Francisco, who granted him an interview. "But it was not what I was looking for." José seized the opportunity to "do the tourist bit," and, while he was in San Francisco it occurred to him to request an appointment with another great chef, Gary Danko, who was causing a sensation at The Dining Room at the Ritz Carlton Hotel. Danko told him that there were no positions available and that the hotel did not have a flexible employment policy, but, nevertheless, to stay in touch. Perhaps he might hear of something, perhaps he could help him find another job.

And so our young chef stayed in touch with Danko, meanwhile finding work at another outstanding restaurant, Chez Michel. Years later, Gary Danko would buy and rename Chez Michel as Gary Danko. "They adored me there, I stayed seven months and I had an incredibly good time." And during this time, Gary and José became friends, even living in the same neighborhood, near the Ritz Carlton. Finally, José obtained work with Danko at the hotel. "Once, we participated in the legendary Napa Valley wine auction, which is a philanthropic event and The Dining Room prepared the main dish; Tom Keller and his team from The French Laundry made dessert; Hiro Sone, from Terra, served a cold potato soup with caviar. That was fantastic, tremendous, we even went to dinner at Madeleine Kamman's home, the renowned cooking teacher and writer."

The world turns. San Juan's restaurants commanded the attention of foreign visitors, philanthropic organizations hosted elaborate events such as A Celebration of Vintage Hospitality, held by the René Aponte Foundation.

Salt Cod 'Serenata' with Sweet Potatoes. Page 159

El Bulli

El Bulli is the culinary mecca belonging to two young Catalonian dreamers: Ferrán Adrià and Juli Soler. When they took over the restaurant, which occupies a beautiful large house hidden in a spot on the Costa Brava called Cala Montjuic, Adrià and Soler were two youths, possessed with great talent and revolutionary ideas.

Soon the Michelin inspector-reviewers noticed Ferrán's cooking and how Juli handled the dining room and wine service. So they earned their first star. I met them when they already had two, and by the time I finally ate at their restaurant, they had three. The Michelin guide states that to them a restaurant has earned three stars when its food, service, and ambiance are so good that the restaurant merits a special trip.

Buffet ready for serving in the Cayey mountains.

Gary Danko, invited to cook one of the dinners scheduled for the festival, brought a team of assistants, including José Santaella. The tastes reminiscent of his childhood, memories of the *playas rumorosas* 'murmuring beaches', as sung by the Puerto Rican El Topo, and the desire to resume the business he had left behind, motivated Santaella to remain in Puerto Rico…At least, for awhile…Because in 1999, he managed to land one of the world's most inaccessible opportunities: a chance to work for Ferrán Adrià, in the kitchen of his restaurant El Bulli, at Cala Montjuic, on the Costa Brava of Catalonia. He spent an entire summer there, amidst gelatins, *espardenyes*, strange-sounding sorbets, in the company of not only Adrià and his cooks and pastry makers, but also many of the top young chefs in Spain.

Although José had spent so much time working in restaurants, it may seem ironic that he chose a different route, albeit still within the world of food. At present, Santaella owns a prosperous business which does catering as well as retailing prepared food. He has a team of cooks ready to meet corporate and individual needs at home or at the office. His clientele is a 'who's who' of Puerto Rican society, while he still seems to be the same chef's apprentice, jovial and simple, who breaks into song while cooking, the same young fellow who gave patés to his teachers and made dessert for his classmates. "I enjoy having clients who know how to eat and who appreciate what I do, as do the Ferré family and Richard Carrión who are among my most loyal clients. Sometimes something unexpected occurs, such as the time I was contracted to prepare a country lunch for Oprah Winfrey, which was held at El Yunque. The following day, she called me at home, from her private jet, to congratulate me and to ask for my recipes. Things such as this compensate for the long hours spent in the heat of the kitchen." José has shared magazine space with celebrities – although never stepping out of his kitchen – when he did the wedding dinner for Dayanara Torres and Marc Anthony; she the Miss Universe of 1993 and he, the singer and actor. The wedding may not have been that of Felipe, prince of Austria and Letitia Ortiz – but it was still quite an event.

Passion Fruit Soup with Goat Cheese Ice Cream and Tarragon. Page 165

"The most important thing for a chef is to travel."

Puerto Rican String Cheese with Okra in Sesame Dressing. Page 154

Where have you not traveled? "I still have lots of ground yet to cover, many places left to go, but I've traveled a lot and have been exposed to many influences...Everywhere I've been, everyone I've worked with, has influenced me and I like all styles. The gelatins of Adrià, Vongerichten's juices, Nobu's sushi...But fusion...I hate...It's that — why that word? Everything is fusion..."

Santaella's food, despite his many peripatetic leanings, remains very personal, as is the kitchen he is developing, which he hopes to display someday at his own restaurant.

How would you define your own kitchen? "It's classic and at the same time, modern. I cook for us in Puerto Rico, for our own particular *gustito* or taste, no matter how sophisticated my kitchen may be." One of his cooks has approached the table where we are seated, bearing platters with a simple lunch for two. "This is a rice with crabmeat...I am a maniac for all sorts of rice. I cook the rice, aerate it to stop the cooking process and then I add all sorts of things...I treat it as the Chinese do...and it turns out divine..." The rice placed on our table has been

served with fried ripe plantains, just as at any *fonda* in San Juan. But these plantains have been chosen and cooked perfectly: They are precisely ripe. The combination is delicious, as José has just finished saying. The dish may reveal oriental influence, but its nature is Puerto Rican, which the Puerto Rican eating it recognizes and savors.

At that moment, someone calls from Barcelona. It is a friend who will take care of other Puerto Rican friends who are traveling. "The guy on the phone is a Catalonian who is like the mayor of Barcelona."

I think about our chat, the simple lunch, about other dishes he's made and that I've had the opportunity to enjoy. I understand perfectly that a family that is comprised of , "everyone is a good cook," also will admire and encourage one another. José ends our conversation with his amusing and loving comment: "Mami, Carmen Laura, is a happy disaster, my great fan. She likes everything I make even though I do not — and might think it awful. "Dammit, Mami," I say, "This tastes like shit!"

Risotto and Tocino Patties with Osetra Caviar in a Champagne Sauce

Serves 6

Risotto Patties

¼ cup olive oil

1 tablespoon unsalted butter

⅓ cup onion, minced

⅓ cup salt pork (tocino), cubed

1 cup arborio rice

⅓ cup Champagne

2 ½ cups chicken broth, with ham, preferably homemade

Salt and pepper

Champagne Sauce

1 cup heavy cream

½ cup Champagne

¼ cup fish broth

Salt and pepper

4 ounces Osetra caviar

Presentation

¼ cup salt pork, cubed

Vegetable oil

Chervil sprigs

The caviar makes this dish pricey and requires some effort, but it will definitely impress your guests. A cava or Californian sparkling wine can be used rather than Champagne. A bit of advice: practice in advance to perfect the risotto.

Risotto Patties

Combine a tablespoon of oil with the butter in a large saucepan and place over moderately high heat. Add the onion and the salt pork and stir while cooking for 2 or 3 minutes, until the onions are soft, but not browned. Add the rice and cover thoroughly with the onion-salt pork mixture. Cook one more minute. Add the Champagne and ½ cup hot broth and stir well. When the rice has absorbed most of the broth, add another ½ cup of broth. Repeat the procedure, adding broth in ½ cup increments until all the broth has been used. Set aside ¼ cup of broth to add at the end.

The rice will take 18 to 20 minutes to cook. When it has softened, yet is still firm, remove from heat. Add the remaining ¼ cup of broth. Season with salt and pepper and stir, thoroughly mixing in the ingredients.

Let cool completely and refrigerate, covered, for at least 3 hours or overnight.

Remove risotto from refrigerator.

Shape by hand into hamburger-like patties, using approximately ½ cup risotto per patty. As you shape them, press down on the tarts, to compact them, so they do not fall apart during cooking.

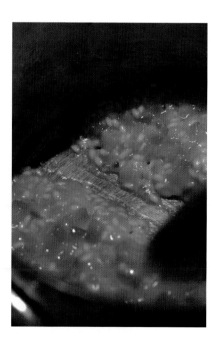

Heat 2 or 3 tablespoons of oil in a 10" nonstick saucepan (If the pan is not a non-stick variety, add more oil to completely cover the bottom). Add as many patties as will fit without touching one another. Cook 8 minutes on each side, until golden.

Champagne Sauce

Add all the ingredients in a saucepan and cook over moderately high heat for 12 minutes, until reduced by half. Correct seasoning.

Presentation

Fry the salt pork in vegetable oil heated in a deep skillet. Fry until crispy. Remove and drain.

Pour some champagne sauce into soup bowls. Place a risotto patty in each bowl. Sprinkle some cracklings over the sauce. Top the patty with caviar. Garnish with 2 chervil sprigs atop the caviar.

Rice with Kumquats and Cilantro

Serves 8

4 cups water

½ cup olive oil

Salt

3 tablespoons orange zest

2 cups rice

½ pound sliced kumquats

½ cup cilantro, minced

½ cup shallots, minced

The Chinese use cilantro in the kitchen, so it is not unusual for Chef Santaella to use ingredients associated closely with that cooking style, such as rice and kumquats (a small citrus fruit with a taste similar to an orange). The dish has truly sensational and exotic aromas.

Boil the water and half of the olive oil in a saucepan. Season with salt and add the orange zest. When the water boils, add the rice and stir twice. When the rice dries, set the heat to low and cover. Let cook until ready, without overcooking.

When the rice is ready, place it in a bowl and mix it with your hands, to aerate and to stop the cooking process. Add the cilantro, the remaining olive oil, the shallots, and the kumquats. Stir and correct seasoning.

Serve on a large serving dish or individual plates.

Salt Cod Serenata with Sweet Potatoes

Serves 12

1 gallon milk

½ gallon water

2 pounds salt cod fillet

1 cup extra-virgin olive oil

1 pound sweet potatoes, peeled and cubed

5 tomatoes, diced

2 heads lechuga del pais, native lettuce,
  hand-shredded

4 purple onions, thinly sliced

6 ripe avocadoes, sliced

6 hard-boiled eggs, cold and sliced

Salt Cod Serenata is a salad made with salt cod and tropical tubers which was a very common lunch in country homes. With its increase in price, however, salt cod's popularity has diminished. It is simple to make and has a single secret: use the best extra-virgin olive oil available and use only real, genuine salt cod, preferably from Norway or Iceland, which, although expensive, is well worth it. I cannot resist recommending a wine to complement this dish: a good cold Albariño, from the Rías Baixas Gallegas.

Pour the milk and the water into a large bowl. Add the salt cod to desalt for 24 hours in the refrigerator.

The following day, fill a large bowl with ice water. Put the salt cod in a saucepan filled with water. Boil for three minutes. Remove, drain, and quickly immerse in ice water to cool. Drain well. Skin, debone, and flake the cod. Add olive oil, mix well, and let chill in the refrigerator for half an hour.

Place the sweet potato in a saucepan filled with water. Boil for 15 minutes or until tender. Drain.

In a large bowl, carefully combine the salt cod, its oil, the sweet potatoes, the tomatoes, the lettuce, and the onions. Serve in a serving bowl, garnished with slices of avocado and boiled eggs.

Lamb Tartare with Pigeon Pea Fritters

Yields 16 canapés

Lamb Tartare

6 ounces lamb loin, minced

2 tablespoons olive oil

½ tablespoon sesame oil

1 tablespoon mint leaves, minced

½ small shallot, minced

Salt and pepper

Pigeon Pea Fritters

14 ounces cooked pigeon peas (may be canned)

2 eggs, slightly beaten

3 tablespoons flour

½ tablespoon baking powder

1 garlic clove, mashed

Salt and pepper

Olive oil

Lamb tartare is reminiscent of the Middle East and Kibbeh. The use of pigeon pea fritters could be messy unless the fritters are well compacted. You may substitute with melba toast.

Lamb Tartare

In a bowl, combine the lamb, the olive oil, and the sesame oil. Mix. Add the mint leaves and the shallot, mix, and season with salt and pepper. Keep in mind that raw meat requires more salt than does cooked meat. Refrigerate until serving.

Pigeon Pea Fritters

Place half of the pigeon peas into the bowl of a food processor and purée. Place the purée into a bowl and add the remaining pigeon peas and the rest of the ingredients, except for the olive oil. Let rest for one hour. Divide into 16 compact portions.

Pour sufficient olive oil into a skillet and place over medium heat. Fry the portions for two minutes on each side or until golden. Remove from heat and drain on paper towel.

Presentation

Just before serving, shape lamb in quenelles using two spoons to mold the lamb. Make 16 portions. Top each fritter with some tartare. Serve as an appetizer.

Rabbit Fricassee in Red Wine

Serves 12

6 rabbit loins and 12 legs

Marinade

6 cups cream

½ cup annatto oil

4 tablespoons dry oregano

1 head garlic, peeled and crushed

½ cup extra-virgin olive oil

3 onions, minced

4 green peppers, minced

½ cup ajíes dulces, minced

½ cup culantro, minced

½ cup cilantro, minced

½ cup green olives, minced

6 carrots, peeled and sliced

1 cup water

1 bottle red wine

Salt and pepper to taste

Puerto Rican rabbits are not as large as their European counterparts, but they have a lot of flavor and plentiful meat. The fried annatto seeds are typical of the island, but this condiment must be used in moderation. It is ideal to use a typical Puerto Rican 'caldero' — a cast-aluminum casserole, as these have a flat bottom and thus distribute heat well. The 'ajicitos verdes dulces' are small, round, sweet peppers.

Rabbit Marinade

In a deep bowl, combine cream, annatto oil, oregano, and half of the head of garlic. Add the cut-up rabbit. Cover and refrigerate overnight.

The following day, place a large, heavy stew pot over high heat and add the olive oil. Fry the onion, green pepper, *ajíes dulces*, culantro, cilantro, green olives, and the carrots. Cook for six minutes. Add the rabbit and its marinade, the water, and the wine. Adjust heat to medium low, cover the pot, and cook for 50 minutes. Uncover the pot and continue to cook for 15 to 20 minutes longer, until the sauce thickens. Serve with white rice, made according to your preference.

Duck Breast in a Molasses and Rum Glaze with Pickled Breadfruit Salad

Serves 6

6 boned duck breasts

Marinade
Olive oil
Peppercorns
½ cup sugarcane molasses
½ cup white wine
¼ cup white rum
Salt
Sage leaves

Breadfruit Salad
1 breadfruit, peeled and diced
3 cups olive oil
1 ½ cups vinegar
Peppercorns
6 onions, finely sliced
3 bay leaves
Salt

Molasses and Rum Glaze
½ cup white rum
½ cup sugarcane molasses

1 tablespoon olive oil

Presentation
6 green onions, whole, cut into a flower shape

The molasses and rum glaze gives this dish a very Caribbean touch, as well as delicious results. Breadfruit, originally from the Pacific islands, has adapted so well to Puerto Rico that it grows wild. It is used in many different ways.

Duck
The day before serving, remove the tough tendon that runs under the breasts. Score the skin in a grid pattern, without touching the meat.

Marinade
In a bowl, mix the olive oil, the peppercorns, the molasses, the white wine, the rum, the salt, and the sage. Cover the ducks with the marinade. Cover and refrigerate overnight.

Breadfruit Salad
The day before serving, boil the breadfruit in a large pot filled with water. Cook for 15 to 20 minutes or until tender yet firm. Remove from fire, strain, drain, and set aside.

Heat the oil in another saucepan and add the vinegar, the peppercorns, the onion, the bay leaves, and the salt. Sauté until the onion has softened. Transfer to a bowl and let cool. Add the breadfruit and mix well. Correct seasoning and refrigerate, covered, overnight. An hour before serving, remove from refrigerator. Serve at room temperature.

Pour the molasses and the rum into a large saucepan. Heat over medium high heat. Reduce for 20 minutes or until the mixture has thickened slightly .

To Cook Duck
Preheat oven to 350°F.
Brush the inside of a skillet with olive oil. Sear the duck breasts over high heat, cooking each side 4 to 5 minutes. Start with the skin side down. When done, transfer to a baking sheet and roast for 8 minutes. The duck should be pink in the center. Remove and slice diagonally into ¼" slices. Set aside, keeping glaze hot.

Presentation

Place the duck slices, fanned-out, off-center on the plate. Place breadfruit
salad opposite. Take care to avoid excess oil, which will run. Top duck with
glaze and garnish with green onions.

Coconut Praline with Grilled Pineapple and Chocolate Sauce

Serves 12

Pineapple

2 fresh pineapples, cored and sliced

1 cup white sugar

Chocolate Sauce

8 ounces semi-sweet chocolate

½ cup whipping cream

Coconut Praline

2 cups coconut, grated

1 cup brown sugar

1 vanilla bean, split open lengthwise

1 pinch cinnamon

4 tablespoons butter

1 lemon, juiced

½ tablespoon balsamic vinegar

½ cup water

Garnish

Mint leaves

Coconut has long been used in traditional Puerto Rican desserts, though, unfortunately, few people still make them at home. This delicious dish of Santaella's is far better when one takes the time to grate fresh coconut meat.

Pineapple

Preheat broiler or salamander. Place pineapple slices on a perforated tray placed over a baking sheet. Dust with sugar and place under heat. When caramelized, turn over. Remove and place on tray. Set aside.

Chocolate Sauce

Place the chocolate and the whipping cream in a saucepan, placed over a double boiler. Stir occasionally, mixing cream and chocolate well, while the latter melts. Remove from heat and set aside.

Coconut Praline

In a non-stick saucepan, place the grated coconut, the brown sugar, the vanilla, the cinnamon, the butter, the lemon juice, the balsamic vinegar, and the water. Cook over low heat, stirring often, until the coconut becomes translucent. Remove from heat and let cool to room temperature.

Presentation

Place some coconut praline in the center of a plate and top with a pineapple slice. Nap with chocolate sauce and garnish with mint leaves.

Passion Fruit Soup with Goat Cheese Ice Cream and Tarragon

Serves 6

Passion Fruit Soup

⅓ cup sugar

1 ½ cups water

1 cup white wine

12 passion fruits, pulp only

½ cup lemon juice

1 ½ cups orange juice, freshly squeezed

Goat Cheese Ice Cream and Tarragon

2 cups heavy cream

½ cup milk

2 tablespoons fresh tarragon leaves, minced

4 egg yolks

1 tablespoon sugar

3 tablespoons light sugar syrup

5 ounces goat cheese, softened

This is a spectacular dessert which combines the tastes of passion fruit, cheese ice cream, and orange juice. If fresh tarragon is not available, substitute with dried.

Passion Fruit Soup

Place sugar, water and wine into a small heavy bottomed sauté pan. Cook over medium heat until it begins to acquire color. Add the passion fruit pulp, and the lemon and orange juice. Cook 2 to 3 minutes and remove from heat. Let cool.

Blend the passion fruit syrup in a blender until puréed. Strain through a fine sieve and refrigerate, covered, until serving.

Goat Cheese Ice Cream and Tarragon

Prepare a large bowl full of ice water.

Place the cream, milk, and 1 tablespoon of tarragon into a saucepan. Bring to a boil. Remove from heat.

Place the egg yolks and sugar in a bowl and beat with an electric beater until thickened and light yellow in color. Slowly add some of the hot cream to warm the eggs. Stir. Pour in the rest of the hot cream, stir, and cook for two to three minutes, or until the mixture coats the back of a spoon.

Place the sugar syrup and goat cheese in another bowl. Add the cream mixed with the eggs and beat with a wire whisk, until soft. Strain through a fine sieve. Add the remaining tarragon and cool over the bowl of ice water. Freeze in an ice cream machine. Keep frozen until serving.

Presentation

Put a ball, a cone, or a cylinder of ice cream in the center of a soup plate. Surround with passion fruit soup.

Terrine of Foie Gras. Page 183

AUGUSTO SCHREINER

THE ALPINE TROPICS

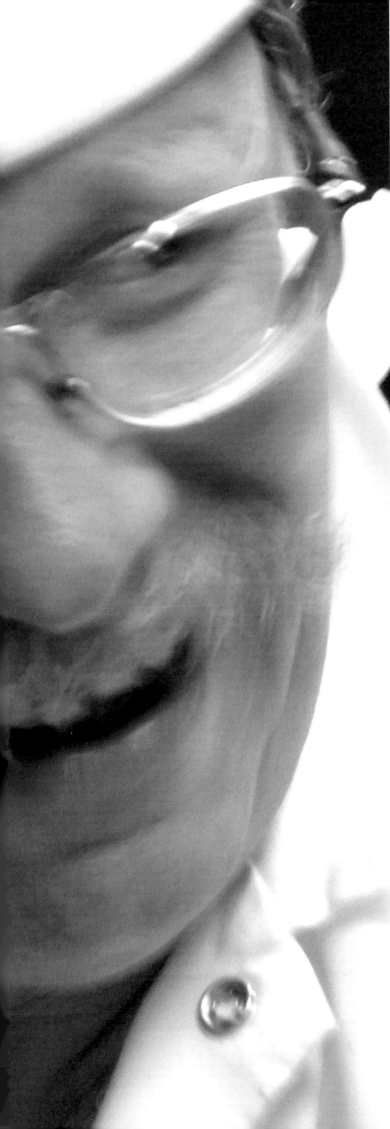

East of San Juan, the Sierra of Luquillo rises to slightly over 1,000 meters. Ever shrouded by leaden skies yielding constant rainfall, nurturing the tropical exuberance of flora and plethora of fauna, this is the rainforest. The heights are woods of pine and trumpet wood and a profusion of giant tree ferns and bromeliads hoarding moisture among their leaves. High on the mountain slopes, just off the narrow Road 186 and one of its branches known as "the three cascades," lies an enclave called Cubuy, where small *fincas* have been turned into weekend homes owned by people anxious to escape the San Juan stridence.

There sits a house that, lacking only a well-fed Swiss cow with its clanging cowbell, could well be an Alpine chalet transported to the tropical hillside. Every Sunday morning, a man with an Austrian accent, a dynamo of medium height, blue eyes and saffron hair, agile and irrepressible with enthusiasm, arrives at this refuge accompanied by his wife. Only a command performance cooking for the International Wine and Food Society, the Chaîne des Rôtisseurs or the Lucullus Circle can lure this man from his sanctuary before Tuesday morning.

Perhaps on a Sunday, Augusto has graced you with an invitation to visit his refuge. You arrive to find him playing with a new toy, such as a machine for raclette-making, or woodworking, while listening to Mozart. Meanwhile, Claudia, his Colombian wife, cares for the orchids and flowers in their beautiful garden.

I well remember an afternoon when several of the chefs featured in this book met at this mountainside chalet. Some came bearing champagne, others a dessert; someone a double magnum of red wine. As Claudia's Doberman Pinschers settled among us, we seated the guests at a long table on a terrace overlooking the ocean and the airplanes taking off from Isla Verde airport. At the center stood Augusto, in animated discourse about *raclette*: what it is; how it is made and served, while he demonstrated the preparation and service. "What a pity," said Augusto. "The clouds didn't clear to let us see the sunset, which is beautiful up here." He and Claudia have transformed that gentle hillside in Cubuy into a corner of Austria in the tropics.

The roads taken, like labyrinthine and narrow mountain roads crisscrossing Puerto Rico, shape people's lives in mysterious ways.

Maine Lobster with Curry Sauce Couscous. Page 184

Augusto's life is no exception. Perhaps his parents secretly hoped, when he served as an altar boy at an ancient village church in upper Austria, that their son would grow up to be bishop of Salzburg, a city only an hour from his village, Hochburg. Silent Night (Stalle Nacht), composed in 1916 by Franz Xavier Gruber, was first sung in a parish near Hochburg. It was, therefore, sung with great fervor in Hochburg at Christmastime.

Ironically, the church where Augusto was an altar boy also had a small plot, property of the Salzburg Franciscan friars. On this land sat a small stable for cows and an old tavern, all of which the monks restored and leased to a person who served a festive dinner every Sunday after mass. The innkeeper hired two or three altar boys to clear the tables of soiled dishes. One day, several young chefs arrived at the restaurant impeccably dressed-out in white, complete with high toques. Augusto stared awestruck. "I was only 12 or 13, and, when I saw those cooks, I was so impressed that I went home and told my father that I wanted to be a chef." The hopes, if there ever had been any, that Augusto become a bishop vanished on the spot. His father found him a steady job with the innkeeper. On Saturdays, Augusto would sleep at the hotel; on Sundays he would clean the wood stoves and light them. Then he would go to church and serve as altar boy, and after mass, he would work the kitchen as a busboy.

At age 15 he was already in culinary school doing an apprenticeship at a hotel, where he also lived. "There were 9 months of practice, 2 months internship at the School of Salzburg and a month of vacation. There I made crèpes for the first time; I diced onions, breaded Schnitzel. I did everything until 5:00 in the afternoon. Training lasted 3 years."

When he finished, Augusto was 18 and had won important prizes, and he dreamed of going to Paris. One day, in a trade journal publication, he saw an ad for a *commis* at a Paris hotel. So then he went to see the Eiffel tower, the grand boulevards, the Opéra, Montmartre, and to work at the Grand Hotel Saint Lazare. But Paris was full of chefs; there were more of them than there were painters. And a young Austrian, just out of culinary school, who spoke no French, had little demand. A *commis* almost 35 years ago was almost a slave. So while he learned French at the Alliance Française and walked two hours daily to just get around, he helped in the kitchen of an old and cantankerous master chef. But

everything has its rewards: each day he learned a little more. "I tried once to get a job at Maxim, the best restaurant in Paris, but they paid so little that it would not even cover the métro."

A year later, a hotel, opening in Düsseldorf, Germany, offered him work. "I earned 10 times what I had earned in Paris, but I saw very strange things happening which I did not like." But Düsseldorf was not Paris, and a few days later, he found work with the institution that he would call home for the next 18 years: the Hilton International hotel chain. "That was a League of Nations…What madness! The kitchen was pure Escoffier and hard and exacting work."

The principal executives and chefs met Sunday mornings at one of their offices to have an *apéritif*, and one day his boss invited him. "Ah! I felt so happy. Now I was really a chef!" That day there was a good-bye party for an experienced chef, Günther Mainka, who was leaving for an exotic location: Puerto Rico and the Caribe Hilton. Chef Schneider, the top chef, regaled the group with his adventures at the San Jerónimo Hilton in San Juan. You can imagine that young Austrian cook's face, who had never heard anything about the Caribbean, as he took in all the tales.

The early 70s saw convulsive politics for some of the islands, which Augusto's destiny did not yet include. Another detour took him to the Bogotá Hilton, Colombia, which proved more significant than he could imagine. His post there was *sous-chef* at the hotel's gastronomic restaurant, Le Toît ("Very French, classic…"), and there he

Far left, preparing the spinach for the lobster dish, page 184. Above, beating egg whites the hard way.

met a young Colombian woman, Claudia, the manager of the hotel flower shop. Soon they made plans for marriage, but the wedding had to wait, as Augusto finally made his way to the Caribbean. "I spent a year alone in Puerto Rico, until Claudia could join me. We had a civil wedding until we could go to Salzburg on my vacation time to marry in the church where I had been an altar boy." Ever since, Augusto received promotion after promotion, until executive chef Emil Graf left to work in Miami and Augusto took his place. "Emil was a great chef, and I learned a great deal from him…the Hilton was a university where we learned about everything, from creative new dishes and menus to personnel and service management, administration… everything."

Little by little, Augusto filled the void left by Emil Graf. His dinners for prestigious wine and food groups were renown. I'll never forget one occasion, while presiding an international newspaper design convention. The awards banquet was held in the ballroom. Suddenly the lights were dimmed, and Augusto entered, carrying a great tray of *flambéed* Cherries Jubilée, followed by a procession of pastry chefs, *sous-chefs*, maître d's and waiters. Six hundred people gave him a standing ovation.

But he dreamed of a country restaurant in the mountains. In 1988, his dreams came true, with improvements. The young Puerto Rican chef Alfredo Ayala decided to sell his San Juan restaurant, Ali-Oli, to concentrate his efforts on a Japanese restaurant and a small seaside guesthouse. Don René Aponte, a friend of the two and a connoisseur of wine and food, served as matchmaker, to everyone's happiness.

Augusto took possession of Ayala's restaurant on September first, 1988. Ayala only took his paintings, leaving Augusto to inherit an intact restaurant; its kitchen stocked with custom-made copper pots from Deliheren in Paris; a refrigerated wine cellar and a small storeroom.

His restaurant was not in the country. But, a few years later, he found the *finca* in Cubuy, and his dream came true, finally.

From Tuesday to Saturday, on the ground floor of the Hotel Excelsior, Augusto ties a bandana around his head like a Japanese chef, puts on an apron and enters his comfortable kitchen, not to leave until three in the afternoon. Then he takes a break until six and works until midnight.

Augusto is a teacher that has trained many young chefs in his kitchen who now occupy important positions. Wilo Benet, who worked with him at the Caribe Hilton and today is chef-owner of Pikayo Restaurant, says, "Augusto is a master teacher. When I don't know how to make a sauce, I grab the phone and ask him, how do I make x sauce? He always finds time and the answer."

Augusto always speaks well of his colleagues and rarely talks about himself. But one afternoon, at the quaint San Juan *fonda*, La Casita Blanca, having a lunch of fried pork and beer, he confessed. "My kitchen has a solid, classic base. I learned from teachers who made me work and who taught me well. Later, at the Hilton, I had the opportunity of working with chefs who knew about cooking, but, once I had my own restaurant, things were different.

"Hotels are one thing and restaurants are another; in

Augusto Schreiner spends his weekends

in the country with his wife Claudia,

sorrounded by dogs, orchids, and

tropical plants. But during the rest of the

week, this great chef hardly leaves the

kitchen of his San Juan restaurant

Blanched asparagus are submerged in iced water to stop their cooking.

the 16 years that I've had my own restaurant, my cooking has changed… I have become more modern, more creative… All the recipes are mine, my sauces are based more on reduction than on stock bases cooked for hours. Occasionally, I'll return to a classic; I cannot escape the connection between my contemporary roots and my training in Paris."

What does this great training chef think of culinary schools? "Some of the kids suffer from indigestion, what with all this about the *nouvelle* Caribbean cuisine. Many lack a solid base of kitchen work and think that because they place a *platanutre* (fried green plantain), they are cooking *nouvelle* Puerto Rican, which is not true. There needs to be more depth to cooking for imagination to flourish."

Augusto also states, "There are many young promising chefs, and some already have their own restaurants. But they have worked hard, they have gone to school and have cooked under good chefs, here and in the United States. One boy was *chef de partier* under Alain Ducasse in New York; another was one of the principal *sous-chefs* under Christian Deluvrier at Lespinasse, also in New York. You can see that they are developing."

Meanwhile, Augusto continues soiling aprons, perspiring in his jackets, smiling impishly under that blond mustache, and teaching anyone who asks how to make Tournedos Rossini. He knows that, and also when to buy Australian Kobe beef and fresh *foie gras* as well. And if cajoled, he will give you a simpler version than that served at one of his dinners for the Commanderie de Bordeaux or the International Wine and Food Society.

Steak au Poivre
Filet Mignon Sautéed with Crushed Peppercorns

Serves 2

The French side of Augusto's experience. A slightly spicy modern version of a classic.

Späetzle

2 eggs

1 cup milk

1 cup water

Salt and pepper

Pinch nutmeg

2 ounces olive oil

2 ½ cups flour

¼ cup parsley, chopped

The filet

2 filet mignons, Angus, 6 ounces each

Salt

Red peppercorns, crushed

Green peppercorns, crushed

Black peppercorns, crushed

White peppercorns, crushed

1 tablespoon olive oil

2 ounces butter

2 shallots, chopped

2 ounces cognac

4 ounces red wine

6 ounces demi-glace

Vegetables

2 ounces green beans

8 whole asparagus

2 ounces, butter

1 cup spinach leaves

Olive oil

Salt and pepper

The Späetzle

Beat the eggs in a bowl with a wire whisk. Add milk, water, salt, pepper, nutmeg and olive oil. Incorporate flour with a wooden spoon, forming a slightly thick dough. Add parsley. Add dough slowly to a *späetzle* machine, or roll and cut in small gnocchi shape.

Bring a casserole filled with salted water to a boil. Add the *späetzle* and cook. When the pasta floats, it is ready. Drain and cool the *späetzle* in ice water.

Filet mignons

Season the filets mignons with salt, and cover both sides with the crushed peppers. Heat the oil in a heavy bottom skillet, and broil the filets until medium rare. Remove. Drain off the oil. Add the butter and sauté the chopped shallots. Return the filets to the skillet. Pour the cognac over the filets and flambé. Remove the filets to a platter. Add the red wine. Reduce until the liquid evaporates and the pan is almost dry. Add the *demi-glace*, and cook until the sauce becomes creamy.

Vegetables

Bring water to a boil in a saucepan. Cook the green beans and the asparagus. Remove; drain in iced water until cool. Sauté in a little butter, seasoning with salt.

Sauté the spinach in another skillet, with a few drops of olive oil. Season with salt and pepper.

To serve

Heat butter in another skillet, and slightly brown the *späetzle*.

Place all the vegetables in the center of the plate and surround by the *späetzle*. Cover each filet with 2 tablespoons of the sauce.

Purple Potato Purée

Serves 6

2 purple potatoes
¼ cup olive oil
Chicken broth
Salt and pepper

The flavor of the Peruvian Andes in the Caribbean.

Peel, cut and boil potatoes, until they soften. Drain and let dry for 2 minutes. Mash the potatoes and add the olive oil, slowly. Add chicken broth should the potatoes dry out. Season with salt and pepper.

Note: To purée, it is preferable to work with hot potatoes. Do not mash excessively to avoid making potatoes gummy.

Terrine de Foie Gras
Foie Gras Terrine

Serves 8

Aspic

1 cup sauternes

1 envelope unflavored gelatin

Terrine

1 ½ pounds fresh foie gras, grade B

1 pound foie gras, grade A

Salt and white pepper

Presentation

Candied fruits

Terrine is the name of an earthenware or cast iron loaf pan. Duck liver cooked this way is simply marvelous.

Aspic

Place the sauternes in a bowl, and sprinkle with the gelatin. Mix and chill in refrigerator. Cut in small dices when hardened.

Terrine

Using a sharp knife, carefully slit open the *foie gras*. Remove all nerves and veins. Place the *foie gras* in a terrine or paté mold, 10" x 3" x 2". Press down hard. Season with salt and pepper and add the Sauternes. Cover, and marinate in refrigerator for 6-8 hours. Preheat the oven to 130°F. Remove the terrine of *foie gras* from the refrigerator. Cover with aluminum foil. Place the terrine in a baking dish in one inch of water. Place in oven and cook in the *bain-marie* for 40 minutes. Remove from oven and let cool. Remove the foil. Take a thick piece of cardboard covered with aluminum foil that is sized to fit the interior measurements of the terrine, and place over the *foie gras*. Place a heavy object (cans or weights) on the cardboard. Refrigerate for 12 hours. Turn over and remove from terrine. Remove excess fat. Cut the terrine in slices that are slightly less than ½" thick. Serve with candied fruits and the aspic.

Wiener Schnitzel
Breaded Veal Scallops ☙ Traditional recipe

Serves 6

6 veal scallops, ½" thick, lightly pounded

A few drops lemon juice

Salt and pepper

All purpose flour

2 eggs, lightly beaten

Breadcrumbs

Lard for frying

6 lemons cut in 6 wedges

Every autumn, Augusto celebrates Oktoberfest and Weiner Schnitzel, breaded veal scallops, appears on the menu of his restaurant. This is Augusto's rendition of a classic Austrian dish.

Flatten scallops a little and sprinkle lemon juice on each side.
Season the meat with salt and pepper, Let rest for 10 minutes.
Dip the scallops in flour, one by one; then dip in beaten eggs and finally in breadcrumbs.

Heat lard in large skillet or frying pan, and fry the scallops, two at a time, over medium heat, until golden brown on both sides. Carefully remove the scallops, and drain on paper towels.

Serve each one with a lemon wedge.

Maine Lobster with Curry Sauce Couscous

Serves 4

Couscous salad

1½ cup chicken broth

1 cup couscous

1 zucchini, finely chopped

1 red pepper, finely chopped

1 small onion, finely chopped

1 small carrot finely chopped

1 chive, finely chopped

Olive oil

Salt and pepper

Lobster

1 live Maine lobster about 2½ lbs.

Court bouillon

Coconut and curry sauce

1 medium onion, chopped

3 garlic cloves, chopped

3 ounces fresh ginger, chopped

1 large yellow apple, diced

2 ripe bananas, chopped

2 ounces butter

5 tablespoons curry

1 tablespoon turmeric

1 tablespoon ground cumin

Salt and pepper

3 cups chicken broth

3 cups coconut milk

To serve

Spinach leaves

Olive oil

Fennel leaves

Coconut has been used in the Caribbean for five centuries; couscous is Mediterranean, and curry takes us all the way to India.

Couscous salad

Bring the broth to a boil. Place couscous into a medium-sized bowl. Pour the broth over the couscous until covered. Cover the couscous bowl with plastic film or cling wrap. Allow the couscous to absorb the broth for 7 minutes. Do not place over heat.

Sauté the vegetables in abundant olive oil for 3 minutes, and remove from heat to preserve bright colors. Place the vegetables and oil over the couscous. Season with salt and pepper.

Couscous may be prepared ahead of time and refrigerated for use the following day.

Lobster

Boil the lobster in the *court bouillon* in a large stockpot for 6 to 7 minutes. Remove. Discard shell. Reserve the lobster meat. Slice.

Coconut and curry sauce

Sauté the onion, garlic, ginger, apple and bananas in butter in a skillet with high sides. Add the spices. Add the broth and the coconut milk. Place in blender and liquefy. Strain and season to taste.

To serve

Wilt a few spinach leaves in olive oil. Remove and dry with paper towel. Place a ring 3" in diameter and 2" in height in the center of the dish, and put the spinach within as a bed. Place a little couscous over the spinach, and squash with the bottom of a bottle. Place the lobster meat in the center. Remove the mold. Surround with the coconut sauce and curry. Decorate the couscous with a sprig of fennel.

Editor's note: Spine or Caribbean lobster may be used as a substitute for Maine lobster.

Sea bass with Saffron Risotto with Calamari Sauce

Serves 4 or 5

Red snapper or yellowtail are fine substitutes for sea bass..

Risotto

1 ounce olive oil

2 minced shallots

1 cup Arborio rice

½ cup white wine

Saffron

Fat free chicken broth, well seasoned

2 tablespoons parmigiano reggiano

3 ounces unsalted butter

Salt and pepper

Squid ink sauce

¼ cup white dry vermouth

½ cup white wine

¼ cup fish broth

¼ cup heavy cream

3 packets squid ink

Lemon juice

Sea bass

2 sea bass filets cut into 6-ounce portions

Salt and pepper

All-purpose flour

Clarified butter

To serve

12 ounces squid rings

Risotto

Heat olive oil in a skillet. Sauté the shallots over medium heat. Do not brown. Add the rice and sauté, stirring constantly until the rice has absorbed the oil. Add the white wine and continue stirring until absorbed. Add the saffron slowly until the rice turns a mustard yellow. Heat the broth. Add the broth slowly and continue stirring until the rice is *al dente* (17 to 18 minutes). Remove from heat. Add the cheese and stir, until melted. Add the butter and stir constantly until well incorporated and the rice becomes creamy. Season to taste with salt and pepper.

Squid ink sauce

Bring the vermouth and white wine to a boil over medium heat. Reduce liquid to one half. Add fish broth and again reduce to one half. Add the cream and simmer over low heat, until slightly thickened. Stir in squid ink and add a few drops of lemon juice.

Sea bass

Preheat oven to 350°F. Season the fish filets with salt and pepper. Place a little flour on a plate and flour the filets on each side.

Heat the clarified butter in a skillet. Sear the filets on each side. Place in the oven, and heat 3 to 4 minutes.

To serve

Pour a little squid sauce on to a plate. Place the Risotto in the center, over the sauce. Sauté the squid for a moment, and toss over fish.

Corn Chowder

Serves 4

3 ears of corn, fresh

3 cups chicken broth

1 small onion

2 stalks celery

Butter

½ cup white wine

2 tablespoon cornstarch, diluted
    in ⅓ cup water

1 quart whipping cream

2 large potatoes, peeled and diced

Salt and pepper

To serve

2 slices bacon, well toasted, cut in
    small pieces

½ avocado, diced

1 bunch cilantro, chopped

1 chive chopped

Corn, a native American staple, in a delicious soup. The taínos ate corn as part of their diet.

Remove kernels from cob, and reserve the kernels and the cob. In a large saucepan, boil the cobs in chicken broth for 20 minutes. Remove from heat, and discard cobs. Reserve water.

In a deep skillet heat the butter. Sauté the onion, the celery stalk and the corn kernels in butter until softened. Pour in the white wine. Add the chicken broth, and cook for 15 to 20 minutes over medium heat. Add the diluted corn starch, the cream and the diced potato. Cook until potato is tender. Season with salt and pepper. Add more corn starch if thicker cream is desired.

To serve

Serve the corn chowder in bowls. When serving add the bacon, avocado, cilantro and chives.

Almond and Chocolate Cake
Kugelhupf

Serves 6

A real delight. Full of calories, but a classic of Central European pastry making.

9 ounces butter

9 ounces sugar

5 egg yolks

Lemon zest

2 tablespoons rum

1 teaspoon vanilla

9 ounces flour

2 tablespoons baking powder

3 ounces heavy cream

3 ounces almonds

3 ounces melted chocolate

3 egg whites

Butter for greasing

Ground almonds

Beat the butter in a large bowl. Add a little sugar and continue beating. Mix in, one by one, the egg yolks, lemon zest, rum and vanilla. Add the flour and baking powder. Add the heavy cream. Divide the batter in equal parts, and pour into two bowls.

Add 3 ounces of ground almond to one of the bowls. Add the melted chocolate to the other bowl. Using a whisk, mix well. Pour into the two bowls, dividing the batter in two equal parts. Beat the egg whites to soft peaks and fold beaten egg whites into batter.

Preheat oven to 325°F. Grease a cake pan with butter, and dust lightly with ground almonds. Add the chocolate batter, and repeat with the vanilla and almond. Bake for 45-50 minutes. It is done when a toothpick, inserted in the center of the cake is removed clean.

Floating Island with Chocolate Hazelnut Pudding and Fruit Purée

An imaginative variation on a classic dessert.

Hazelnut and chocolate pudding

8 tablespoons butter

2 ounces 10x sugar

6 eggs, separated

4 ounces almonds, blanched and ground

4 ounces bittersweet chocolate, grated

2 ounces sugar

Butter for greasing pan

Floating island

2 cups milk

½ teaspoon vanilla extract

¾ cup sugar

1 cup egg whites

1½ cup sugar

3 eggs yolks

Mango sauce

1 fresh ripe mango

3 tablespoons sugar

A little lemon juice

Strawberry sauce

Fresh strawberries

A little lemon juice

¼ teaspoon kirsch or white rum

Kiwi sauce

3 fresh kiwis

4 tablespoons sugar

A little rum

Chocolate sauce

6 ounces bittersweet chocolate

½ cup heavy cream

¼ teaspoon Frangelico hazelnut liqueur

Hazelnut and chocolate pudding

Cream the butter with the 10x sugar in an electric mixer for about 10 minutes until creamy. Beat in the egg yolks one by one. Incorporate ground almonds and grated chocolate.

Preheat the oven to 300°F. Beat the egg whites and the sugar to soft peaks, and fold in chocolate. Grease individual baking dishes with butter and powder with sugar. Turn the mixture into the mold, and bake in *bain marie* for 40 minutes.

Floating island

Heat the milk, vanilla and ¾ cup sugar. Beat the egg whites and the 1½ cup sugar and make a meringue. Using an ice cream scoop, form meringue ovoidal islands. Place on milk mixture and cook over low heat. Do not let milk boil. Turn several times till slightly stiffened. Remove with a napkin and place on a tray. Dilute the egg yolks with a little milk and add to the sauce pan with the rest of the milk. Cook over medium heat, stirring constantly with a wooden spoon. Do not let it boil. When it creams and coats a spoon, remove from heat. Strain and chill over ice.

The fruit and chocolate sauces

For the mango sauce, process all the ingredients and strain. For the strawberry sauce, process strawberries and lemon juice in a processor. Strain. Add the kirsch or white rum. For the kiwi sauce, process all the ingredients in the food processor and strain. For the chocolate sauce, heat the chocolate and cream until they reach a liquid mixture. Remove from heat, and add the liqueur.

Presentation

Place a little of each sauce in the 10 o'clock position, in large dessert plates. Place one floating island in the 2 o'clock position and the pudding in the 5 o'clock position. Cover the pudding with chocolate sauce.

INTER

Guineos, Félix Medina, 1906

LUDE
(3)

FOO-FOOS, MOFONGO, MANGÚS
AND OTHER TASTY THINGS

He who has never traveled thinks only his mother knows how to cook.
African Proverb

The Antillean slave trade lasted almost four centuries, it's legacy burnt a swath of racism, which, like the termite, has eaten into our societies, and has endured until the present. Nevertheless, let's try to look beyond racism and to admit, openly and without prejudice, that all of us who live in the Antilles are touched by Africa. Each time that we listen to Maelo Rivera or Celia Cruz; that we read Sir Derek Walcott or Nicolás Guillén, that we savor *empanadas* from Loíza along with a good stewed okra with mofongo there is an orisha laying his hand on us. Luis Pales Matos has made us well aware by use of the vivid metaphor: "Here come the drums! Take care, white man for they reach you…"

That presence is so strong, that there are some who assert that we in the Caribbean eat far closer to the way Blacks eat than we do to the European way of eating, and that African heritage dominates the cooking of the Caribbean Basin. One cannot deny the strong Black influence in our culinary practice; it is a strong common denominator in the Antilles. But, I humbly believe, that what differentiates the cookery of one island from another is the particular European colonial heritage: English, French, Dutch, Danish, and Spanish; plus the influence of the Chinese, Indonesians, and Indians of India, all of whom arrived in conditions of semi-slavery.

If things would exactly be according to the former opinion, there would be little difference between the food of Martinique and that of Curaçao, or between the food of Jamaica and that of Puerto Rico. That is not the case; by merely crossing the imaginary 'frontier' between Saint Maarten and Saint Martin, one confirms this difference of cuisines, yet I must be honest and tell you a short anecdote.

Years ago, I was in Miami attending a Caribbean culinary competition, which culminated with a grand party to the rhythms of calypso and reggae. The young men and women, almost all Blacks, on the culinary teams from the different countries, had set up their kiosks around the swimming pool. They set aside classical cooking and the inventions of nouvelle Caribbean cuisine; they rolled up their shirtsleeves, and cooked as their mothers and grandmothers had taught them. That day I was able to better understand the cooking from the Lesser Antilles, and I made a note of an observation: "The truth is the Blacks are the the the cooking soul of these islands, and, besides, they cook while dancing." But, I must add, each one cooks and dances with the personality and nuances, pertinent to his respective circumstances.

Although Puerto Rico always had a large population of the poor and Black, the percentage is not as high as that in the Lesser Antilles, Haiti or Jamaica. Neither had Puerto Rico the ritual food offerings of the Afro-Caribbean religions, such as there were and are in Brazil, Haiti, and Cuba. But we have seen a kitchen for the rich and another type of cooking for the poor, among whom, many were Black or mulatto or mestizo. Does this co-existence of two types of cooking affect or change the existence of a national cuisine? No, because a similar phenomenon has occurred in other places. We see the dichotomy between popular cooking and haute cuisine in European countries. Foodstuffs that were used by the poor, today are gourmet. The potato that saved Europe from famine, is served at moneyed tables as Escoffier's Pommes Anne. In Puerto Rico, *funche*, which was humble food, is dressed in formal attire by Franco Seccarelli when he serves polenta to accompany a dish of shellfish or fish. Salt cod, which was daily lunch for many in the island's towns, now is the exquisite dish which José Rey presents fried in tempura, and José Santaella takes humble okra to an elegant country buffet.

It's that cooking is not static, suspended in time and space as a monument to the tastes of a given

Land Crab Empanadas. Page 202

The ships that

arrived from Africa

brought along fruits,

seeds, and vegetables

that were new to

Puerto Rico, as well as

the ancestral and

tribal tastes of the

Black cooks

Mofongo. Page 260

From left to right, a 'vegigante' ready for carnival, various mortar and pestles, Doña Verena Pizarro Osorio, in the town of Loiza, offers an 'empanada'.

land. As do other cultural expressions, cooking evolves. It evolves, changes, it undergoes periods of abundance and prosperity and richness, and moments of scarcity and vicissitudes; it exhibits ethnic and geographic specificity, and extends its influences, making its way into our pots and pans, yet no one knows how.

For example, perhaps French cooking might not have become The French Cuisine if Catherine de Medici had not married Henry II of France, taking with her to Paris a battalion of Italian cooks who taught the French at least two things: how to eat with a fork and the art of pastry making. In our case, what would our cooking be like if the Africans had not arrived? I don't know. But it would be very different. On the other hand, how would they cook in Africa if there had not been slavery in America and if the slave ships had not returned to Africa laden with our garden products?

But let's take a look at what, for hundreds of years, they put in our *ollas* (pots), the dingas and mandingas who cooked in the huts at the sugar mills and in the Spaniard's homes, used whatever was at hand, because, for many years, in Puerto Rico they lamented, "One must eat what the island produces because very little arrives from Spain." Oil, vinegar, chickpeas, ham, spices, cheese, etc. arrived late and in meager quantities, so that, as the Cubans say, "When there is no bread, there is cassava", applied literally to Puerto Rico, as cassava was the 'daily bread' or staple for Blacks, *mestizos*, mulattos and poor whites, including soldiers.

The slaves who reached Puerto Rico came from such different places as the Gulf of Guinea, Sudan, Senegal, and Bantu Africa. Different numbers of slaves arrived in different periods; in the sixteenth century, relatively few arrived, while in the nineteenth century, the number of slaves increased greatly because the sugar industry needed workers.

Those who arrived in the sixteenth century had perhaps never seen a white man; those who arrived in the nineteenth century had undergone the influence of three hundred years of European colonization and were familiar with more ingredients, dishes, and

Top right, Sweet 'Cassava' Tortillas. Page 200

cooking techniques. They knew more and had savored more tastes, and it occurs to me, that that could have influenced the development of our cooking at the beginning of that century.

How do the Sub-Saharan contributions reveal themselves in our kitchen? In several ways: foodstuffs with African origins, such as the gandul or pigeon pea. African names of dishes and products: *fritangas*, a derivation of fricanga, an African word. The use of strong condiments, such as ajíes or hot chili peppers, to mask the problem of food conservation or spoilage. Lastly, certain culinary skills, such as deep frying (in palm oil in Africa, in lard, here). What are some of the fritters called in the Lesser Antilles? Accra: the name of the capital of Ghana. For a long time, the most common food in the country was very simple: the king plantain, which was abundant in Africa. Plantains of multiple varieties adapted extremely well to the Caribbean. When did dishes such as *mofongo, fu-fú, mangú, pasteles*, fried ripe plantain, *platanutres*, etc. appear for the first time? Their origin is lost in time, but I would bet anything that it was the African cooks who transformed the

most elementary dish in Puerto Rican mestizo cookery, boiled green plantains, into more complex affairs. From the beginning the pots attended by the Black women were filled fraternally with African plantains and Indian tubers: tubers such as cassava, *yautía* (taro), *ajes* (sweet potato), and *lerenes* (water chestnuts), to which *ñame* (igname) was added, this last, as African as the slaves.

The slaves came accompanied by their different eating habits, depending upon which country or tribe of origin, which changed and adapted to the island's products as well as to those from abroad. The slaves' food was more or less, regulated by ordinance, but certainly the governing principle was not the sabrosura of the food, but rather a full belly. The slave owners had to maintain a very delicate balance when feeding the slaves, as strength was required for work, while spending the least possible in feeding them.

The greatest concentration of the Black population was in the coastal zones where sugar cane could be planted, therefore, where most sugarmills were

In front, Taro Root Friters; behind, 'Ñame' Puffs. Pages 199 and 203

From there to here and back again

Perhaps the most significant agricultural legacy that Africa left America is the plantain and the banana, which for the poor population was the most common foodstuff. It was the origin or ingredient in many dishes of the Caribbean popular cookery, such as *pasteles, mofongo, platanutres* and *tostones*, and the different varieties of *sancocho*. Originating in Southeast Asia, it acclimated well to Guinea's gulf region in Africa, from where it traveled to the Canary Islands and from there to Hispaniola, where it was planted by Fray Tomás de Berlanga in 1516.

Two other food products, very popular in Puerto Rico, which came from Africa, are the igname or *ñame*, an original ingredient of foo-foo, father of *mofongo*. The others are *gandules* or pigeon peas, which are extensively cultivated in the Dominican Republic. Each time you go to the Plaza del Mercado for a guinea hen to stew it *criollo*-style, think of how it got its name: hen from Guinea, from where it is supposed to have originated. If you go to France and would like to eat guinea hen, you have to order *pintade*, and, in Italy it is called *faraona*.

On the other hand, the Caribbean sent Africa pimentos both sweet and hot, pineapple, peanuts, cassava, and *yautía* (taro), plus the recipe for callaloo, that is cooked using taro leaves. In South Cameroon, there is a dish with an unpronounceable name , Kpwem, which is also known by its French name: *Feuilles de Manioc* (cassava leaves). Who would have told the Taínos that the *yautía* and cassava would become Africa foodstuffs? Such is life...and cooking.

located. It is no coincidence that our most interesting popular food comes from the coastal area extending from Boca de Cangrejos — where slaves fleeing from other islands had founded San Mateo de Cangrejos — to Río Grande. One must walk into the kitchens of Piñones, Jobos, and the Medianías to see for oneself, Black hands mashing together cassava, pumpkin, plantain, and coconut water to understand our African culinary roots.

Don't be surprised that something else reached us from Africa, too. At the end of the eighteenth century, Spanish and European immigrants, such as Canary Islanders, Majorcans, and Corsicans, climbed the mountains to cultivate a shrub that yields a small red fruit: coffee. Another contribution Africa made to our kitchen, this time not by the slaves, who barely worked on the coffee *haciendas*, but by the fruit of the coffee plant. Where was this plant from? Ethiopia; from where it traveled to the Middle East, where the Turks baptized it *kahve*, it continued to Europe, where its consumption became immensely popular and from where it was propagated in Central and South America. Puerto Rico, with its latitude near 19°N, proved to be a marvelous climate and *terroir* — as wine makers would say — for the cultivation of high quality coffee. Its fame was such that the Pope drank coffee from Adjuntas and Lares. Production fell off greatly after the arrival of the Americans, for economic and commercial reasons, but this African product has never left Puerto Rican tables, whether filtered through a *media* (stocking) or made in a gleaming Italian expresso machine. Recently, it has recovered considerably the fame it enjoyed at the end of the nineteenth century and there are many connosieurs, today, who say that Puerto Rican coffee is the best in the world.

Coffee, rum, and tobacco. Tobacco is neither food nor drink. We have have already touched on the subject of rum, but we still have to take a look at the other Africa, that of the Moors, who populated Al Andalus. They bequeathed to us the stills which distill rum and the sugar that sweetens coffee, and were expulsed from Castile, about the period in which the controversial Juan Ponce de León arrived at what are today the Ruins of Caparra.

Traditional Puerto Rican Sauce from Salinas. Page 75

Masks from Loíza

Serves 12

Masa or dough

15 to 20 green bananas (finger bananas), peeled and grated

1 cup annatto coloring (oil)

2 cups chicken or beef broth

Salt to taste

Filling

2 or 3 garlic cloves

1 teaspoon salt

1 tablespoon vinegar

¼ pound ham, diced

2 pounds pork or 3 pounds chicken breast, diced

Vegetable oil

3 or 4 cilantro sprigs, minced

2 culantro leaves, minced

2 ajíes dulces, minced

1 medium onion, finely chopped

1 small green pepper, finely chopped

1 medium tomato, finely chopped

¼ cup annatto coloring (oil)

1 small can tomato sauce

½ cup water

½ teaspoon oregano

1 tablespoon capers

Pasteles

¼ cup raisins

1 small can Spanish pimentos, cut in strips

12 pimento stuffed olives

1 can chickpeas, cooked in water

Plantain leaves

Parchment paper

Thin twine

Annato coloring (oil)

Doña Marina López is as active at age 90 as she always was. She was a pioneer in Puerto Rican culinary education and taught for 30 years in San Germán. She also taught at the Kitchen Shop in San Juan. Doña Marina says that the typical pastel takes green banana only, without any other tuber. "The green banana is from the mountain, the plantain from the coast". Doña Berta Cabanillas, author of 'Cocine a Gusto', holds that slaves working at sugar mills invented pasteles.

Masa or dough

Put the grated bananas and ½ cup annatto coloring (oil) into a large cauldron. Depending on the type of banana, it could require some more oil. Slowly add the broth, until reaching desired consistency. The type of banana or plantain will determine the amount of broth used. The dough must be soft. Add salt to taste. Mix the dough well. Cover and reserve while the filling is prepared.

Filling

Mash the garlic and the salt in a mortar. Place the ham and the pork or chicken in a saucepan. Add the mashed garlic and salt. Add the vinegar and scrape bottom to incorporate the garlic; stir well. Fry in some oil over medium heat. Brown the meat without cooking it.

Put the *cilantro*, the *culantro*, the *ajíes*, the onion, the green pepper, and the tomato in another cook pot or cauldron. Fry in the annatto coloring. Add the tomato sauce, the water, the oregano, and the capers with some of their liquid. Stir well and cook for 15 to 20 minutes over medium heat. Correct seasoning. Add the meat, ham and garlic. Mix well.

Pasteles

Boil salted water in a large cook pot. Cut out the hard ridges of the plantain leaves and divide the leaves into 12 pieces. Scald, drain, and dry. Spread a little coloring oil onto each piece of leaf. Put more or less 2 tablespoons of the dough onto each leaf and spread into a rectangular sheet. Top the *pastel* filling with 2 or 3 raisins, several Spanish pimento strips, olives and a few chickpeas, thus insuring that each *pastel* has some of each ingredient. Repeat with remaining dough.

Fold the leaf containing the *pastel*, so that the bottom of the dough covers the top part. Fold a second time. Wrap in a second plantain leaf or in parchment paper for pasteles. Make small *pasteles*, so that there is a fair balance between *masa* and filling.

Place two *pasteles* together – folded-sides facing each other – and bundle, tying together with the twine.

Put the *pasteles* into the boiling water and cook, covered, for one hour. Turn after half an hour. When cooked, remove the *pasteles* from the pot, cut the twine, unwrap the leaf covering, and remove *pastel*. Serve hot.

Editor's note: Annatto coloring is made by frying annatto seeds over low heat in lard or vegetable oil, until fat turns orange colored. Do not let it brown.

Frituras de yautía
Taro Root Fritters

2 pounds yautía or taro root, peeled, washed and
  chopped
2 garlic cloves, crushed
2 egg yolks
¼ teaspoon salt
¼ teaspoon sesame seeds, crushed
¼ teaspoon baking powder
1 teaspoon butter
Milk (optional)
Vegetable oil to fry

'Yautía', or taro root was a staple for the Taino Indians who inhabited the Antilles. The fritters are an African legacy as they reach us through the Moors of North Africa who populated Al-Andalus and also through Sub-Saharan Africa, where they are very popular especially on the West coast. The French Lesser Antilles call the fritters 'accras', their African name, which coincidentally is the name of the capital of Ghana.

Grate the taro root or mash in a mortar

In a bowl, combine the grated *yautía* or taro root, the garlic, the egg yolks, and salt. Add the crushed sesame seeds, baking powder and the butter. If necessary, add milk. Mix well. Make a very small ball of batter and test for salt. Pour oil into a deep skillet; fry over medium high heat. Fry the remaining fritters until golden. Remove one by one with a perforated spoon and drain on paper towels.

Tortillas dulces de yuca
Sweet Cassava Tortillas

Yields 12 tortillas

8 pounds cassava, peeled and chopped

12 ripe coconuts

2 tablespoons aniseed

¼ pound butter

2 pounds sugar

Ginger to taste

Powdered cinnamon to taste

Plantain leaves

These sweet tortillas and the land crab empanadas are a specialty of the coastal area between Piñones and Río Grande, even extending further East. Although the principal ingredient is cassava, the method for masa and the use of coconut reveal the influence of African slaves. 'Burén' is a Taíno word meaning the ceramic griddle that the Indians used for baking cassava; currently, iron is used, but the system is similar.

The Baptist church of Medianía Alta organizes 'jueyadas' (crab parties) to collect funds, in which the ladies of the church make land crab empanadas, cassava tortillas, arepas and yaniclecas typical of the area. This recipe and that of the crab empanadas are Mrs. Emma Carrasquillo's, who has taught this tradition to the sisters at the church and has very kindly given them to me.

This technique — and that of the crab empanadas — is complicated and its mastery requires practice. Time savers include using store-bought cassava meal or flour and coconut milk, but the Loiza cooks maintain that the results are not the same.

Dough

Grind the cassava in a meat grinder. Place the ground cassava on a piece of cheesecloth or other porous fabric to permit squeezing out the excess water. Squeeze the grated cassava until it is very dry and then place it in a bowl.

Place a strainer or sieve over another bowl. Sift the ground cassava through the sieve to make finer flour.

Pour ground and sifted cassava into a *caldero* or cook pot placed over medium heat. Stir constantly until it acquires a thicker consistency. Avoid leaving it on the burner for very long, as it will become lumpy.

Split open the coconuts and extract the pulp. Grate the coconut meat and put into a bowl. Add water gradually and squeeze the mixture. Filter the extracted liquid through a sieve, to produce thick coconut milk. Reserve some milk to dampen the plantain leaves.

Pour the remaining coconut milk into a bowl. Add the aniseed, the butter, the sugar, the ginger, the cinnamon, and the cooked cassava and combine well; make a thick batter. Taste, and add more sugar if needed. Divide the batter into 12 portions.

Tortillas

Dampen a plantain leaf with coconut milk. Pour some batter onto the leaf and spread evenly, shaping it into a rounded patty. Heat a cast iron skillet, a griddle, or a *burén* over medium heat. When hot, add the patty on the plantain leaf. Cook until the tortilla starts to cook, then turn to finish cooking on the other side. Always keep patty on the plantain leaf. Continue turning until the tortilla has browned slightly.

Serve the tortilla alone or atop the plantain leaf. Repeat with the remaining tortillas.

Editor's note: If the griddle or *burén* is large, several tortillas may be made simultaneously.

Tostones volaos
Soufflé Plantain Tostones

Criollo Sauce

1 tablespoon ground garlic

1 cup tomato sauce

¼ cup olive oil

Salt and pepper to taste

Tostones

4 green plantains, peeled and cut into 5 or 6 slices

Salt

Corn oil

'Tostones Volaos' are the Puerto Rican equivalent of the French pommes soufflés. It is said that they were created by doña Angelina, who was the cook at Los Robles Restaurant in Salinas, where they are very popular today. The recipe for the criollo sauce comes from Moncho Carro, owner of the small restaurant Chef Ramón, also in Salinas.

Criollo Sauce

Put all the ingredients in a bowl and mix well. Transfer to a serving dish.

Tostones

Put a folded napkin on the work surface. Keep a smoothing-iron or a heavy mallet handy.

Work with one plantain at a time. Pour a lot of oil into a caldero or heavy bottomed cook pot and heat over medium high heat. Fry 5 or 6 plantain slices until they float. Remove from pot and drain. Slightly raise the heat.

Place a plantain slice on the napkin. Fold the napkin over the plantain and quickly flatten the plantain with 2 blows. The slice should be very thin, and its edges intact so that the steam does not escape. Put in a strainer to drain oil. Repeat the procedure with the remaining slices.

Fry the flattened plantains again in the hot oil until golden. Remove from oil and drain in a strainer. Repeat with the rest of the plantains.

Serve with criollo sauce.

Empanadas de Jueyes
Land Crab Empanadas

Yields 15 empanadas

6 ripe coconuts

2 green peppers, minced

10 to 12 ajíes dulces, minced

6 long leafed culantro (recao) leaves, minced

6 oregano brujo leaves, minced

8 garlic cloves

Salt to taste

5 packets sazón with annatto

5 packets sazón without annatto

2 pounds crabmeat (jueyes)

8 pounds cassava, peeled and chopped

12 large plantain leaves

Annatto seeds, ground

½ yard cheesecloth

'Oregano brujo' (warlock's oregano) is large-leafed and totally different from small-leafed oregano, which looks like marjoram. The process of making the empanadas should begin with making the 'adobo' for the dough, as the 'adobo' should be thoroughly cold.

Coconut milk adobo

Split the coconuts and extract the pulp. Grate the pulp and place in a bowl. Gradually add water to the grated coconut and squeeze the mixture. Filter the extracted liquid through a sieve, pressing down, to extract the coconut meat.

Pour the coconut milk into a saucepan and cook over medium heat. Add the peppers, *ajíes*, garlic, *culantro*, *oregano*, *sazón* with and without annatto, salt, and one pound crabmeat. When the mixture comes to a boil, turn off and let cool.

The coconut milk *adobo* must be cold to be used correctly in this recipe. It will be used to prepare the crab filling, to dampen the plantain leaves, and in the preparation of the cassava dough.

Crabmeat Filling

When the coconut milk *adobo* mixture has cooled, the surface will have a thick coating. Remove the coating with a spoon and put it in another saucepan. Reserve the remaining coconut milk *adobo*. Cook for a few minutes; stir occasionally. Add the remaining pound of crabmeat and continue to cook until thickened. Reserve to use as the filling.

Remove another layer of the coconut milk remaining in the first saucepan. This layer will not be as thick as the first. Pour this layer of milk into a bowl. Reserve for future use in dampening of the plantain leaves.

Cassava dough

Grate the cassava. Place the grated cassava on a piece of cheese cloth or other porous fabric. Squeeze the grated cassava until it is very dry and then place it in a bowl.

Place a sieve over another bowl. Scrape and press the grated cassava through the sieve to make a finer flour. Sift all the cassava.

Gradually place the grated cassava into a *caldero* or cook pot, and set over medium heat, stirring constantly, until thickened. Add some ground annatto for color. Avoid leaving over heat very long; otherwise the dough will become lumpy. Let it cool and put in another pot.

Empanadas

Take a plantain leaf that has been blanched or exposed to heat. Dampen it with the reserved coconut milk.

Follow a procedure similar to that for making pasteles (see recipe in this chapter); pour some *masa* onto the leaf and spread the *masa* evenly. Fill with crabmeat mixture and wrap the leaf as for pasteles, but do not tie with twine. If the *empanadas* are not to be eaten immediately, freeze for later.

Heat a skillet, griddle, or *burén* over medium heat. Place the *empanada*-filled plantain leaf on the cooking surface. Cook for a few minutes, then open the leaf to check the cooking process. Close well and turn the *empanada*, without removing it from the plantain leaf. Let it continue to cook. Continue turning, until the dough has cooked and has browned slightly. The plantain leaf will always burn slightly.

When the *empanada* is well-cooked, remove from heat along with its plantain leaf or by itself. Repeat process for the remaining *empanadas*.

Buñuelos de ñame de doña Carmen Aboy Valldejuli
Doña Carmen Aboy Valldejuli's Ñame Fritters

1 pound ñame, peeled and cut into chunks

½ quart water

1 tablespoon salt

2 tablespoons lard or vegetable oil

6 tablespoons all-purpose flour

2 tablespoons milk

½ teaspoon salt

1 egg

Vegetable oil for frying

Powdered sugar, sugar syrup, or jelly

This recipe belongs to Doña Carmen Aboy Valldejuli, one of Puerto Rico's great cooking teachers. Her book, 'Cocina Criolla', has gone through more than 50 editions since it was published in 1954. It is considered the 'Culinary Bible' for brides. The 'ñame' is a tuber of African origin; it has become well-acclimated to the Antilles. It was a staple in the slaves' diet. In English, it is called yam.

Boil the water with a tablespoon of salt. Add the *ñame*, cover, and boil over moderate heat for 40 minutes or until tender. Remove, drain, and mash.

Add the rest of the ingredients and mix the batter. Deep-fry by tablespoonfuls until golden. Drain on paper towels.

Serve with powdered sugar, or accompany with sugar syrup or jelly.

Editor's note: If the griddle or *burén* is large enough, several *empanadas* may be made simultaneously.

Rice Croquettes. Page 225

FRANCO SECCARELLI

THE TASTE OF UMBRIA
ON CRISTO STREET

Above, the first step in making egg pasta.
Opposite, shaping the rice and mozzarella croquettes by hand.

The taste of his native Umbria and the wise teachings of a mother merged in Franco Seccarelli, so that when he crossed the Atlantic to establish his own restaurant in Puerto Rico, he was already endowed with the qualities of a great chef

Autum is our favorite season for travel in Europe, perhaps because the leaves turn red and gold, the frenzy of the grape harvest is at full force, wild mushrooms are for sale by the roadside, partridge, hare and venison appear on myriad menus, and all restaurants experience a renewal. So when an invitation arrived from the Slow Food movement requesting my participation as judge at the Bologna Slow Food Awards in October of 2000, it could only have been heaven-sent.

As soon as I told Franco Seccarelli, the chef and proprietor of the romantic Italian restaurant Il Perugino on Cristo street in Old San Juan, he commented, "If you go to Italy this autumn, we must get together, as I will be there. You should also spend a few days at my home near Assisi."

It was agreed. On October 7, Madame Villon and I had hardly settled into our hotel in Milan, when we received a telephone call from Franco. He and his lovely wife Sandra were in Milan, and we were to meet in front of the Cathedral. Shortly after meeting, the four of us arrived for lunch at Visani, a classic of Milanese cooking.

To eat with Franco Seccarelli at Visani, a restaurant of great tradition, is to embark upon a course in Italian gastronomy. Franco is not only an excellent cook, but he is also a philosopher of cooking who is passionate about the culinary treasures of his native country.

That afternoon, while we lunched, he recounted the story of each of the dishes we had ordered. "This is not common veal, this is *agresto nerveti*: milk-fed veal, which in Italy is different from Puerto Rico because the veal in Italy is not as young; it has already fed on grass… This *risotto saltalto* is different; notice that it is almost like a rice pudding, with a lot of saffron…" Thus explaining dish by dish, until Sandra's Milanese arrived. "See?" asked Franco pointing, "If the *costoletta alla Milanese* is boneless, *non é legitima* (not authentic)."

We finished our long lunch, said goodbye with hugs and kisses and went our

Foie Gras with Caramelized Onions. Page 226

separate ways. After Milan, a long highway journey awaited us, crossing the Apennines to reach Perugia. Twelve days after our Milan lunch, Vittorio – married to Franco's Aunt Anna Maria – lit a fire in the fireplace at Franco's house. And at sundown we toasted my birthday with young wine made in his garage, next door to Franco's house.

"My father and mother lived in that house and I spent my childhood there," Franco said. "With the olive trees surrounding the house and the 200 more that I planted, soon I'll be producing olive oil." That place in Umbria, high in the hills where Francis of Assisi and his monks had walked, seemed wrought from a canvas of Giotto or Il Perugino. I understand why Franco, searching for a name for his restaurant in that far off Caribbean island, would think of Il Perugino.

Perugia is a city that hosts an annual grand jazz festival as well as the Eurochocolate festival. It's also where Franco grew up, surrounded by the aromas and tastes of olive oil, cheeses, sausages, lake fish and white truffles of Umbria. Franco seems to have been predestined to become a great chef. His parents met at the restaurant in the Brufani Hotel, which still exists in Perugia. His father was a waiter in the hotel dining room, and his mother the young private chef at the residence of the owners of the hotel.

Carlo Seccarelli and Alma married and opened a *trattoria*, Girarrosto (rotisserie), with a partner from whom they soon separated. In two years, they sold their part of the *trattoria* to the partner and opened La Lanterna, a more elegant restaurant, which they owned from 1953 to 1984. It was there that Franco learned what a kitchen was. "I was in elementary school, and when I wasn't in class, I was in the kitchen and she was teaching me; I remember that she taught me to make mayonnaise using two forks," Franco said, gesturing as though vigorously whisking the eggs and oil.

But his mother not only taught him her cooking secrets, she also revealed the secrets of the business, such as purchasing. Alma knew who was who among her purveyors and by a mere touch she could gauge the freshness of a cut of beef or veal. "My mother was something; she made me go every

Saturday 30 kilometers outside Perugia to see a shepherd named Matteo, who lived with his sheep, to buy cheese, because the man made an unequalled Pecorino." Keeping his eyes open in the kitchen, burning his fingers, cutting himself with the knives, Franco learned to cook, little by little, with his mother and his Aunt Anna Maria. And equally important: "My mother taught me to eat."

Military service in Italy took Franco away from the kitchen for a time and also out of the technical school where he studied telecommunications. But cooking was his vocation. Soon he was working in a hotel in Perugia and catering suppers and activities on his own, until an interesting opportunity presented itself: to go to England to work as a first assistant at the Westley Court Hotel in Birmingham. "It was a big hotel that did a lot of weddings and very little creative cuisine, but I was already 32 or 33 years old, and I had to learn quickly what I had not learned in culinary school …and to improve my English."

Meanwhile, Franco had met a young Puerto Rican student in 1987, who convinced him to come seek his fortune in Puerto Rico. In the Caribbean, a new world of colors, sounds, customs, and tastes awaited the Italian who had only left Umbria to go to gray Britain. Here in San Juan, he soon met Juanita, a marvelous Dominican cook who had a contagious laugh and worked along side him in the small kitchen of Amadeus in Old San Juan. Juanita had worked early in her career in the kitchens of Ali Oli, the splendid restaurant owned by chef Alfredo Ayala.

So the young Italian joined the San Juan fraternity of chefs, and, from one day to the next, Franco switched from milk-fed veal, Umbrian lentils, truffles, and porcini mushrooms to guava and passion fruit sauces, pigeon peas and conch.

But in Italy he had learned the most important lesson: "My mother gave me the best sort of schooling: she trained me to taste." I have never known a great chef who did not have the heightened sense of taste to which Franco alludes, as it is something that one either has or does not have. Franco has it, and it is evident in his cooking – this and something else. Each time I ask a great cook what is most important in cooking, I always hear: "A sense of proportion." Franco expresses it another way: "Cooking is all about balance. It is not good if you can't recognize each of the ingredients that have gone into a dish. Cooking is simplicity." This is reflected in the use Franco makes of aromatic herbs. "If I use rosemary, I don't add anything else. If I put in basil, it is only basil. I do not mix flavors and aromas". His lentil soup is a tribute to simplicity, and to reverence, which is an ingredient he considers superb. Franco's respect for the quality of ingredients is such that he affirms, "I never use a griddle because you can never clean it well, and it becomes saturated with unpleasant odors. Fish, poultry and meat I always do on the grill, in the oven, or steamed. And I only use Italian virgin olive oil."

"I have the feeling that my mother, Alma, should also sign all of my recipes because of their intrinsic balance and simplicity"

When Franco opened Il Perugino on April 1, 1989, the restaurant was located on Cristo Street between Caleta de San Juan and Fortaleza, on the ground floor of a colonial house, until he decided to seek a new location. One of Il Perugino's painted angels must have touched Franco with its wing, for he soon found a new site on Cristo Street, 20 meters from the Old San Juan Cathedral. Early in 1994, he renovated the building, moving to the upper floor while converting a dry well in the middle of the restaurant into a wine cellar which *sommelier* Marcos Mercado maintains well stocked with an excellent selection of Italian wines. Although Il Perugino's cooking has always been creative, after the move, it became more personal, always rooted in the traditions of his native Umbria,

but perhaps a little more influenced by the new gastronomic currents that converge in today's Italy. "My favorite restaurants in Italy are not necessarily the most famous. I really like La Tenda Rossa, to which Michelin has awarded two stars, located in San Casciano in Val di Pesa, near Florence. In Rome, Sans Souci was very good and continues to be good, but the owner, who is a friend of mine, sold it and recently opened the Bellavista at the Splendid Hotel."

I also asked Franco what he thought of Felidia in New York? "Felidia is very good. I met Lydia Bastianich when they invited me to cook at an Italian food festival in New York to commemorate the tenth anniversary of the James Beard Foundation Awards four years ago. She is very nice, and she must have liked what I cooked because she came to my station several times to try what I had made."

As Seccarelli has stated, "I don't wish to criticize the modern cuisine of which I am part, but only that which pretends to invent without logic, which mixes for the sake of mixing, where there is no balance of tastes. There are those who don't respect the personality of the ingredients, their freshness, or their fragrance. One cannot renounce innovation, but instead must respect the harmony of tastes and simplicity."

I still remember a night when friends invited us to dine at Il Perugino with the well known chef Jacques Pepin and his Cuban wife Gloria. Franco came to the table to see how everything was and to present us with a bottle of Vega Sicilia Reserva Unico, just as Pepin was trying a white polenta with shrimp that had come as an appetizer. Pepin stopped eating, looked at Franco and said to him, "White polenta, I didn't know it existed." Franco looked at him, smiled and shrugged his shoulders modestly.

The moment that clients learn that certain ingredients have arrived, they scramble for reservations, in anticipation of savoring dishes such as the sensational *Fettuccine con Tartufo Bianco*.

"My clients trust me. Fifteen years ago they began to tell me 'do as you wish,' placing themselves in my hands."

Until recently, the walls of Il Perugino, were covered with photos of celebrities who had dined there, from Luciano Pavarotti, the Infanta Pilar of Spain and Piero Antinori, to the current governor of Puerto Rico, whose official residence is only two blocks away. The president of Puerto Rico's most important bank, Richard Carrión, lives near the restaurant and often dines there. "In 15 years, Richard has never dined from the menu. He calls when he is coming, and I have to wrack my brain to decide what to cook for him that I had not cooked yesterday or the day before. It is hard, but he has never returned a dish."

Another of Franco's neighbors is the Archbishop of San Juan, Monsignor Roberto González, who walks a few meters from his residence to the restaurant. "His tastes are simple, a pasta with vegetables, an arugula salad, but, like a good Puerto Rican, he always leaves a little room in his stomach for dessert." In 2002 Franco and Sandra accompanied him and his delegation to the Vatican for the beatification ceremony of the Puerto Rican Charlie Rodríguez. "It was the only time that I have ever flown from San Juan to Rome non-stop. It was very emotional, a unique experience, because Charlie is a true saint."

I can just imagine the reaction of Franco's family and friends in Perugia, had they seen Carlo and Alma's little boy traveling with his friend, the Archbishop, to see the Pope. Who could have imagined it? Surely, Alma, surrounded in heaven by Il Perugino's cherubim, would follow the journey saying: "God bless you, my son, but make sure the veal is good, and cook with the best oil you can find; it's all in the taste."

Altromondo

In the old part of Perugia, close by the Piazza Italia, Anna Maria, Franco Seccarelli's aunt, has a restaurant called Altromondo, which has garnered two forks in the Michelin Guide for many years.

Anna Maria does not look her age, and works long hours in the restaurant as if she were still her big sister's apprentice. She is an enchanting woman who maintains Altromondo's atmosphere of a family kitchen, with service that makes many consider it one of the best, if not the best, restaurant in the city. I have not eaten in any other restaurant in Perugia, so I really cannot pass judgment. But I will tell you it is well worth the trip, just to eat her *antipasti*, particularly her rice fritters with mozzarella.

A shrimp and scallops ragú with black olives and basil will soon cover a dish of tagliolini. Page 220

Tagliolini al ragù di capesante e gamberete
Tagliolini with Scallop & Shrimp Ragù

Serves 4

Scallops and shrimp make a beautiful combination in this delicious dish.

Tagliolini

1 pound of fresh egg pasta (see recipe page 218)

Ragù

10 unshelled shrimps, 21/25 size

½ cup of extra-virgin olive oil

4 or 5 garlic cloves

4 fresh basil leaves, minced

4 black seedless olives, finely chopped

1 sliced hot pepper (optional)

1 cup fish broth

4 large fresh sea scallops, diced

Fresh parsley, finely chopped

Salt

Tagliolini

Divide the egg pasta in two. Flatten each half with the palms of your hands. Shape each into a rectangle and flour lightly. Set the rollers of the pasta machine to the widest setting and feed the dough through the machine opening. Repeat, this time decreasing the width by one setting. Continue this cycle, each time decreasing the width by one setting, so that the dough becomes progressively thinner. Flour dough as you work.

Cut the long sheet into 14" long pieces. Fold the thin dough in half, lengthwise. Fold again. Cut the dough into ⅛" inch ribbons. As you unroll the pasta, you unroll the finished tagliolini.

Ragù

Peel and devein the shrimp, reserving the shells. Slice the shrimp lengthwise.

Heat the olive oil in a large heavy skillet over medium heat. Add the garlic, the shrimp shells, basil, olives, and hot pepper (optional). Cook until the garlic is golden. Add the fish broth and stir until the oil emulsifies, then add salt. Cook over low heat for about 10 minutes. Remove skillet from heat. Discard the garlic and shrimp shells. Reserve half of the liquid.

Add the shrimp and the scallops. Bring a large pot of salted water to a boil. Add the pasta, cooking until *al dente*. Drain and add to the shellfish in the skillet. Cook over medium heat until shellfish is done, 2 or 3 minutes. Make sure that the pasta does not dry out; should this happen, add a little of the reserved sauce. Add parsley and stir.

Serve on warm plates, placing the pasta in the center. Surround with the shrimp and scallops.

Pasta al dente

To determine whether pasta is *al dente*, take a piece out of the pot and bite into it. If it does not feel raw, yet still gives some resistance when you bite it, it is *al dente*.

Fettuccine fresche al tartufo nero
Fettuccine with Black Truffles

Serves 4

Fettuccine

1 pound fresh egg pasta

8 tablespoons butter

4 o 6 tablespoons of water

1 whole black truffle

3 ounces black truffles, preferably fresh, finely diced

8 tablespoons parmigiano reggiano cheese, freshly shaved or grated

When white truffles are in season, Seccarelli uses these rather than black truffles.

Divide the pasta dough into two equal pieces. Flatten each half with the palms of your hands and lightly dust with flour. Set the rollers of the pasta machine to the widest setting and feed the dough through the machine. Repeat, this time decreasing the width by one setting. Continue this cycle, reducing the width by one setting until you achieve the desired width (setting 4 or higher).

Fold the dough in half, then fold again. With a knife, cut the roll into ¼" ribbons. As you unfold the pasta, you unfold the finished fettuccine. Bring a large pot of salted water to a boil . Cook the fettuccine for a maximum of three minutes or until *al dente.*

In a large skillet heat the butter, plus 4 to 6 tablespoons of water, over medium heat. When the butter has melted, add the fettuccine. Toss well. Remove from heat. Using a truffle slicer or a very sharp knife, slice the truffles. Add the Parmesan cheese and cut a bit of sliced truffle. Stir well and add a little more water, if necessary.

Serve in bowls. Scatter with truffles.

Serves 4

This simple filling transforms a classic pasta into a heavenly delicacy.

Filling

6 ounces fresh spinach

2 tablespoons unsalted butter

6 ounces cleaned chicken liver, diced

½ ounce black truffle, minced

1 egg, beaten with 1 tablespoon water

1 truffle, julienned

Salt and white pepper

Ravioli

1 pound fresh egg pasta

3 tablespoons butter,

Diced parmegiano reggiano, freshly grated

1 egg beaten

1-2 tablespoons of water

½ black truffle, julienned

Filling

Clean the spinach, removing stems. Place the leaves in a pot or large saucepan without adding anything. Cook over low heat until the moisture has evaporated. Set aside.

Heat ½ tablespoon of butter in a skillet, then sauté the chicken livers for one minute, just until they turn pink inside. Remove from heat, slice, and allow to cool. In a food processor, coarsely chop and mix the liver, the spinach, the truffles, and the egg. Put the filling in a bowl, adding the remaining butter. Season with salt and pepper to taste. Refrigerate, allowing mixture to harden slightly.

Ravioli

Divide the dough in two. Feed the dough through the pasta machine, dusting with flour to prevent sticking, until thin sheets of pasta dough have been produced. Place half of the stretched dough on the work surface. Drop a bit — about the size of a walnut — of the spinach, liver, egg, and truffle mixture, at 2" intervals between each ravioli. Using a small paintbrush, brush with beaten egg between fillings. Cover with the other half of the pasta. Press down on the edges with your fingers, thus eliminating air pockets. Cut the ravioli with a ravioli cutter (a small wheel with teeth) in 2" x 2" squares.

Bring a large pot of water to a rolling boil. Add the ravioli and cook 6 to 8 minutes, or until *al dente*. Remove from heat and drain well. Place the pasta in a skillet; add butter and one or two tablespoons of water. Remove from heat and add the grated cheese and julienned black truffles.

Truffles

Fresh truffles are only available at the end and begining of the year. They are very expensive and
have to be purchase through a distributor. "Summer truffles", though not as good, can be used.
Although preserved truffles do not have the same aroma as the fresh ones, they are less expensive and available all year-round.

Suppli di riso
Rice Croquettes

Serves 10

4 tablespoons butter

3 tablespoons extra-virgin olive oil

¼ piece onion, finely minced

1 pound rice (short or medium grain)

Water

½ pound parmigiano reggiano,
  freshly grated

1 pound fresh mozzarella di buffala

4 or 5 eggs, beaten

Toasted bread crumbs, finely ground

Salt

These savoury croquettes were a specialty of Franco's mother and are included here as a homage to his native Umbria.

Heat the butter, oil and onion, until the onion wilts and is soft and tender. Add the rice. Add water each time the rice seems to dry out. When the rice has reached the *al dente* stage — after cooking for 10 or 11 minutes maximum — and is dry, remove from heat. Add the *parmigiano reggiano*. Place on a chilled platter to cool.

Cut the mozzarella into ½"cubes. Compress and shape the rice by hand, then place a mozzarella cube in the center. Close your hand and shape the croquette into a ball. Coat with breadcrumbs. Dip in the beaten egg, and again coat with breadcrumbs. Shape the croquettes. Pour the oil into a skillet or deep fryer, and preheat to 350°F. Fry for 2 minutes or until the croquettes are golden brown and the mozzarella inside has melted.

Gnocchi di zucca al tartufo bianco
Pumpkin Gnocchi with White Truffles

Serves 4

½ pound pumpkin, peeled

1 egg

Nutmeg to taste

Salt to taste

White pepper to taste

1 cup grated parmigiano reggiano

All-purpose flour

2 tablespoons of butter

1 white truffle

If you are a gnocchi fan and can afford the truffles, you must try this unique recipe.

Preheat oven to 250°F. Cut pumpkin into slices ½"-thick and place on a cookie sheet. Bake for 30 minutes, until the pumpkin has lost its moisture and begins to brown and stick to the baking sheet. Remove from oven. Let cool.

Process pumpkin in a food processor until it has the consistency of a purée that can be shaped or manipulated. While processing, add the egg, the nutmeg, the salt and pepper. Remove from the processor bowl, and add half of the Parmesan cheese. Thoroughly dust your hands with flour, so that the dough does not stick to them as you work. Pull the dough into a long slender cylinder, and cut the gnocchi in 1" lengths. Bring a large pot of salted water to a boil. Place the gnocchi in the boiling water, just a few at a time. Remove these as soon as they float to the surface. Drain and place on paper towel.

Repeat the process with the remaining gnocchi. In a skillet, heat the butter with a little water. Add the gnocchi and season with salt and pepper. Remove from heat and add the remaining parmigiano. Finely slice the truffles with either a truffle slicer or a sharp knife. Place gnocchi in the center of the plates, topped with sliced white truffles. Serve.

Chef's note. Gnocchi should be served as soon as they are prepared.

Serves 4

½ **pound fresh *foie gras* in ½"**
  slices
5 tablespoons unsalted butter
½ cup dry white wine
1 large onion, thinly sliced
Salt and white pepper
Finely minced parsley

A delicious and very original way to prepare duck liver.

Season the *foie-gras* with salt and pepper. Place half of the butter, the wine, the onion, and a pinch of salt and pepper in a deep skillet. Cover and cook over low heat for approximately 20 minutes, being careful not to let the wine evaporate; should this occur, add a little water. Onions should remain white and very soft in a creamy base.

Heat the remaining butter in a skillet. When it has reached medium heat, add the slices of *foie-gras* and cook each side for approximately 30 seconds . Divide the caramelized onion onto four plates, arranged as a bed for the *foie- gras*. Place the *foie-gras* on top of the onions. Top with minced parsley.

Beef Tenderloin Perugino alla Ghiota
Filetto Perugino alla ghiotta

Serves 10

Beef tenderloin with a personal touch: Franco Seccarelli's wonderful sauce.

1 beef tenderloin (about 5 pounds)
  ready to cook

4 cloves of garlic

Salt and white pepper

½ pound sage

4 cups dry white wine

1 cup extra-virgin olive oil

½ onion

1 tablespoon capers

1 lemon, peeled

½ celery stalk

1 pound chicken livers, cleaned

Preheat oven to 400°F. Place the tenderloin, seasoned with garlic, salt and pepper in a glass oven-proof pan with olive oil and few sage leaves. Roast for 15 to 20 minutes, turning every 5 minutes and basting with ¼ cup of wine. Cook until a meat thermometer inserted deep into the filet, reads 135°F., for medium rare (adjust time to allow for personal preferences).

To prepare the sauce, pour the remaining ½ cup of extra-virgin olive oil in a deep skillet. Add garlic, remaining sage, onion, capers, lemon, celery stalk, and chicken livers. Cook over medium heat, occasionally adding some of the white wine, for 3 minutes. Cook until the wine evaporates. Remove from heat, and blend in a food processor or a blender. Place the sauce in a saucepan and add the remaining wine. Simmer at medium heat for 2 minutes. Cut the tenderloin in ¼" thick slices, and cover with sauce.

Red Snapper Filet with Basil and Tomato
Filetto di pesce al basilico e il pomodoro

Serves 4

The aromas of Caribbean basil go hand in hand with the tomato, and add a masterful touch to this fish from our coastal waters.

10 green basil leaves, finely chopped

2 tablespoons extra-virgin olive oil

¼ cup of water

Salt and white pepper

2 tablespoons unsalted butter

4 garlic cloves, finely minced

4 red snapper filets, approximately
  3 ounces each

3 ounces tomato, peeled, seeded and diced

Make a raw *salsa*, combining basil, extra-virgin olive oil, water, salt and pepper in a bowl.

Preheat oven to 400°F. Butter the bottom and sides of a glass baking dish.

Scatter the garlic and a little *salsa* in the pan. Add the fish fillets and cover with *salsa* and tomato. Bake for 4-6 minutes. Remove and cover with salsa.

Thin Apple Tart à la Mode. Páge 246

DANIEL VASSE

A TEACHER FROM
THE LAND OF BUTTER

No one who sees Daniel Vasse riding his super-

motorcycle on Highway 31, between Palmas and San

Juan, would ever imagine that the motorcyclist is a

highly sensitive chef who is genuinely concerned

with the future of young Puerto Rican chefs

One day, I sat down in front of the TV and, by chance, happened upon a relatively unknown movie channel just in time to catch the beginning of a film that glued me to the screen for two hours. It had only three principal characters: a United States politician (Sam Waterston, the prosecutor in *Law and Order*), his friend, a poet (John Heard), and a beautiful Scandinavian scientist (Liv Ullman). Their conversation was an absorbing philosophical dialogue which seemed like a verbal game of chess for three. The successive images and the play of light, ever-changing throughout the day, were a remarkable visual feast. The action advanced as the threesome debated; they wandered onto terraces, through cloisters, into dungeons, crypts, and monk cells, into a maze of corridors, and up and down infinite stairways in one of the most extraordinary places in the world, Mont Saint-Michel.

I have been to Mont Saint-Michel only once, and its memory left me with the desire to return in autumn, to linger in a Gothic chapel and listen to the mass sung in Gregorian chant; to stray closer to the sheep for a better view, to watch them graze on the grasses of the salt marshes; to savor an omelet at the Bistro de la Mére Poulard; and to spend a night there, awakening at dawn to the sound of the abbey's bells.

Many people who travel to France think only of Paris, Champagne, Provence, Bordeaux, and the Côte d'Azur. Although Le Mont Saint Michel is the second most popular destination (after Paris), many visitors forget about the cold, wineless North; the land of hardly people and fierce fighters who survived by the sword for centuries, turning back waves of invaders along the coasts of Normandy. It is a curious fact that if Henry Plantagenet, a Norman, had not married

Eleanor of Aquitaine, perhaps the wines of Bordeaux might never become as famous as they are today. Eleanor's dowry was the entire Duchy of Aquitaine, extending from the Pyrenées to Anjou, and ever since then, the United Kingdom has been one of the most important customers of Bordeaux wines.

"I was born 4 years after the Allies landed in Normandy, but at home everyone talked a great deal about the invasion which had marked the beginning of Hitler's defeat. My parents helped the Résistance and my six older siblings, although very young at the time, still have memories of the assault (Le Débarquement)." Daniel Vasse, with grey hair and brown eyes, looks Norman, albeit a Norman well-acclimated to the Caribbean's warm waters. His three restaurants are located literally on the water: Chez Daniel on the marina at Palmas del Mar; The Grill, next door to Chez Daniel (open only during high tourist season); and Daniel by the Sea, at the Palmas Beach Club.

"My parents were from Villebaudon, not far from the beaches of Aromanches and Omaha, where thousands of American soldiers died. This village is located on the road that goes from Aromanche, passes thru St. Lo, and ends at Avranches. We call this road *La Route de la Liberté*." Mont Saint Michel is just 23 kilometers from Avranches.

Provence, on the Mediterranean, is the land of olive oil, aromatic herbs, and tomatoes; Normandy is the land of cattle, horses (the celebrated Percherons), an abundance of butter, gallons and gallons of thick cream, tons of cholesterol, and millions of apples. Normandy is to France as Asturias is to Spain; neither makes wine. Asturias ferments

Palmas del Mar

Palmas del Mar is a controlled-access resort located in southeastern Puerto Rico, about an hour from San Juan. It covers 2,750 acres and has 3 miles of beachfront facing the Caribbean Sea. It combines hotels, private homes, and condos in a setting that includes two 18-hole golf courses, more than 20 tennis courts, a private beach club, an equestrian center, a marina, water sports facilities, a co-op for professional fishermen, and several restaurants.

Red Snapper Roses on a bed of Leeks with Ginger Cream. Page 242.

apples to produce *sidra* (cider); Normandy makes cider as well, while calvados, distilled from apples, is the northern counterpart to cognac.

"But you know something? Even though my kitchen still reflects my Norman roots, I do not flambé my dishes with Calvados. I use Barrilito Rum instead, because in Normandy we use Negrita Rum, which is made in Martinique." All of Daniel's family, starting with his father, who was a butcher, work in what Daniel calls *métiers de bouche*, "professions of the mouth." They are bakers, butchers, pastrymakers; everyone's occupation has to do with food.

Of course, Daniel learned to handle knives as a child, and by adolescence had begun to work at restaurants, the classic French route to mastering the cook's trade. "France did not have culinary schools back then; one had to go to school in Switzerland or Germany, which was very expensive." But life itself charts its course, and one day Daniel found himself a thousand kilometers to the south, in Le Boulou, close to the Catalonia border. He had married a girl from the Pyrénées, and he was hired as a chef at a casino. "I worked like a slave, and after a year I asked the owner for a raise, but instead he offered me either to work as chef at a camping project or to establish a restaurant at a resort in Puerto Rico. The casino owner had bought land at Palmas del Mar, southeast of the city of San Juan, where he and a partner were building a marina and planned to build a restaurant.

Daniel and his wife Lucette had never heard of Puerto Rico, and they had no idea where it was located. "I thought it was in Portugal." They searched through maps of Portugal and couldn't find Puerto Rico. So they continued looking; eventually a tiny dot on a map identified with the words: Puerto Rico. In 1982 the couple brought their 9 year-old twin daughters, Céline and Sévérine, to Palmas del Mar, where they spent the season. "It was not easy, we didn't speak English or Spanish. Just French." The following year they returned, this time to stay. "We worried that the girls might not adapt, but as it turned out they quicky began speaking English and Spanish at school. My clients enjoyed my food, especially my lobster grilled with butter, which I did without boiling it first."

Eventually, the Frenchman who held the contract with the marina departed, and Daniel and Lucette quickly saw the possibility to open up their own restaurant. In 1985 Palmas del Mar welcomed Chez Daniel. Their clientele grew rapidly. Two years later, the couple decided Daniel needed an assistant in the kitchen, someone familiar with preparing French food. Lucette needed help in the dining room as well. Daniel consulted his brother, a pastrymaker who owned a pastry shop in Paris. He had a *chef pâtissier* whose sister and her fiancé had just finished culinary school. They thought about the offer, accepted, and have been at Palmas del Mar for 18 years now. "Frank is my shadow; his cooking is one hundred percent my style. This is the best thing that ever happened to me. He is *chef de cuisine* at Chez Daniel and at The Grill and she is maître d' at Chez Daniel." Frank and Valérie have settled at Palmas del

Facing page, on top, Frank Arnould, Daniel Vasse's right hand, helps him in the kitchen. This page, Duck Confit with Potatoes Sarladaise. Page 243

The chefs prepare a rack of lamb. Page 245

Mar, and they have a 10 year-old daughter who is like a grand-daughter to Daniel and Lucette. They are not yet grandparents; the Vasse twins are now 30 years old, and one of them is the Banquet Manager at San Juan's Ritz Carlton.

Upon arriving in Puerto Rico, Daniel received an invitation to join the Chef's Association. At the first meeting he attended, he met several German, Austrian, Swiss, and French colleagues. When the meeting ended, Daniel addressed the group, saying: "I see that 80 percent of the chefs here are European. Has it occurred to you that unless we train young Puerto Ricans, gastronomy has no future?" Thus, Daniel began to dedicate some time to educating chefs, holding classes at Palmas del Mar, at the now-closed The Kitchen Shop in San Juan,

and at the Humacao campus of the University of Puerto Rico. He also collaborates in many food and wine events. But his baby is the *Festival de la Buena Vida*, an annual event that raises money for community service. "Each year we auction a dinner for 8 to 12 people, which I cook at a private home, with help from members of the Festival Committee. That evening, someone acts as *sommelier*, others are waiters or waitresses, someone takes care of valet parking, etc. People have a great time; those who buy the dinner arrive in formal dress; they drink fine wines, they eat well, and a significant sum of money is raised for charity."

Daniel has witnessed first hand the dramatic development of gastronomy in Puerto Rico over the last several decades. He recalls the change with a Norman refrain: "Oh, the *crêpe* has turned." The contributions he has made over the last twenty-odd

Some time ago, a family who lives in Palmas del Mar celebrated their daughter's wedding reception at Chez Daniel, and they requested that Daniel prepare an unusual wedding cake, something very French. The chef brainstormed until it occurred to him to mention a *Croquembouche*, which he described to the bride as a pyramid, tall and cone-shaped, built up of small balls made of *pate-à-choux*, which could have different fillings and are assembled and glazed with caramel.

The bride loved the idea, but Daniel pondered the logistics. "Calculating the number of guests, 600 balls of *pate-à-choux* had to be baked and filled on the morning of the wedding. But the caramel had to be added at the last minute, because the humidity would cause the caramel to run."

Everything turned out just as planned. The dessert sat on a cake base, on an enormous round tray that rested on a kitchen table, which had to be carried with utmost care. When the cooks lifted the tray, they could not fit the *Croquembouche* through the doorway: it was a couple of inches too high. "Imagine what a huge problem it was! We all looked at each other, thinking the same thought: unless the doorframe was dismounted, the dessert would not make it into the dining room. Someone miraculously found a carpenter, who took apart the doorframe, we took the dessert into the dining room, and the doorframe was reassembled." And, best of all, the bride was delighted with her *Croquembouche*, so different from any of the wedding cakes at her friends' weddings.

Valerie Arnould, coordinates with Daniel Vasse the last details for lunch.

years have been considerable. "It has been very fulfilling to be part of this growth; one becomes aware of the development later on."

What does this chef say about his own cooking? "I am a French chef who uses the ingredients that are available here – so much more is available today compared to twenty years ago – but my kitchen is still French."

Has progress been made in culinary education for young aspirants? "Not all schools in Puerto Rico are good, but there are a couple that stand out and there are some talented young graduates who are full of potential. But the young kids have to be aware that graduating from culinary school does not transform them into chefs. I see them wearing a toque and a jacket embroidered with "chef so-and-so," and I ask them: are you a chef?

Whose boss are you? Because chef means boss, chief. You are just a cook. If you work hard and work well, you will become a chef."

Daniel does not have much spare time, although he tries to play tennis. He also loves to ride his motorcycle, which looks like a two-wheeled Mercedes Benz, all over the island roads. Yet, his truest passion is the proffesion he has dedicated his life to: "Cooking is like a drug, as absorbing as religion can be. You have very little free time; you are not free Saturdays and Sundays; it's a demanding profession. While others enjoy Christmas Eve, you spend it in the kitchen. But, if you accept this, and work well, cooking will give you lots of satisfaction."

Quiche aux Oignons
Onion Quiche

Serves 8

Pâte Brisée

1 cup all-purpose flour

6 tablespoons butter, very cold, diced

2 eggs

2 tablespoons water

Salt

Filling

3 tablespoons butter

2 large onions, thinly sliced

1 cup water

Thyme

Pinch of salt

3 eggs

½ cup heavy cream

Nutmeg

Salt

Pepper

1 cup Swiss cheese, coarsely grated

4 tablespoons butter, very cold, diced

Nostalgia is the mood that Chef Daniel has created with these recipes. The traditional quiche from Lorraine (east of Paris) calls for bacon rather than onions, but the onions in this adaptation are an excellent substitution. Try to make the pie dough. It will taste much better than store-bought.

Pâte Brisée

Pour the flour into a medium sized bowl. Add the butter. Add the eggs, water, and salt together. Flour your hands and knead the dough and shape into a ball. The dough should be firm, but you should be able to see little bits of butter. Cover with plastic wrap and refrigerate for 30 minutes.

Preheat oven to 325°F. Flour your work surface and roll out the dough with a rolling pin, making an 11" circle. Spread the dough unto a round quiche or pie pan.

Filling

Place butter in a skillet. Sauté the onions in the butter and water until tender. Season with thyme and salt.

Place eggs, cream, nutmeg, and pepper in a bowl and mix. Add the onions and the Swiss cheese. Mix well. Pour into the pie shell, top with the diced butter and bake for 40 to 50 minutes or until golden and puffy.

Paté de Foie de Volaille
Chicken Liver Paté

Serves 12

1 pound fresh chicken livers, thoroughly cleaned
** and membranes removed**
5 eggs
4 tablespoons all-purpose flour
1 cup heavy cream
4 tablespoons cognac or brandy
Thyme
Salt and pepper
Butter, to grease the pâté pan

To serve

Unsalted butter

This simple paté is very easy to make and is excellent served as a tapa or appetizer. Serve with the best possible toast.

Place the chicken livers in a food processor and process until liquid. Sieve the purée through a streiner, pressing with a spatula. Set aside.

Combine the eggs, flour, cream, cognac or brandy, thyme, salt, and pepper in a bowl. Mix well. Place the bowl over another bowl filled with ice. Carefully fold the chicken liver purée into the mixture.

Preheat oven to 350°F. Grease the bottom and sides of the pan with butter. Fill the pan with the liver pâté. Cover with pan's lid, or with tin foil.

Bake in a doble boiler for 1 hour and 45 minutes. Let cool to room temperature. Refrigerate for 24 hours.

Serve on buttered toast.

Gratin Dauphinois
Potatoes au Gratin

Serves 6

This is a classic potato recipe. Over the years variations have evolved.

8 ounces unsalted butter

1 cup fresh milk

1 cup heavy cream

6 Idaho potatoes, medium sized, peeled
  and sliced as finely as possible

4 garlic cloves, minced

Salt and pepper

Nutmeg

1 garlic clove split in half, lengthwise

Butter

Heat a saucepan over medium heat. When hot, add the butter, milk, and heavy cream. Stir well. Add the sliced potatoes in layers. Spread minced garlic on each layer with salt, pepper, and nutmeg to taste, between each layer of potatoes and on the top.

Cook for 20 minutes.

Preheat oven to 325°F. Rub ½ garlic clove on the bottom and sides of an 8" x 8" baking dish. Grease the inside surfaces with butter. Add the potatoes with the sauce. Bake 10 to 15 minutes, or until golden. Serve with any roasted meat.

La Côte de Veau Normande
Veal Chops with Mushrooms and Calvados

Serves 2

Almost all dishes à la Normande contain cream, butter, cider, calvados or apples. This recipe includes butter, cream, calvados and cider. Austrians — like Augusto Schreiner — and Italians bread the chops and fry them; these are completely different. If you cannot find Norman cider, you may use Asturian.

2 veal chops, 8-10 ounces each

2 shallots, minced

4 white mushrooms

1 ounce Calvados

¾ cup cider or white wine

¾ cup heavy cream

2 tablespoons butter

1 tablespoon vegetable oil

Salt and pepper

Presentation

2 sprigs thyme

Heat the butter and oil in a frying pan or skillet, over medium heat. Add the veal chops and panfry for 5 minutes on each side. Remove chops from pan and set aside.

In the same pan, fry the shallots and mushrooms until softened. Add the veal chops and flambé with the calvados. Immediately add the cider (or wine) and reduce by half. Add the heavy cream. Season with salt and pepper. Simmer over low heat for one minute.

Presentation

Place a veal chop in the center of a large plate and cover with the sauce. Garnish with a sprig of thyme. Can be served with pasta or sautéed potatoes.

La Rose de Cartucho aux Poireaux, Creme de Gingembre et Tomates Grillées
Red Snapper Roses on a Bed of Leeks with Ginger Cream and Grilled Tomatoes

Serves 2

10 ounces "cartucho" or red snapper fillet, very thinly sliced

1 leek, cut in 1" slices

2 tablespoons butter

1 teaspoon sugar

1 one-inch piece fresh ginger, peeled and sliced

Salt and pepper

1 cup heavy cream

1 teaspoon gingerroot, peeled and grated

½ lime

2 small ripe tomatoes, cut in halves

Pinch of fresh garlic

2 tablespoons dry white wine

To serve

White rice, cooked

'Cartucho' is a deep-water fish, belonging to the snapper family, which has delicious meat. Ginger was one of Puerto Rico's primary exports during the Spanish regime.

On a greased piece of waxed paper, form the fish slices into spirals, going from small to large, creating two roses, 3" in diameter each.

Place the leek slices in a small saucepan, cover with water, and butter, sugar, a slice of ginger, salt, and pepper. Cook over low heat for 10 minutes. Remove, drain and set aside. Keep hot.

In another saucepan, mix the heavy cream with a teaspoon of grated ginger, salt and pepper. Simmer over very low heat for five minutes. Add a few drops of lime juice and strain.

Season tomatoes with a pinch of garlic, salt, and pepper, and grill.

Preheat oven to 375°F. Season fish roses with salt, and pepper and moisten with a splash of white wine. Oven roast for eight to ten minutes, taking care not to overcook fish.

Presentation

Place a bed of white rice in the center of a plate. Cover with the drained leeks, followed by the fish. Garnish with the grilled tomatoes. Surround with ginger sauce. Serve immediately.

Confit de Canard et Pomme Sarladaise
Duck Confit and Potatoes à la Sarladaise

Serves 2

4 duck thighs
1 garlic bulb
2 bay leaves

Marinade

1 cup rock salt
1 teaspoon black pepper, ground
1 teaspoon thyme leaves
2 cloves, slightly crushed

Potatoes

3 Idaho potatoes, peeled and sliced
1 black truffle, sliced (or 1 teaspoon truffle pieces)

Duck confit is a traditional and delicious way to prepare duck which has its origins in the French country kitchen. Be patient, it is essential for duck to cook slowly so that it does not become leathery. The classic Potatoes à la Sarladaise are easy to prepare, as they are not boiled before frying. If you put the duck into a glass or ceramic jar and cover with a layer of duck fat or pork lard and refrigerate, it will last several days and will also acquire more flavor.

Marinade

In a bowl, mix salt, cloves, and thyme. Completely cover both sides of the duck thighs with this mixture. Refrigerate for four hours.

Preheat oven to 300°F. Remove the duck thighs from the refrigerator and, using a paper towel, remove all the salt. Do not use water. Place the duck thighs in a heavy bottomed cook pot. Add garlic and bay leaves. Cover and roast for two hours. Remove from oven, place the duck thighs on a tray, cover, and keep them hot. Leave oven on.

Potatoes

Strain the fat from the pot. Clean the pot and pour strained fat back into it. Sauté the potatoes with the truffles over medium heat, until cooked but not soft.

Place the duck thighs over the potatoes and finish cooking in the oven for 10 minutes.

Presentation

Place some of the potatoes and truffles in the center of a plate and top with duck thighs, crossed, so as to appear to be seated on the potatoes.

Carré d'Agneau au Chèvre avec une Purée de Carottes
Rack of Lamb with Goat Cheese Crust and Carrot Puré

Serves 4

A carré, or rack, has 15 lamb chops. One half of a rack has 8 chops; the other half has the remaining 7. To better display the dish, the racks are frenched, which means that the bones are shaved.

Crust

1 egg

2 tablespoons Dijon mustard

2 ounces goat cheese

½ cup thyme, minced

Salt and pepper

Crust

Place the egg, mustard, cheese, and thyme into a bowl. Mix well. Season with salt and pepper.

Rack of Lamb

2 frenched racks of lamb, center cut

1 cup bread crumbs

1 onion

Rack of Lamb

Preheat oven to 350°F. Cut away excess fat from racks with a very sharp knife. If the butcher did not "French" the bones, do so now by removing the meat from between the chops until bones are clean. Spread the crust mixture onto the rack. Cover with breadcrumbs.

Place the racks in an ovenproof baking dish and surround with the onion. Roast for approximately 30 minutes for medium-rare meat. Remove from oven and set aside. Take onions and meat juices out of the pan and set aside.

Sauce au jus

½ cup wine vinegar

1 cube veal or meat bouillon

1 cup water

1 tablespoon cornstarch

Sauce au jus

Put the onion and meat juices into a skillet. Cook the onion over moderate heat for two minutes. Deglaze the skillet juices with vinegar. Add the bouillon cube and the cup of water. Stir, add cornstarch, and cook over medium heat while stirring until the sauce thickens.

Carrot Purée

2 pounds carrots, peeled and sliced

1 teaspoon garlic, minced

8 tablespoons butter

Salt and pepper

Purée

Boil the carrots in a saucepan until tender. Remove from pan and drain well. Place carrots and minced garlic in a food processor and blend until puréed. Add butter and mix, with three or four pulses of the processor.

Season with salt and pepper. Transfer to a bowl. Set aside, keep hot.

Presentation

Thyme sprigs for garnish

Presentation

On the bottom half of a plate, place five spoonful of carrot purée. On the top of the plate, place several sprigs of thyme. Slice the racks into individual lamb chops and place them in a fan over the thyme. Pour the sauce over the meat.

Tarte Fine aux Pommes à la Mode
Thin Apple Tart à la Mode

Serves 2

Tarts

2 puff pastry disks, 6" diameter each

2 red apples

2 tablespoons brown sugar

2 ounces butter, at room temperature

Ground cinnamon

Presentation

2 scoops vanilla ice cream

Daniel could not be a true Norman chef without offering a classic recipe from his region, where apples abound and are used to make calvados, one of the world's best distilled spirits.

Preheat oven to 380°F. Cover a baking sheet with a silpat liner or parchment paper. Place the two puff pastry disks on the baking sheet.

Peel the apples, cut in half, seed and slice as thinly as possible. Place the sliced apples, in circles on each pastry disk. Dust with brown sugar and spread with butter. Sprinkle cinnamon on top. Bake for 20 minutes or until golden.

Presentation

Remove tarts from the oven and place each on a serving plate. Serve hot with a scoop of ice cream on each tart.

Editor's note: Frozen puff pastry may be used – once thawed.

Profiteroles au Chocolat
Profiteroles with Chocolate Sauce

Serves 6

Pâte à Choux

2 cups water

1 tablespoon sugar

9 tablespoons butter

½ teaspoon salt

9 ounces all-purpose flour

6 eggs

Chocolate Sauce

2 cups milk

6 ounces dark bittersweet chocolate

2 tablespoons unsweetened cocoa powder

10 tablespoons sugar

2 tablespoons butter

Filling

Vanilla ice cream

This is a classic of French cuisine which is always a favorite. Chef Daniel indicates the classic vanilla ice cream filling for profiteroles, but they can also be filled with whipped cream.

Pâte à Choux (Puff Pastry)

In a large saucepan combine the water, sugar, butter, and salt. Bring to a boil over medium heat. Add flour and stir rapidly with a wooden spoon, to avoid lumps. Reduce heat to low and continue stirring, until the mixture draws away from sides of the the saucepan. Turn off heat and add the eggs, one by one, mixing each into the batter.

Preheat oven to 350°F. Place batter in a pastry bag. Cover a baking sheet with a Silpat liner or parchment paper. Pipe out small balls of batter. Bake for 30 to 35 minutes or until golden.

Chocolate Sauce

Place milk, chocolate, cocoa powder, sugar, and butter into a saucepan and cook over low heat for 15 minutes, or until the mixture has become a creamy liquid.

Presentation

Cut off, but do not discard, tops of puff pastry. Fill with vanilla ice cream. Cover the ice cream with the reserved pastry top. Place in the center of a dessert plate and cover with chocolate sauce. Serve immediately.

Fondant de Chocolat et Glace au Miel
Chocolate Fondant and Ice Cream with Honey

Serves 6

This dessert is a chocoholic's dream and it has a million calories, but it is delicious. I suggest practicing this recipe before attempting to serve it to guests, as the oven temperature or the baking time may require adjustment. Puerto Rico used to produce and export cacao, until a plague destroyed the crops in the eighteenth century.

Fondant

2 eggs

6 tablespoons sugar

8 tablespoons butter

4 ounces dark bittersweet chocolate, chopped

5 tablespoons all-purpose flour

6 small chunks same chocolate

Presentation

Vanilla ice cream, to accompany cake

¼ cup of honey

6 chocolate cigarettes

Fondant

Preheat oven to 375°F. Place eggs and sugar in a bowl and beat, using an electric hand beater or a full-size electric beater. Beat until the ingredients turn light yellow.

Melt butter and chocolate in a double boiler, stirring occasionally. Add the egg and sugar mixture. Slowly add the flour and fold gently with a spatula.

Grease and dust with flour individual porcelain or glass molds. Half fill each mold with chocolate batter. Place a piece of chocolate inside each. Pour in the rest of the batter almost to the rim. Bake for eight minutes.

Presentation

Unmold cake onto a dessert plate. Serve hot, with a scoop of vanilla ice cream, glazed with honey. Trim with a chocolate cigarette.

Editor's Note: Use the best quality of chocolate available.

INTERLUDE
(4)

MOFONGO WITH KETCHUP
AND HELLMANN'S IN PARIS

Norman
Rockwell

A great coincidence and some vast differences: Juan Ponce de León, a Spanish conquistador, and General Nelson Miles, an American, both landed at the Bay of Guánica in Southwestern Puerto Rico. The first disembarked in 1508, and bore the cross of the Spanish Catholic Kings; the second, in 1898, opened doors for the Protestant religions. The Spaniard, with the culinary tradition of olive oil, wine, and spices; the American, with canned food, Corn Flakes, and Campbell's soups. Miles' landing accompanied a major dietary scandal, since more US troops died of botulism caused by spoiled rations of canned meat, than there were war casualties during the entire Spanish-American War.

Until today, Puerto Rico has felt the impact of the American kitchen. What first comes to mind is the hamburger and the hotdog, but history is not that simple. Just as Spain has bequeathed cooking produced by a mixture of races and religions, so has the US. It has brought us more than canned or preserved foods: centuries of tastes go back to the Native American nations that populated the country, from Sonoma to Minnesota and from Kissimmee to Lake Huron. Add waves of immigrants from African slaves to blue-eyed Swedes and undocumented Mexicans, and you'll understand that many people have contributed to the complex American cook pot.

Our old cast iron skillets, with their *criollo* aromas, accommodated the new tastes brought along by the new housewives who came to live in Puerto Rico carrying baggage that included customs, implements, and recipes. Some of these women delighted in the sweetness of our fruit, and a pinch of our seasoning slipped into their stoves; thus began another process of culinary 'creolization'.

In 1917, US citizenship was granted to Puerto Ricans: 18,000 were drafted during World War I and thus, had to eat American food rations. The US Army diet included bacon, baked beans, hominy, corned beef, peanut butter, beef, and noodles, and turkey and gravy. That same year, the war effort sent the first wave of Puerto Rican men and women to work in stateside factories and on US farms, thus filling the vacancies left by Americans who were serving on the front in the Armed Forces.

Since then, the Puerto Rican diaspora to the US, whether caused by unemployment, need or simply the desire for economic improvement, has forced hundreds of thousands of Puerto Ricans to adapt, as best they could, to a very different climate and culture. The first generations of emigrants always find it difficult to adapt to the food habits of the host country and live with nostalgia of their native foods, but the second and third generations are born and brought up eating another sort of food, which they come to call their own. This occurred with the Europeans who came to Puerto Rico; it happens to the emigrants who go to El Barrio, Orlando or Chicago.

Their native land weighed heavily in their minds and the Nuyoricans created associations, organized parades, founded museums, and continued to keep their culture alive. When one sees the Federal Department of Agriculture confiscate plantains and bananas from Puerto Ricans traveling to the US, or the plastic containers filled with frozen *pasteles de masa* (making this dish is a Christmas ritual islanders still practice, even on the mainland), one becomes aware of the nostalgia for food from home.

After the 1950s, the island's economy improved, and we became aware of American food in other ways. With the advent of the jet plane and concomitantly, cheap air travel – despite its abominable 'tourist class' meals- travel increased to destinations all over the US, whether for vacations or to visit family, and with it, exposure to what is eaten in los *niuyores*. Also, the large contingent of Puerto Rican university students who leave Puerto Rico year after year to study in the US and who often must learn to cook not what they ate in Puerto Rico but what is eaten where they study, although some proudly show the cookbook by doña Carmen Aboy that Mami sent them.

During that period, gastronomy in Puerto Rico was transformed – and, in the United States, as well. In 1961, Julia Child

Corned Beef Alcapurrias. Page 262

Meat Stuffed Cheese. Page 261

returned to the US from France and two years later, revolutionized TV cook shows (on PBS) becoming the precursor to the Food Channel. Julia and others in the culinary world preached the return to values of regional cookery, forging an opening to the changes. The day she died, the New York Times, in August 2004, wrote an elegy to her: "Julia Child, the French chef for a Jell-O Nation."

An ironic allusion, as the third millennium begins for American housewives of various ethnic origins continue to depend on semi-prepared and canned foods, such as the proverbial TV dinner, which began its long run in 1954. The 1950s and 1960s also brought a new era of US cookbook publishing. Forty years ago, there was a paucity of titles, light years from what one sees today in a Border's or in a Barnes and Noble. This has contributed to expand our culinary horizons.

A while back, I said that the US cook pot was complex. Imagine 1968: Time-Life Books published the Cookbook Series Foods of the World, dedicating 9 volumes out of a total of 24 to US regional cookery. Precisely that complexity turns the US influence on Puerto Rican cooking into a tangled path through a labyrinth.

The introduction of the supermarket in the 1940s is a more controversial point. Many find them a blessing, while many consider supermarkets a necessary evil in today's world. Moreover, they criticize them for contributing to the extinction of the typical *Plaza del Mercado* and small food and convenience stores. But one must look at the other side of the coin. That is, supermarkets represent a point of sales for products made or assembled here on a commercial scale. And also, as a friend told me: "People in Puerto Rico changed their way of eating with the advent of supermarkets, because products formerly unavailable began to appear on the shelves."

To this one must considerer another phenomenon which has multiplied in the last two decades: fast food chains. Their worldwide impact is such that in 1986, the journalist Carlos Petrini created the Slow Food movement, which at present has extended to over 100 countries, as a counterbalance to the uniformity of 'fast food' and to protect regional cuisines from extinction. If you've harbored any doubt that Puerto Rico has fallen prey to 'fast food', just take a stroll through the food court of any shopping center.

Several years ago, Madame Villón and I were visiting the best 'gourmet' store in the world: Fauchon, at Place de la Madeleine in Paris. We browsed through the products displayed on the shelves: goose foie gras and duck foie gras from Périgord and Alsace, ciders from Normandy, black truffles, summer truffles, truffle oil, vinegars from all over France...when my eyes focused on several huge jars with an extremely familiar blue label. I could not believe my eyes, so I drew closer. Yes, there at Fauchon, at Place de la Madeleine, amidst such an aristocratic array of preserves and condiments, sat that exotic sauce which is always present in our fridge: Hellman's mayonnaise.

Do you need more? To the disappointment of many Parisians and to the resignation and acceptance of others (because not only tourists frequent them), McDonalds and Pizza Hut compete for space with traditional bistros along Paris boulevards. De Gaulle, who said that no one knows the difficulty of governing a nation that produces 400 different cheeses, is no doubt, turning over in his grave. Globalization is a two way street. Our supermarkets are replete with North American products, but Caribbean products have successfully and considerably invaded the US market in the US.

Their defenders justify the distribution of low cost food, but another negative effect is the loss of domestic cooking habits and skills which teaches people to become accustomed to food that lacks character. But there is a fast food worth singling out: pizza. This cheese favorite has made history, although our pizza owes more to New York than to Naples. Every young child baseball, basketball, or soccer match concludes with the coach and teammates having a pizza.

When one talks about 'American food', one must tread carefully, because much of it is no longer the monotonous and bland food of earlier years; one now finds good recipes of American food, with Oriental, Mexican, Caribbean and French influence, of course. Our housewives (and many men) have learned to cook well via cooking classes, TV, newspapers, magazines, and the Internet. As they learned, they devised variations of the recipes and these variations led to criollo adaptations of American dishes, such as the addition of passion fruit or guava to cheesecake or cheese soufflé, as did Wilo Benet in one of his recipes.

Giovanna Huyke could offer us examples of her creations, as could Aaron Wratten, with his tropical chocolate cake, which reminds me of the cake made by my mother, a native of New Orleans. Melquíades Tirado's *alcapurrías criollas* are filled with corned beef, like that the American soldiers carried in their backpacks.

If you'd spy on the cooks, both men and women, you'd find them sneaking in a package of *sazón* (criollo seasoning) or a few cilantro leaves, to a chicken or shrimp recipe with names as American as Teddy Roosevelt. Of course, there are extremely curious cases of culinary symbiosis, such as the Christmas turkey seasoned *criollo* style, stuffed with *mofongo*, by our friend Adita Mattei. The Puritan colonists of New England would have condemned her to the stake, even if, when serving the turkey, someone added ketchup to the *mofongo*.

Another positive aspect of our gastronomic world resides in the fact that young people interested in pursuing the culinary arts have enjoyed access to culinary schools in various states — as well as in Puerto Rico. This, along with the employment opportunities in mainland restaurants, has contributed to expanding our culinary horizons. The last point means that

New York is to a young chef from Guayanilla, the equivalent of what Paris is to a kitchen hand from St. Honoré les Bains. And the chefs featured in this book express the following: to work alongside a good chef is a better education than what any culinary school can provide.

The new American cuisine has unquestioned French influence and many first class French chefs are trailblazers as they establish grand restaurants in New York, Los Angeles, San Francisco, Chicago, Las Vegas, and Orlando. No one doubts that New York rivals Paris as the Gastronomic Capital of the World and that has opened new horizons for the chefs and food-lovers in Puerto Rico: it is not the same to reach Le Bernardin or Alain Ducasse by means of a three hour flight, as it is to undertake a transatlantic crossing to France.

Another fact that is either forgotten or ignored: nearly 200 years ago, poor Corsican countrymen, with Italian surnames, arrived in Puerto Rico, with permission to work only in agriculture. Corsica had belonged to Italy until 1768, when France purchased it, and those immigrants were called *los franceses* (the French). They cultivated coffee and citron and had the reputation for eating well. Some of my friends from Yauco tell me tales of how when a French ship docked in Ponce, the Corsicans would contract the ship's chef and would take him to their mountain homes to cook at their parties. Doña Marina López says they established stores which sold French products, including truffles. Their recipes must be sought from old papers stored in the attics of the Corsicans' descendants.

French cooking is pervasive worldwide and at the beginning of this millennium, we find a Puerto Rico that is open to a multitude of influences, which are enjoyed primarily when dining at fine restaurants, or at home on special occasions. But, when one goes to the Sunday buffet at la Casita Blanca in Villa Palmeras, we realize how hard it is to change culinary habits acquired in one's own childhood or handed down as an inheritance. Here, Puerto Ricans enjoy drinking *maví* and serving themselves straight from the cook pots; stewed goat kid, pigs' feet, salt cod with eggplant, rice with chicken, arroz *pegao*, and stewed red kidney beans, with a *tembleque* for dessert, black coffee

and a *chichaíto* or liqueur after the huge lunch.

The great chef Alain Chapel spoke of what he called the traditional kitchen and the kitchen of the imagination. Throughout this book we have seen the interweaving of tradition and imagination and how each enriches the other. The chefs that we feature demonstrate that they are capable of maintaining extremely high standards in their kitchens and, independently of their nationality, dig into the Caribbean tradition to add and to include in their cooking, so that the new generation of *Boricua* chefs does not lose our ancestral tastes.

I haven't taken a vacation for two years, so that rates high among my plans for the rest of the year. I hope to spend a few days with my children and grandchildren in Miami, to watch the World Series, to savor the barbecued meat made by my son Jorge, and to enjoy watching him light a good Havana cigar after lunch.

This image brings to mind a few thoughts. Of course, the ball game was played by the Taínos for centuries before Abner Doubleday made baseball popular in the US. The word barbecue is derived from *barbacoa*, an Arawak word with several meanings: a four legged table, a watchtower, and a wooden grill for cooking their small animal prey. The Havana cigar? Fray Bartolomé de las Casas had already described it at the beginning of the sixteenth-century, as what the Indians of Hispaniola did: "They lighted one end of the musket and they sucked the other end…the smoke…and…called tobaccos."

Doña Marina

I had the privilege of getting to know doña Marina when both of us taught at The Kitchen Shop, owned by Dolly Colón, a kitchen store and a wonderful cooking school at Plaza Las Americas.

At age 90, doña Marina reflects upon her life's experience of Puerto Rico's modern cooking. Born in Yauco, by age 9 she was helping her mother, who owned a small hotel, to stuff a turkey with truffles. She wanted to become a lawyer, but instead, became a professor of home economics, which she taught in San Germán for 30 years. She was an eyewitness to the transformation of Puerto Rico. Recalling the 1940s and 1950s, she says: "Despite the U.S. influence and those of other immigrations, Puerto Rican cooking remained vigorous and always prevailed." Curiously, Puerto Rican cooking began to influence the tastes of the foreigners who lived on the island.

Although doña Marina is a widow and no longer cooks very much, she is still fascinated by cooking. "I cannot resist a good recipe in a magazine, I must clip it out and save it. I wish there had been culinary schools in my time, because I'd had gone to study to become a chef."

A Historic Menu

The proliferation of food and wine societies, several of which are international, have been a great contribution to the development of gastronomy in Puerto Rico. Actually, there are more or less a dozen that remain active. The most important, among the international, are the International Wine and Food Society (IW&FS), la Chaine des Rotiseurs, la Confrerie des Chevaliers du Tastevin and the Commanderie de Bordeaux. The Cofradía Puertorriqueña del Vino and Los Amigos de la Buena Mesa, are very active among the local ones. IW&FS was founded by André Simon in Europe in 1933 and was established en Puerto Rico in 1963, with the goal of promoting gastronomy on the island. It only has 64 members and its first formal activity was celebrated in the Swiss Chalet on March 18, 1964, and was prepared by the respected chef Hans Mooseberger. The menu was completely French, including the wines (except for the Madeira at the end).

Passion Fruit Cheesecake

Yields one cake

Pie Crust

¼ cup butter

1 ½ cups ground Graham crackers

Cheesecake

10 ounces cream cheese, softened

1 cup sour cream

3 small eggs, separated

½ cup sugar

¾ cup passion fruit juice

1 teaspoon lime

1 envelope unflavored gelatin

2 tablespoons water

Passion Fruit Syrup

1 cup frozen passion fruit juice concentrate

¾ cup sauternes wine

1 tablespoon white rum

This recipe combines a classic of the New York Jewish Kitchen (The cheesecake at Junior's, in Brooklyn, is famous) with passion fruit, which grows in the Caribbean and northern South America. The recipe can also be made with guava or pineapple. There are millions of recipes for cheesecake, as each housewife in the United States has her own recipe.

Crust

Remove the bottom of a 9" spring form.

In a small saucepan, melt the butter over low heat. Turn off heat and add the ground Graham crackers. Mix well.

Thoroughly cover the bottom of the pan with the Graham cracker mixture. Press firmly into place. Reassemble the pan and butter the inside walls.

Cheesecake

In an electric beater, beat the cream cheese with the sour cream, the egg yolks, and 6 tablespoons of sugar, until well-mixed and soft.

In a small saucepan, bring the passion fruit juice and 2 tablespoons of sugar to a boil. Remove from heat and let cool for 3 minutes.

In a small bowl, mix the water with the powdered gelatin. Add passion fruit juice and stir well. Do not allow lumps to form.

Add the gelatin to the cheese mixture and beat at low speed until well-mixed.

In a bowl, beat the egg whites to soft peak stage. Fold into cheese mixture. Pour into pan. Refrigerate for 8 hours.

Syrup

In a saucepan over medium heat, bring the passion fruit concentrate and ½ cup sauternes to a boil . Reduce, stirring, to one third. Add the rest of the wine and rum, stirring thoroughly, and cook for three minutes.

Let cool and serve with the cheesecake.

One 12 pound turkey, rinsed and dried

Turkey Seasoning

Ground garlic

Powdered seasoning (your choice)

Salt and pepper

Olive oil

Several packets *sazón* with culantro and annatto

Butter

Mofongo

8 very green plantains, peeled

2 pounds bacon

20 garlic cloves, peeled

Salt

Gravy

The turkey's pan juices

1 tablespoon cornstarch

Worcestershire sauce to taste

Salt to taste

Water

Adita Molini, daughter of Corsicans and married to a Corsican, was born in Yauco. Adita used to run a catering business. At Christmas time her work had her roasting about 25 turkeys and stuffing them with 'mofongo', a monumental task that left her completely exhausted. "If I see another turkey and one more tablespoon of 'mofongo' I'll explode!" she exclaimed when December 24th rolled around.

Stuffed turkey for Thanksgiving or Christmas is a custom imported from the US, where turkey can be dressed with, among other things, corn stuffing or oysters. Adita turned this into a criollo dish by filling it with mofongo. As you'll see, the turkey's seasoning is not measured. "I do it by eye," says Adita. She makes 'mofongo' with boiled plantains, which is healthier, but many cooks prefer to lightly fry them without browning the chopped plantain.

Turkey Seasoning

In a bowl, mix the garlic, the powdered seasoning, salt and pepper, olive oil and *sazón*. Rub thoroughly over both the inside and outside of the turkey. Carefully tuck *adobo* under turkey breast skin, so it will be thoroughly seasoned. Cover with aluminum foil and refrigerate for two days.

Mofongo

In a large pot, boil the plantains in salt water. Meanwhile, in a very hot skillet, fry the bacon until crisp. Remove and drain on paper towel. Set aside the bacon fat, transferring it to a small bowl.

When the plantains have softened, process them in a food processor along with the garlic, the bacon and its oil, until everything has been well-ground and the mixture is manageable. When the *mofongo* has cooled, shape it into balls and stuff the turkey. Repeat rubbing turkey with the seasoning and the butter.

To Roast Turkey

Preheat the oven to 325°F. Cover the turkey with aluminum foil and roast for 25 minutes per pound or until browned and thighs are cooked. Occasionally baste the turkey with its own juices or drippings. Remove the aluminum foil 45 minutes before the turkey is ready, so as to let brown. Remove from oven and let rest.

Gravy

In a saucepan, combine the pan juices, the cornstarch, the Worcestershire sauce, and a little water. Cook and stir until thickened. Correct seasoning.

Keshi Yena
Meat-stuffed Cheese

Yields one cheese

1 round of Edam or Gouda cheese, whole

Filling

Lard or olive oil

2 onions, finely chopped

1 criollo green pepper, finely chopped

3 tomatoes, peeled and seeded, finely chopped

2 cloves crushed garlic

1 tablespoon chopped parsley

1 teaspoon oregano

2 teaspoons chopped cilantro

1 bay leaf

1 tablespoon Worcestershire sauce

**½ cup alcaparrado (capers, pimento and olives
   condiment)**

2 tablespoons dark raisins

1 pound lean pork, ground

1 pound beef, ground

Salt and pepper

To Bake

Plantain leaves

I hadn't eaten 'Queso Relleno' for so long that I had almost forgotten about it, until recently, when I sat down to reread the delicious Elogio de la Fonda (In praise of the fondas), written by the Puerto Rican author Edgardo Rodriguez Juliá. The book includes the essay Cena Navideña (Christmas Dinner), which mentions, among a litany of Christmas dishes, what he calls 'exquisitez dominguera'(Sunday delicacy): 'keshi jena' from Curaçao. Holland has reached us bathed in tropical Caribbean waters. What is different about the Puerto Rican interpretation? We bake it wrapped in plantain leaves and we use cilantro. Keshi jena means stuffed cheese in Papiamento.

Leave cheese at room temperature overnight. The following day, carefully remove the red paraffin. Cut ½" off the top, as though removing a lid. Carefully scoop out the interior, leaving a ¾"-thick shell resembling a hollowed-out grapefruit.

Filling

In a large, deep skillet, heat the lard or olive oil over moderate heat. Fry the onion and the green pepper, until softened. Add the tomato and the garlic, stir and cook until tender. Add the herbs, the Worcestershire sauce, the *alcaparrado,* and the raisins. Stir well and cook for 2 minutes. Add the meat, stir well and season with salt and pepper. Raise heat slightly and cook, stirring occasionally, until the meat begins to brown. Correct the seasoning and stir well. Remove from heat.

To Bake

Preheat oven to 350°F. Carefully stuff the cheese with the filling, pressing with a spoon. Wrap in plantain leaves.

Place the cheese in a baking dish with 1" of water. Bake for one or one and a half hours. The cheese should have melted somewhat, mixing into the filling.

To serve, cut into wedges.

Corned Beef Alcapurrias

Yields 36 small alcapurrias

Filling

2 ½ twelve-ounce cans of corned beef

Homemade sofrito

¾ cup tomato sauce

Salt and pepper

Masa or dough

2 ½ pounds yautía (taro root)

5 green plantains

2 pounds calabaza (pumpkin)

¼ gallon annatto coloring (oil)

Vegetable oil for frying

These marvelous alcapurrías stuffed with corned beef were invented, if one can attribute such a popular dish to a single creator, by Melquíades Tirado, the chef and owner of the lovely restaurant, El Mesón de Melquíades, high in the mountains of Jájome, in the center of Puerto Rico. For those unfamiliar with the very typical Puerto Rican 'alcapurria', let me point out that this is a croquette, usually filled with meat or crabmeat ('jueyes'); the masa which envelopes the filling is made of green or ripe plantain or yautía (taro root). Melquíades has retired, but the Mesón continues to be open to the public several days a week (especially on weekends).

Filling

Place the corned beef and the *sofrito* in a skillet over medium heat. Add the tomato sauce and season with salt and pepper to taste. The corned beef should not be too moist. Remove from heat and set aside to use as the filling for the *alcapurrias*.

Masa or dough

Grate the taro root, plantain, and pumpkin. Place them in a deep bowl, and mix well with a large spoon. While kneading, slowly and sparingly add the annatto oil; too much could be disastrous. When everything has been thoroughly mixed, cover and refrigerate for one hour, until the dough becomes firm.

Alcapurria

Place the dough and the corned beef on a comfortably ample work surface. Take a saucer and cover with a square of wax paper. Place a tablespoonful of the dough in the center of the paper. Spread out and fill with ½ tablespoon of corned beef. Fold and shape, aided by the wax paper, into a rectangular *alcapurria*.

Heat vegetable oil in a *caldero* or deep aluminum casserole. Deep fry until crispy. Drain on paper towels.

Yields one cake

8 eggs, room temperature, separated into yolks
  and whites
2 cups sugar
2 eight-ounce packages cream cheese, room
  temperature
Grated zest of 2 limes
1 ½ cup sugar

This is a delicious Corsican dessert which is still popular in Corsica and which doña Anita Gatell included in her book, 'Cocinar Cantando' (Cooking and Singing), which was published in 1972 as a fundraiser for the Oratorio San Juan Bosco. The book was a success and sold out quickly. Unfortunately, it has not been republished. The recipe, which I reproduce exactly as written, was given to me by doña Palmira Borrás, a grandniece of Mrs. Gatell who was born in Yauco.

The Corsicans, who came to Puerto Rico at the end of the eighteenth century and the beginning of the nineteenth, had a cooking style greatly influenced by the Italians, because not until the mid-eighteenth century did Corsica become part of France.

Preheat oven to 325°F. Beat the egg yolks with the sugar, cream cheese, and lime zest. Fold in the egg whites, beaten to soft peak stage. Pour the batter into a well-buttered cake pan 18"x 12" x 2". Bake until slightly golden.

AARON WRATTEN

COOKING IN PARADISE

Grilled Lobster Ratatouille. Page 280

Perhaps you are old enough to remember the movie The Endless Summer? It is the story of an idyllic summer in the lives of two young surfers who travel around the world in search of the perfect wave. Their journey takes them from California to Hawaii and from Australia to Ghana. One of the beaches where the action takes place is a pristine beach where the ocean's fury devours the surfers, only for them to reappear, triumphant, riding their boards, conquering the enormous waves. Not only are the waves impressive, the beach is paradise. Renowned for its surf, the beach too is magnificent with coconut groves giving shade to multi-color flowers, as well as peopled with friendly fishermen who coexist with the visitors.

It is not Waikiki, in Hawaii; this beach is located on the west coast of Puerto Rico, a refuge for people who don't mind the three hour drive from San Juan, some of whom make the pilgrimage to check out the waves, others who seek only to spend a relaxing, idle weekend at the beach.

Rincón has fallen prey to its own success and to rampant development for tourism, just as have many other picturesque places in remote locations. A Hungarian dreamer whose name is Telehl, and three Americans, all slightly eccentric and possessed of a singular vision, are those responsible for the creation — long ahead of its time — of a small corner of paradise, the Horned Dorset Primavera.

Mr. Telehl and his wife arrived at that isolated spot, just a speck lost to the world, and they bought a *finca* on the coast which sheltered a small beach. They began building their dream hotel, literally with their own hands. Mrs. Telehl's death left the Hungarian disconsolate. He thus sold the property to three Americans who had reached Rincón literally fleeing the harsh winters of upstate New York: Syracuse, reputed to suffer among the harshest winters in the United States.

One of the Americans, Harold Davies, was a professor of literature at the University of Syracuse. The others, Stanley and Bruce Wratten, owned a successful four-room inn and restaurant in a town called Leonardsville on the outskirts of Syracuse. Davies was also the Wratten's partner in that venture. The threesome decided to complete Telehl's project, hired a Puerto Rican architect to design the project, which was given a sui generis interpretation. The hotel would barely disturb the existing vegetation and topography, and no two rooms would be alike. A common terrace would overlook the magnificent sunsets, the occasional whale breaching near the horizon, the changing sea and cloud flecked skies, from Maní beach — near the city of Mayagüez — to Mona Island, 45 miles off the coast.

The Wrattens and their families worked as cement block-layers, painters, and promoters of their small hotel, which opened its doors in the early '90s. "I came down in 1986 and worked very hard painting walls, laying cement blocks, doing whatever was needed." The speaker is young and slender, possessing a ready smile. He is Aaron Wratten, Stanley's son, who has developed a curious relationship with the Horned Dorset Primavera, akin to someone who has a girlfriend he will neither leave nor marry. "The Hungarian really pinched pennies. He collected hundreds of empty beer cans, which he stuffed into the large holes in the cement blocks used for building the walls, so that the mortar used by the block-layers would only bind the blocks into place. That way, the cement couldn't fill all the holes in the blocks, which saved a whole lot of cement."

Primavera was the name the Hungarians had originally given the property; the Horned Dorset was the name that Wratten and Davies added to the first. Their Leonardsville inn was named the Horned

Harold's Madrid-Style Gazpacho. Page 277

The red snapper filets with ginger butter on banana leaves are ready to go to the oven. Page 282

Chocolate Rainforest Cake. Page 286

Dorset, after the celebrated breed of sheep possessed of a peculiar quality: both male and female are horned; the ram exhibits those enormous, curved horns that one sees represented in the graphics for the zodiac sign of Aries. Neighbors from Rincón don't call the hotel by its complete name. To them it is – perhaps nostalgically – just Primavera.

Aaron speaks almost flawless Spanish, albeit nuanced by *puertorriqueñismos* and colloquialisms spiced with local humor. His Syracuse birth and upbringing not withstanding, his command of Puerto Rican slang is total, acquired during the long days and nights spent in the kitchen with his helpers. He is the chef at the Horned Dorset Primavera, and although the hotel advertises French cuisine in its promotional literature, the description is not quite accurate, because as Aaron says himself, "It's French cuisine with Puerto Rican ingredients." The hotel restaurant – its formal dining room – offers three menus daily: six dishes, one a Provençal menu, another a tropical menu and a menu dégustation. Doctor Jeckyll and Mr. Hyde. Whether French, or more or less French, matters not, Aaron's cooking is young, modern, and honest. The restaurant ranks among the very best outside of San Juan, a fact confirmed in that The Horned Dorset Primavera is the only island member of the Relais et Châteaux organization, whose motto is "excellence in the five c's: Courtoisie, Charme, Caractère, Calme, Cuisine."

Aaron spent his childhood and adolescence with his parents in the Northeast, amidst bitterly cold winters, apple orchards, and sheep, at times helping out in the dining room and kitchen of the familly restaurant in Leonardsville.

Then one day, in the mid '80s, he decided to go to France. "I spent two months in Brittany, staying with a family; friends of a friend of a friend. I managed to get accepted to the Groupe Ferrandi cooking school, which belongs to the Paris Chamber of Commerce." Aaron, who barely spoke French and had little experience in the kitchen, thus found himself at a strict, classic cooking school, where everyone had to work 10 hour days. "But you know what? They really teach you to work."

Soon after, he came to Rincón for the first time, not to paint landscapes or still lifes, which his mother had taught him to paint, but to paint walls at the half-built hotel. Naturally, if there was no hotel, there were neither guests nor a kitchen in which to practice the skills he had acquired in Paris. "I cooked at Harold's house, fooling around with him, because he loves to cook and is one of the best cooks I've ever met." To hear Aaron tell it, Harold is a legendary character who owns a vast library and who, at the slightest provocation, will catch a plane or embark on a cruise ship to discover new worlds, despite his having already covered

Mango chutney with raisins. Page 278

Aaron Wratten comes from a family that owns a popular inn, both hotel and restaurant, near Syracuse, New York. Yet it was difficult for him to decide upon cooking as his profession

Mango Tarts with Vanilla Ice Cream, garnished with hierbabuena leaves. Page 284

Parsnip and Celery Root Soup

Yields 3 quarts

Vinegar reduction

1 cup balsamic vinegar

The sopa

1 medium onion, julliened

2 celery stalks, finely sliced

2 garlic cloves, peeled and sliced in half, lengthwise

2 tablespoons vegetable oil

2 pounds parsnips, peeled and diced

2 pounds celery root, peeled and diced

1 bay leaf

1 pinch nutmeg

8 cups chicken or vegetable broth

Salt and pepper

½ cup whipping cream (optional)

Parsnips look like white carrots but have a softer texture and are much sweeter. They provide a nice balance when mixed with the earthy perfume of celery root. The chef drizzles reduced balsamic vinegar over the top for its contrast in flavor and color.

Vinegar reduction

In a small saucepan, over medium heat, reduce to half the balsamic vinegar.

The soup

In a heavy stockpot, cook the onions, celery, and garlic in the vegetable oil over medium heat. Stir frequently until softened, about three minutes. Add the parsnip, celery root, bay leaf, nutmeg, and the chicken or vegetal broth. Bring to a boil, lower heat, and let to a simmer. Skim off any oil or foam that comes to the surface. Simmer for ½ hour or until all the vegetables are very soft. Allow to cool to room temperature.

Purée the soup in a blender in small batches until completely smooth. Pass this through a fine sieve or chinois, to insure a smooth texture.

Return the soup to a pot and bring to a boil. Add the heavy cream (optional) and bring to a boil again. Season with salt and pepper to taste

Presentation

Serve hot in soup bowls. Sprinkle with the vinegar reduction.

Harold's Madrid-Style Gazpacho

Serves 6

The gazpacho

2 slices white bread

1 ½ cups water

3 cucumbers, centers removed, diced

1 green pepper, finely sliced

1 red onion finely sliced

16 ounces canned tomatoes, drained

½ tablespoon ground cumin

Mayonnaise

1 egg yolk

Red wine vinegar

1 garlic clove, mashed

½ cup extra virgin olive oil

Salt and freshly ground pepper

Condiments

1 cucumber, peeled, seeds removed
   and finely chopped

1 fresh tomato, seeds removed
   and finely chopped

1 green pepper, seeds removed
   and finely chopped

A less common version of a very popular dish. Harold Davies, 'the arbiter of taste' of the Horned Dorset and the chef's culinary mentor, passed it on to him. It is simple to prepare, healthy, and refreshing.

The gazpacho

Place the bread in a bowl with the water and allow it to soak for a few minutes.

Combine the diced cucumber and sliced green pepper and onion in the bowl with the bread and water. Add the canned tomatoes and cumin. Toss everything together and process in a blender until smooth. Transfer to a bowl and refrigerate, covered.

Mayonnaise

In a 2-quart mixing bowl, combine the egg yolk and vinegar. Add the garlic and the egg. Whisk in the olive oil in a slow trickle to make a mayonnaise. Whisk in a little soup to dilute, then whisk the soup into the mixture. Season to taste with salt and freshly ground black pepper. Cover and refrigerate until ready to serve.

Condiments

Place each condiment in a separate bowl.

Presentation

Serve the soup in chilled bowls and pass the condiments separately.

Land Crab Patties with Chutney

Serves 4

The chutney

2 cups white vinegar

½ cup red wine vinegar

2 cups brown sugar

2 teaspoons freshly-grated ginger

½ cup tamarind juice frozen concentrate, or ¼ cup seedless tamarind paste

2 cinnamon sticks or ¼ tablespoon ground cinnamon

⅛ teaspoon ground cloves

2 cilantro seeds

8 cups mango pulp, peeled and diced

1 cup raisins

The land crab turnovers

1 pound land crab (jueyes) meat

½ onion, finely sliced

½ red pepper, seeded and finely diced

1 tablespoon olive oil or clarified butter

1 egg

2 tablespoons mayonnaise

1 tablespoon Dijon mustard

A few drops Tabasco

A few drops Worcestershire sauce

Dash ground cumin

2 leaves sage, bruised

2 tablespoons parsley, finely chopped

1 tablespoon cilantro, finely chopped

½ teaspoon celery seeds

Dash salt

Dash white pepper

1 cup, approximately, breadcrumbs

2 ounces clarified butter o light vegetable oil for frying the turnovers

You will end up with more chutney than you need; just store it in the refrigerator for a future use. It is best to cook the chutney in advance and let it rest in the refrigerator for 24 hours

The chutney

In a heavy bottomed saucepan, combine all ingredients except the mangos and the raisins. Cook slowly and reduce for ten minutes, stirring occasionally. Add the diced mango and the raisins. Continue cooking for half an hour or more, stirring occasionally to prevent the chutney from sticking to the bottom. The chutney will be ready when the syrup starts to thicken. It will become thicker as it cools.

Transfer to a covered glass container. Keep tightly covered in the refrigerator for up to two months.

The land crab patties

Squeeze excess liquid from the crabmeat. Examine carefully and remove any shell pieces.

Sautée the crabmeat in olive oil or clarified butter in a heavy skillet, over medium heat, for one minute. Remove from stove and cool to room temperature.

In another skillet or frying pan, sauté the onion and red pepper in butter or olive oil, over medium heat, until tender.

In a bowl, combine the egg, mayonnaise, Dijon mustard, sauces, cumin, and herbs, and mix well with a wire whisk. Add the sautéed onion and red pepper, and the crabmeat. Season with salt and pepper. Add a handful of breadcrumbs and mix well. It shouldn't be too thick, but no excess liquid should seep out as you form a sample patty with your hands. If necessary, add more breadcrumbs, but be careful not to make the mixture too thick or dry.

Make 2" diameter patties, about ¾" thick. Coat both sides lightly with breadcrumbs. Cover and refrigerate.

At serving time, sauté crab patties in clarified butter or light vegetable oil in a heavy bottomed skillet or frying pan. Brown for 2 minutes on each side. Drain on paper towels and keep warm.

The vinaigrette

1 tablespoon red wine vinegar
4 tablespoons extra virgin olive oil
Salt and black pepper

To serve

4 cherry tomatoes cut in half
A few leaves of Bibb or Boston lettuce and
**   watercress for garnishing**

The vinaigrette

In a bowl, mix the vinegar and olive oil, beating vigorously with a wire whisk. Season with salt and pepper.

To serve

Place the lettuce and watercress leaves in the center of serving plates. Sprinkle with the vinaigrette. Place two patties over the lettuce, one resting partially on top of the other. Put 2 tablespoons of chutney on the side of one of the patties. Garnish with two half-cherry tomatoes.

A tip from the chef: The patties are simple and can be prepared quickly. You can prepare them one day in advance, and keep them in the refrigerator. Then you only need to coat them with breadcrumbs and fry them.

Grilled Lobster Ratatouille

Serves 6

This is a reworking of a traditional French vegetable dish. The chefs loves the way grilling intensifies the flavor of lobster tails.

Grilling oil

4 garlic cloves, peeled

Leaves of one rosemary sprig

1 pinch dried oregano

1 pinch red pepper flakes

Black pepper

1 cup extra virgin olive oil

Cilantro and basil purée

2 tablespoons cilantro leaves, finely chopped

2 tablespoons basil leaves, finely chopped

1 garlic clove, finely chopped

2 tablespoons extra virgin olive oil

The vegetables

1 eggplant, cut into ½"-thick long strips

1 zucchini, cut into long strips

1 summer squash, cut into ½"-thick long strips

1 purple onion, cut into ½"-thick strips, lengthwise

1 red pepper, seeded and cut into ½"-strips, lengthwise

2 tomatoes, seeded and quartered

Salt

The lobsters

2 spiny lobsters, 2 pounds each, or 2, 1-pound Caribbean lobster tails, coarsely chopped

For serving

6 tomatoes for stuffing

Presentation

12 small basil leaves

Grilling oil

In a blender, combine all the ingredients for the grilling oil and purée for 30 seconds. Reserve.

Cilantro and basil purée

In a blender, combinethe ingredients and purée. Reserve.

The vegetables

Lay the eggplant on a plate and sprinkle liberally with salt on both sides. Allow to sit for ½ hour to remove some of the bitterness. Wipe off all excess moisture and salt.

Lay the vegetables on a tray and brush both sides liberally with the grilling oil (or dip in the oil, removing the excess with your fingers). Season lightly with salt.

The lobsters

Remove the lobster meat from the shell by using kitchen shears. Discard the shells. Split the tails in half lengthwise. Season the tails with salt and a few spoonfuls of grilling oil.

Grill the vegetables one at a time until cooked through. The zucchini will take about a minute per side, the eggplant a little longer. Cook the peppers on the skin side only. Scrape off what skin you can with a paring knife when they have cooled. Do not try to cook the tomatoes too long or they will fall apart. The onions should be cooked the longest, on the coolest part of the grill, until they are soft but not burned.

The lobsters

Lastly, cook the lobster tails just until done. They should be barely opaque in the center.

Let everything cool. Dice everything into ¾" pieces and combine in a bowl. Don't worry if it looks like a bit of a mess. This is rustic.

If you are preparing dish in advance, store in the refrigerator, covered.

For serving

Preheat oven to 325°F. Cut a ½-inch slice off the top of the tomatoes. and carefully scoop out the insides with a melon-scoop or teaspoon to form a bowl. If they don't sit straight, cut a very thin slice off the bottom, being careful not to make a hole in your bowl. Stuff the tomatoes very full with the lobster mixture and place them in an ovenproof dish, allowing a space between them so they heat evenly. Bake in the oven for twenty minutes or until warm in the center.

Presentation

Garnish with a sprig of basil and a few drops of Basil Cilantro Purée.

Red Snapper Steamed with Banana Leaf and Vegetable Slaw

Serves 4

This is a delicious way to cook red snapper, because it keeps all the flavor of the fish.

Ginger-lemon butter

2 garlic cloves, lightly mashed

1 one-inch piece fresh ginger, peeled and grated

The juice of one lemon

The juice of one lime

¼ cup parsley, finely chopped

¼ cup cilantro leaves, finely chopped

½ pound butter, at room temperature

Dash Cayenne pepper

The vegetable slaw:

1 red pepper, julienned

1 medium zucchini, julienned

1 medium red onion, julienned

¼ head green cabbage, julienned

2 medium carrots, julienned

1" piece ginger root, julienned

The Fish:

4, 8-ounce portions of red snapper filets, with the skin on, but pin bones removed.

Ginger - lemon butter

4 pieces of fresh banana leaf, roughly the size of the fish portions

The ginger-lemon butter

In a food processor, put all the ingredients and process until purée is creamy.

Cut a piece of plastic wrap 18" long. Pour the ginger-lemon butter over the plastic wrap, on a long wide strip. Form like a sausage, 1 ½" in diameter. Twist the ends. Refrigerate until very hard.

The vegetable slaw

In a bowl, toss all the vegetables together. Grate the ginger on the finest side of the grater. Place the ginger pulp in a coffee filter, fold in quarters and squeeze the juice over the vegetables. Season lightly with salt and refrigerate.

The fish

In a deep skillet with a tight fitting lid, large enough to comfortably accommodate the four fish filets, place up to 1 inch of vegetable slaw in the bottom of the pan including the juice that has collected at the bottom. (If you have extra slaw, cook it in a separate pan at the same time as the fish, with a little olive oil.)

Score the fish through the skin several times. This keeps it from curling up as it cooks. Season the fish lightly with salt and place on top of the vegetables. Unwrap the butter, slice four ½" rounds, and place one on each filet. Place a banana leaf atop each one. Add ¾ cup water to the pan. Cover pan with aluminum foil and cover with the lid. (Be careful the lid does not seal too tightly or it could explode when heated.)

Start over a high fire. Watch the edges for steam. When the pan begins to boil, lower the heat to a simmer. Cooking times will vary. A ½" thick filet may cook in 3 minutes, whereas an 1½" thick piece may take 10 minutes or more. The point is to cook the fish slowly without overcooking it. (When you decide to check it, be very careful of the steam that will escape when you first open the foil. Wear an oven mitt to be safe and keep your face away.)

The skin side will cook last. It should be firm, but not hard. If you're not certain, poke a knife between the slits in the skin and peek at the center. It should just be opaque. If it is too close to call, just put the lid back on for a minute but take it off the burner. It will 'carry over', or continue to cook, by the heat in the pan.

To serve

Remove the banana leaves and place in the center of serving plates, place a portion of vegetable slaw and a fish filet on top. Spoon over them any juices in the pan. Cut a thin slice of the butter and place on the fish to melt as you serve it.

Mango Tart

Serves 4

- 4 six-inch puff pastry circles, thawed
- 4 tablespoons mango paste
- Pinch cinnamon
- 2 medium-large mangos, peeled and sliced in 3" thin slices
- 2 tablespoons sugar for sprinkling
- Vanilla ice cream (optional)

These are fairly simple to make. The trick is to slice the mangos very thinly and arrange them nicely on the puff pastry.

Lay puff pastry sheets on a lightly floured surface and dust lightly with flour. Cut four 6" circles from the pastry using a coffee saucer and a sharp knife. Place the circles on a lightly greased cookie sheet and return to the refrigerator.

Warm the mango paste in a small saucepan. Add a little water and mix well with a wire whisk, so that it has the consistency of jelly. Add the cinnamon and allow to cool.

Divide the mango paste into four portions and place in the middle of each pastry circle. Using the back of a teaspoon, spread the paste out toward the edges, leaving clean a ½" border around the edge, like a pizza. Place a spoonful of chopped mango in the centers only.

Trim off any remaining flesh from the pit of the mango and chop into small pieces. Try to keep the slices of mango together. One at a time, gently fan the mango slices out, like cards. Pushing them with cupped hands, form the slices around into a circle, the same size as the pastry. With a wide spatula carefully pick up the circle of mango slices and place it atop the pastry. (If this fails, simply place the pieces one by one in the form of a lady's fan until you get all the way around.)

Preheat oven to 450°F. Sprinkle the tarts lightly with sugar. If possible, place the tray on a second empty tray. (This will help prevent burning on the bottom.) Place in the oven. After five minutes, when tarts begin to bubble, lower the oven to 350°F. Remove as soon as the edges begin to puff and brown, being careful that they do not burn on the bottom.

Serve warm with vanilla ice cream (optional).

Lime Granité

Yields 3 cups

¾ cups sugar

2 cups water

4 or 5 green limes, to make ½ cup of juice

A few drops Barrilito Rum, 3 star

At the restaurant, Wratten serves a granité, or 'ice', before the main course. The purpose of this is to 'cleanse the palate' of the preceding courses' flavors. A granité is like a sorbet, but it has a more granular texture and does not require an ice cream machine to make it.

Bring the water and sugar to a boil. Split the limes in two, and squeeze the juice to make ½ cup. Save the empty shells for later. Strain the juice and mix with the sugar syrup. Place in a plastic or metal container and freeze overnight.

If you plan to serve the granité in a lime shell, scrape them clean with a spoon. Cut the bottom tips off, so they will sit flat, and freeze them.

Remove the granité from the freezer and allow it to soften, without melting. With a heavy fork, break the mass into finer and finer pieces (or scrape with a spoon) until you have slush. Return to the freezer until it becomes firm again. Scoop the granité into the frozen lime shells and drizzle a few drops of rum over the top just before serving them.

Chocolate Rainforest Cake

Serves 12

This is a Tropical version of the classic German Black Forest Cake. Make the cake part one day in advance. Put the whipped cream on it when you are almost ready to serve it.

The Cake

1 ¾ cup sugar

⅔ cup vegetable oil

3 eggs

1 ⅓ cups water

1 ½ cups all-purpose flour

2 teaspoons baking soda

½ teaspoon baking powder

⅞ cup cocoa powder

Pastry cream

2 cups milk

2 cups coconut milk, unsweetened

1 cup sugar

½ cup cornstarch

4 eggs

1 tablespoon butter

½ teaspoon vanilla extract

Syrup

½ cup water

½ cup sugar

¼ cup Barrilito Rum 3 Star

Garnishes

1 cup macadamia nuts

1 can sweetened coconut flakes

To Assemble

2 ripe bananas, peeled and sliced ¼" thick

1 cup whipping cream

2 tablespoons 10x sugar or 1 tablespoon
  granulated sugar

Dash vanilla

An 8-ounce block of semisweet chocolate

The cake

Preheat oven to 400°F. Lightly grease a 9"cake pan and cut a parchment paper circle (the paper sold for wrapping *pasteles* is good for this) or wax paper to fit the bottom. Mix together the sugar, oil, eggs, and water.

Sift the dry ingredients together and stir into the liquid. Mix until smooth. Pour into pan with paper bottom and bake at 400°F for 45 minutes, or until a toothpick inserted in the center comes out clean. It should be higher in the middle than around the edges. Let cool in the pan and refrigerate covered, overnight, before slicing.

Pastry cream

Bring the milk and coconut milk to a boil in a heavy 2-quart saucepan. In a medium-sized bowl, whisk the eggs, sugar, and cornstarch together until smooth. Whisking constantly, slowly incorporate the hot milk into the eggs. Return the mixture to the saucepan and whisk constantly over high heat until it begins to thicken. Remove from the fire and continue stirring for a few seconds to avoid lumps forming. Return to a low fire and cook for half a minute more to make sure the starch is completely cooked.

Remove from the fire, stir in the butter and vanilla. Cool and store covered with plastic wrap on the surface of the pastry cream, in the refrigerator, until needed.

Syrup

Bring the water and sugar to a boil. Cool and add the rum.

Garnishes

Toast the two ingredients separately, either in a frying pan over low fire stirring often, or on a cookie sheet in a 400° oven. Either way, watch carefully and remove when just lightly browned. The nuts will take considerably longer. When they are cool, crush the nuts lightly into coarse ¼" pieces.

To assemble

Remove the cake from the pan and remove the paper from the bottom of the cake. With a long serrated knife, cut a little off the top of the cake to make it almost level, but not less than 2 inches high. The top will end up in the middle of the cake, so don't worry if it looks less than perfect. Carefully cut the cake into three even layers.

On a tray, platter, or cardboard cake round doyle, start with the middle layer first. Lightly coat it with the syrup or drizzle it with a teaspoon. It should be damp but not soaked through.
Stir the pastry cream to loosen it. Spread a layer of the pastry cream ¼" thick, or more. Sprinkle with one quarter of the nuts. Distribute evenly over the middle layer.

Continue with the second layer (use the top here, but put it upside-down). Repeat as above with the syrup, nuts, cream, and banana. Place the last layer (the original bottom) upside down. Coat lightly with syrup. Return cake to the refrigerator.

Save these last steps for as close to serving as possible, no more than an hour before.

Whip the heavy cream with the sugar and the vanilla. Spread thickly over the top of the cake, but not the sides. Sprinkle with remaining nuts and some toasted coconut. Finally, shave generous amounts of chocolate over the cake with a vegetable peeler or a small knife.

RECIPE INDEX

Papaya dries at Dong Nguyen's farm.

CREDITS AND PERMISSIONS

Page 2
Luis G. Cajiga, 'Calle Mercado', 1953, oil
Estudio Cajiga, San Justo 205, Old San Juan, PR
www.estudiocajiga.com
Collection of the Museo de Arte de Ponce
Fundación Luis A. Ferré, Inc., Ponce, Puerto Rico

Page 3
Francisco Oller, 'Bodegón con Aguacates y Utensilios',
1890-91, oil on canvas, 21" x 32 1/2"
Collection of the Museo Histórico de Puerto Rico de la Corporación de las Artes
Musicales
Currently on loan to the Museo de Arte De Puerto Rico

Page 5
Oscar Colón Delgado, 'Jíbaro Negro', 1941, oil on canvas, 40" x 29"
Collection of the Puerto Rican Institute of Culture

Page 7
Carmelo Sobrino, 'Sandía', 1997, oil on canvas, 33" x 42"
Courtesy of Mrs. Myrna I. Vega

Pages 8-9
Digital illustration of multidisciplinary artists Néstor Otero
and Annex Burgos. Pages from the artists' book 'Diálogo con objetos cotidianos',
published by the experimental press 'Mandíbula', founded by both in 2001. These
illustrations, like the book, were created using the programs Photoshop and PageMaker.

Page 11
Antonio Martorell, 'Service Compris', 2003, plaster, acrylic, and charcoal on canvas,
60" x 72"
Artist's collection

Page 12
José L. Díaz de Villegas y D'Estrampes
'El Pique de las Siete Lunas', 2001, oil on canvas
Collection of the Meduña-Ferré family
Courtesy of Cyril and María Luisa Meduña; José L. Díaz de Villegas

Page 68
Myrna Báez, 'Mangle', 1977, acrylic
Collection of the Museo de Arte de Ponce
Fundación Luis A. Ferré, Inc., Ponce, Puerto Rico

Page 128
Juan Sánchez Cotán, 'Quince, Cabbage, Melon and Cucumber', c 1602,
oil on canvas, 27 1 /8" x 33 1/4 ."
San Diego Museum of Art (Gift of Anne R. and Amy Putnam)

Page 191
Félix Medina González, 'Guineos', 1906, oil on canvas, 22" x 30"
Collection of the Puerto Rican Institute of Culture

Page 251
Norman Rockwell, 'Freedom from Want', 1943, oil
Norman Rockwell Art Collection Trust,
The Norman Rockwell Museum at Stockbridge, Massachusetts
Printed by permission from the Norman Rockwell Family Agency
Copyright © 1943 the Norman Rockwell Family Entities

A Note On The Type

The text of this book was set in Spectrum, a face designed by the Dutch typographer Jan van Krimpen in the early 1940s. It was designed for a Bible — which was never printed — for the Spectrum publishing house in Utrecht. The Dutch foundry Enschedé issued the face in 1952 and the British firm, Monotype, issued it in 1955.

Spectrum is a modern descendant of the Venetian faces of the sixteenth century. Elegant and reserved, it is admired for its flexibility and legibility, even in smaller point sizes.

The secondary face is Meta, designed in 1991 by a German, Erik Spiekermann, for FontShop and expanded since then. Meta was designed as a general application sans serif type family. Its subtly modulated lines have an angular finish, for a touch of informality.

"It is in artistic expression that we see what it is to be human, and what is possible for human beings to be. That this has been the purpose of BAM for the past 150 years—and that it will continue as far as it is possible to see— is what we might call a magnificent and inspiring spectacle."

FROM THE INTRODUCTION BY CHARLES MEE

The Complete Works

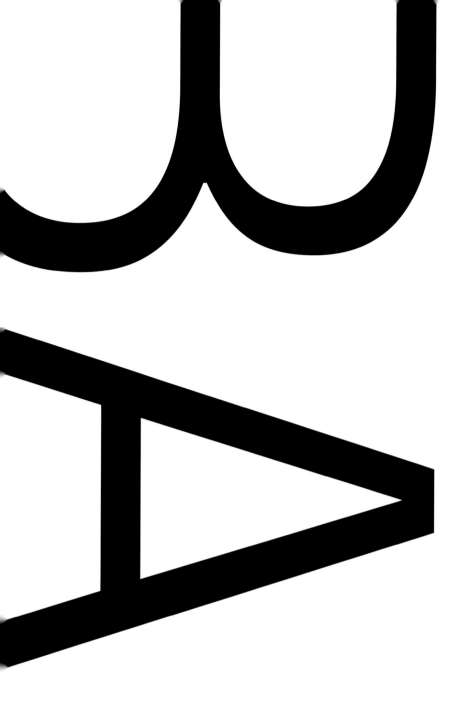

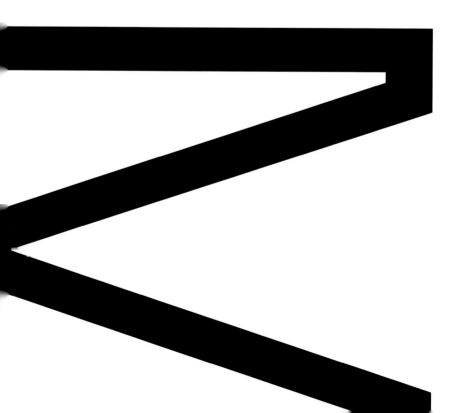

Edited by Steven Serafin

Brooklyn Academy of Music
in association with
The Quantuck Lane Press

contents

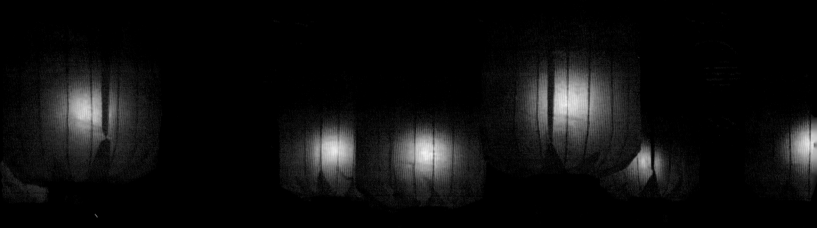

Jin Jia in *Raise the Red Lantern*,
National Ballet of China, 2005.
Photo: Jack Vartoogian

Top: Karen Brooks Hopkins.
Photo (detail): Erin Trieb

Bottom: Joseph V. Melillo.
Photo (detail): Timothy
Greenfield-Sanders

The Brooklyn Academy of Music (BAM) has stood the test of time for more than 150 years, enduring fire, flood, the Great Depression, and a host of other formidable challenges, all thanks to the extraordinary commitment and support of many people who, over 15 decades, have committed themselves to the institution's vitality and survival.

This publication, BAM's first official written history, is dedicated to those individuals who never wavered in their belief that BAM has been and always will be a shining light among the cultural treasures of New York City and throughout the world.

BAM would like to thank the following individuals, groups, and organizations for their steadfast and loyal support:

> Members of the BAM Board of Trustees since 1861, including current leadership: Alan H. Fishman, chair, and vice chairs William I. Campbell and Adam E. Max;

> Members of the BAM staff since 1861, including current executives: Alice Bernstein, Matthew Bregman, Lisa Mallory, and Keith Stubblefield;

> All BAM donors past, present, and future, for providing the resources that have allowed the institution to endure for 150 years;

> The incredible supporters of this book, for their belief that the BAM story finally needed to be told, especially James H. Ottaway Jr., honorary editor and loyal friend to BAM;

> JPMorgan Chase, BAM 150th anniversary sponsor.

We are forever indebted to the borough of Brooklyn and the city of New York, which more than once have prevented the wrecking ball from tearing down the building, and whose elected officials over the years have understood BAM's unique role in enhancing the vitality of New York City, including current leadership: Mayor Michael R. Bloomberg; Marty Markowitz, Brooklyn borough president; Christine C. Quinn, speaker of the New York City Council; and Kate D. Levin, commissioner, New York City Department of Cultural Affairs. Special thanks also go to former mayor Edward I. Koch and Howard Golden, former Brooklyn borough president, for their exemplary support of BAM's capital projects.

We also salute the authors, editors, designers, and creative team whose work made this publication a reality, including the invaluable contribution of James L. Mairs and Austin O'Driscoll of the Quantuck Lane Press.

BAM also wishes to acknowledge Joan K. Davidson and Furthermore, a program of the J.M. Kaplan Fund, as well as The Bay and Paul Foundations, for their underwriting support; the Robert W. Wilson Charitable Trust and Francois Letaconnoux for their contributions to the Harvey Lichtenstein Oral History Project; and Charles & Irene Hamm, The Gladys Krieble Delmas Foundation and Leon Levy Foundation for their support of BAM's archival work.

Additional thanks go to BAM trustee Ronald E. Feiner, who allowed us to borrow many items from his archival collection that are featured throughout this book.

Finally, thank you to our loyal BAM audience, who are the most adventurous theatergoers on the planet, and to the legions of creative artists who have graced our stages and screens for a century and a half. You are the very best part of what makes our civilization humane and transcendent.

In closing, our mantra: "BAM is not a job, but a crusade!"

Karen Brooks Hopkins
BAM President

Joseph V. Melillo
BAM Executive Producer

From Harvey Lichtenstein
BAM President and Executive Producer Emeritus

I would like to say thank you to all the people who have helped to resurrect BAM: those who have worked there and, of course, the artists here and abroad who have entrusted their works to BAM. And then there are the people on the other side of the curtain: the audience. My thanks for supporting BAM for all these years and into the future. Without your encouragement and support, we could not exist. But together we have brought life to a grand old theater, and, I am sure, will continue to do so. And thanks for the assistance through the years from the city of New York and the Brooklyn borough presidents—and to the citizens of Brooklyn and all of New York. Thank you.

From Kate D. Levin
Commissioner, New York City Department of Cultural Affairs

Through decades of resilience, reinvention, and an unstoppable commitment to bringing together the finest artists and audiences, BAM has profoundly shaped its neighborhood, our city, and the world's cultural life.

Top: Harvey Lichtenstein.
Photo (detail): Lois Greenfield

Bottom: Alan H. Fishman.
Photo (detail): Barry Burns

From Marty Markowitz
Brooklyn Borough President

BAM is the big stage for Brooklyn, the nation, and the world—the epicenter of the cutting edge, the locus of hip, and the historic grande dame of the Brooklyn theater. The borough of Brooklyn is proud to have such an important institution among its cultural treasures.

From Altria Group, Inc.
Sponsor of Part III, Scenes from the Next Wave

Altria Group is proud of its long association with BAM, especially our role in helping present the Next Wave Festival. All of us congratulate BAM on celebrating its 150th anniversary.

From the Edward John Noble Foundation
Sponsor of Part II, Harvey Lichtenstein and the BAM Renaissance

In celebration of BAM's 150th anniversary, the Edward John Noble Foundation is proud to support the chapter that chronicles the dynamic and visionary leadership of Harvey Lichtenstein.

From Alan H. Fishman
Chairman, BAM Board of Trustees

I have had the great privilege of being associated with BAM for more than 25 years. While that seems like a long association, it pales when compared to a 150-year-old institution. I would like to believe that the BAM of today compares adequately to the BAM of yesterday. The BAM family has worked hard to make those who created this wonderful institution proud. Thanks to all for that, and let's go forward with respect for the past and genuine excitement about the future.

A Family Tree Grows Deep in Brooklyn

by James H. Ottaway Jr.

The 150th anniversary of the Brooklyn Academy of Music reminds me of my 100-year-old mother, Ruth Blackburne Ottaway, telling me stories of her growing up at 259 Henry Street in Brooklyn Heights, attending Packer Collegiate Institute for 12 years, and often going to dances at BAM as a teenager during the "Roaring Twenties" in what would later become the Lepercq Space and is now the home of the colorful BAMcafé.

My mother was delighted when I told her that I was working on the campaign committee for major gifts for the first BAM endowment in the 1990s, and later contributed to the BAM cinema programs for teenagers in Brooklyn high schools. There is a plaque in a wall niche at the back of the Howard Gilman Opera House commemorating my mother's family history in Brooklyn and at BAM.

The oldest roots of our family tree growing in Brooklyn go down deep into the 19th century when my mother's great-great-grandfather John Woodward, who captained a company of Brooklyn volunteers in the Civil War, was a founding trustee of the Brooklyn Institute of Arts and Sciences, which merged with the Brooklyn Academy of Music and formed a cultural partnership with the Brooklyn Botanic Garden, the Brooklyn Children's Museum, and the Brooklyn Museum, where his statue still stands. He left his whole fortune to the Brooklyn Museum.

The youngest roots of our family tree in Brooklyn have grown from Woodwards to Blackburnes to Harts— my mother's maiden name—to three Ottaways, who are today principal owners and operators of the Brooklyn Brewery. They are my brother David, a director of this fast-growing brewery; his son Eric, who is general manager; and his son Robin, who is sales manager. Robin's daughter Avery is in preschool at Packer, where 12 members of our extended family have gone to school since 1916, when my mother first attended. Eric and Robin are expanding the capacity of the Brooklyn Brewery from 10,000 barrels a year today to 120,000 barrels in two years, playing their part in the present-day "Brooklyn Renaissance" along with the always innovating Brooklyn Academy of Music.

Congratulations to Karen Brooks Hopkins, president, and Joseph V. Melillo, executive producer, and all of the creative geniuses who have led BAM to its highest levels of both performance art and financial stability in your 150th anniversary year, from your admirer James H. Ottaway Jr.

James H. Ottaway Jr., principal sponsor of this publication, served on the BAM Endowment board of trustees. In 2003, he retired as a director and senior vice president of DowJones & Company and chairman of the Ottaway Newspapers group.

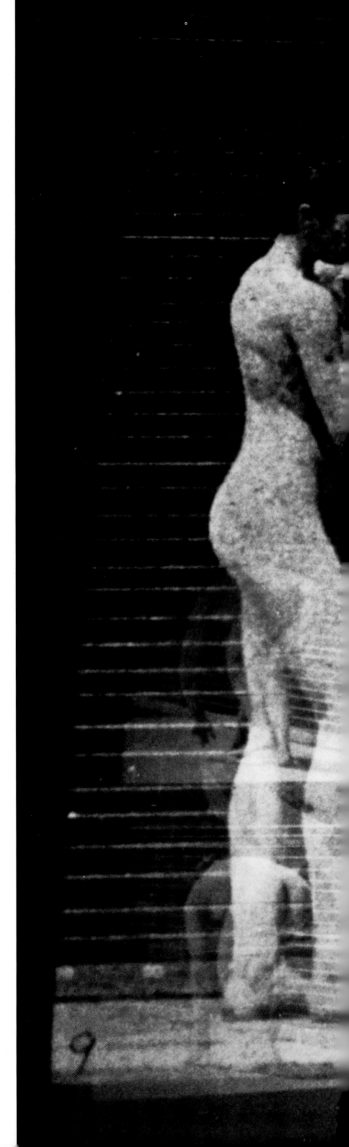

by Charles Mee

We live in a world these days where it's taken for granted that the Brooklyn Academy of Music is one of the greatest cultural institutions on the planet. And yet, not long ago—certainly within my own lifetime—it was a big, old, dark, neglected pile of stones off Flatbush Avenue where no one I knew ever thought to go.

The first time I ever walked into the theater at BAM was completely inadvertent. A friend had invited me to see a theater piece called *The Photographer / Far from the Truth*, inspired by the work of the 19th-century photographer Eadweard Muybridge, whose obsession with animal and human locomotion led him to develop a photographic means to project a series of images that had been captured by a set of still cameras: galloping horses, running bison, nude women descending staircases. I knew Muybridge's work, and I thought it was great, but, of course, I knew no one could make a good theater piece out of it. Still, I went anyway, because I had nothing else to do, and I thought it might be kind of exciting to venture out into the unknown wilderness—and stop for some cheesecake at Junior's.

And then the piece was absolutely, completely amazing. Directed by JoAnne Akalaitis of the experimental theater troupe Mabou Mines and designed by Santo Loquasto, it had music by Philip Glass, with lighting by the brilliant Jennifer Tipton, choreography by David Gordon, and a wonderful book by Robert Coe—a collage of music, movement, and text that was absolutely fantastic. It was, as it turned out—in the fall of 1983—the very first production of BAM's brand-new Next Wave Festival. And it was so wonderful that I condescended to go back to BAM for another Next Wave piece—this time it was the Trisha Brown Dance Company, with visual presentation by Robert Rauschenberg and music by Laurie Anderson, whom I had last seen in a loft on Broome Street in SoHo, with the audience sitting on the floor.

And then came Lucinda Childs and her company in a program that included a set designed by Frank Gehry and music by John Adams. And then Lee Breuer and Bob Telson with *The Gospel at Colonus*—Clarence Fountain and the Five Blind Boys of Alabama playing the role of Oedipus, backed by a gospel chorus of what seemed like several hundred thousand singers. Amazing. So the next year I became a subscriber, and that was the year of Meredith Monk and Ping Chong; Remy Charlip; Steve Reich; Bill T. Jones/Arnie Zane, with sets by Keith Haring, music by Peter Gordon, and costumes by Willi Smith; the Mark Morris Dance Group—and the completely stunning production of *Einstein on the Beach*, created by Philip Glass and Robert Wilson.

And then the next year Pina Bausch brought her Tanztheater company from Wuppertal—the ultimate dance-theater; then came Mechthild Grossmann,

The Photographer/Far from the Truth,
Philip Glass and Robert Coe, 1983.
Photo: Johan Elbers

Clarence Fountain and Isabell Monk (featured) in *The Gospel at Colonus*, Lee Breuer and Bob Telson, 1983. Photo: Beatriz Schiller

Laura Dean, Reinhild Hoffmann, Susanne Linke, and one of my favorite pieces of all time in the Next Wave: *The Birth of the Poet*, written by the fabulously scatological Kathy Acker, directed by Richard Foreman, with scenery and costumes designed by the wonderful SoHo artist David Salle—and what I remember is that people (almost immediately) started walking out. Often they would be so upset that they would stand up to leave, and sit down again, and stand up again, and sit down again, and stand up again, and go out into the aisle and stand there, and then turn and leave in disgust, or sometimes call out some insult at the stage before they turned and left, or sometimes walk to the stage and yell at the actors. One woman walked down to the edge of the stage and, in a swivet, not knowing just how to express her scorn and contempt properly, finally opened her purse and looked for something—anything she could find—to throw at the actors before she turned and left in a rage. By the time of the intermission in the Opera House—a

theater big enough to seat, it seemed to me, half of Brooklyn—there were only 23 of us still there, and I couldn't help thinking: This is like the good old days in Paris. This must be what it had felt like at an opening night for Alfred Jarry and Serge Diaghilev and Erik Satie.

And then the next year there was Merce Cunningham and John Cage, the Impossible Theater, Anne Teresa De Keersmaeker from Belgium, Molissa Fenley and Dancers, John Zorn, the Kronos Quartet, Eiko & Koma, and the Flying Karamazov Brothers. And by the 1987 Next Wave, when Peter Brook did *The Mahabharata* in BAM's Majestic Theater (renamed the BAM Harvey Theater as a tribute to longtime president and executive producer Harvey Lichtenstein), I was sitting in the front row with my feet grounded on a stage covered with dirt—for the full nine hours.

And then it turned out that the Next Wave was only part of the offerings at BAM. As the fall came to an end, it was time to buy tickets for the upcoming Spring Season, which each year contained some of what's next and much of what has proven to be enduring in the world of theater, dance, music, and opera. As I overheard one audience member say to his partner, as they walked into the lobby of the Harvey, "All I need is food, clothing, shelter, a happy family, and tickets to BAM, and then I have a complete life."

And finally, as time went on, the Next Wave and the Spring Season were not all that was going on at BAM. The newly created four-screen theater, BAM Rose Cinemas, was showing first-run films and classics. BAMcafé was hosting free live music and spoken word performances: jazz, Afropop, world rhythms, swing, mambo, gospel. BAMart was putting on exhibitions in fall and spring, many of them featuring emerging, Brooklyn-based artists—along with visits from the likes of Louise Bourgeois, Chuck Close, and William Wegman. Meanwhile, if you happened to have kids, there were weekend performances for young people in the BAMfamily series and the BAMkids Film Festival. For those who wanted to get inside the minds of some of the artists who were bringing their work to BAM, there were the Artist Talks—chats with Peter Brook and Bill T. Jones and Steve Reich, Trisha Brown and William Christie and Robert Lepage.

And yet it turns out that the BAM I knew was not the first BAM but the second BAM, and these people I loved so much—Pina Bausch and Robert Wilson and Jan Lauwers and the others—were not, after all, the first people ever to appear at BAM but part of an extraordinary legacy of art, culture, and community. In fact, the first-ever opening night at BAM was more than 150 years ago—January 15, 1861—with a performance of music that included works by Mozart and Verdi. In its early years, BAM played host to distinguished productions of opera and theater and a remarkable array of famous speakers and celebrities, from Frederick Douglass to P. T. Barnum. At that time, BAM was on Montague Street in Brooklyn Heights. Then in 1903 the first BAM burned to the ground. But by 1908 a new BAM was built—this time at its present location on Lafayette Avenue—and Enrico Caruso sang Charles Gounod's *Faust*, and the glory of the past returned. Still, after World War II, along with many other American cultural institutions—indeed, along with many American central cities, as interstate highways and suburbs flourished—BAM struggled to survive and declined into that neglected "pile of stones."

The renaissance at BAM was brought about by Harvey Lichtenstein, who arrived on the scene in 1967 and set about making what the *New York Times* declared "the foremost showcase for contemporary experimental performing arts in the United States." Or, as Lichtenstein himself said at one point, he thought he would like to make Brooklyn into the Left Bank of New York. Not long after Lichtenstein launched the rebirth of BAM, he brought in Karen Brooks Hopkins and then Joe Melillo to help him

manage the tempest he had set in motion. And so, when the time came in 1999 for Lichtenstein to turn the enterprise over to someone else, his chosen successors were already well versed in the "BAM culture," knowing everything that had already happened and what ought to happen next. Together, they had it in mind to transform a wonderful, adventurous theater into a unique institution, at once local and global in its aspirations—a center for the arts that would endure forever.

As it happens, my first sojourn to the "Left Bank" and the beginning of the Next Wave Festival was also when I returned to playwriting after an absence of nearly 25 years. I had written plays for off- and very-off-Broadway in the early sixties, performed at Caffe Cino in the West Village, La MaMa in its earliest days, and upstairs at St. Mark's Church in-the-Bowery. And, at the same time, I had become immersed in anti–Vietnam War activities, writing polemical rants for any offbeat downtown newspaper that would publish them, which led to writing more generally about American foreign policy, about the origins of the Cold War, and, finally, about American international relations—not as a historian engaged in a disinterested pursuit of the truth but as a citizen activist speaking to fellow citizens, hoping to have some influence on the conduct of U.S. foreign policy.

In short, I got caught up in things that I couldn't get out of and had nothing to do with the theater for all those years. I was consumed with art and archaeology and history and politics. But finally, in the early eighties, I made my way back to writing plays, my first and greatest passion—the thing I had always wanted to do in life. Since I came back to it so late in life, I was too old to think of having a career as a playwright. I just wrote what I loved. Still, after all those years away from the theater, I couldn't remember what was possible to do onstage. And then, when I stumbled into BAM for the first time, I knew I had come home.

"Good writers borrow," T. S. Eliot once said. "Great writers steal." At BAM, I knew I had come to the right place: a thieves' paradise—for writers, well, yes, but also for dancers, for musicians, for visual artists, for anyone walking in off the street looking for astonishment, for pleasure, for inspiration, for life. If you want to write a play, think of the music of Philip Glass and Laurie Anderson, the dance of Trisha Brown and Lucinda Childs, the spectacles conceived by Frank Gehry and Robert Rauschenberg. And if you want a text to put in the midst of all this, fine, steal one. I realized, watching things at BAM, that I didn't know what other people liked, but I knew what I loved. When I walk out the door after a performance at BAM, I don't need to ask the people I'm with, "Did I like that?" or "What was my favorite part?" No, I know what I love. So in my own work, I do what I love.

Mechthild Grossmann, a member of Bausch's company, did a solo show in 1985 in the Lepercq Space, the big black box theater that is now home to BAMcafé. She stepped up to a microphone and told the story of Antigone: "Act One, Scene One . . . Act One, Scene Two . . ." and so on. The whole story in outline. And then she turned around and sat atop a grand piano and sang a song. And then she got down from the piano and sat in a bathtub. And we all sat in the audience, watching and, in our minds, placing these events, one after another, into the frame of the Antigone story she had just told us. Only last year, almost 25 years after I saw her Antigone, I stole Grossmann's whole dramaturgical strategy for a piece I "wrote," inspired by the story of Thyestes.

Robert Woodruff, who in 1986 directed the Flying Karamazov Brothers in *The Soldier's Tale* at BAM, once said of the designer George Tsypin, who in the following year designed *Zangezi*, directed by Peter Sellars, with music by Jon Hassell, "I love to direct a play designed by George Tsypin because Tsypin designs a set you cannot stage a play on. And so, if I work on a set of Tsypin's, I'm forced to be more resourceful than I would be otherwise." And ever since Woodruff told me that, I've always tried to write Tsypin plays—plays that cannot be done onstage, scripts that purposely contain an array of obstacles so that the director and designers and actors are forced to be more "resourceful" than they otherwise would be, to come up with things no one would ever have thought of if the play had been easy to stage.

In 1999, when Jan Lauwers brought his Needcompany from Brussels to BAM to do *Morning Song*, I was struck by how his company of actors was, itself, implicitly a cosmopolitan global society composed of seven different nationalities. They are, even before they begin to get along together onstage, the European Union in a nutshell—indeed, a distillation of today's global society. "There's a quotation from Einstein," Lauwers has said, "in which he says that nationalism is the childhood disease of civilization. But at the same time, when an artist brings things from his own nationality into his art—his art is enriched. So I combine the Turkish dancer with the Argentine actor in *Morning Song*—to see what happens."

And what happens often in a Lauwers production is a whole new idea about the nature of theater. "It was John Cage who said once," Lauwers recalls, "that you need at least five different sources of energy at the same time to have good theater. And so . . . by changing the idea that theater has only one center into the idea that there isn't a center, but a series of off-centers, I discovered freedom in theater. So whether one sings a song, tells a story, or dances, without a center everything is important and it is the public, and every individual, who makes up his own story." In short, Lauwers lives in a multinational democracy,

where no one story is privileged above all others, no one destiny, no one family narrative dominates the known world, but rather many points of view, many sets of values, many histories and ideals for the future learn to coexist.

This is called globalism, but it might also be called Brooklyn, a cluster of neighborhoods whose population is largely foreign-born—not second or third generation, but foreign-born—the embodiment of a vibrant, resourceful cultural identity. Exactly the right place for BAM—and for me. I moved to Brooklyn 15 years ago, and over the past 10 years BAM has put on several of my plays, to my great delight. The first was *Big Love*—inspired by one of the oldest plays in the Western world, *The Suppliant Maidens* by Aeschylus—a piece that has a great deal of music and dance and physical theater as well as text. Some producers wanted to move *Big Love* to Broadway, but I said no finally, not just because they wanted to replace our actors, who had worked so hard and so beautifully on the piece, but because I felt the play belonged at BAM, where a playwright can keep company with Pina Bausch and Robert Wilson and Jan Lauwers and Jennifer Tipton and Ivo van Hove and, well, Shakespeare—and with Brooklyn.

The second piece of mine at BAM was *bobrauschenbergamerica*, a collage of scenes inspired by the work of Robert Rauschenberg. I love collage and the way that it doesn't privilege one image—one image or vision or way of seeing things—above all others but rather marshals a myriad of visions, and says we must pay attention to all of them, expand our understanding and imagination to see what sort of world can contain them all. This seems to be the most appropriate art form for the global society in which we live. And when the play was presented in the Harvey as part of the Next Wave Festival, Rauschenberg himself was in the audience.

In the late nineties, I had learned enough from BAM that a number of theaters and collaborators were content to work with me, and I came to be overloaded with possible projects—with more than I could possibly do, especially more than I could do while still holding down a job to support myself. And so, in a lighthearted moment, I emailed my old friend Dick Fisher. Dick and I had met when we first came to New York in our early twenties. And while I had gone into every money-losing venture I could find, Dick had thought it would be fun to be an investment banker, and he became, in time, the president and chairman of Morgan Stanley—and, as it happens, the first chair of the BAM endowment campaign. But he was not the sort who was consumed by his job—he and his wife, Jeanne, loved the arts: theater, painting, music, literature. The most open, receptive, nonjudgmental, patient, interested mind—that was his genius, and the spirit he shared with Jeanne.

In any case, late one evening, I wrote to him what I thought was a moderately amusing email, saying I had projects to do with lots of people, but every play I wrote lost me money, and I couldn't afford to pay the rent and feed my children—and so I wondered: How would he like to start a playwriting company with me? He would put in all the money and I would write all the plays.

And the next morning, Dick called to say he had discussed the idea with Jeanne and said with earnest, "We'd love to do it!" And with that—that easily, that quickly, that simply—I was finally, at the age of 60, able to spend my life doing what I love. All the time, day and night—at my desk, in the garden, wandering the streets, in a café. And what is certainly even more astonishing, there were no strings attached. Jeanne and Dick never made a suggestion, or a criticism, about my plays, either directly or indirectly. And so, one day, when Dick mentioned that he had seen a show at a gallery on the Upper East Side that he thought I'd like, I had no hesitation to drop in on a show of the work of Joseph Cornell. I walked into the gallery, stopped just inside the door, looked around, and thought: *This is a theater piece.*

And so I wrote *Hotel Cassiopeia*, which became the third work of mine to be done at BAM. It was performed, like *bobrauschenbergamerica*, by the SITI Company, directed by my very close friend Anne Bogart. Anne and I have worked together for more than 20 years now, and I love her. In fact, when my wife, Michi, and I got married, Anne conducted the wedding ceremony. And when we did *Hotel Cassiopeia*, Michi was in the cast. So my life and my friends and my wife and my imagination and my plays all live together in the same universe. And when we go out at night, we'd rather go to BAM than anywhere else—to the Next Wave and the Spring Season and the BAM Rose Cinemas and DanceAfrica and the BAMcafé—to hear the Brooklyn Sax Quartet, Rha Goddess, Ismail Lumanovski and the New York Gypsy All-Stars, the international dance band Charanga Soleil, and the Arab ensemble Tarab, with a mix of North African folk songs and flamenco, the psychedelic art rock of Gary Lucas and Gods and Monsters, live jazz, R&B, world beat, rock, pop, experimental, classical, and more—because BAM is home.

With all this activity, it's hard to imagine that anything else could ever happen at BAM—but, of course, no one should ever think we have come to the end of new ideas at BAM. Obviously, BAM hadn't yet published a history of itself. And so here it is—the BAM book—a narrative chronology, from the beginning to the present, with more than 350 images of artists and performances—the barest suggestion of all the stunning art that we are now privileged to take for granted at BAM.

Aristotle said that human beings are social animals. He thought that a person alone on a desert island was not quite human—that we become who we are in our relationships with others. And the art form par excellence of relationships, of their simplicity and purity and complexity and mystery, is theater, opera, dance, and, now, cinema—that extraordinarily complex constellation of music and movement, dance and text, media and visual art. It is in artistic expression that we see what it is to be human, and what is possible for human beings to be. That this has been the purpose of BAM for the past 150 years—and that it will continue as far as it is possible to see—is what we might call a magnificent and inspiring spectacle.

Sam Williams and Chas Elstner in *The Soldier's Tale*, Flying Karamazov Brothers, 1986. Photo: Tom Brazil

Opening Night

From the opening night speech by Simeon B. Chittenden, Brooklyn Academy of Music, January 15, 1861

Ladies and Gentlemen: When I accepted the novel and difficult part assigned to me in the arrangements of these entertainments, it was with the distinct and good understanding that I was to be supported where I now stand, by the presence of my associate directors. And when I prepared a few simple words with the purpose of speaking them to you, one of those bewitchingly fair ladies dashed my work—and, according to present indications, my 24 associates—into oblivion, by the intimation that whoever appeared in front of these footlights tonight would be required to sing. (*Applause.*) It may seem to you a very wonderful thing that one lady should thus dispatch 25 vigorous gentlemen. (*Laughter.*) But I assure you that the only wonder in the case consists in the fact that I remain to tell the tale.

Two hundred and forty years ago the good bark *Mayflower*—you may have heard of her—landed 100 passengers at Plymouth. They came to this country to colonize and build up a new nation, and that was no small undertaking considering that they had to fell the forest, till the soil, build their houses, establish roads, make laws, build churches and schoolhouses, and fight the Indians. These old Puritans had no time for amusement: when not at work, they had to watch and pray. But it is not so with us, their descendants. We have need enough to pray, but we have to work but little to secure plenty of leisure, and we are very apt to get into mischief, as some of us have lately done—into politics—(*applause*) and so we have concluded to amuse ourselves with an Academy of Music. (*Loud applause.*)

Two hundred and thirty-eight years after the Pilgrims landed, seven gentlemen called a meeting of their fellow citizens to see if the means could not be secured for the erection of a hall worthy of a great and populous city that had not any such convenient establishment. At that meeting a committee of 25 was appointed to take the subject in hand. They proceeded with the work. I have just told you how 24 of the committee were incidentally disposed of. (*Laughter.*) But I will not detain you with any recital of the difficulties that attended us in our earlier efforts. We did not dare at first to let anyone know that we contemplated the erection of so comprehensive and complete an establishment as this, or one so costly or elegant.

Moreover, we wanted a great place where men of all parties and creeds can meet on common ground in time of need and time of danger, to devise measures of local beneficence and philanthropy, or to lay on the altar of our country all personal and party considerations, that we may unite together as one man to redeem the nation, and transmit to unborn generations the precious and free institutions that for more than 80 years have been the hope of the race. (*Applause.*) And so for these purposes we built our Academy of Music. As I am a member of the building committee, it may be unbecoming in me to say anything in favor of the building; but I may repeat the words of Webster, on a far different occasion: "There she stands—judge for yourselves." (*Applause.*)

Ladies and Gentlemen, the Brooklyn Academy of Music is no longer a myth, but a present and grand reality. (*Applause.*) It denotes an era in our history, and henceforth it should be a power in our midst.

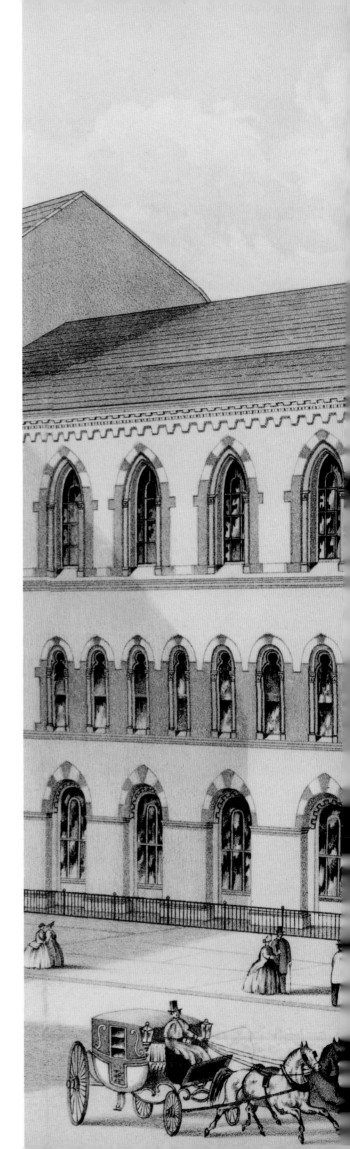

by Phillip Lopate

The Brooklyn Academy of Music, acknowledged as
the oldest performing arts center in the United States,
had its inception at a meeting in October 1858 at the
Brooklyn Polytechnic Institute that assembled the
core of Brooklyn society: among them, Henry E.
Pierrepont, A. A. Low, Simeon B. Chittenden, and
the Reverend Richard Salter Storrs. These were
men of substance and character who had a hand in
so much of Brooklyn's cultural and physical development, converting it in the 19th century from a
genial backwater to a modern metropolis. The
owner of ferry companies, warehouses, and real
estate, Pierrepont was known as the "first citizen"
of Brooklyn for having laid out much of its street
pattern and was also active in creating Green-Wood
Cemetery, Montagu Park, and the Astronomical
Society of Brooklyn; Low, a prosperous tea importer
with a large fleet of clipper ships traveling to and
from China, helped to finance the first Atlantic
cable and served on the governing boards of the
Packer Collegiate Institute and the Brooklyn Library;
Chittenden ran a dry goods business and invested in
bringing rapid transit to Brooklyn; Reverend Storrs
was pastor of the Church of the Pilgrims, the first
Congregational church in Brooklyn, who adminis-
tered foreign missions to China, Japan, Turkey, and
Africa, and helped found the Long Island (later the
Brooklyn) Historical Society. They were worldly,
well-traveled men and seasoned pragmatists who had
the ability to turn necessity and vision into reality.
A. A. Low told those at the Polytechnic meeting,
"If we want this thing let us determine to have it,
and not consider the thing done with the passing of
a few resolutions."

The founding fathers of the Academy were,
in short, the White Anglo-Saxon Protestant elite
of the community—the civic-minded WASPS of
yore—who established the city's great museums,
opera companies, symphony orchestras, and public
parks, not to mention its universities, libraries, and
hospitals. We may never know the precise combination of altruism, noblesse oblige, vanity, economic
incentive, and desire to please their wives that motivated them, but we can be grateful that they acted
as they did. These were the men who had already
organized Brooklyn's first symphony orchestra, the
Philharmonic Society, in 1857; now they met to
create a venue for regular classical music and opera
performances in Brooklyn. There were already irregular
concerts scattered about Brooklyn, in churches or
acoustically ill-suited halls. There was also a plethora
of musical offerings in Manhattan, at Niblo's Garden,
the Academy of Music on East 14th Street and Irving
Place, Castle Garden, and the Great Hall at Cooper
Union. But to get to them from Brooklyn meant

Architectural rendering of the first
Brooklyn Academy of Music,
ca. 1861. Courtesy of BAM Hamm
Archives Center

Part I

Academy of Music, Brooklyn.

waiting for a ferry to cross the river, then another conveyance to the performance, and then reversing the process, which added up to hours of transportation, an intolerable nuisance in uncooperative weather. No, what was wanted was a lyric hall closer to home. At first the group sponsored concerts at the Brooklyn Atheneum, a local cultural center, but the room was too small to accommodate the crowds, and in the end they decided to bite the bullet and erect a proper music hall.

An ample enough property was acquired on busy, commercial Montague Street, between Court and Clinton Streets, in the heart of Brooklyn Heights, a block away from City Hall (now Borough Hall). A committee of prominent city patriarchs was appointed to raise the necessary funds and another formed to select an architect. Henry E. Pierrepont, the latter committee's chair, wrote to his fellow members recommending Leopold Eidlitz, a well-regarded architect known mainly for designing churches and synagogues, who trained in the office of the highly respected English-born architect Richard Upjohn: "Mr. Eidlitz is the architect of St. George's Church, the Metropolitan and the American Exchange Banks and other buildings in New York of great architectural beauty, and originality of design. We are informed he is reliable in his estimates. . . . The Moorish style of architecture which he has adopted is new to us, and seems strange, and not adapted to secular buildings—but before rejecting that style we must pause before the fact that the new Covent Garden Theatre in London, which is of acknowledged elegance, is built in that style. Perhaps our taste then may need schooling from experience, and considering Mr. Eidlitz's acknowledged

talents and taste and proficiency in his art, it might be safe to put ourselves in his hands."

As the academy was intended "for the purpose of encouraging and cultivating a taste for music, literature and the arts," there was considerable debate concerning what to name the institution. Both "Musical" and "Lyric" Hall were rejected in favor of "Academy of Music," despite the existence of a rival namesake situated directly across the river. The plan for incorporation was finalized in March 1859, and a joint stock corporation was formed to sell shares for $50 each to prosperous members of the Brooklyn community, with the goal to raise $150,000. As such, writes curator and theater historian Mary C. Henderson in *The City and the Theatre*, the Academy fit "the pattern previously set in the building of earlier opera houses. It was erected with money raised by private subscription and it was located near its fashionable audience." The building ended up costing $200,000, and, according to theater scholar Paul Nadler, when the Academy opened "the directors proudly proclaimed it fully paid for, not a penny in debt, though it later came out that there was in fact a 'considerable debt' which was not retired until mid-1862 at the earliest."

It was a precarious moment to undertake such a lofty enterprise, with the country plunged into civil war, but in other respects the time seemed ripe. As recently as 1855, Brooklyn had annexed Williamsburg and the town of Bushwick; its population had grown to more than 266,000 by 1860, in the process laying claim to the title of third largest municipality in the United States, behind New York and Philadelphia. That boast, heard often on the lips of Brooklynites, also carried with it a duty to shed provincial ways and acquire cultural sophistication. As A. A. Low put it trenchantly in a speech at the initial meeting at the Polytechnic Institute: "I hold that we often err in thinking and styling our city the third city of the Union. That the city contains a large number of men, women and children we are ready enough to admit; but until it possesses larger attractions to men of letters, men of science and culture, to men of intellect, in fact to men of every walk and condition of life . . . until it possesses these things in as large a measure as some other cities of the country such as Boston, Baltimore, Cincinnati and St. Louis and many others, I would be slow, for one, to style our city the third city in the Union." Others allowed themselves to fantasize about the importance of the new music hall; one enthusiast remarked in the *Brooklyn Eagle* that the Academy would "be to Brooklyn what the Temple was to Jerusalem, the Parthenon to Athens, or St. Peter's to modern Rome."

When the Academy opened its doors in January 1861, it was greeted with considerable fanfare, but not without a measure of disappointment. Eidlitz was something of a structuralist, who attempted to "express" the interior functions of the building in its exterior design. The result, to critics of his day, was somber, with both Gothic and Moorish trappings, and lacking in the sort of decorative putti carvings and gilded ornamental hodgepodge that many expected in a concert hall. "There is but little tawdry or florid decorations anywhere," announced the *Brooklyn Eagle*, "the gayer colors are completely excluded, and gilding is almost completely ignored, still the bright red upholstery and the heavy purple curtains of the boxes relieve wonderfully when the place is lighted up, what otherwise would be exceedingly gloomy." Likewise the *New York Times* gave it a mixed review: "The first glance, probably, will not please," it said, "for it seems to present a huge mass of red brick, with a multitude of little windows patched over it," before acknowledging that the interior was handsome and the exterior tastefully solid, and concluding, "The oftener we see the building, the better we like it." Destroyed by fire in 1903, all we have to judge the edifice today are photographs and drawings, which suggest something of the medieval air of Old Prague. In any case, Eidlitz—who went on to design the Temple Emanu-El with Henry Fernbach and the Tweed Courthouse, among many distinguished buildings, and to redesign the New York State Capitol with H. H. Richardson and Frederick Law Olmsted—never built another auditorium.

The First Brooklyn Academy of Music

The Brooklyn Academy of Music was inaugurated with great pomp on January 15, 1861, with a program that included Mozart, Donizetti, Verdi, and Friedrich von Flotow. The following week the First Lady, Mary Todd Lincoln, attended its first opera, Saverio Mercadante's *Il Giuramento*. Though the Academy, as its name pointedly indicated, was to be devoted to music, its organizers were quite conscious that it had another community-defining purpose. As recorded in the *Brooklyn Eagle*: "Up to this time—while we claim to be the third city of the Union—we have not had a single public building worthy of a decent country town. We regard the inauguration of the Academy of Music as an era in the history of Brooklyn, not alone because it makes accessible a refined enjoyment; not alone because it will tend to encourage and foster local trade and business, and keep thousands of dollars here that would otherwise be spent in New York; not because it will make Brooklyn more desirable as a place of residence even; but because we regard it as an indication that our citizens will not be content with having Brooklyn any longer an overgrown village, an incomplete chrysalis—a city without the accessories that make city life bearable and enjoyable." On the second of two opening nights, one for the music hall and another for the ballroom, Simeon B. Chittenden said in his speech that the Academy would be a place to welcome national as well as foreign dignitaries, and, emphasizing the immediacy of the concurrent Civil War, its civic function would be as "a great place where men of all parties and creeds can meet on common ground in time of need and time of danger."

Above all, the founding fathers stressed that the Academy was to be a place for "innocent amusements," which meant music, not drama. "Let us encourage here whatever is pure and admissible: let us discourage every entertainment to which we would hesitate to invite our sons and daughters," proclaimed Chittenden. "Let me say here, that no one of us proposed to build a theatre, nor do we propose to allow this building to be used for theatrical purposes." His position no doubt was influenced by the negativism toward play-going that persisted from the 1849 Astor Place Riot, the result of a professional rivalry between the American actor Edwin Forrest and the English tragedian William Macready that was aggravated by class differences among audiences, which ended in one of the most violent incidents in the history of the theater. In addition, most of New York's theaters featured minstrel shows, a popular form of entertainment that was also looked down upon by more sophisticated audiences. Chittenden and other Academy leaders of the institution even drew the line at allowing "improper" musical spectacles, such as the supposedly indecent opera *La Traviata*. Verdi's ennobling treatment of the courtesan Violetta and her extramarital affair did not sit well with the more pious citizenry of Brooklyn. We may smile today at such Victorian prudishness; what is harder for us to grasp is the degree to which the moral causes of the day, such as abolitionism, temperance, and sexual purity, whether sterling or dubious in retrospect, were championed by the community at large.

Social class also factored into the initial prohibition of theater. The Academy's founders had wanted a place where they and their wives could dress to the nines, see and be seen, "a place to make visible one's bank account and social standing," as noted by Mary C. Henderson, in an atmosphere of elevated, approved classical music and opera. The biggest shareholders were guaranteed the best seats. Many lesser stockholders, however, worried that the Academy would never turn a profit or break even if it restricted itself to opera and symphony. Theater, by far the more popular art, would have to be allowed in for the operation to succeed. Brooklyn's high society was simply not large enough to fill a 2,200-seat auditorium; like it or not, social inferiors would have to be enticed to buy tickets. But the fashionable world was resistant not only to the thought of compromise but to the idea of cohabitation with a less refined segment of the local populace.

A delicious send-up of this snobbish attitude appeared in a hoax letter to the *Brooklyn Eagle*, penned by a pro-drama stockholder: "We, Messrs. Low, Benson, Sloan, &c., want a place of amusement kept open for the exclusive use of our respectable selves and families, (in short, for our set) where the amusements are of such a character that the general public will care nothing about them, and will not frequent the house; or, if they do come, they must be content with such diet only as is palatable to us. And you, our dear Brother Stockholders, (but not of our set) must help us bear the expense of this nice arrangement. You must be content to get no interest for your investment and to see the Academy closed eight months a year, because, forsooth, should we open it for the Drama, or amusements that the general public taste approves, it might interfere with the delightful reunions of the Balcony and Dress Circle, where we and our set take care to secure the best seats."

Division between elitism and populism arose from the start, posing a continuous challenge to the Academy of merging community and cultural identity. What could be morally wrong, argued supporters of drama, about Shakespeare, whose works were the object of enormous cultural enthusiasm in 19th-century America? Other shareholders claimed they had been assured on the sly that theater would be permitted, or else they would never have invested. Apparently, the fundraisers had told each group, pro- and anti-drama, what it wanted to hear. However, after the Academy ill-advisedly allowed a lecture on the breaking of wild horses, with live subjects onstage, it became more difficult to argue against nonmusical performances. The purists caved in; the pro-drama faction carried the vote. By the end of 1861, not only were dramatic productions on the boards, initiated on December 23 with a performance of *Hamlet* that had E. L. Davenport in the title role, but even *La*

Traviata, "the story of the poor demimondaine," was mounted at the Academy, thanks to the patience of opera impresario Jacob Grau. It proved to be a huge success and soon became "Brooklyn's favorite opera," according to the music critic of the *New York Times*, Charles Bailey Seymour. "No other opera draws such crowded houses, and on no occasion do the good people so liberally patronize librettos and bouquets as when *La Traviata* is on the bills. . . . Mr. Grau deserves from Brooklyn hearty recognition of his services."

Jacob Grau ferried the same opera singers between the New York and the Brooklyn academies of music. In one period of nasty snowstorms when the New York house shut down, the enthusiasm of Brooklynites for their new opera house resulted in all performances being shifted there. New York's critics suddenly had to alter their condescending tone. "Opera thrives in Brooklyn, whilst it starves in New York . . . the metropolis finds itself in the humiliating position of playing second fiddle to the sister city, which supports opera three nights in the week, while New York can only support two," wrote the *Herald* critic, Edward G. P. Wilkins. The critic for the *Tribune*, William Henry Fry, chimed in: "Every performance [in Brooklyn] thus far has been a success. On Saturday night . . . the Brooklyn musical fanatics turned out in crushing numbers and dazzling gaiety to enjoy the woes of *Lucia di Lammermoor* and her unfortunate tenor of a sweetheart." Still, New York sophisticates tended to scoff at Brooklynites as cultural parvenus: "The aristocracy, the wealth, the talent, the beauty, the fashion of Brooklyn, it seems, rush three nights out of the week to the Academy of Music on Montague Place, dressed almost to death. . . . Several tailors who were on the point of bankruptcy have been put upon their feet by the demand for dress-coats; the dealers in bouquets have realized fortunes; hack drivers are full of orders, and the milliners and mantua-makers are half wild."

From the start, the Academy had established itself as a profit-making enterprise; it charged rent for each performing group, even the Brooklyn Philharmonic. When it raised its rental price to $250 a night, resulting in a standoff with impresario Grau, the *Times* critic Charles Bailey Seymour sniffed delightedly: "There was a danger a week ago, that New York might become a sort of suburb to Brooklyn, so fervently did the newly ignited operatic fires burn in that city, and so dimly were they kept alive here. To avert this calamity, the directors of the Montague-street Academy have been kind enough to raise the rent of their house." The critic for the *World* was even more emphatic: "This retaliatory measure will possibly necessitate a general return to the indigenous amusements of the sister city—baseball, tea parties, and crossing the ferry."

If Manhattan symbolized the polarities of rich and poor, Brooklyn embodied a more middle-class residential identity as "the city of homes and churches."

Illustration of the Brooklyn and Long Island Sanitary Fair, 1864. Courtesy of BAM Hamm Archives Center

The provincial chauvinism of Brooklyn's elite, heard, for instance, in Simeon B. Chittenden's boast that the Academy had been "built by Brooklyn hands, by Brooklyn bricks, and by money from Brooklyn pockets," can be understood partly as a defensive reaction to the sneering of New Yorkers across the river. For the moment, Brooklyn was trying to feel itself a city in its own right, not a mere suburb of New York. However, by the end of the 19th century—on January 1, 1898, to be exact—it would amalgamate with Manhattan, Staten Island, Queens, and the Bronx, and see its status reduced to being merely one of the five boroughs of New York City. Brooklyn's decision to consolidate was motivated chiefly by economics. According to historian Ralph J. Caliendo, it was "so deeply in debt that it could not build desperately needed water mains, sewer lines, or schools. Property owners there . . . favored consolidation so that their communities could draw from real estate taxes in central Manhattan." The opening of the Brooklyn Bridge in 1883 would also greatly increase the interdependence of the two cities,

Frederick Douglass. Photo: Time Life Pictures/National Archives

while emphasizing the importance of Brooklyn as a bedroom borough for Manhattan workers. Seth Low—the son of founding father A. A. Low—former mayor of Brooklyn and soon to become the reform mayor of New York City, drafted the proposal for consolidation, and Brooklyn voters, however reluctantly, approved it. Whatever the injury to its pride, Brooklyn continued to grow dramatically in population for decades after consolidation; in retrospect it seems to have been both inevitable and a wise course of action. But in 1861, and for much of the second half of the 19th century, Brooklyn would continue to dream autonomous big-city dreams, with its new Academy of Music at its center.

The Academy and the Civil War

The 1863–64 season at the Brooklyn Academy of Music was marked by a memorable two-week event that opened on February 22, 1864: the Brooklyn and Long Island Sanitary Fair, a fundraiser for the U.S. Sanitary Commission, a forerunner of the Red Cross that treated sick and wounded soldiers and saw to their comfort, while making sure that their recuperating wards were clean and hygienic. The fair, kicked off by a grand parade of the entire military force of the city passing in review before the Academy, attempted to re-create the great market fairs of Europe. Its central bazaar held dozens of booths with technological displays and items donated for sale, plus a "Skating Pond," a mirrored trompe l'oeil exhibition; a "Post Office," where letters from the fair could be posted to friends; and a huge soda fountain, free of charge for fairgoers, set up by a local Court Street druggist. The Academy was decorated with immense red, white, and blue bunting and an American eagle suspended from the ceiling. Three temporary buildings had been erected alongside and across the street from the Academy, with large dining rooms for the hungry customers. The fair raised over $400,000 for clothing, food, medical supplies, and other provisions for the Union Army, more than any other fundraiser for the Sanitary Commission held in the Union, and was deemed a magnificent success.

Among the most prominent members of the Sanitary Commission, George Templeton Strong, New York lawyer, man-about-town, charitable board member, and inveterate concertgoer, noted in his journal, one of the most insightful American diaries of the 19th century: "November 21, [1863,] Saturday. Thursday night Ellie and I, with [Henry W.]Bellows, his wife and daughter, went to [the] Brooklyn Academy of Music. I rode outside on the box. The Rev. Henry Ward Beecher delivered an address about his experiences in England. Proceeds of the performance for the benefit of the Sanitary Commission. As representatives of the Sanitary Commission, we were received with distinguished consideration, admitted through the stage door, shewn into the Committee Room, introduced to the reverend, and accommodated in a special proscenium box. The house was large and intelligent. Capital address and enthusiastically applauded.... His matter and his manner were excellent. I never heard so good a popular address. Beecher stands up for the English people and maintains that we have their sympathy. His speech was an argument against the bitter anti-Anglicanism now prevalent."

Henry Ward Beecher, the charismatic Brooklyn preacher, was but one of the many well-known orators who spoke at the Academy of Music. Virtually every important politician, activist, writer, and explorer of the day addressed the hall: abolitionist and social reformer Frederick Douglass, Elizabeth Cady Stanton, Lucy Stone, and Julia Ward Howe, appearing on behalf of women's suffrage; P. T. Barnum; Oscar Wilde; Mark Twain, with his writer friend George Washington Cable; Bret Harte; General Philip H. Sheridan; Henry M. Stanley, the "hero of the Dark Continent"; Matthew Arnold; and Arthur Conan Doyle, to name just a few. Theatergoers saw the most famous actors of the day, usually with pick-up companies and abridged scripts tailored to highlight the stars: Edwin Booth in *Hamlet*, *The Merchant of Venice*, *The Iron Chest*, and *Richelieu*, as well as the soon-to-be-infamous John Wilkes Booth in *Richard III* and *The Marble Heart*; Edwin Forrest in *King Lear*, *Jack Cade*, *Virginius*, and *Othello*; Kate Bateman as Julia in *The Hunchback*; Joseph Jefferson in *Rip Van Winkle*; Charlotte Cushman as Lady Macbeth; and Laura Keene in *She Stoops to Conquer*. The first Academy would later play host to luminaries such as Steele MacKaye, Dion Boucicault, Lillian Russell, and Mrs. Fiske, as well as the inimitable Sarah Bernhardt and the legendary Eleonora Duse, all eyes concentrating on her still presence, who electrified the Academy's audiences in *Camille* and commanded "the staggering prices for Brooklyn of $5 for an orchestra chair."

In those years, it seemed, all important civic rites and celebrations had to be held at the Academy. On April 17, 1865, three nights after the assassination of Abraham Lincoln, the Academy of Music was filled to overflowing with mourners—as noted by historian Henry R. Stiles, "one of the most solemn and impressive demonstrations that had ever taken place in Brooklyn." When the Brooklyn Bridge finally opened, on May 24, 1883, the festivities were housed there, with President Chester A. Arthur and Grover Cleveland, then governor of New York, in attendance. When Ulysses S. Grant passed away in 1885, memorial services took place at the Academy. The importance of the Academy to the greater good of the community was characterized early in its history by numerous sources, but none with more simplistic eloquence than what appeared in a description of the

Eleonora Duse. Photo: Hulton Archive

Academy in the aptly titled 19th-century guidebook *The City of Brooklyn*: "Here Brooklyn gathers, and speaks, acts, or gives, whenever her public spirit is invoked, or some question of local or national import needs the attention of her citizens, and here art, science, religion and amusement, hold their levees."

The first Academy was said to have the best acoustics of any music hall in the region. Curiously, there was a difference of opinion among music aficionados, who championed its sound, and theater patrons, who thought its large proportions swallowed up normal speech. In 1863 the *Brooklyn Standard Union* critic harrumphed, "It is only those rough parts of tragedy, which are usually howled by the actors, that reach the first row in the balcony and Gilmore might as well try to throw a 30 pound ball into Charleston, from his present position, as Edwin Booth [endeavors] to make one syllable of the finest passages of *Richelieu* strike the 'dull, cold ears' of the family circle." Even if this had been true, it did not prevent Booth from mounting many seasons of classical repertoire at the Academy. He chose the Brooklyn hall to give his last public farewell appearance, in *Hamlet*, of course, on April 4, 1891. Otis Skinner played Laertes and Helena Modjeska was Ophelia to Booth's superannuated Danish prince. The anonymous reporter for

Edwin Booth. Photo: Napoleon Sarony

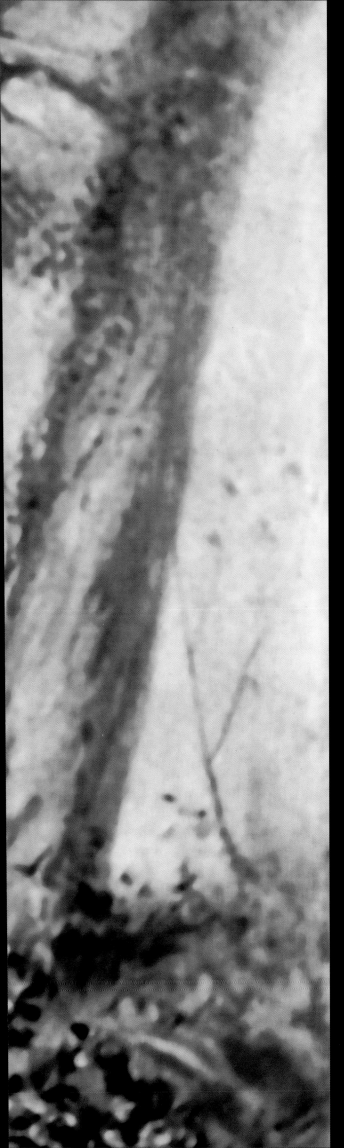

by Roger Oliver

In a manner of speaking, Edwin Booth went into the family business. His father, Junius Brutus Booth, began his acting career in his native England before settling in the United States, where he achieved great success, especially in Shakespearean roles. Two of Edwin Booth's brothers—Junius Brutus Jr. and the infamous John Wilkes Booth, assassin of Abraham Lincoln—also became actors but never achieved the stature of their father and more illustrious brother. The three brothers acted together only once, in 1864, in a production of *Julius Caesar*.

It was not until after his father's death that Edwin Booth first gained notoriety for himself in such Shakespearean roles as Petruchio, Benedick, Romeo, and Shylock. The last role was one he continued to perform throughout his career, along with Othello, Iago, his father's calling card Richard III, and King Lear. But it is for his performance as Hamlet, Shakespeare's Danish prince, that Booth is best remembered. He performed it from 1853 to 1891, when, at the age of 57, he gave his final performance of the role and of his career at the Brooklyn Academy of Music.

In addition to bringing new measures of subtlety and introspection to his acting, Booth was known for his innovations as an actor-manager. He founded his own theater so that he could stage scenically elaborate productions and edited a series of promptbooks that prolonged the lives of these productions. His continuing legacy to the acting profession is the Players Club on Gramercy Park in New York City, which he established as a meeting place for actors and where he lived until his death. Revered as well as emulated, Booth was a commanding presence on the stage, his reputation enshrined in the annals of American theater by Eugene O'Neill in his Pulitzer Prize–winning play *Long Day's Journey into Night*: "That from Booth," proclaims the character of James Tyrone, "the greatest actor of his day or any other!"

Edwin Booth

the *World* gushed, "*Hamlet* was the play and the big auditorium was packed to its utmost capacity, mainly by ladies. It was not only one of the finest gatherings that had ever assembled in the City of Homes, but one of the most demonstrative as well. When the curtain fell upon the last act there was a storm of applause."

The Academy's theatrical performances were not always so mainstream or erudite—sometimes the bill of fare might be "Refined Vaudeville for Refined People," which featured Wormwood's Monkey Theater, billed as "Positively the Greatest Trained Animal Act in the World"; a dramatic sketch like "Josephine vs. Napoleon"; or a popular spectacle like "Buffalo Bill" Cody in his famed Wild West show. There were also novelty acts, such as the magician Herrmann, "the greatest living prestidigitateur"; a "Hungarian band" from Budapest and Siberian bloodhounds; as well as ventriloquists, comedians, and clowns—a miscellany of entertainment, writes Maurice Edwards, ranging "from the sublime to the ridiculous." In addition, the Academy routinely played host to large high school and college graduations, and several local amateur groups, such as the Amaranth Society and the Gilbert Society, performed comic plays with enthusiastic regularity, picking up the slack when theatrical bookings began to decline at the first Academy, in the last decade of the 19th century. Then again, theater had always taken a back seat to concerts, operas, lectures, and social affairs; music continued to dominate the schedule, as the Academy's founders had intended.

The Golden Age of Music and the Great Fire

It was in the area of classical music that the first Brooklyn Academy made its deepest, most lasting contribution to American culture, by helping to

stabilize the presentation of a full repertoire and offering a venue to various orchestras, opera companies, and solo performers. The central figure in this flowering was the conductor Theodore Thomas, who took over the Brooklyn Philharmonic in the early 1860s and built it into an efficient, artistic unit, at the same time developing an eponymous orchestra for select performances and conducting the New York Philharmonic across the river. A man of clearly staggering energies and discipline, he was also a crusader who saw his mission as educating the public to serious music, which usually meant German music, though his programs were commendably catholic. The music critic James Gibbons Huneker summarized his impact thus: "It is no exaggeration to state that Theodore Thomas did more for orchestral music in North America than any previous conductor. His influence was profound and far-reaching. His was a household name wherever a love of good music was to be found."

After a tenure of nearly three decades, wishing to extend his reach beyond Brooklyn and New York, Thomas accepted an offer to take over the Chicago Symphony and gave his final concert at the Academy on April 18, 1891. New York's music life, long dependent on him, was suddenly faced with a vacuum. Leopold Damrosch assumed the baton at the New York Philharmonic, but the Brooklyn Philharmonic simply stopped functioning. Why is not entirely clear, though Maurice Edwards, in his invaluable book *How Music Grew in Brooklyn: A Biography of the Brooklyn Philharmonic Orchestra*, offers various speculations, from laziness to frugality to sectarian politics. In short order, the Boston Symphony Orchestra approached the Brooklyn Philharmonic's directors and offered to take over its next season's concerts. The offer was accepted, leading to one of the most rewarding, long-lasting alliances between two cultural institutions. For the next 75 years, which encompassed the musical directorships of Pierre Monteux, Serge Koussevitzky, and Charles Munch, the Boston Symphony, probably the most highly regarded orchestra in the land, made regular visits to Brooklyn.

As a means to fill the vacuum left by Thomas's impending departure for Chicago, the distinguished conductor Anton Seidl started his own modestly sized orchestra, the Seidl Society. A most celebrated performance occurred at the Academy on March 31, 1890, when Seidl conducted Wagner's *Parsifal* with an expanded 84-piece orchestra, and the "huge audience (every seat and standing place was taken) was considered the most distinguished—in bearing, in attire, in pedigree—in the building's history." As described by Joseph Horowitz in his book *Wagner Nights*, "The significance of the '*Parsifal* Entertainment' was threefold. It was a milestone in introducing Wagner's final opus to the United States. It stirred dreams of a New World Bayreuth in Brooklyn. . . . It was a high culture/High Society hybrid peculiar to the late Gilded Age, when Wagner reigned supreme: a concert as devoutly serious as its trappings were glamorous."

The success of *Parsifal* launched a series of Seidl Society concerts at the Academy; in addition, the Academy made economically minded arrangements with a number of cultural institutions to share opera companies and symphony orchestras, where an expensive opera production might help pay for itself by rotating four nights in Manhattan and three in Brooklyn. The New York Philharmonic came to have its own regular season at the Brooklyn Academy of Music. European orchestras of the highest caliber often stopped in Brooklyn during their tours of the United States. The D'Oyly Carte Opera Company offered meticulous productions of Gilbert & Sullivan. Many world-renowned virtuosos of the day had recitals at the Academy, including pianist and composer Louis Moreau Gottschalk, the European diva Adelina Patti, Lilli Lehmann, Marie Van Zandt, Ole Bull, Ignacy Jan Paderewski, Fritz Kreisler, and Josef Hofmann, the "Wonderful Child-Pianist." Big names were needed to fill such a large auditorium. The more prosperous members of Brooklyn's immigrant population, which had grown exponentially at the turn of the century, wanted to see luminaries from their native lands.

Sad to say, the first Academy building on Montague Street was not properly maintained for much of its later history; repairs were deferred or done on the cheap, and it developed a reputation as a "dirty old palace of art." Even sadder, it burst into flames and burned to the ground in a single day, November 30, 1903. Inadequate water pressure for fire hoses and the preponderance of wood inside the building, in balconies and supports, made its complete destruction inevitable. "The heat in the street was so intense that plate glass windows two hundred feet away were cracked and shattered. . . . With the effect of a volcano the roof crashed down into the flames, carrying everything before it and sending up a great shower of sparks almost to the height of a skyscraper," reported the *New York Herald* the next day. A few weeks later that same newspaper carried a follow-up story with the headline "A FIRETRAP DESTROYED," and pronounced the fire a "blessing to Brooklyn." Others took a more sentimental, melancholy tack: "Its every timber was filled with cherished memories. . . . The grim old pile was sacred to us," one reader wrote in the *Brooklyn Eagle*. Another called it "the finest of our Brooklyn buildings and quite the equal of any theater built in America or abroad in the last sixty years."

Total damages were estimated at $273,000, but New York real estate being what it was and is, a development group came forward immediately and offered the Academy's directors $600,000 for the site—the charred but still valuable land on Montague Street. Ironically, the Academy's stock rose after the fire like a phoenix from the ashes. With some cash in hand from the land sale, the directors lost no time starting to raise the rest of the money—over one million dollars—to erect a bigger, better, and safer structure. There was never any doubt that the Academy should be rebuilt, and soon. Brooklyn would "die socially, educationally, musically and to some extent politically" without a new Academy of Music, wrote one *Eagle* reader in a letter. In the interim, concerts, recitals, and lectures were held at substitute Brooklyn locations, including the Baptist Temple, Association Hall, and the historic Plymouth Church.

Martin W. Littleton, the Brooklyn borough president who spearheaded the rebuilding drive, sent an appeal to prominent Brooklynites, out of which would grow the so-called Committee of 100: "We have made up our minds, that with your help and the help of Brooklyn people, an Academy of Music can be built. I know it is not necessary for me to urge upon you the many reasons why we need in Brooklyn

Ignacy Jan Paderewski, 1895. Photo courtesy of BAM Hamm Archives Center

such an Academy, for we all feel that there should be a place where our ever swelling population might gather to gratify its passion for music, to satisfy its thirst for knowledge, to minister to its love for social communion and to appeal to its patriotism in the great struggles of popular politics." Note how these multiple uses were already woven into its identity. For better or worse, it has never been possible for the Brooklyn Academy of Music to dedicate itself entirely as a musical venue in the manner of Carnegie Hall, the Metropolitan Opera, La Scala, or most renowned concert halls. The Academy has always had to juggle expectations of high art and community function, to play a local civic role as well as a world-class cultural role. That necessity has been both its burden and glory—its destiny, in a word.

Rebirth and Revival

The new Brooklyn Academy of Music was incorporated on April 13, 1904, and ground was broken for the building in the following year. The site chosen to house the Academy, on Lafayette Avenue between Ashland Place and St. Felix Street, was at the edge of two neighborhoods, Fort Greene and downtown Brooklyn. With Fort Greene's elegant brick row houses and brownstones, the planned convergence of train lines—the city's mass transit and the regional Long Island Rail Road—and the site's proximity to the major traffic arteries of Flatbush and Atlantic Avenues as well as to the commercial district of Fulton Street, with its department stores and movie theaters, the new location seemed poised to become the next hot area, the very next heart of Brooklyn. We must defer for the moment the question of why this did not come to pass, and merely note that it seemed a wise decision at the time. The October 15, 1908, issue of *Architecture* magazine deemed it "without question . . . the best site in Brooklyn."

A design competition was held for the selection of an architect, and this time the Academy's directors elected to go with a firm that specialized in theater architecture. Henry B. Herts and Hugh Tallant— "who are perhaps only beginning to receive their due as being among the best architects of New

The Brooklyn Academy of Music, Brooklyn, N.

York City," notes architectural historian Francis Morrone—were responsible for the gorgeous Art Nouveau–style New Amsterdam Theater, the Beaux Arts–style Lyceum Theater, the Liberty, the Gaiety, and the lavish Folies Bergère (later the Helen Hayes Theater); after they dissolved their partnership, Herts went on to design the Shubert, the Booth, and the Longacre. Herts and Tallant were superb not only at elegant exteriors and poetic interiors but at the technical and acoustic aspects of theatrical construction. They surpassed themselves in meeting the complex challenges of the new Academy of Music, giving Brooklyn, in Morrone's opinion—and most of us would concur—"one of the borough's great buildings."

The structure had to be massive and supple to satisfy the varied purposes envisioned for it: musical, educational, dramatic, and social. There would be a 2,200-seat opera house; a 1,400-seat concert hall, with the illustrious Frothingham pipe organ, primarily for chamber music and popular lectures; a 400-seat lecture hall; a large ballroom or banquet hall, 40 feet wide and 180 feet long, accommodating at least 600 people, for "those civic and social gatherings which will enable us to meet face to face, to take each other by the hand, and to feel our common duties as citizens of a great City and of a great Republic"; plus a spate of classrooms and administrative offices, all under one roof. The main facade of the building, in the Italian Renaissance style, was composed of cream-colored brick above a gray granite base—marble had been initially proposed but rejected as too expensive—and the architects made it a point to order bricks with as rough and variegated a texture as possible to avoid the flat wallpaper look of much modern brick. Singled out for special praise was the innovative, ornamental use of polychromatic terra cotta. The handsome cornice, mingling blue, red, yellow, and sienna colors, contained 22 full-sized lion heads with red tongues. Along the top of the building were carved the names of famous opera and symphony composers. Of note, the ornate cornice was removed in 1952, due to physical deterioration that was deemed too costly to repair. Later, the historic preservation community lamented its destruction, and the cornice was replaced in 2004 as part of the building's renovation.

The building's main facade ran 190 feet down the entire block of Lafayette Avenue and included five metal doors through which all were expected to enter, thereby circulating guests through a grand foyer of 5,000 square feet before siphoning them off to their respective events. And of course the building was fireproofed to within an inch of its life. *Brooklyn Life* assured its readers of "the pains taken to ensure the safety of the public. With the structural work of brick and steel and the floors all of dolomite laid over cement, there will be comparatively little to burn and that little will have scant chance against the downpour of water from the huge tanks on the roofs that will

Frieda Hempel, *Bulletin of the Brooklyn Institute of Arts and Sciences,* 1921. Courtesy of BAM Hamm Archives Center

be operated automatically." The mural decorations were entrusted to the American Impressionist painter William de Leftwich Dodge, who had earlier adorned the Library of Congress. This time there were also plenty of plaster putti, generating another controversy thanks to their exposed genitalia; the architects agreed to drape the private parts of only those putti closest to the audience.

The cornerstone was laid on May 25, 1907, and the building was completed on September 15, 1908. The present home of the Brooklyn Academy of Music opened a mere five years after the fire, first with a recital on October 1, 1908, by the popular mezzo-soprano Madame Ernestine Schumann-Heink, and then with an inaugural gala performance on November 14 in the Opera House of Charles Gounod's *Faust,* featuring Geraldine Farrar and Enrico Caruso. The operatic and symphonic components carried on in the new building with renewed passion and distinction. "Indeed, what followed was what might be called the second Golden Age of Music in Brooklyn, if we consider the last 10 to 15 years of Theodore Thomas's tenure the first Golden Age," wrote Maurice Edwards. "Starting with that first year of the new Academy, the Metropolitan Opera was invited annually to present full seasons in Brooklyn. Thus during the new Academy's first winter season, Brooklynites were privileged to hear [Arturo] Toscanini conduct the Met, and during the second, [Gustav] Mahler. . . . Most of the great stars—including [Nellie] Melba, Farrar, and Caruso—appeared there frequently." In addition to their operatic roles, many of the major

Enrico Caruso in *Pagliacci*.
Photo: Hulton Archive

by John Yohalem

Long before radio broadcasting began, the Metropolitan Opera earned national fame by touring the nation. In San Francisco, Enrico Caruso's Don José in *Carmen* on April 17, 1906, is sometimes associated with setting off the earthquake that leveled the city hours later. Trapped in a quivering hotel, Caruso vowed never to return—but soon he was drawing witty caricatures of his distraught fellow singers. Caruso's cartoons of musicians were almost as well known as his voice; he gave them to friends and editors, refusing remuneration: "I can't take money for something that gives me so much pleasure."

The Met often visited the Brooklyn Academy of Music, at the uncomfortable first Academy building on Montague Street, and then at the elegant new structure whose Opera House was inaugurated by the Met's company on November 14, 1908, with Charles Gounod's *Faust*, starring Caruso and Geraldine Farrar. Caruso, then 35 years old, had made his Met debut in *Rigoletto* on opening night of the 1903 season, and the beauty and size of his voice—and his across-the-footlights charm—made him more than a public figure: a popular hero. He sang every Met opening night but one in the 17 seasons that followed, and he brought many of his most famous roles to the Academy, in *Aida*, *La Gioconda*, *Tosca*, *Marta*, *La Juive*, and *Pagliacci*. Unusual among tenors of his— or any—generation, he was as effective in gracious, old-fashioned bel canto operas like *L'Elisir d'Amore* as in the new, more intense creations of Puccini and Leoncavallo, as well as in the stentorian hero roles of French grand opera, such as Samson and Vasco da Gama.

Caruso's voice, suave musicianship, and personal magnetism would have made him famous in any era, but he happened to be the foremost tenor in the Italian repertory when electronic recording was perfected and was among the first musicians to exploit the new technology successfully. As a result, he became the first singer with a worldwide public—millions knew and loved the sound of his voice, even if they had never been within a thousand miles of an opera house.

singers were also heard in recital, including Frieda Hempel, Johanna Gadski, Maria Jeritza, Louise Homer, and Feodor Chaliapin. Among the musicians featured were many of the most prominent pianists, including Percy Grainger and Sergei Rachmaninoff, and violinists, such as Jan Kubelik, Jascha Heifetz, Mischa Elman, and Efrem Zimbalist.

In the early years of the new Academy, there were also visits by the Boston Symphony Orchestra, conducted by Max Fiedler; the New York Philharmonic; and the newly formed New York Symphony Orchestra, led by Walter Damrosch. Notable operatic performances included Geraldine Farrar in *Madame Butterfly*, Emma Eames in *Tosca*, Leo Slezak in *Otello*, Emmy Destinn in *Aida*, Lucrezia Bori and Umberto Macnez in *Rigoletto*, and Alma Gluck in *La Bohème* as well as recitals by Irish tenor John McCormack, Yvette Guilbert, and Mary Jordan. The most dramatic moment in Academy history occurred on December 11, 1920, when Enrico Caruso, by now a regular at the Academy, while singing Nemorino in Act 1 of Donizetti's *L'Elisir d'Amore*, suffered a throat hemorrhage and began to spit blood. "Members of the chorus passed him towels which he coughed into and then dropped in the pit," wrote David McCullough. Local legend

has it that he died that night onstage, but the story is apocryphal and the Academy can only take credit—or discredit—for hastening his end, which occurred nine months later in Naples, Italy. Yet simultaneously the Academy attended to the needs of other segments of the community—the Anti-Profanity League threw a "benefit concert for the relief of the people of Southern Italy who have been affected by Earthquake, Fire and Tidal Wave," the Association of Master Plumbers sponsored a dance, the Orphan Asylum Society of Brooklyn held a Diamond Festival Ball, a reception was given for Ireland's diplomatic mission. In short, it was business as usual.

The Brooklyn Institute of Arts and Sciences

What was different about the new Academy was the extensive educational program that it offered, which turned the Lafayette Avenue building into a kind of "open university." Public lectures being a form of popular entertainment at the time, there were, as before, addresses by public figures such as Booker T. Washington, William Jennings Bryan, Jacob Riis, and the young Winston Churchill; former presidents William H. Taft and Theodore Roosevelt, the latter on "What it Means to be an American," as well as future presidents Woodrow Wilson, Franklin D. Roosevelt, and Calvin Coolidge; poets of the day like Carl Sandburg, Edna St. Vincent Millay, and Rabindranath Tagore; noted authors like H. G. Wells, Sinclair Lewis, and Sherwood Anderson; sudden celebrities such as Helen Keller and her teacher Anne Sullivan; Rear Admiral Robert E. Peary on "The Discovery of the North Pole"; and aviator Amelia Earhart—not to mention a presentation on Oberammergau and the Passion Play, illustrated by "A Very Complete Series of Lantern Photographs," and an ongoing series by the ever-popular Burton Holmes, the American traveler, photographer, and filmmaker whose documentary "travelogues" introduced Brooklynites to the world and brought the world to Brooklyn.

More intriguing was the expanded roster of educational courses and lectures given weekly at the Academy by its self-styled departments: among them, philology, geology, philosophy, pedagogy, music, political science, entomology, electricity, and microscopy. All of these classes and talks were sponsored by the Brooklyn Institute of Arts and Sciences, a cultural and educational institution founded in 1823 as the Brooklyn Apprentices' Library (later the Brooklyn Institute). The Institute was reincorporated and renamed in 1890 and in that same year merged with the Brooklyn Academy of Music. As an umbrella organization of the borough's major cultural institutions, the Brooklyn Institute of Arts and Sciences

ANNA PAVLOWA

The Incomparable

Mime

Assisted by

LAURENT NOVIKOFF

and

ALEXANDRE VOLININE

Her

Ballet Russe

and

Symphony

Orchestra

Two Ballets, "Coppelia," by Delibes, and "Flora's Awakening," by Drigo, will be introduced in addition to the usual divertissements.

Thursday Evening, October 16 at 8:15 o'clock	OPERA HOUSE	ACADEMY OF MUSIC

Tickets Now on Sale

To Members with Weekly Ticket..........................$1.00, $1.50, $2.00; Boxes, $2.00, $2.50, $3.00
To Persons not Members ....$1.50, $2.00, $2.50; Boxes, $2.50, $3.00, $3.50

No War Tax

50

would come to include the Brooklyn Museum, the Brooklyn Children's Museum, and the Brooklyn Botanic Garden; for over half a century, it was joined at the hip to the Brooklyn Academy of Music, and in retrospect it is unclear whether the Institute swallowed the Academy or the Academy swallowed the Institute. Without question, however, the Institute played a significant role in the development of the present-day Brooklyn Academy of Music.

The relationship between the Institute and the Academy originated at the old Montague Street building, where the Institute had offered a modest program of lectures. But in the plans for the new Academy of Music, the Institute, which at this point was more fiscally solvent than the Academy, decided to move in and share the new facility and help defray costs, while greatly increasing its educational offerings—hence part of the need for such a large building, with lecture hall, classrooms, and a floor of administrative offices. In effect, the above-mentioned disciplines were not "academic" departments, in the sense that the term is understood today. However, even if they were skeletal one-person affairs, it is admirable that the Institute was able to field such an ambitious, encyclopedic enterprise. It is hard to picture even the spatial arrangements of such an endeavor, except as a rabbit warren of desks occupying the third floor of the new building.

"The lectures are too numerous to count, unless one sums up the whole with the public addresses and exhibitions, which reach a total of 490, afternoon and evening events under the auspices of the Brooklyn Institute," summarized the *Musical Courier*. "If every man and woman in Brooklyn cannot find 'culture' now, it will not be the fault of . . . the Brooklyn Institute." These courses and talks were offered to the general public for a nominal admission fee. The underlying assumption was that the average person had a right to the world's knowledge; one did not have to be admitted to an institute of higher learning to listen to a discourse on the new physics or the new poetry. The Brooklyn Institute often drew on university faculty for its lecturers, in return offering instructors the soul-broadening chance "to meet audiences non-academic in character, but made up of people who are in the midst of the problems of life and thought." The Institute's offerings at the Academy became a model for what would develop into university extension teaching, a fact of which it was proudly aware: "The work that was commenced . . . at the Institute . . . is now being done by hundreds of other institutions throughout the country— notably by Columbia University, the University of Chicago, the Society of University Extension Teaching in Philadelphia."

Under the tireless direction of Franklin W. Hooper from 1888 to 1914, the Institute also issued a twice-monthly *Bulletin*, which was overtly patri- archal and unapologetically stodgy. In addition to items about upcoming events at the Academy, there were articles of general interest and edification, about paintings in the Metropolitan Museum, the Battle of Brooklyn in the Revolutionary War, Halley's Comet, and a plethora of obituaries. The *Bulletin* regularly carried photographs of distinguished gray-bearded, bald-pated men, reminiscent of the founding fathers, with clearly gerontophilic enthusiasm—such as no magazine would dare today, at the risk of alienating its youthful demographic. There were event announce- ments and program descriptions as well as advertise- ments for fur coats, Columbia phonograph records, Sohmer pianos, and oriental rugs. The *Bulletin*, despite the democratic philosophy of the organization's educational program, was addressed largely to the Institute's higher-income, paid-subscription base.

In one issue, we find the following message to opera subscribers: "Please notice that at the end of the performance carriages will advance to the carriage exits on Ashland Place and St. Felix Street in order as they stand *and not in response to carriage calls*. The numbers of the first carriages in line on both side streets will be posted on number carrying machines, one at each end, in the main lobby, thereby notifying patrons that the numbers announced are approaching the exits. Patrons are requested to stay inside the main lobby in order that they may see their numbers when placed on the indicators, and thus avoid congestion at the doors. They may pass into the outer lobbies at each end of the main lobby when their carriage numbers are posted. They are urgently requested to take their carriages as quickly as possible—if they do not their carriages will have to move on and again take their place in the line later on."

The leading families who frequented the Academy in its early years still had to choose between arriving in their own carriages or taking a horse- drawn equivalent of a cab—a decision magnified by the appearance of the motor car—but what made their situation more poignant was the knowledge that merely by their attending an opera in Brooklyn, their social brethren across the river would scorn them for being in that leprous category Edith Wharton described in her novel *The Age of Innocence* as peren- nial "new people." After the consolidation of the five boroughs in 1898, there was no longer any hope of Brooklyn's competing meaningfully with Manhattan as a "sister city." The fact that oil magnate John D. Rockefeller, a prominent fixture in New York society and a virtual stranger to the Academy, had donated $20,000 to the new building meant it was also no longer possible to boast that every nickel had been raised in Brooklyn, which represented a turning point in the history of the institution.

A figure of three million annual users had been projected—too optimistically—for the new Brooklyn Academy of Music. The September 17, 1910, *Bulletin* was able to boast that the Department of Music "has

Isadora Duncan. Photo: MPI

by Rachel Straus

Before the rise of Isadora Duncan, dance in America was a vaudevillian entertainment, closer in spirit to the circus than the opera house. But with the 1898 revival of the Olympic Games, the alteration of dance's reputation commenced. Duncan, a San Francisco–born ingenue, surmised that if the roots of dance stemmed from ancient Greece, birthplace of the Olympics, then its low reputation in puritanical America might receive reconsideration. When a U.S. newspaper announced in 1901—"Like an Ancient Greek Bas-Relief Come to Life She Astonishes Paris"—Duncan's goal of transforming dance into art with a capital "A" had begun.

Duncan further consecrated dance by connecting it to avatars of individualism, Walt Whitman and Friedrich Nietzsche. With this intellectual staging, she redefined the female dancer as one who authors her own movement. Her muse was none other than herself. Casting off the Victorian corset, Duncan employed her entire body to explore weightlessness—and gravity. She shirked ballet's five positions of the feet for continuous motion based on walking, skipping, running, and leaping. She spurned the idea of physical control, replacing it with corporeal release. Yearning and searching became her subject matter. Duncan broke convention, devoting entire evenings to solo dancing. Through romantic music—Schubert, Chopin, Gluck, Brahms— her body resembled a cresting wave, emotion upwelling from what she described as "the luminous manifestation of the soul." While Duncan's magnetic stage presence inspired, her extemporaneous political diatribes in criticism of capitalism incited controversy. She exhorted the rich to underwrite art.

In 1908, Duncan's troupe was the first dance company to perform at the Brooklyn Academy of Music, paving the way for modern dance; previously, operas that included ballet sections had been presented. However, in 1913, tragedy struck Duncan when her two children drowned. She created one of her most dramatic dances, *Marseillaise*, in response to her loss and the devastation wrought by World War I. Looking in performance less like a nymph and more like a monumental statue, she insisted—despite considerable outcry—that symphonic works were suitable for dancing. In 1927, her accidental death by strangulation immortalized her fame. In three decades, Duncan helped America embrace dance as a legitimate art form worthy of the opera house stage. She remains an icon of modern dance.

steadily grown until its present membership of 2,658. It is believed to be the largest musical organization in the United States." On the other hand, another *Bulletin* article at year's end warned that many thousands of dollars had been lost "in the giving of operas and concerts during the coming season. The chief lessons of the year have been that we have had too much opera, that too high prices have been paid to [operatic] artists"—that musicians in symphonies and chamber groups had been "underpaid" and attendance had suffered at their events.

The truth was that the extraordinarily diverse, distinguished musical fare being offered year-round at the Academy, whatever the genre, was not attracting audiences sufficiently large enough to break even. Even sold-out houses might not pay all the expenses of elaborate musical productions. The broader understanding that high culture could probably never pay for itself and that it would have to be subsidized, by either the state, corporate sponsorship, or both, had not yet sunk into general consciousness. The Academy, ignoring its deficits, persisted in trying to build over time an appreciation among the Brooklyn public for the best in classical music. As wryly noted by Marilyn V. Baum, the Brooklyn Academy of Music may have been not only the first performing arts center in America but also "the first to introduce the concept of deficit spending in the arts." Debt would continue to plague the Academy. However, for the moment, its successful educational lecture program was helping to subsidize its musical offerings.

Dance and Theater

In its new home, the Brooklyn Academy of Music became increasingly hospitable to dance, and to the emerging American art dance in particular. Isadora Duncan was innovating the solo dance, molding, in skimpily draped outfits, poses drawn from Greek statues into a flowing sequence of movements, at the same time as she was pioneering choreography to symphonic music rather than pieces written expressly for dance. On December 15, 1908, Duncan danced on the Academy stage to three movements from Beethoven's Symphony No. 7, with Walter Damrosch conducting his New York Symphony Orchestra. In 1910, Anna Pavlova (or Pavlowa) performed the first of a series of engagements with her partner Mikhail Mordkin, introducing Brooklyn audiences to the pointed-toe techniques of classical Russian ballet. Ruth St. Denis, the high priestess of mystic dance, appeared with her company in the following year and returned in 1923 with her husband and manager, Ted Shawn, and the exotic Denishawn dancers. "The standard Denishawn concert evening began with a benediction," wrote Elizabeth Kendall in her book *Where She Danced*, "Ted Shawn in long white robes dancing 'The Lord Is My Shepherd'; it wended its way through a variety of Duncan-and-Pavlova-esque 'Nature Rhythms,' some St. Denis–style Orientale vignettes, and finished up on a modern note: a mix of ballroom duos and Ballets Russes–type solos—in all, 33 dances."

In the 1930s, Shawn would bring his own company, Ted Shawn and His Men Dancers, to the Academy. But by then a new force had galvanized the American art dance—Martha Graham, originally trained in Denishawn, purified what had once been semi-amateurish eclecticism into a hieratic, ceremonial spectacle, at once more intellectually rigorous, more psychologically intense, and more formally shaped. Graham was both an extraordinary soloist and an ensemble choreographer, dedicated to teaching. Her first appearance at the Academy was on February 24, 1933; thereafter, she performed frequently at the Academy throughout her career. Other modern dance companies to perform at the Academy during the same period included those led by Doris Humphrey and Charles Weidman (with José Limón), Anna Sokolow, Hanya Holm, and Helen Tamiris.

Theater in the new Academy did not flourish as robustly as dance. There were too many competing legitimate playhouses in Manhattan and in Brooklyn to justify a full-fledged dramatic schedule, and indeed the Academy hosted no theatrical events between 1911 and 1915. Nevertheless, before and after that interregnum, there were significant moments. Before: *The Warrens of Virginia*, produced by David Belasco, with Mary Pickford, Emma Dunn, and Blanche Yurka; the Ben Greet Players performing plays by

Shakespeare; a series of dramatic readings by Leland Powers; productions by the New Theatre Company of *Twelfth Night* and John Galsworthy's *Strife*, with Maude Adams and John Drew; as well as an engagement by the venerable actress Ellen Terry. And after: beginning in 1916, when Sarah Bernhardt made her Academy debut, followed by the next year, when she returned to the Academy at age 73, post–leg amputation, and triumphed in the role of Camille, also playing Mme. X, Hecuba, Joan of Arc, Cleopatra, and L'Aiglon—all told, six roles in three nights and three matinees. Bernhardt breathed new life into the Academy, and in the next decade many major American and European actors would appear on the Academy's stage, including Ruth Draper, Walter Hampden in the role of Hamlet, Cornelia Otis Skinner, romantic actor E. H. Sothern, and the widely popular British actress Mrs. Patrick Campbell.

Growing Brooklyn and the Great Depression

By 1923 Brooklyn's population had grown to more than two million inhabitants. It was growing faster than any other locality in the country; apartment houses, tenements, and one- or two-story family houses popped up seemingly overnight, following the subway and bus lines that had penetrated deeply into the borough. The good news for the Academy was that it now had a much larger population base from which to draw. The bad news was that the borough's geographical area was now so far-flung, so extensive, that it became difficult to think of Brooklyn as having a center, and the train lines were all so connected to Manhattan that it was as easy to get to Carnegie Hall or the Metropolitan Opera from Far Rockaway as it was to get to Lafayette Avenue and Ashland Place.

José Limón and Charles Weidman in rehearsal, 1939. Photo: Gjon Mili

In 1929, the Academy gained a new neighbor half a block away: the Williamsburgh Savings Bank, for many years the tallest and only skyscraper in Brooklyn. It has since developed iconic status as a symbol of Brooklyn; at the time, it seemed proof, if proof were needed, that the immediate area around the Academy of Music was destined to become the borough's true magnet. But 1929 was famous for another reason, as we know—the start of the Great Depression. It put the kibosh on neighborhood development and started a steep decline in Fort Greene's property values. As the business community faltered, so did donations, contributions, and ticket sales dramatically ebb. Undaunted, or perhaps deciding that tough times required distraction, the Academy mounted in its 1933–34 season a stream of headliners, Maurice Edwards recounts: "singers Lotte Lehmann, Richard Crooks, and Lawrence Tibbett; pianists Walter Gieseking, Artur Schnabel, and Vladimir Horowitz; violinists [Jascha] Heifetz, [Nathan] Milstein, and [Yehudi] Menuhin; guitar great [Andrés] Segovia; plus the American Society of Ancient Instruments and the Ballet Russe de Monte Carlo." In addition, there were performances by Martha Graham and La Argentina, recitals by Lily Pons and José Iturbi, and lectures by Frank Lloyd Wright, Edward Steichen, Gertrude Stein, and Theodore Dreiser. Yet unfortunately, at the same time, some of the Academy's alliances with other institutions began to unravel. Due to budgetary constraints, the New York Philharmonic and the Metropolitan Opera stopped visiting the Academy, in 1933 and 1936, respectively.

Here let us note the differing fortunes of the Academy's musical programs and the Institute's educational offerings. A mildly gloating letter from the Institute's then director, Charles D. Atkins, in April 1932 states, "We are in the home stretch of the most hectic season ever faced, breathing a bit heavily from the depression, otherwise sound in all activities. Music events have taken a steep nose dive and will not, I fear, ever recover, but in general lectures it would not be a surprise to find we have set a new peak in attendance for the year." In that same year, Atkins wrote a friend, "The Brooklyn Academy of Music (not the Institute) is in a bad way financially; it is the only home we have and the Trustees fear, I believe, that we will have it on our hands before long. They have just had to place a second mortgage of $100,000 on the Building of which we have taken $25,000." This letter was prescient: as it transpired, the Institute would have to bail out its impecunious landlord. "In the years following the opening of the new Academy," wrote Marilyn V. Baum, "the Institute assumed more and more of the Academy's financial responsibilities. In return, the Academy stockholders gradually donated up to 40 of their corporation shares to the Institute. But the Academy's annual deficits became increasingly larger. The reported deficit for 1935 was $47,000, and the accumulated deficit was $445,508. . . . The Academy went bankrupt in 1935 and had to be saved from foreclosure and possible demolition. At this point, Brooklyn Borough President Raymond V. Ingersoll stepped in with a plan to save the Academy."

Essentially, Ingersoll brokered a shotgun marriage by which the reluctant Institute would take complete ownership of the Academy, which it did in 1936 by purchasing the facility to provide a permanent home for the Institute. A fundraising drive was formed to subscribe 5,000 new members to the Institute as a means of generating the necessary additional funds for the transaction.

The Julius Bloom Era

An institution does not survive 100 years, much less a remarkable 150, without a few dedicated, inspiring leaders along the way. Julius Bloom began working at the Academy in 1936, about the same time the financial deal to rescue it was being put into place; in 1938, he was promoted to associate director, and two years later, in 1940, he was named the director. From the beginning of his tenure, he faced one budget crisis after another but did not slacken in his determination to offer the best cultural fare to Brooklyn, in the process turning the Academy into what *Variety* called "the biggest show biz factory in the world." In addition to running the Major Concert Series with headliners and further promoting modern dance as an Academy staple, Bloom started an "Appreciation Series," in which artists gave lectures and recitals to demonstrate their art. The calendar of events for the 1938–39 season, for example, included recitals by Jascha Heifetz, Kirsten Flagstad, Marian Anderson, Jussi Björling, Myra Hess, and Yehudi Menuhin; the Boston Symphony Orchestra, conducted by Serge Koussevitzky, and the Budapest String Quartet; dance performances by the Ballet Russe de Monte Carlo, Doris Humphrey, Esther Junger, and Uday Shankar, the pioneer of modern dance in India; and lectures by Carl Sandburg, Bertrand Russell, Thomas Mann, composer Aaron Copland, and the dance critic John Martin. Extending the concept of adult education to bring more people into the building, he also offered the community "a variety of courses and clubs on astronomy, natural history, photography, creative writing, foreign languages, and child care," reported Geoffrey S. Cahn in his article "Rebirth, Struggle, and Revival: The Brooklyn Academy of Music, 1908–Present." Bloom was especially keen, Cahn noted, in reviving the Chess Club, which he accomplished and which attracted the 12-year-old Bobby Fischer, future grandmaster and world champion, who honed his skills at the Academy.

"A voice like yours is heard only once in a hundred years."
ARTURO TOSCANINI

"One of the greatest living singers."—THE NEW YORK TIMES.

"A voice that ranks with the first of the world." —CHICAGO TRIBUNE.

MARIAN ANDERSON

GREAT AMERICAN NEGRO CONTRALTO

In Recital

MONDAY EVENING   MARCH 28

at 8:30 o'clock

OPERA HOUSE   ACADEMY OF MUSIC

ELEVENTH RECITAL IN THE SERIES

Music and the Dance

STANDING ROOM ONLY: Members, $1; Non-Members, $1.50.   NO TAX

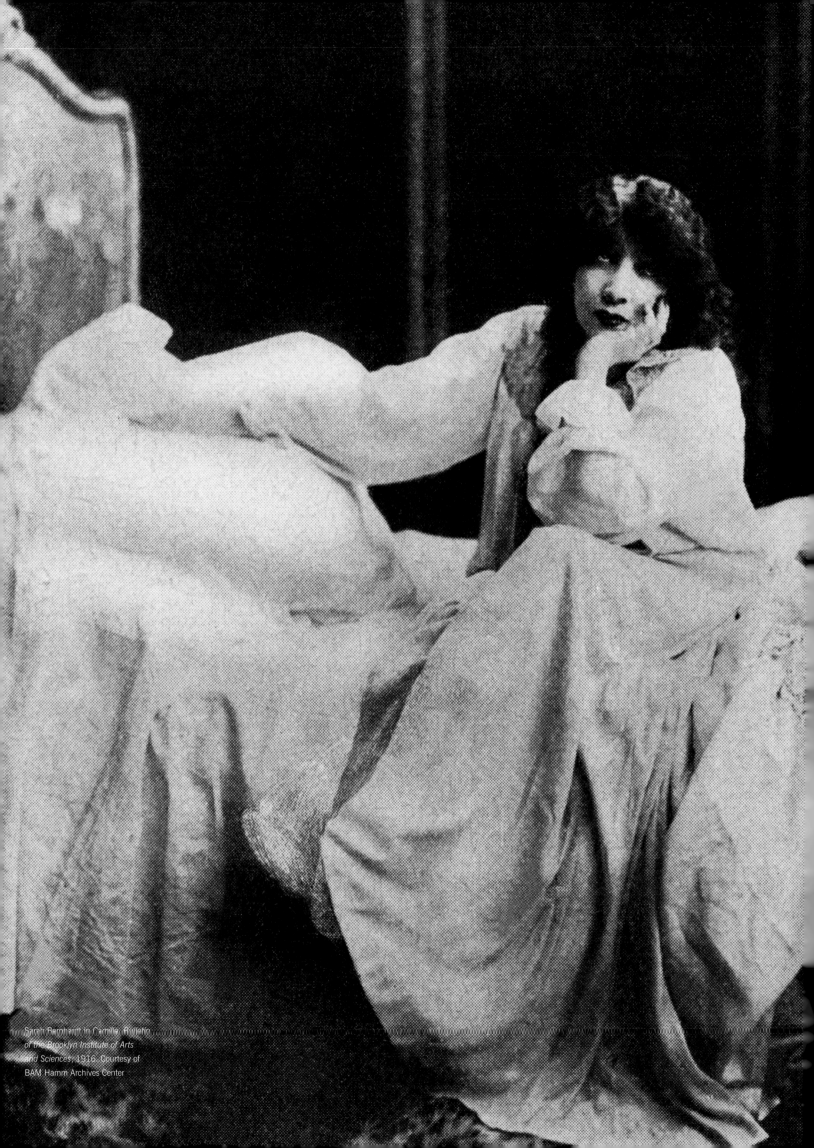

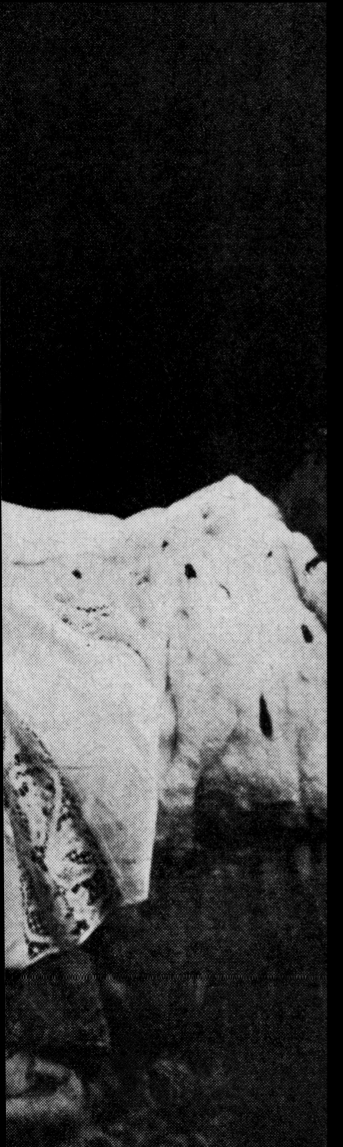

by Roger Oliver

Mark Twain once wrote, "There are five kinds of
actresses: bad actresses, fair actresses, good actresses,
great actresses—and then there is Sarah Bernhardt."
He was far from alone in his adulation. Victor Hugo,
Oscar Wilde, D. H. Lawrence, and even Sigmund
Freud sang her praises in extravagant terms. American
stage actress Laurette Taylor deemed that Bernhardt
reigned when "the theatre was so magnificent as to
be almost unreal," while Ellen Terry, the queen of an
English acting dynasty, called her nothing less than
"a miracle." In a career that encompassed more than
150 roles and 10,000 performances, she became
known simply as "The Divine Sarah."

Born in Paris, Bernhardt established her reputation on
the Parisian stage playing classic and contemporary
roles at the Comédie-Française and the Odéon. Forming her own company, she became one of the first
international superstars, touring throughout the rest
of Europe and Great Britain as well as Denmark,
Russia, Egypt, Australia, and even Tahiti. She made
nine tours of the United States, traveling at one point
on a private train from coast to coast. Her repertoire
ranged from classic roles, including Racine's Phèdre,
Lady Macbeth, and the title role of Hamlet, to historical
figures Cleopatra and Joan of Arc, to such melodramatic
characters as Tosca, Fédora, and Théodora, written
expressly for her by Victorien Sardou, and—perhaps
her signature role—the ill-fated courtesan Marguerite
Gautier, the "lady" of the camellias. She first appeared
at the Brooklyn Academy of Music in 1916 and returned
the following year, despite a leg amputation, to portray
six different roles in six performances.

The descriptions of her performances as well as the
many photographs taken during her career suggest a
larger-than-life quality to her acting that emphasized
passion and extravagance more than verisimilitude
and nuance. Arguably the most famous actress of the
19th century, Bernhardt was at once scandalous and
eccentric, formidable and seductive—a woman of
independence whose private life paralleled the flamboyance and intensity she brought to the stage.

Sarah Bernhardt

Erick Hawkins (featured) in *Appalachian Spring*, Martha Graham Dance Company, 1944. Photo: Jerry Cooke

One of Bloom's projects was to try to revive the Brooklyn Philharmonic, long dormant since the defection of Theodore Thomas to Chicago. He pulled together a professional orchestra under the troika leadership of three young directors in 1941, and for the second season he snared Sir Thomas Beecham, then in New York as conductor at the Metropolitan Opera, to moonlight at the helm of the revived Brooklyn orchestra. "And indeed, Sir Thomas stayed on to lead a four-concert series in the Opera House, the second program of which featured Virgil Thomson's suite, *The River*." The concerts were received ecstatically by the press, and Bloom's hopes and those of many others were high. "Beecham himself was ready to carry on," wrote Maurice Edwards. The great conductor refused to believe that Brooklyn could not maintain an orchestra presenting concerts regularly throughout the season: "What are four concerts a year in a city of I-don't-know-how-many millions? . . . Immortality is in front of us. I'm throwing you the challenge." But the challenge proved too daunting, even with such a world-renowned musical star as Beecham promoting it; there was insufficient long-range support for the undertaking, and the dream of a Brooklyn orchestra was once again put on hold.

It would seem that the moneyed elite of Kings County—not all of them, not entirely, not immediately, but as a class—had begun to drift away from supporting local Brooklyn institutions, or at least from adopting them as their special arena for the enactment of social prestige. The Great Depression of 1929, which lasted through the 1930s, had dried up a considerable

amount of available funding and caused those with money to be cautious about donating it or making a public display. No longer sure the spectacle of their wealth would be appreciated as it once was by the masses, as in the days when social lions drove carriages each afternoon through Prospect Park, they began to lie low. Not that there was a shortage of well-heeled people in the borough, but wealthy Brooklynites with aspirations to social position were slowly coming round to the realization that acceptance into the upper regions of society ultimately depended on their getting placed on the boards of opera companies, symphony orchestras, museums, universities, and hospitals in Manhattan. Thus began the gradual process by which the Brooklyn Academy of Music, originally established for the "Beauty, Wealth and Fashion of Brooklyn in their own Opera House," as an 1861 *Brooklyn Eagle* headline put it, evolved into an institution catering to a more middle-class clientele. As for the millions who had swarmed into the borough, causing its population to swell to a peak of 2,738,000 by 1950, most were poor, working-class immigrants who were too busy trying to survive to contemplate paying for an evening at the symphony.

The Academy was again on the brink of financial collapse in 1951–52, and there was serious thought given to selling the building to Long Island University for $550,000. William Zeckendorf, the colorful realtor and chairman of the university's board of trustees, announced to the press that a deal had been struck for converting the building to classrooms, with the Opera House to be turned into a gymnasium. Again, a Brooklyn borough president, John Cashmore, stepped in and worked out a rescue operation, this time with a more permanent solution to save the Academy. In effect, the city of New York took title to the Brooklyn Academy of Music and leased it back to the Institute for 100 years at $1 a year. The city also promised to absorb the Academy's annual maintenance costs up to $75,000 a year. In addition, the Institute had to agree to operate the Academy as it had since 1936 and "to spend up to $250,000 on restorations."

Bloom continued to place his bets on big names, musical stars like Risë Stevens, Jan Peerce, and Helen Traubel, Vladimir Horowitz and Igor Stravinsky, Regina Resnik, Paul Robeson, and Rudolf Serkin, Patrice Munsel, Richard Tucker, and Roberta Peters; authors such as Aldous Huxley, Langston Hughes, Robert Frost, Pearl Buck, and Eugene O'Neill; actresses like Lillian Gish, Eva Le Gallienne, and Elsa Lanchester; and dance companies like Martha Graham, Agnes de Mille, and José Greco. He was even willing to flirt with the lesser-known avant-gardists. In 1948, Pearl Primus appeared with her company, and in 1952, Bloom launched the Theater for Dance with Merce Cunningham, Jean Erdman, Erick Hawkins, and Donald McKayle. He also initiated a series of dramatic readings that included Charles

Laughton, Sir Cedric Hardwicke, Charles Boyer, and Agnes Moorehead performing George Bernard Shaw's *Don Juan in Hell* as well as *John Brown's Body* by Stephen Vincent Benét, with Tyrone Power, Judith Anderson, and Raymond Massey. Simultaneously, he managed to get a resident orchestra off the ground yet again, this time as the Brooklyn Philharmonia under the inspired leadership of conductor Siegfried Landau. In 1955, he offered subscribers some 300 events for a $15 subscription fee, and the Academy drew an audience of half a million customers. But after that peak, attendance resumed its steep decline; the deficit kept growing.

A harried Bloom, running out of ideas for the Academy's salvation, gave an understandably bitter interview to a local journalist in the *New York Herald Tribune*: "Why is it . . . that a New Yorker who will pay $6.60 for a concert in Manhattan won't take a 20-minute subway ride to see the same program in a better concert hall with better acoustics and at one-half the price? Because it's in Brooklyn; something about the mere mention of the name makes New Yorkers smirk. . . . It takes every waking moment and a fair share of mumbling in my sleep to plot against the Brooklyn Prejudice and think of ways to bring people across the river and into the arts." In a sense, Bloom wanted it both ways. On the one hand, he would assert his local vision: "The Academy was under no obligation to compete with Carnegie Hall—an exalted national institution." He saw his mission as being "to create for the community what Carnegie Hall could in no way do." On the other hand, he would fume to a *Daily News* reporter: "Some people . . . would like to think of us as a country cousin. But there is no operation in Manhattan that has such a span of activity. I can't think of any type of program that is not represented here. . . . Just name it and we've got it."

With television in the 1950s keeping more and more of the Academy's former patrons at home, Bloom concluded, "Only the unique will draw cash customers from the other boroughs." So he tried to offer exclusive performances of name artists. But Carnegie Hall and the Metropolitan Opera continued to emit a mystical aura that convinced potential concertgoers that the music to be heard there was somehow better. The true "Brooklyn Problem," which Bloom could not bring himself to admit, was not just that the other boroughs were snobbishly condescending toward Brooklyn but that Brooklynites themselves were snobbish, conforming obediently only to signals from the national media centered in Manhattan, and would not take local offerings seriously unless they were first approved by authorities across the river. The larger paradox was that it wasn't enough for Brooklyn's most ambitious cultural institutions, such as the Academy of Music or the Brooklyn Museum, to ably serve the local population, however many millions that base

may contain; for them to succeed, they also had to win the respect and patronage of Gotham and the world beyond. Ironically, in 1957, Bloom abruptly quit the Academy after serving it for 20 years and moved to Manhattan to become the executive director of Carnegie Hall.

The Changing Neighborhood

Starting in the 1950s, Brooklyn fell into a social and economic decline as well as an emotional tailspin. It suffered a series of losses none of which seemed that significant at first but together proved devastating. First, the local breweries went out of business, then the *Brooklyn Eagle*, and then even the beloved Dodgers baseball team moved away, leaving Ebbets Field to the wrecking ball. Finally, the federal government closed down the Brooklyn Navy Yard. Brooklyn had been a stronghold of the working class, but when several hundred thousand manufacturing jobs left Brooklyn in the 1960s it broke the backs of the neighborhoods. Decades of massive disinvestment accompanied the

Agnes Moorehead, Charles Laughton, Charles Boyer, and Sir Cedric Hardwicke in *Don Juan in Hell*, George Bernard Shaw, 1951. Photo: John Chillingworth

deindustrialization process, starting with the redlining—the refusal to grant mortgages—by local banks of whole minority districts.

The original thinking behind situating factories in New York City, the densest population region, had been to take advantage of its large workforce and to minimize the cost of transporting goods to potential consumers. But by the 1950s, the unionized workers were commanding higher wages than elsewhere, and manufacturers began opening plants in the South as well as in Asia and Latin America. At the same time, the multistory factory had given way to a preference for one-story horizontal sheds that demanded more low-cost land than was available in metropolitan New York. The lack of sufficient back space for containerization also led to the transfer of the operation from Brooklyn and Manhattan to the ports of New Jersey. To complicate matters, thousands of migrants of color—African American, Hispanic, and West Indian—arrived in Brooklyn looking for work at precisely the moment when the borough was losing thousands of entry-level, unskilled jobs. In the same period, coincidentally or not, thousands of middle-class white families fled the city to pursue the suburban American dream. "Between 1940 and 1970 the middle-class white population moved to suburban areas, creating a loss of more than 682,000 people. The black population, generally poorer, had increased to 549,000," write Barbara Parisi and Robert Singer in *The History of Brooklyn's Three Major Performing Arts Institutions*.

One of the places in Brooklyn that African Americans settled from the 1950s onward was the Fort Greene–Bedford-Stuyvesant area. It had some beautiful housing stock—solid brownstones and five-story walk-up apartment buildings—but property values had been dropping since the Depression, and many stately homes had been sliced up into smaller units to accommodate the labor force at the Brooklyn Navy Yard. There were also a number of SRO (single-room occupancy) hotels that contained a goodly share of people on welfare, as well as public housing, like the Fort Greene projects, that began promisingly but became increasingly dangerous and blighted as they became racially segregated. During that time, a large part of the Academy's audience, it would seem, came from middle-class, mostly Jewish neighborhoods like Flatbush, where classical music was still revered and Metropolitan Opera radio broadcasts with Milton Cross, or the painful sounds of a child practicing the piano, could be heard. This was the milieu from which sprang Harvey Lichtenstein, who would try as quickly as possible, when he took over the institution in 1967, to attract audiences different from his parents' generation. These aging concertgoers were increasingly reluctant to venture into the neighborhood around the Academy, and would either make the excursion into Manhattan or sometimes attend concerts at other

more conveniently located venues like Brooklyn College's Center for the Performing Arts.

The area around the Academy was termed a "transitional zone," which is often code for decline, gentrification, or the invasion of one ethnic group and the flight of another. In urban design terms, what "transitional" means is neither here nor there. It must be said that, aside from the risk of crime, there was something about the specific environment around the Academy building that made it an awkward, not entirely appealing destination. Being in a transitional location between commercial and residential areas of Brooklyn, it was never properly integrated into either. It sat in a kind of cul-de-sac, cut off as it was by two major thoroughfares. To its west, scruffy Flatbush Avenue failed to became a fashionable shopping street and seemed more like a highway, a six-lane traffic conduit feeding into the Manhattan Bridge. Atlantic Avenue, to the south, was another intimidating, highway-like moat that was treacherous to cross on foot. It stood semi-derelict for decades, awaiting some grand development—originally, it had been offered to the Brooklyn Dodgers for a new stadium, but they chose to move west to Chavez Ravine in Los Angeles. Both Flatbush and Atlantic Avenues were subject to almost continual repairs and reconstructions, which fed the choppy experience of crossing a construction site to get to a monumental, somewhat forbidding music hall. Contributing to the impression of isolation was the fact that the Academy building's western flank did not abut directly on Flatbush Avenue but rested on two-block-long Ashland Place, which sliced off a triangular piece of street-pie just to the east of Flatbush. The building's entrance was cocooned on Lafayette, a rather short avenue that neighborhood people rarely used to get from one

Opposite: Rudolf Nureyev, backstage at BAM, 1962. Photo: Arthur Todd

Above: Pearl Lang. Photo: Ray Fisher

Martha Graham, *Bulletin of the Brooklyn Institute of Arts and Sciences*, 1933. Courtesy of BAM Hamm Archives Center

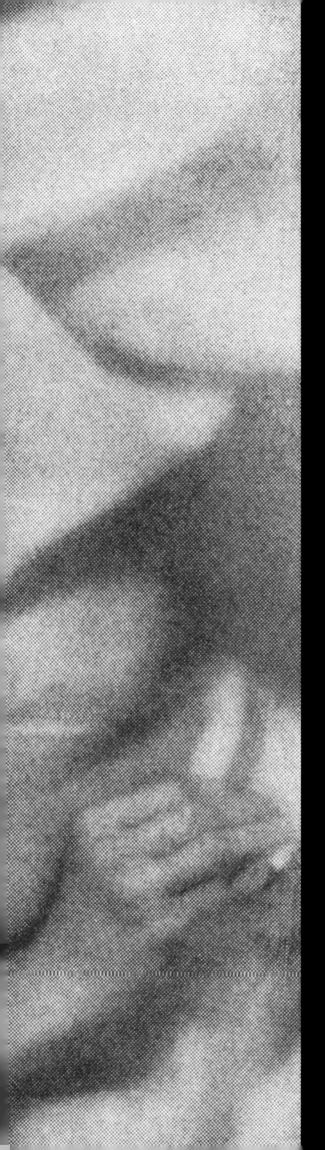

by Susan Yung

Martha Graham is, and will remain, one of the most influential choreographers in the history of modern dance. She created a rich, versatile technique that has held its own as an expressive language. When combined with the stories she carefully chose to tell, her dances reached operatic heights. The act of breathing, coaxed into a contraction, formed a cornerstone of Graham's technique. The related tilting of the pelvis provided an impetus for myriad movements. She used gestures and repeating linear patterns to evoke states of mind, mixing the body's organic curves and the jarring angles of flexed joints. Combined with sets, costumes, and music, her interpretations of Greek myths created indelible manifestations of age-old archetypes. She was unafraid to magnify and stare unflinchingly at the darkest of psychological states, but she was not above poking good fun at herself.

As dynamic an individual as she was on- and offstage, Graham was the consummate collaborator. Her artistic partnerships epitomized a collective effort; Noguchi's sets and Halston's costumes remain vivid in the mind's eye, in tandem with her choreography. She created weighty roles for her company's typically muscular men and physically challenging, searing portraits for the women—a number of which she performed, unforgettably. Many of her dancers developed their own remarkable styles and went on to form internationally renowned companies—Erick Hawkins, to whom she was married from 1948 to 1954, Pearl Lang, Merce Cunningham, and Paul Taylor, among others.

Graham's varied early experiences include dancing at Denishawn for eight years and performing in a revue. Teaching at Eastman School of Music, she developed her trademark style. She formed her company in 1926, ultimately choreographing 181 works. In 1933, her company first appeared at the Brooklyn Academy of Music, where it would return numerous times before the performances that took place in 1994 to celebrate the 100th anniversary of Graham's birth. After her death in 1991, the fate of her estate—most importantly, the rights to her dances—became the subject of heated dispute and has served as a cautionary lesson for choreographers. The company and school that bear her name continue to advance Graham's legacy, teaching her pliant technique and commissioning new work while keeping her powerful oeuvre vibrant.

place to another. It was quiet, a good thing for a music hall, but it felt deserted, with very little pedestrian traffic. Theaters in large cities are often placed at busy, floodlit intersections, dependent as they are on impulse customers who pass the marquee and think, *Why don't I go in and see if there are any tickets left?* Such was not the Academy's lot. If you encountered the building at all, it was likely because you had gone out of your way to seek it out.

Always Darkest Before the Dawn

The period following the departure of Julius Bloom through the mid-1960s is spoken of in the institutional literature as a dark time, when the Academy leased out part of its rooftop studios to a judo academy and its ballroom to a boys' prep school; when it went so far as to offer free gifts to subscribers that included a salad set, a three-piece set of luggage, a wonder knife, a hair dryer, and an electric coffeemaker; when it was reduced to renting out the Opera House to gospel revivals and "muscle shows"; and when it operated at only 30 percent of its capacity. There are two ways of looking at these facts: what an indignity, what a humiliation, the Academy had never sunk so low; or, isn't it kind of admirable that it was still plugging away, trying to recruit members by any means necessary, even salad bowls or patching in a judo school.

Pearl Primus. Photo: Baron

While it is true that the Academy enjoyed its finest hours when it benefited from visionary leaders such as Theodore Thomas, Franklin W. Hooper, Julius Bloom, and Harvey Lichtenstein, it is also true that for a nonprofit institution to survive 150 years, it has to find ways to tread water during periods of mediocre leadership and economic downturn. In effect, there was something equally commendable, if not heroic (if of a different order of heroism), in those responsible for keeping the institution afloat during its darkest hours.

William McKelvy Martin, who took over for Bloom, was by all accounts an ineffectual leader. But somehow he gave enough encouragement to conductor Siegfried Landau that the Brooklyn Philharmonia could follow up its successful Beethoven festival with adventurous programming that included Elliott Carter's Symphony No. 1; Verdi's *Requiem*, a first in Brooklyn since the 1903 Academy fire; Mahler's *Songs of a Wayfarer*; Honegger's *King David*; and Strauss's *Salome*. Somehow he enticed the New York Philharmonic to come back in 1960 and put on another series of concerts at the Academy, conducted by Leonard Bernstein. Somehow the programming was loosened up to permit an evening of *Comedy in Music* with Victor Borge; a series of jazz concerts with the likes of Duke Ellington, Louis Armstrong, Dizzy Gillespie, Dave Brubeck, and Count Basie; and even pop singers like Johnny Mathis and Ray Charles—unfortunately, too little, too late. Somehow he promoted the newly formed Brooklyn Opera Company as well as the Brooklyn Civic Ballet and the Equity Library Theatre; Tyrone Power returned to the Academy stage, with Faye Emerson and Arthur Treacher in Shaw's *Back to Methuselah*, and was followed by the appearance of Bette Davis and Gary Merrill in *The World of Carl Sandburg*; Rudolf Nureyev would make his American debut at the Academy with the Chicago Opera Ballet in 1962, shortly after defecting from the Soviet Union, and in the next year the instantly famous pianist Van Cliburn would give his only New York concert. Somehow the dance companies of Pearl Lang and Paul Taylor would put on a memorable series of programs in 1964, followed in the next year by those of José Limón and Merce Cunningham, just as the Academy was about to experience its transformation and renaissance.

Consider the dance companies that performed earlier at the Academy, such as Martha Graham, Anna Sokolow, Merce Cunningham, Jean Erdman, Erick Hawkins, José Limón, Katherine Dunham, and Paul Taylor. What is striking about this list is not only its quality but that it shows the degree to which the avant-garde was welcomed into the programming mix that constituted the Brooklyn Academy of Music prior to the tenure of Harvey Lichtenstein. There would seem to be more continuity between the former, allegedly impossibly frumpy, musty Academy

Agnes de Mille (seated) in rehearsal.
Photo: Gjon Mili

and the hip, post-1967 one than is generally acknowledged, but the "cutting edge" element was not formatted or packaged as such, in so clever and insistent a manner. Perhaps, too, there was less of a distinction then between blue-chip high culture and bohemian "downtown" culture. An artist like Agnes de Mille or Paul Taylor could straddle both worlds. To simplify a complex cultural shift, what happened in the radicalized antiwar climate of the 1960s is that "high culture" became tainted with a fat-cat establishment brush and forfeited a good deal of its credibility. Classical music had been mocked for some time as longhair, but now it had somehow lost its power to intimidate. The previous balance between high culture and pop culture was shattered; rock music and television grew immeasurably in importance, and high culture was trumped decisively by the advancement of pop—the world had changed.

In Hollywood movies of the 1940s, there were black-and-white melodramas about tortured, sensitive conductors and classical pianists. In the 1950s, the action in a romantic comedy or musical would sometimes pause for a piano solo by José Iturbi or an opera singer like Lauritz Melchior or Robert Merrill singing an aria—Mario Lanza and Anna Maria Alberghetti were in fact movie stars—or George Balanchine would choreograph lush ballet sequences for Technicolor movies. On radio and television variety shows, classical music still held its own as an entertaining supplement, with a presumed appeal for the average American audience. However, by the late 1960s, all such interludes had disappeared. Vanished. The classical music roster of an impresario-agent like Sol Hurok—once a celebrity name himself—could no longer be marketed as assuredly to audiences. Whether it was Isaac Stern or Pablo Casals, Rudolf Serkin or Eugene List, the Academy's Opera House would still remain half empty. A new strategy was needed, a new philosophy, a new approach, something had to be done, and without a moment to lose—as they say in the comic books—*KA-BLAM! POW! BAM!*

"A new strategy was needed, a new philosophy, a new approach, something had to be done, and without a moment to lose—as they say in the comic books—*KA-BLAM! POW! BAM!*"

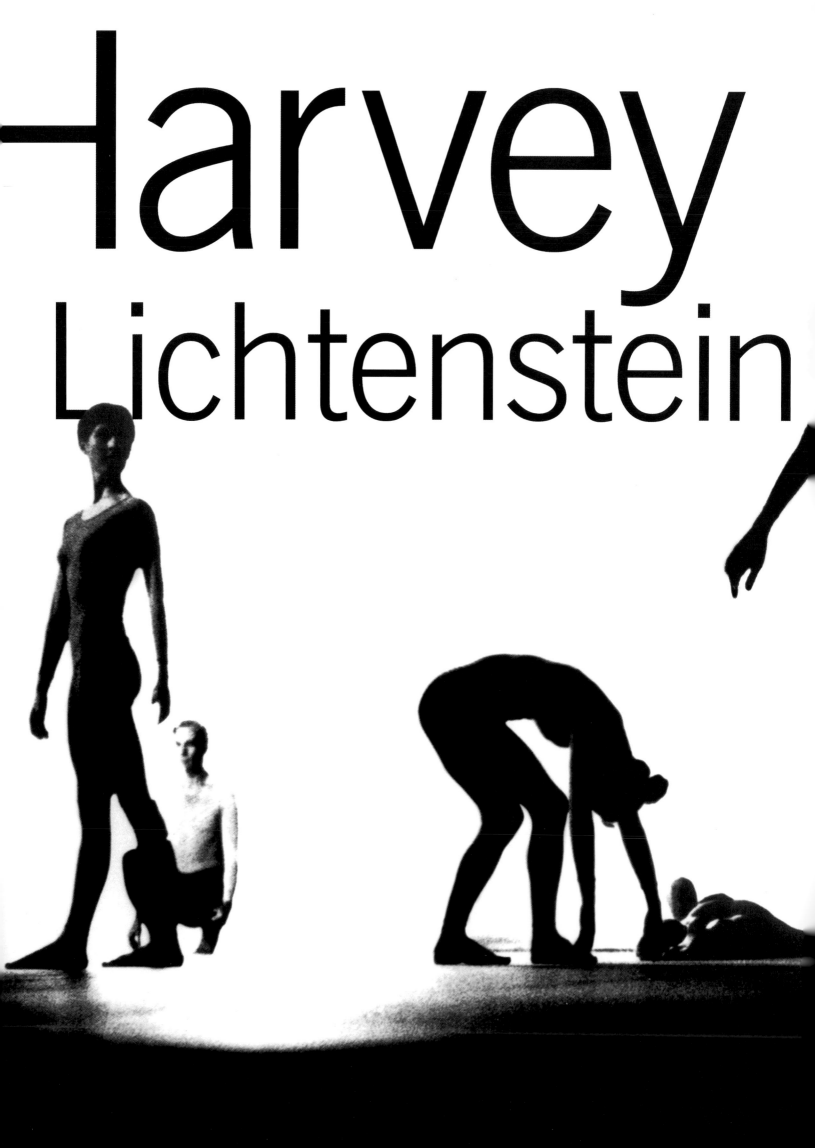

Harvey
Lichtenstein

and the

BAM
Renaissance

Renting the Opera House

by Robert Wilson

The first time I went to BAM was to see the Living Theatre in the late 1960s. It was an extraordinary experience to see provocative visual theater in a classical proscenium arch. It was unlike anything I had ever seen before. It was so different from any theater in Manhattan. It was thrilling. I also saw, around the same time, Merce Cunningham perform at BAM. Seeing his work *Canfield* at the Opera House, with its choreographic patterns like a Jackson Pollock painting, was mind-boggling. These two events changed my life forever.

After seeing these works I began to make my own theater. In 1969, I presented a work called *The King of Spain* at the Anderson Theatre on the Lower East Side of Manhattan. The work was performed in a proscenium arch. I knew at the time that I wanted to break away from the performance art scene of the sixties, where theater was happening on rooftops, in parking lots, in alleyways, and on the streets. I wanted to work within the frame of the box. I called Jane Yockel, who was working with Harvey Lichtenstein, and made an appointment to meet him at BAM. I liked Harvey from the beginning. I told him that I had seen Broadway plays and didn't like them. And operas at the Met and didn't like them either. But I liked very much the work of George Balanchine and the New York City Ballet as well as Merce Cunningham and John Cage. I tried to explain something about my work. I told him that for me all theater is dance. Harvey, having been a dancer, seemed to understand. My work was about stillness and the movement within stillness. It was developed abstractly and with time-space constructions of theme and variations. I explained that I was fascinated by the two-dimensionality of the proscenium arch, where one side is hidden from the public. I told him my idea about *The Life and Times of Sigmund Freud*. It was a silent work in three acts, and it was not a historical but a poetic presentation of his life. The first act was set on the landscape of a bright, midday sunny beach, the earlier years of his life; the second act set in a gray Victorian drawing room, the middle years of his life; and the third act in a dark cave, the last years of his life and his death.

I told Harvey that if he presented the work in the Opera House, I would pay 50 percent of the costs. He agreed, and the work was performed in the fall of 1969 and again in the spring of 1970. It received a very negative review by Don McDonagh in the *New York Times*. He said, "The work described itself as a dance play in three acts but any resemblance to plays was purely coincidental. A stranger strolled by during the first intermission and asked whether I had any idea of what was going on. 'Very little,' I had to confess." Harvey said the fact that many people walked out and that the press was bad didn't matter. He liked the work very much and was interested in what I wanted to do next. Some weeks later, Richard Foreman wrote a very favorable review in the *Village Voice*. Harvey called to tell me about the review and said this would be a passport for us to do other work. In 1971, I presented *Deafman Glance*, and at Harvey's suggestion Ninon Tallon Karlweis came to see it. She had brought the Living Theatre, Eugène Ionesco, and Jerzy Grotowski to New York. As she had taken Peter Brook to Europe, she wanted to bring my work as well. *Deafman Glance* was presented at the Festival of Nancy and then went to Paris and played for several months to a sold-out house of 2,200 people each night.

The press and public reactions were overwhelming. *Le Monde* proclaimed that once in a lifetime we witness such a miracle in the theater. French surrealist Louis Aragon wrote an "open letter" to his deceased friend André Breton, who had shared his aestheticism and political ideology, saying that this was the most beautiful thing he had ever seen in his life and it was what they had hoped the future would be. As a result, my theatrical career was established. I will always be indebted to Harvey for having had the vision and courage to present those early works of mine at BAM, and, of course, for presenting those that followed in the next decade—*The Life and Times of Joseph Stalin*, *The $ Value of Man*, and *Einstein on the Beach*.

Previous page: *Canfield*, Merce Cunningham Dance Company, 1969. Photo: James Klosty

Opposite: Michel Sondak and Robyn Evans in *The Life and Times of Sigmund Freud*, Robert Wilson, 1969. Photo (detail): Martin Bough

by John Rockwell

Harvey Lichtenstein arrived at BAM in 1967, but BAM wasn't BAM yet, with all the exuberant connotations of an acronym that only began to be used formally in marketing materials in 1973. In 1967, it was still the Brooklyn Academy of Music, the Academy for short—names that evoked a grand past but a gravely imperiled present. The real story of its renaissance, and its path toward the future, began in 1966.

It was in that year, as the subcultural hippie revolution was polarizing the city and the nation, that Seth Faison, Brooklyn born and bred, became chairman of the Academy's governing board. "Everybody was expecting it to die," he said later, "and nobody wanted to be involved with something that was dying." The gloom was highlighted in a director's report dated June 9, 1966, from William McKelvy Martin to the board of the Brooklyn Institute of Arts and Sciences, the umbrella organization with its own board of trustees that included BAM along with the Brooklyn Museum, the Brooklyn Children's Museum, and the Brooklyn Botanic Garden. Martin referred to the previous season almost apologetically as "equally arduous and financially disappointing," with an operating deficit that was two and a half times greater than anticipated, a decline in the already unstellar attendance, and a marked deterioration of the surrounding neighborhood.

Attached to this gloomy screed was a presentation by Faison entitled "The Future of the Academy." In it Faison argued that "any new programming should be unique or have some element of control by the Academy," meaning less reliance on dispensations from Manhattan organizations and concert agencies that treated BAM as yet another provincial stopover. He called for greater institutional fundraising but added that "the only way to attract such foundation or governmental support would be to create and launch innovative programs or approaches not already being taken." He sought to "increase the percentage of quality programs not otherwise available in the City or by Academy centered groups." Our aim, he went on, is "to attract an increasing share of the *total* City population." At the same time, he wanted to emphasize "program approaches of national significance" intended to develop an interest and pride in the heritage of the local African American community.

Faison, in other words, wanted to engender just the kind of programming that Lichtenstein would undertake when he arrived the following year. Martin gave notice, a search committee for a new director was formed, Lichtenstein was offered the job in the fall of 1966, and he was unanimously confirmed at a board meeting on January 31, 1967. At that meeting, Faison described him as, among the four finalists for the job, "the most eager of them all to grapple with the problems of the Academy." He started work on March 1.

Imago, Alwin Nikolais Dance Company, 1968. Photo (detail): Robert Sosenko

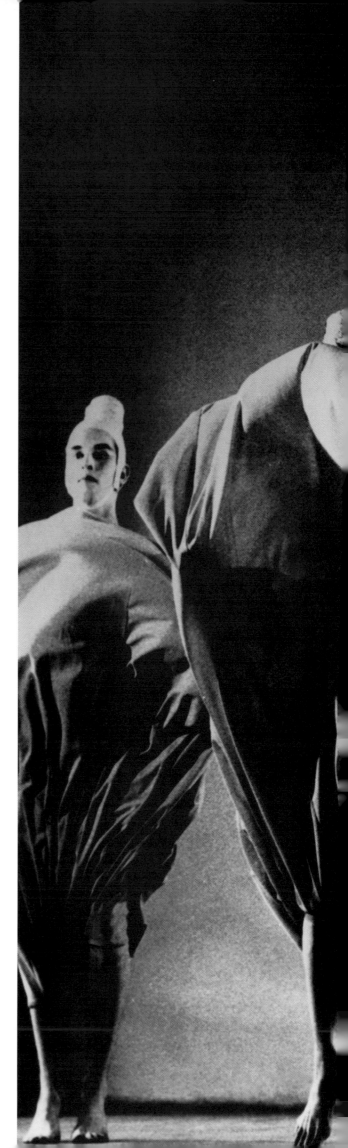

Lichtenstein was the youngest of the final candidates, but he had a background—and, no doubt, a go-getter personality—that rightly appealed to Faison. Born in Brooklyn in 1929, Lichtenstein came from a working-class family. His father was a Polish immigrant, the son of a rabbi, who married a woman whom Lichtenstein remembers as "a good solid Jewish mom." He was raised mostly in Brooklyn and for some time in far Manhattan, and he graduated from Brooklyn Technical High School and Brooklyn College. As a child, he suffered from asthma—still having to control it with medications into adulthood—and had a best friend who loved classical music, Toscanini especially.

During college, he became interested in dance, initially in the Martha Graham performances he first saw at a Broadway theater where his girlfriend was ushering. He began dancing himself, broadened his interest beyond modern to include ballet, went to the American Dance Festival when it was still at Connecticut College, gravitated down to Black Mountain College in North Carolina when it was a Cage-Cunningham-Rauschenberg nest, and spent time at Bennington College, where he enjoyed being one of the few straight male dancers in a bevy of females. By the mid-1950s, he was dancing in several New York companies, among them those of Sophie Maslow and Pearl Lang, and spent a year in the New York City Opera corps de ballet. By all accounts, including his own, he was more a vivid onstage personality than a polished technician.

In the late 1950s, Lichtenstein decided to move on from dance; his father had died and he felt financially responsible for his mother, and he had married, with a son to come. So he got a job as a fundraiser for Brandeis University near Boston. But he missed the arts, and in 1964 he learned of a Ford Foundation program to train arts administrators. Accepted into the program, he wound up being placed first at the New York City Ballet, where he developed a fascination with George Balanchine, then at City Opera, and at both companies was instrumental in pioneering subscription plans as well as fundraising. Morton Baum, then a cultural power broker in Manhattan and chairman of both City Ballet and City Opera, advised him that Brooklyn was a lost cause, especially with the advent of the glamorous, glittering Lincoln Center. But when Lichtenstein told him that the Academy was proposing to pay him $16,000 a year, Baum said he couldn't match that, and off Lichtenstein went, back to Brooklyn.

The Academy he took over was a far cry from what it is today. The downstairs Opera House and Music Hall were dilapidated. The second-floor ballroom—later the Lepercq Space—was rented out to a boys' prep school. Farther upstairs was a judo academy. The programming was heavy on classical music, with itinerant virtuosos dispensed from the big midtown Manhattan agencies, touring orchestras, the

Academy-based Brooklyn Philharmonia under its founder Siegfried Landau, and an excess of lectures, drowsily attended by a declining number of aging "members."

From the first, Lichtenstein and Faison decided that they had to enliven this dreary round with a few key events squeezed into and around prior commitments, designed to attract the attention of Brooklynites but especially of Manhattan reviewers and audiences. In other words, they had to have BAM offer things that couldn't be seen elsewhere, that would establish it with a fresh image as an innovative center.

Before we get into the details of how they did that, it would be profitable to sketch an overview of Lichtenstein's 32-year tenure at BAM and more narrowly of his first 15 years there, up to the inauguration of the Next Wave Festival in 1983. That span can be broken down into clearly delineated segments. At first, in the late 1960s and early 1970s, he concentrated on dance, modern dance in particular, with a few striking innovations, such as Sarah Caldwell, Merce Cunningham, Martha Graham, Eliot Feld, the Living Theatre, Jerzy Grotowski, the Chelsea Theater Center, Robert Wilson, and Peter Brook. Gradually, the mustier offerings at BAM thinned out, the leases for the prep school and judo academy expired, and the Brooklyn Philharmonia was vitalized with the appointment in 1971 of Lukas Foss as music director.

Peter Brook's BAM debut in 1971 signaled the beginning of a shift of emphasis from dance to theater, which dominated the most visible programming for the rest of the 1970s. Big names, especially British big names, became the preferred method of attracting

Opposite: *Frankenstein,* Living Theatre, 1968. Photo: Daniel Vittet

Below: *Seraphic Dialogue,* Martha Graham Dance Company, 1968. Photo: Martha Swope

Merce Cunningham in his *Antic Meet*,
1958. Photo (detail): Richard Rutledge

by Nancy Dalva

Merce Cunningham stood at the nexus of classicism and modernism the way Russian-born choreographer Michel Fokine stood at the nexus of classicism and romanticism. Cunningham stripped his choreographic process of all but the essential element of movement, excluding decor, narrative, music—anything decorative or extrinsic. These were later added back, their invention left to others—including John Cage, Robert Rauschenberg, and Jasper Johns—without much, if any, collusion. All but an early few of his 150 works were made in silence. The independence—indeed the primacy—of choreography thus established, Cunningham next began to break down movement into increasingly small increments and began to divide up the body as well. To the lower-body positions of ballet, he added a flexible and dynamic torso; later, he would choreograph for the arms without regard to the lower body, giving them "facings" and directions all their own. The same, too, for the head.

Meanwhile, he broke dance out of the proscenium and began to assemble and reassemble his dances without regard to a "front," fracturing and refracting the stage picture in the way that Cubists broke up the visual plane of a painting. This fragmentation mirrors the breakdown of syntax and the concurrent notions of simultaneity and multiplicity of associations that arose in modernist literature, and in computer coding the breakdown of information into digital bytes. Cunningham was also an early adopter of new technologies, including video and computer programming. All along, his use of chance procedures at some point in the making of every piece was a way to remove some of the effects of personal choice and habit and willful control, and can be viewed as a kind of personal Taoism.

Cunningham was born in Centralia, Washington, one of three sons of a lawyer father and a gadabout mother. He first studied dance with the vaudevillian Maud Barrett, then studied modern dance at Seattle's Cornish School, where he met Cage; in 1939, at the Bennington School of the Dance at Mills College in Oakland, California, he met Martha Graham, whom he followed to New York. In the summer of 1953, while in residence at Black Mountain College in North Carolina, he formed the Merce Cunningham Dance Company. More than a dozen company engagements at BAM over the years include the troupe's venue debut in 1966; its first extended season in 1968; *Split Sides* (2003), with live music by Radiohead and Sigur Rós; and the celebration of Cunningham's birthday with the premiere of *Nearly Ninety* in 2009. Two weeks before he died in July of that same year, at age 90, he was in his studio with his dancers, working on something new.

attention to BAM. This corresponded with a shift in Lichtenstein's tastes—ever open to new excitements—toward a newfound passion for theater and actors. But the collapse in 1981 of the second of his two efforts to establish a BAM Theater Company, an overt attempt to create a true American repertory theater ensemble, led to the worst of BAM's periodic budgetary crises and to what Lichtenstein still remembers as the "biggest disappointment" of his career. The programming emphasis shifted quickly and decisively to the kind of striking innovation, particularly avant-garde innovation, that would flower first in the two seasons of the Next Wave series, in 1981 and 1982–83, and that served as a stalking horse for the Next Wave Festivals from 1983 to today, chronicled in the later chapters of this book.

When Lichtenstein was offered the job in the fall of 1966, he was faced with a 1967–68 season that was already largely planned, full of concerts and lectures but with too many stretches when the theaters would be dark. He wanted something striking to launch his tenure, to "keep BAM in the public eye." Throughout his BAM career, he recalled much later, he sought "a big opening and a big closing." For him, the way to do that was to attract critics from Manhattan, who came to Brooklyn hardly at all before he arrived and only selectively thereafter. He wanted "to make sure we had the things that would attract them," to create "a kind of aura about BAM," to make everyone realize that "BAM was being resurrected somehow from the dead."

In the fall of 1966, he heard about a new touring company, the American National Opera Company, founded by Sarah Caldwell, the imposing if eccentric conductor and opera impresario from Boston. He booked them to open his first season with three operas in a single weekend—Berg's *Lulu*, Verdi's *Falstaff*, and Puccini's *Tosca*, with the vivid Australian soprano Marie Collier. *Lulu* especially, still in its incomplete two-act version, was a big novelty at the time and attracted the Manhattan movers and shakers—and critics. The engagement was not without its Caldwellian quirks, including her refusal to halt rehearsals, Lichtenstein ordering his stage crew to stop working, her sleeping on the stage floor all night, and a delayed curtain for the Saturday evening *Tosca* as the changeover from that afternoon's *Falstaff* took longer than Caldwell had anticipated. But Lichtenstein's opening salvo still counted as a hit, putting BAM on the map in a way that it hadn't been for decades.

The other major innovation that Lichtenstein was able to work into that first season was a weeklong run of the Merce Cunningham Dance Company in May 1968. Dance had played a role in the Academy's programming before 1967, but only in one- or two-night stands of companies that were touring or on run-outs from across the river, rather like the classical virtuosos farmed out from the Hurok agency or Columbia Artists Management. Lichtenstein and

Faison decided early on to emphasize dance. It was relatively inexpensive to present, Lichtenstein knew the field, and the time and place were right for a center for American modern dance when the Ford Foundation had just poured enormous support into Balanchine and ballet. Not that Lichtenstein was mounting a counterattack: "I wasn't fighting Balanchine; I wasn't fighting ballet. I was just trying to make a home for what I thought was important work that wasn't being seen."

Cunningham's eight-performance stand at BAM was the first major season anywhere in New York for an abstractionist who could make Balanchine look like a purveyor of story ballets. Some people booed *Winterbranch*, with its music by La Monte Young and

decor by Robert Rauschenberg, but Lichtenstein—
it's difficult not to refer to him as Harvey, since
everybody did and does and since now there's a
BAM theater actually called the Harvey—and many
others became lifelong devotees. *RainForest*, with an
electronic score by David Tudor and floating silver
pillows from Andy Warhol, made a special impression.
That engagement inaugurated a long relationship
between BAM and the Cunningham company,
including a residency. It also helped bring Lewis Lloyd,
who had helped run the Cunningham organization,
to BAM as a key early assistant to Lichtenstein.
And it was certainly the kind of "big closing" that
Lichtenstein always sought.

The next season, the first for which Lichtenstein
could take much fuller responsibility—even with the
ongoing visiting orchestras, touring orchestras, lectures,
and rentals—contained more dance than ever. The
music programming—still essentially farmed out to
independent ensembles—seemed a little friskier,
as did the intermittent film series. But Lichtenstein
arranged to open the season with another exotic
blockbuster, the kind that would blossom when the
idea of a "next wave" came to define BAM in the
1980s. That was the occupancy of the Academy in
October 1968 by four productions from Julian Beck
and Judith Malina's Living Theatre. Nudity in their
Paradise Now invoked the interest of the Brooklyn
Police Department, but a settlement was reached

Merce Cunningham (featured) in
Walkaround Time, Merce Cunningham
Dance Company, 1968.
Photo: James Klosty

Above: Raymond Andrews and Sheryl Sutton in *Deafman Glance*, Robert Wilson, 1971.
Photo: Martin Bough

Opposite: Ryszard Cieslak (featured) in *The Constant Prince*, Jerzy Grotowski / Polish Laboratory Theatre, 1969. Photo: Theodore Brauner

whereby the Academy agreed to confine it to within the theater. *Paradise Now*, with its determined vision of anarchic sixties bliss, won the most attention, but the company's *Frankenstein*, which ended with an elaborately constructed, truly terrifying monster filling the backstage wall of the Opera House, was what stuck in most viewers' memories, including Lichtenstein's. He does recall, however, encountering a puzzled Academy guard in the lobby after *Paradise Now*. "You know," Lichtenstein says the guard said, "we go through the theater in the morning and we clean up and stuff, and when I go up in the balcony it's full of underwear."

Later that same month, Martha Graham opened the now much expanded, much trumpeted Festival of Dance. Some Manhattanites were still wary of braving the wilds of Brooklyn; the critic Clive Barnes had an American friend who decided to pass on the Graham season because he "would wait till she goes to London." But overall the engagement attracted audiences from all over the five boroughs and beyond to line up at the box office. Those who skipped Brooklyn missed the Graham company at its latter-day height and when Graham herself was still dancing. Not quite two years later, on the eve of yet another Academy engagement, word got out that she had given up dancing, and she blamed Lichtenstein for the press leak—he denies having said anything himself, though he concedes that "someone in the press department" might have done the deed.

The 1968–69 dance program, bolstered by several key foundation, government, and private grants, included all manner of other choreographers, all in runs that exceeded the earlier one-night stands. The season included Cunningham, Anna Sokolow, Erick Hawkins, Paul Taylor, Alwin Nikolais, Alvin Ailey, José Limón, and the young Twyla Tharp. Dance continued to be an Academy mainstay until well into the 1970s; the sometimes acerbic critic

Arlene Croce thought it "the best dance theater in New York." Even when dance was supplanted thereafter by theater as the programming focal point, it remained a key to BAM's image.

Some companies drifted away over time. Ailey was in residence for a couple of years but yearned for the bright lights of Manhattan and eventually made his base the New York City Center, where his company still performs its main annual New York season. But Cunningham stayed far longer at BAM, and Tharp became a regular for a while, even establishing her office on an upper floor. She grew into a star at BAM, with long seasons that made money for her and the Academy. Temperamental as always, she had an up-and-down relationship with Lichtenstein, who has his own flashes of temper, too—a story that extends past the end point of this chapter.

Lichtenstein's attention to modern dance did not preclude ballet. The Harkness Ballet appeared at BAM, and the American Ballet Theatre—before it, too, found new opportunities in Manhattan—was in residence for a while during the late 1960s. A highlight of those engagements was the guest appearances of the intensely theatrical Italian Carla Fracci and the elegant Dane Erik Bruhn. The Pennsylvania Ballet was a regular visitor from 1973 to 1980. A bolder effort in terms of risk for the Academy's still delicate finances came in the fall of 1969 with the establishment of a resident troupe, the American Ballet Company, led by the 27-year-old choreographer Eliot Feld, a protégé of Jerome Robbins. However, reviews were mixed, attendance disappointing, and fundraising insufficient, and the company was disbanded after two years.

The attention-getting import of the 1969–70 season was Jerzy Grotowski and his Polish Laboratory Theatre that fall. Grotowski was highly selective, not to say picky, about where he would perform, and having rejected all the spaces in and around BAM, he eventually chose the Washington Square Methodist Church in Greenwich Village. Grotowski was fierce about capping attendance at no more than 100 people for each performance of the company's three productions, all were in Polish (before the age of supertitles), and the action wasn't at BAM or even in Brooklyn. But Grotowski was still presented by the Academy, and hence the season redounded to its credit and attracted enormous attention in New York's theatrical, artistic, and journalistic communities.

Another long-standing relationship began in 1969 with the director-designer Robert Wilson's *The Life and Times of Sigmund Freud*. One of Wilson's early dreamscapes with an amateur cast, it did include one uncredited guest appearance by Jerome Robbins in the title role. Robbins was a friend and admirer of the young Wilson, an admiration attested by Robbins's glacial ballet *Watermill*, which premiered at Lincoln Center in 1972. In the previous year, the Academy presented another Wilson epic, his *Deafman Glance*,

by Roger Oliver

In 1971, a headline in the *New York Times* questioned whether the Chelsea Theater Center was "America's Most Exciting New Theater?" and Martin Gottfried's article answered in the affirmative. Established in 1965, the Chelsea presented its first three seasons in Manhattan and in 1968 became the resident company at BAM, which coincided with BAM's emergence as one of the most ambitious and adventurous venues in contemporary American theater.

For artistic director Robert Kalfin, who formed a partnership with Michael David, the company's repertoire at BAM was envisioned as a mix of new plays, "unknown" classics, and plays that had been largely forgotten or overlooked—works by major African American playwrights, including *The Gentleman Caller* by Ed Bullins and *Slave Ship* by LeRoi Jones (now Amiri Baraka); groundbreaking British and European plays, including Edward Bond's *Saved*, Jean Genet's *The Screens*, Peter Handke's *Kaspar*, and Stanislaw Ignacy Witkiewicz's *The Crazy Locomotive*; plays by major writers known primarily for their work in other genres, notably Allen Ginsberg's *Kaddish*, Isaac Babel's *Sunset*, and Isaac Bashevis Singer's *Yentl the Yeshiva Boy*, adapted with Leah Napolin; and innovative and nontraditional music-theater works, including John Gay's *The Beggar's Opera* and the Kurt Weill / Bertolt Brecht collaboration *Happy End*.

One of the most successful Chelsea productions was Hal Prince's environmental staging of Leonard Bernstein's *Candide*, with a new book by Hugh Wheeler and additional lyrics by Stephen Sondheim and John Latouche, which opened at BAM in 1973 and then moved to Broadway, where it ran for nearly two years. After a decade, in 1978, the Chelsea ended its residency at BAM as it struggled for survival, but it remained a significant part of the BAM experience that attracted an array of talented, often emerging, artists, including Glenn Close, Alan Schneider, Willa Kim, James Woods, Frank Langella, Tovah Feldshuh, Des McAnuff, Christopher Lloyd, and Meryl Streep.

Theater Center

Chelsea

just before it transfixed Parisian intellectuals and made
Wilson a star in artistic Europe. The 12-hour production—14 at the premiere, to Lichtenstein's extreme
displeasure—*The Life and Times of Joseph Stalin*, shown
at BAM in 1973, incorporated both *Freud* and
Deafman Glance along with other earlier Wilson work.
It remains a memory of near-religious epiphany for
those of us who loved it—others hated it, or were
at least bored to distraction, and there were plentiful
walkouts. *Stalin* was followed in 1975 by *The $ Value
of Man*, after which there was a hiatus for Wilson at
BAM until the revival in 1984 of *Einstein on the Beach*.
Not that engagements like Cunningham's or Wilson's
attracted big crowds: "There were times, when Merce
performed, when I would be in tears, practically,"
says Lichtenstein about surveying the empty seats.
"When we did *Stalin*, we had tiny audiences, four,
five hundred people." This was in the 2,100-seat
Opera House.

Early in his career as a theater administrator,
Lichtenstein's taste was still very much evolving.

Wilson struck him at first as excessively amateurish,
and the director's eccentricities and self-indulgences
drove him nuts—as in that two-hour overrun at the
first performance of *Stalin*. "I put on *Sigmund Freud*
before I saw it," he said. "Someone told me about it.
I didn't quite know what was going on." He warmed
to the greater professionalism of *Deafman*, conceding its
"fantastic" stage imagery, and, after 1979, to Wilson's
use of professional European actors and opera singers.
He missed the original 1976 *Einstein on the Beach*
altogether, even at its Metropolitan Opera House
performances, catching up to it only when he himself
produced its revival eight years later.

In the late 1960s and early 1970s, Lichtenstein
relied on trusted friends and advisers to alert him to
work worth pursuing. Key among them was the
theater agent Ninon Tallon Karlweis, based in New
York and Paris, who alerted him to, among others,
Grotowski and Peter Brook. Lichtenstein loved
Karlweis, especially because, he says affectionately,
she had total recall of performances she slept through,

and she slept through them all. She also served as a tutor to Robert Wilson in those years, introducing him to the work of the classic European playwrights, composers, and authors. Paul Lepercq, who came on in 1972 as board chairman, was another early supporter and adviser, and he backed up his recommendations with financial support. Lepercq was also one of the first to alert Lichtenstein to Twyla Tharp and, later, Pina Bausch.

Still, from early on, Lichtenstein would travel to see things himself, and ideally would not present work in New York that he hadn't seen. His trips were mostly to Europe; he didn't much cultivate the Asian work that later became more prominent at BAM, and he tended to delegate the African and Asian dance and music the Academy sponsored. It was Karlweis who oversaw an ambitious Afro-Asian Festival starting in the fall of 1971. Becoming the American director of the Spoleto Festival in Italy from 1971 to 1974 provided Lichtenstein some distraction from his Brooklyn responsibilities but also bolstered his European contacts. Those contacts bore fruit, especially his connections to British theater. On the continent, at first he had mixed luck; he failed to secure Bertolt Brecht's Berliner Ensemble from Communist East Berlin, but he did land Grotowski and, later, the Comédie-Française.

Not all the organizations that operated more or less independently within BAM ran counter to Lichtenstein's vision for the Academy as an innovative magnet. In 1968, he arranged for the lively, inventive Chelsea Theater Center, which had been operating in inadequate space in Manhattan, to come to BAM and take over the 199-seat fifth-floor theater. The Chelsea, in the persons of Robert Kalfin and Michael David, operated on its own but with Lichtenstein's blessings. It offered new plays, often with a political agenda, bold productions, striking young actors, and free admission. Its first major success at BAM was *Slave Ship* by LeRoi Jones (now Amiri Baraka), and the list of authors subsequently presented reads like a who's who of late-20th-century stagecraft, including but hardly limited to Jean Genet, Peter Handke, William Golding, Christopher Hampton, Edward Bond, Allen Ginsberg, and Isaac Bashevis Singer, as well as Brecht and Kurt Weill, whose *Happy End* featured Christopher Lloyd and "Meryl Streep before she was Meryl Streep," as Lichtenstein put it. Martin Gottfried began a 1971 *New York Times* article with "The most exciting new theater in America is the Chelsea Theater Center at the Brooklyn Academy of Music."

Hal Prince's Chelsea production of *Candide*, which opened at BAM in 1973, went on to a two-year run on Broadway and was subsequently revived at the New York City Opera. The Chelsea attracted attention from Manhattan, from downtown denizens and more conventional theatergoers, and several of its productions were extended off-Broadway, including *Slave Ship*. But the company also drew audiences from what Pete Hamill in a 1969 *New York* magazine article called the "new people" beginning to gentrify BAM's borough; all told, some 70 percent of the Chelsea's audience came from Brooklyn. The relationship with BAM lasted until 1978, when Kalfin and David split up. The Chelsea name went back across the river, but the Chelsea residue—renamed the Dodger Theater and still very much active—stayed on at BAM for two more seasons.

Back in 1969, Lichtenstein met Peter Brook through Karlweis and Grotowski and was inspired to go to England to see Brook's *A Midsummer Night's Dream* with the Royal Shakespeare Company in the summer of 1970. It was the beginning of a long, warm relationship between Lichtenstein and both Brook and the company, and of Brook's decisive role at several key junctures in BAM's history. Lichtenstein looks back on that fresh, minimalist, mesmerizing *Dream* as "maybe the greatest production I've ever seen." He was determined to bring it to BAM, but David Merrick, the most fearsomely powerful producer on Broadway, wanted it, too, for a limited run and a national tour. Lichtenstein went to see Merrick, who according to Lichtenstein simply eviscerated him—rather like Sol Hurok had done once, too—treating him like a presumptuous Brooklyn bumpkin. "It was brutal," Lichtenstein recalls. Yet when Lichtenstein wants something badly enough, he is persistent. He kept working and managed—through a Brook-loving board member, David Picker, who ran United Artists—to arrange for a two-week BAM run after the eight-week Broadway engagement, followed by Merrick's national tour. What appealed to Brook, beyond Lichtenstein's dogged enthusiasm, was his willingness to offer less expensive tickets to those who

Meryl Streep and Christopher Lloyd in *Happy End*, Kurt Weill and Bertolt Brecht / Chelsea Theater Center, 1977. Photo: Martha Swope

couldn't afford Broadway prices. Brook went on to help redesign the ballroom at BAM into the flexible Lepercq Space and inaugurate it with his *Conference of the Birds* in 1973, and to play a major role in the transformation of the Majestic Theater—now the BAM Harvey Theater—which opened in 1987 with Brook's *The Mahabharata*.

Lichtenstein's passion for Brook and his go-for-broke tenacity in winning Brook for BAM provides key insights into his personality. Harvey Lichtenstein is a fan; he can be depressed when he has nothing much to do but is almost childlike in his enthusiasm. His outlook is optimistic even if his private moods may seem pessimistic. He is an emotional more than an intellectual person. He makes decisions by instinct. "He reacts with his gut, not his mind," said his second wife, Phyllis. More often than not his taste proved both exciting in itself and in tune with that of his audience, or of the audience he helped shape through his BAM programming. It was his overall personality, charms and seeming warts together, that allowed him to achieve the remarkable things he achieved. I

cannot count the number of times that, scuttling out of the auditorium after a performance, I've found Harvey standing at the top of the aisle, his eyes glittering with enthusiasm, oblivious to all else, clapping as hard as he could and "grinning like a stage-door fan," as Ben Brantley put it in a *New Yorker* profile.

Lichtenstein rarely allowed himself to be trapped by fashion, by others' perceived opinions of what was good and what was not. "What I've learned is to really keep yourself open to stuff," he remarked. After decades in the administration business, he says he still has no real idea what will attract audiences: "Who the hell knows what draws?" So he trusts his own passions instead, and more often than not people trusted him back and agreed with him enough to buy tickets, to subscribe, to come back for more.

Yet periodically Lichtenstein did overreach, often abetted by larger economic crises in the city and the country. The financial structure of the Brooklyn Institute, of which the Academy was a member when Lichtenstein arrived, allowed the larger body to cover some of his deficits, giving him a certain latitude in his early years at BAM. Eventually, however, the other institutions within the Institute grew restive at having to bail him out, and the result was that the Academy was spun off on its own in early 1971 as the St. Felix Street Corporation. The city owned the land and the building (parking lots included), the Academy paid no rent, and the union deals were not punitive. Still, suddenly responsible for its own budget, and laboring under the deficit from the demise of the Feld ballet company and the expenses of the *Midsummer Night's Dream* production, BAM found itself in a financial hole. Lichtenstein remembers sleepless nights and his terror that the whole house of cards might collapse. The board was not as financially supportive as it later became, and fundraising was still underdeveloped, despite Lichtenstein's success in drumming up grants for some of his ventures. Sometimes payrolls had to be delayed, and there was his constant fear that they wouldn't be met. The crisis reached its nadir at the end of 1971. The budget and attendance had tripled, but the staff had stayed small and the deficit had grown. "We were really in trouble, and I couldn't meet the payroll. I was up most nights. I just couldn't—I didn't know what I was going to do. Those years, of '71, '72, '73, were really difficult."

Though he tried to scale back the schedule and the budget, he also kept on trying to open and close big and keep BAM in the public eye. One such effort was an engagement in 1971 for Maurice Béjart, the vivid, not to say lurid, French choreographer. Lepercq, himself French, had encouraged and supported Lichtenstein to book Béjart. Lichtenstein thought Béjart was "terrific," and certainly his dancers—including Suzanne Farrell, during her hiatus from the New York City Ballet—were terrific. But Béjart was "creamed" by the conservative (or tasteful, as they

Below: *A Midsummer Night's Dream*, Peter Brook / Royal Shakespeare Company, 1971. Photo: David Farrell

Opposite: Ben Kingsley and John Kane (featured) in *A Midsummer Night's Dream*, Peter Brook / Royal Shakespeare Company, 1971. Photo: David Farrell

Chuck Davis (featured) in *DanceAfrica*,
African American Dance Ensemble.
Photo courtesy of African American
Dance Ensemble

by Susan Yung

DanceAfrica, founded in 1977 by artistic director Baba Chuck Davis, is BAM's longest-running annual program. This festival, which traditionally takes place on Memorial Day weekend, summarizes so much of what BAM has come to represent. It brings to Brooklyn accomplished and eclectic companies from throughout the African continent and the global expanse of the African diaspora. In addition, with troupes from the New York area participating each year, it showcases both well-known and emerging companies. Since 1997, these have proudly included the BAM/Restoration DanceAfrica Ensemble, comprising students from the Bedford Stuyvesant Restoration Corporation in Brooklyn, who also dance with the festival's visiting companies after a period of in-depth training. BAM's fall Next Wave Festival hews to a similar framework—international companies alternate with New York's finest, including a good number from neighboring Brooklyn.

In the 1960s in New York, Davis studied and performed dance and drumming before forming the Chuck Davis Dance Company in 1968. The company first performed at BAM in 1977, constructing an African village in the Lepercq Space; the following year, an outdoor bazaar was added. Davis invited four companies to perform in addition to his own, which is now based in Durham, North Carolina, where Davis was born and where it has had a long-standing relationship with the American Dance Festival. Since then, DanceAfrica has had more than 80 companies perform, boasting up to 25 troupes in one milestone festival; typically, three to five a year perform. Companies have visited from numerous countries—Gambia, Zaire, Uganda, and Ghana, as well as Cuba, Peru, and Haiti—with each one sharing its distinct style of dancing, drumming, and costumes.

While the heart of DanceAfrica is centered in the mainstage performances, the festival—which has expanded to several cities, including Chicago and Washington, DC—has grown to include many components. In addition to the bazaar, offerings include workshops, films, art, and live music. BAM often has held off-site celebrations at the nearby Weeksville Heritage Center, one of the first communities established in New York by newly emancipated African American slaves. Integral to DanceAfrica are the construction of a memorial room, a libation pouring ceremony, and the honoring of the Council of Elders, who attend the performances in full ceremonial garb. But it is the presence of Davis—recognized as one of 100 Irreplaceable American Dance Treasures—that completes the DanceAfrica experience, reminding us to be constantly respectful of one another with his irresistible call and response: *Agoo! Améé!*

Chuck Davis and DanceAfrica

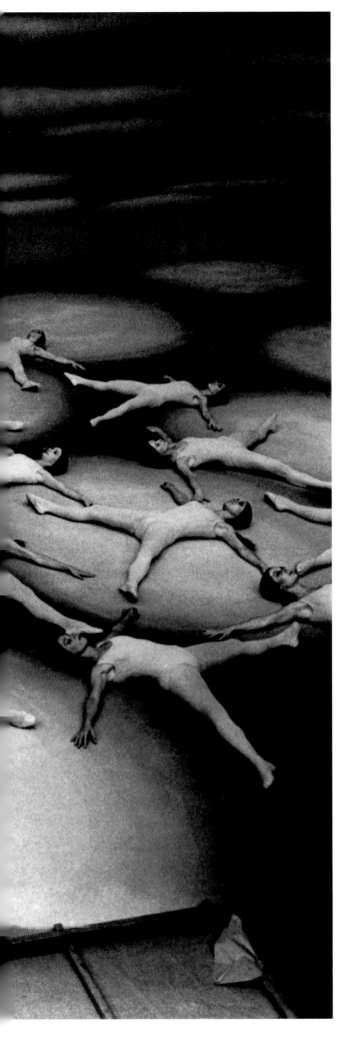

saw it) New York dance critics. Those same critics disdained most European "contemporary ballet" as vulgar and unballetic, which didn't stop Lichtenstein from presenting the likes of John Neumeier, Jiří Kylián, Hans van Manen, and Mats Ek, who almost all got "hammered," in Lichtenstein's recollection. In the 1971–72 season, there was the Afro-Asian Festival, which brought dance and music from Cambodia, Senegal, Morocco, Iran, India, and Sierra Leone, followed the next season by Mali, India, and Turkey (the Whirling Dervishes).

Although one pillar of Faison's 1966 plan for the revitalization of the Brooklyn Academy of Music had been outreach to the surrounding African American community, that effort never really quite took off in Lichtenstein's early years—though not for want of trying. Often under the guidance of Mikki Shepard, who in 1988 cofounded the 651 program (later 651 ARTS), the Academy tried all manner of African American and Hispanic theater, dance, jazz, and popular and soul music, especially in the budgetarily constrained years of the early 1970s, along with youth and education programs. One problem, Lichtenstein thinks in retrospect, was that BAM had not found itself in the marketing arena, especially for African American and Hispanic communities. BAM undertook "populist things that we felt would have a real resonance in the community," says Lichtenstein. "They were terrific concerts, but they didn't draw the kind of audience we expected. We really didn't understand how to promote it."

Beyond marketing, popular music audiences, whatever their color, are not always comfortable in theaters and concert halls normally devoted to high art; there are acoustical problems—too much reverberation for amplified music—and image problems. And pop stars often tour when they have a record to promote, not when an impresario wants to slot them into a crowded schedule.

Besides popular music, there was the Jamaican National Dance Theatre Company, which appealed to the Afro-Caribbean community in Brooklyn and helped lead to Chuck Davis's still-flourishing annual DanceAfrica program in the late spring. There was African American dance, notably with Ailey and a Dance Black America festival in the late 1970s; African American theater from the Chelsea Theater and the Black Theater Alliance; and a Hispanic series called Festividad. Overall, on paper and in retrospect, BAM's offerings geared at least in part to the African American and Hispanic communities look more interesting, varied, and extensive than they are sometimes perceived to be. They insulate Lichtenstein from charges of tokenism, that he didn't do enough to make contact with BAM's immediately surrounding community.

Despite his boyhood enthusiasm for the popular, low-priced Lewisohn Stadium concerts and Toscanini, and aside from the theatricalized

Le Sacre du Printemps, Maurice Béjart/ Ballet of the 20th Century, 1971. Photo: Robert Kayaert

flamboyance of opera and his persistent if not always successful efforts to establish a real opera presence at BAM, Lichtenstein did not invest enormous energy toward classical concerts in BAM programming. He had inherited a millstone of mostly middlebrow programs from visiting orchestras, Brooklyn Philharmonia concerts, and touring virtuosos. However stellar some of them may have been, they did not lure Manhattanites, who could hear the same artists at the revitalized Carnegie Hall, the flashy new Lincoln Center, and such ancillary venues as Town Hall, Hunter College, and the 92nd Street Y. Lichtenstein steadily pared down the itinerant orchestras and soloists, but his major steps in enlivening concert music at BAM came with his role in the appointment of Lukas Foss to conduct the mostly independent Brooklyn Philharmonia (later Philharmonic) and in bringing in the violist Scott Nickrenz in 1973 to lead the chamber music programs, which still appealed especially to the aging German-Jewish population of Brooklyn. Nickrenz enlisted a raft of brilliant young players, many now familiar to the Chamber Music Society of Lincoln Center, Carnegie Hall, and the world. There was also a curious Nickrenz sideline in the late 1970s in country and old-time American music concerts.

Foss's predecessor, Siegfried Landau, had done some laudable work, as had Thomas Scherman's Little Orchestra Society, even if Lichtenstein now recalls their Brooklyn concerts as "dress rehearsals" for their

Sue's Leg, Twyla Tharp Dance Company, 1976. Photo: Paul Kolnik

subsequent Manhattan showcases. Foss, who stayed on in Brooklyn until 1990, represented real change. He was a lively personality, a noted composer, and a still-undervalued conductor. He—along with the orchestra's longtime executive and artistic director and chronicler, Maurice Edwards—injected all manner of new and unusual music into the programs, especially with his marathon concerts and his Meet the Moderns series from 1975. In that Foss was heartily encouraged by Lichtenstein, despite Lichtenstein being "turned off by the avant-garde in music," meaning not the Steve Reichs and Philip Glasses he fostered but such rigorous "uptown" modernists as Elliott Carter, Milton Babbitt, and Charles Wuorinen. Foss was socially and musically friendly with a wide swath

of composers and conductors, including Leonard Bernstein, who slipped in at one Meet the Moderns concert to conduct his Symphony No. 2 with Foss at the piano. The critic Alan Rich wrote in a 1972 *New York* magazine article that "Foss has been working hard to change the image of the Brooklyn Philharmonia from just a nice pickup orchestra giving imitations of Manhattan-establishment concerts into an ensemble with a programming personality of its own."

With opera, BAM never really found its footing until the advent of spring opera performances in the 1980s, above all with William Christie at the helm. "I was anxious to get some opera, and was ready for anything," Lichtenstein says. The two major efforts, both post-1983, were a venture with the agent and opera administrator Matthew Epstein and a plan to make BAM the home for James Levine's once cherished, now seemingly abandoned "mini-Met." Before them, Lichtenstein tried all manner of smaller companies, starting with Caldwell in 1967. Dating back even before his arrival, there were ensembles led by Boris Goldovsky and Felix W. Salmaggi, then one by Vincent La Selva, the Eastern Opera Company, the North Shore Friends of Opera, the Metropolitan Opera National Company, and, perhaps most interesting, Ian Strasfogel and his New Opera Theater, along with the Chelsea Theater's occasional quasi-operatic ventures, like *The Beggar's Opera, Candide,* and *Happy End.* Most of these treated BAM as a tour stopover or were too small-scaled to make much of an impact beyond Brooklyn. Strasfogel's chamber-opera productions of repertoire ranging from Monteverdi to Viktor Ullmann to György Ligeti were a notable exception, but, says Lichtenstein, "they didn't really catch on."

What the public sees on BAM stages is what defines the Academy's public image. But as with Faison's role in Lichtenstein's assumption of the directorship—his title morphed over the years to executive director, then president—backstage maneuverings played as crucial a role in BAM's evolution, not least in the area of fundraising. There were several prominent board figures in the 1970s, among them Donald M. Blinken and Leonard Garment. But far and away the most important for Lichtenstein was Paul Lepercq, a dapper French investment banker linked with the Schlumberger–de Menil Franco-American oil empire—or, as Lichtenstein likes to put it, "the Schlumberger gang." Lepercq met Lichtenstein in 1969, encouraged and helped him bring Béjart to BAM, and in 1972 became board chairman. "I was in Spoleto," recalls Lichtenstein, "and I said to Paul, 'Paul, I'd like you to come on the board,' and he said, 'Yes, chairman maybe. And, you know, I make a contribution. A hundred thousand dollars.'" This was in the years when BAM ticket prices still hovered in the $5 range. Later, he upped the ante to $200,000.

Lepercq played a crucial role in transforming a collection of political hacks, social ornaments, and

Peter Brook.
Photo (detail): Martha Swope

by Roger Oliver

Now in his seventh decade of making theatrical magic, there is little doubt that stage and film director Peter Brook is one of the most important figures in contemporary theater. He directed his first production as an 18-year-old Oxford University student, and three years later, after productions of Shaw, Ibsen, and Shakespeare at the prestigious Birmingham Repertory Theatre, he made his debut at the Shakespeare Memorial Theatre at Stratford-upon-Avon, the precursor of the Royal Shakespeare Company. Early productions at Stratford included *Titus Andronicus* with Laurence Olivier and Vivien Leigh and *The Tempest* with John Gielgud.

It is with three landmark productions for the Royal Shakespeare Company that Brook achieved worldwide fame. The first was his highly acclaimed *King Lear*, produced in 1962 with a stellar cast—Alec McCowen, Diana Rigg, Alan Webb, and Irene Worth—led by an unforgettable performance by Paul Scofield. Two years later, in 1964, his theatrical realization of Peter Weiss's *Marat/Sade* demonstrated his ability to dazzle audiences with contemporary as well as classical texts. It was in 1970, however, with his startling and innovative production of *A Midsummer Night's Dream*—presented at BAM in the following year—that Brook took his rightful place as an unparalleled theater artist.

That same year, Brook left London for Paris and, with Micheline Rozan, founded the International Centre for Theatre Research. After a three-year theatrical odyssey to Africa, the Middle East, and the United States, working with a multinational group of actors, Brook returned to Paris and established his company at the Bouffes du Nord theater, where he created a series of productions that sought to develop a new international theater language. One of the high points of the Centre's work was the production in 1985 of *The Mahabharata*, longtime Brook collaborator Jean-Claude Carrière's three-part, nine-hour dramatization of the ancient Indian Sanskrit epic. BAM's landmark presentation of *The Mahabharata* in 1987 catalyzed the discovery of what became the BAM Harvey Theater. Although many of Brook's subsequent productions have been smaller in scale, he continues to experiment and to explore in a restless search for new forms of theatrical expression.

Peter Brook

Christopher Walken and Irene Worth in
Sweet Bird of Youth, Tennessee Williams/
American Theatre Season, 1975.
Photo: David H. Fishman

noncontributors into a working board finally ready to raise the money to ameliorate BAM's chronic deficits. "He really ruled that board," said Lichtenstein. "We had a board that really didn't come through. 'You know,' he says to the board, 'in the French cavalry, there are cooks and there are riflemen, but there's one thing they all do. They can all a ride a horse.'" By which he meant raise or donate serious money. "One night," Lichtenstein went on, "he said to me, '*Ami*, there are five or six people I'm just going to let go. I'm going to tell them they're not doing the work.'" So he let them go, while Lichtenstein fretted. "Then he took me out to dinner at Luchow's on 14th Street and ordered a bottle of good French champagne. And he said, 'Let's celebrate.' He was a character." Later, Lichtenstein himself, having learned his lesson, fired another board chairman, who refused to donate more than $5,000 per year. And then he and his chief fundraiser went for their own celebration, this time at the bar of the St. Regis Hotel.

Lepercq was more than a character; he was a mentor. In 1971, Lichtenstein had remarked to a reporter that he was "convinced being President of the United States would be easy after running the Brooklyn Academy of Music." Lepercq took it upon himself to provide Lichtenstein regular lessons in managerial technique. He helped Lichtenstein reshape and augment his staff, meeting regularly with him and his department heads for early morning rye bagels and coffee at Lepercq's Park Avenue office. The tutorials ended in 1976, when Lepercq relocated his business back to Europe.

By then, Lichtenstein had evolved a managerial style that served him well until and beyond his retirement. The first step was surrounding himself with a supportive staff. Charles Ziff arrived in 1973 as director of promotion and audience development and helped refine and automate BAM's marketing, including the formal use of the name "BAM." That punchy acronym did more to enliven the Academy's image than anything other than the equally catchy rubric "Next Wave." Lichtenstein's two most significant staff hires in the 1970s were Judy Daykin, who began as general manager, or second in command, in 1974 and stayed at BAM for 13 years, and Karen Brooks Hopkins, who came to the development department in 1979 and shortly afterward was promoted to vice president for planning and development, all before she was 30.

At first, Lichtenstein had trouble balancing the need for strong support with a fear that too-strong associates might undermine his control. "During the early years," he recalls, "it was musical chairs. I was still trying to understand and run the place. I was distracted for three years, to some extent, with Spoleto. I was sort of beginning to get it together, but it took a number of years, because it was totally new to me. Running a theater was new to me, understanding what a box office was, understanding stage management was all new to me. I had never run a theater. Lepercq was a good teacher. And then when I got Daykin, things really began to stabilize. That was a good seven, eight years. Before her, I held things pretty close to my chest or vest or whatever. I was a lone ranger; I ran this place out of my hip pocket. I was feeling, you know, 'I'm just learning, I really don't know, I feel inadequate.' I was going and going and going, but still the idea of opening myself up scared me, because everyone would see how much I didn't know. With Daykin, things changed. I felt very comfortable with her. I didn't feel any competition. She was a real, real partner."

With his board and staff more settled and the hard years of the early 1970s behind him, Lichtenstein could establish his managerial personality. He even had a lobbyist working for him at City Hall—Gordon Davis, later a New York City parks commissioner, chairman of Jazz at Lincoln Center, and briefly president of Lincoln Center itself. Lichtenstein's style and tactics as an administrator were always based on his passion for certain artists and for BAM and his willingness to pursue projects without quite knowing yet how he would pay for them. That allowed him to accomplish an enormous amount, far greater than a more cautious person could have achieved. But it sometimes got him into trouble. As early as his quest for Brook's *Midsummer Night's Dream*, he recalls, "I was making all kinds of crazy promises and then reneging because there was no way I could keep them, financial things. I remember promising the Royal Shakespeare Company millions of dollars to do it at BAM, which I didn't have. And then I had to backtrack. I mean, it was wild."

"The thing that is key to understanding Harvey is that his greatest attribute is also his greatest flaw—and that is he will bet the ranch every time on what he believes in," said Hopkins, now BAM president, in Ben Brantley's *New Yorker* profile. But that "greatest attribute" usually outweighed any flaw. Like any good impresario, Lichtenstein always sought the best possible deal for BAM, even if he alienated some of the artists he engaged. He would pressure foreign governments for aid, particularly in air transportation on national airlines. He would insist that companies fundraise themselves to support their engagement. As early as Robert Wilson in the late 1960s, he provided the stage and stagehands and box office and chipped in a modest amount of money, but otherwise Wilson was on his own. Lichtenstein had a reputation for declining to sign contracts until the last minute, after a company had committed to come to BAM and couldn't easily back out, and then insisting on further concessions. "Sometimes I made deals that were rather harsh on the companies, which they

didn't appreciate," he concedes. But he had a tight budget, and he was trying to do as much as he could, for BAM and for New York audiences. And he didn't always alienate the artists whom he admired and cultivated. The sometimes hypersensitive choreographer Bill T. Jones once described Lichtenstein's managerial style as "fatherly but not paternalistic."

Throughout the 1970s, with government and foundation grants and increasing board support, BAM was able to upgrade and reinvent its physical plant. In 1973, with the prep school lease expired, the second-floor ballroom was transformed into the Lepercq Space, a sorely missed arena that now serves as home to the BAMcafé. In 1976, the Music Hall, the smaller of the two ground-floor theaters, was redesigned into the 1,000-seat Carey Playhouse, ideal for spoken drama. It has since become the BAM Rose Cinemas, but now BAM has the Harvey two short blocks away.

Sheila Reid and Ian McKellen in *The Wood Demon*, Actors Company, 1974. Photo: Donald Cooper

The Chelsea's fifth-floor theater, now used mostly as a rehearsal space, was upgraded with additional offices and storage areas. Finally, in 1978 came a long-planned total renovation of the entire building, including the Opera House.

But before that came an incident both potentially tragic and ultimately inspiring. On Labor Day morning of 1977, a water main broke beneath Ashland Place next to BAM. Lichtenstein rushed in from East Hampton. Both ground-floor stages and half the orchestra seats in each theater were submerged in 24 feet of water and mud. The basement was waterlogged, and with it the Chelsea Theater's sets, props, and costumes. There was no insurance. But then something remarkable occurred: the city and the staff and the board all pitched in for an extraordinary rescue effort. Helen Hayes agreed to lead the emergency campaign. Donations poured in almost as quickly as the water. Help came not just from the city but from the state and federal governments. Foundations, corporations, and individuals all over

the country pitched in. Nearly one million dollars was raised. Mayor Abraham Beame appointed an 11-agency task force and enlisted 400 city workers for the cleanup crew, and the fall season improbably opened on schedule on October 15. "It was extraordinarily reassuring to feel the wave of support that embraced us," Lichtenstein wrote in his annual report.

If dance dominated the late 1960s and early 1970s, theater, and especially British theater, came to the fore in the 1970s. This partly reflected Lichtenstein's newfound passion for theater, sparked by Brook and the Royal Shakespeare Company. And partly it was a deliberate strategy to distance himself from the Grotowski/Wilson kind of avant-gardism— a move he regretted, and one that still cropped up occasionally, as in the production in 1976 of *The Red Horse* by the experimental theater troupe Mabou Mines, along with various postmodern dancers, and that returned with a vengeance in the Next Wave. Instead, he gravitated toward what he now describes as "maybe not groundbreaking in the sense of what

Below: Richard Pasco and Ian Richardson in *Richard II*, Royal Shakespeare Company, 1974. Photo: Donald Cooper

Opposite: Tony Church (featured) in *Lear*, Royal Shakespeare Company, 1975. Photo (detail): Joe Cocks Studio Collection

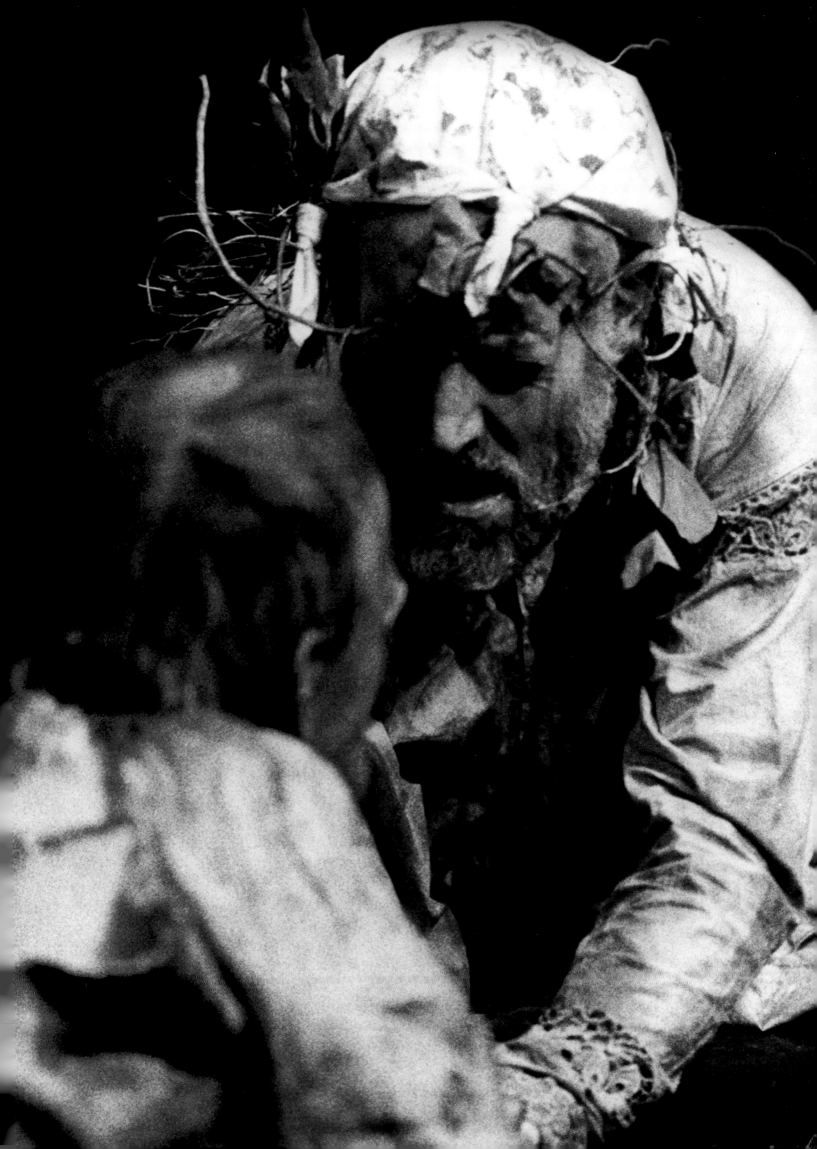

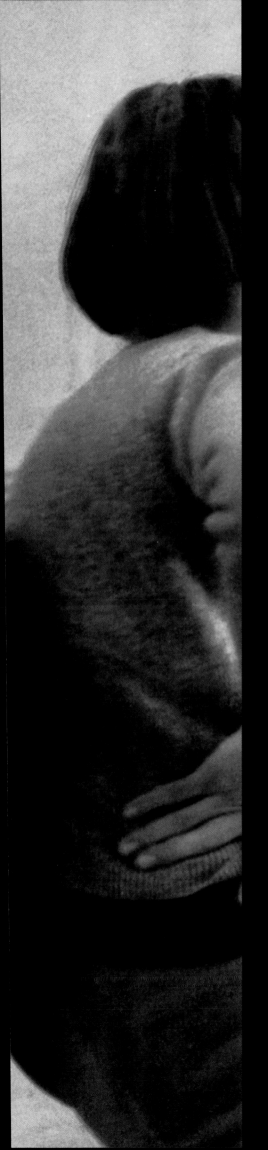

by Susan Yung

Twyla Tharp may have more popular breadth than any of her choreographer peers, though it's hard to say how she is best known. It could be for her Broadway shows, such as *Movin' Out*, for which she won a Tony Award; for the films she's choreographed, including *White Nights*; or for the three books she has authored. Or because she has embraced all types of music, from classical to chart-topping pop. What is certain is that she has never compromised on concept, technique, or principle throughout her prolific career.

In her early work from the 1960s, Tharp disassembled, analyzed, and re-created conventional jazz and modern movement, turning it inside out, running it in retrograde. She crafted roiling, cursive phrases that flowed seamlessly or darted unpredictably. It was too technical to be called strictly postmodern, despite the loopy, relaxed demeanor and the dollops of pedestrian movement. In the 1970s, she began working with Mikhail Baryshnikov—then a guest principal with the American Ballet Theatre (ABT)—who, with a similar compact build, mop of hair, and physical genius, became a male doppelgänger for Tharp. On him, she could satisfactorily combine jazzy, pelvis-swiveling movement with bravura ballet, topped off with his irresistible charisma. She choreographed *Push Comes to Shove*, featuring Baryshnikov, for ABT in 1976, and began choreographing more with ballet.

In addition to making inroads into opera houses, Tharp ventured onto Broadway in 1981 with *The Catherine Wheel*, a collaboration with musician David Byrne. The explosive culminating segment, "The Golden Section," is today performed as a self-contained piece by marquee companies, including Alvin Ailey American Dance Theater, and is considered a "Mt. Everest" of dance, something to be conquered rather than simply performed. Her company premiered *In the Upper Room*, to David Byrne's music, in 1986. Combining brisk ballet with what resemble aerobic exercises, it remains a litmus test of top ballet companies' technical and adaptive capabilities. *The Catherine Wheel* and *In the Upper Room* were performed in 1987 during a monthlong run at BAM, along with many other Tharp works, including classics such as *Baker's Dozen* and *Nine Sinatra Songs*. Tharp has pushed the definition of musical theater with her Broadway paeans to Billy Joel, Bob Dylan, and Frank Sinatra, letting the oft-familiar music fill ears while her choreography visually tells the story, eliminating spoken text's primacy.

Toward the end of ABT's rendition of *Upper Room*, exhaustion sets in, but the dancers tap into deep reserves of skill, muscle memory, and will, and soldier on to a rousing finale. The same might be said of Tharp throughout her work's journey.

Twyla Tharp

we do with the Next Wave, but really important. It kept BAM in the public eye, and we were reviewed. People took it seriously."

That they did, and the British companies attracted a middle-class public from far beyond Brooklyn. The *New York Times* even ran a map showing people how they might get to the distant, exotic borough. The 1973–74 programs, which Lichtenstein called a "breakthrough season" after the forced austerity of the early 1970s, included a much-ballyhooed British Theater Season, also known as Shakespeare-upon-Flatbush. It was the culmination of the relationships he had forged previously with Brook and the Royal Shakespeare Company. Coming to know them was, he says, "a terrific learning experience. I was really captured by the theater." The Royals opened the British season in January 1974 with *Richard II*, with Ian Richardson and Richard Pasco alternating as the king and Bolingbroke, and continued with

three other productions. They were followed by Ian McKellen's Actors Company, with works of R. D. Laing, Anton Chekhov, William Congreve, and Shakespeare—notably, a new production of *King Lear*. Frank Dunlop's Young Vic was the third installment in the British season, starting with *The Taming of the Shrew*, with Jane Lapotaire and Jim Dale; followed by Molière's *Scapino*, again with Dale and with the young Ian Charleson; and Terence Rattigan's *French Without Tears*. Edith Oliver in the *New Yorker* called *Scapino* "a treasure chest—a glorious cornucopia of every kind of comedy, with no theatrical tradition left untapped."

The Royals returned the next season with a repertoire that included Maxim Gorky's *Summerfolk*, directed by David Jones, who was soon to play an even larger role in BAM's theatrical endeavors. The American Bicentennial celebration in 1976 included a third Royal Shakespeare stand, along with the Abbey Theatre of Dublin, including Sean O'Casey's

Rosemary Harris, Tovah Feldshuh, and Ellen Burstyn in *The Three Sisters*, BAM Theater Company, 1977.
Photo: Martha Swope

Cleavon Little in *Joseph and the Amazing Technicolor Dreamcoat*, Tim Rice and Andrew Lloyd Webber, 1976. Photo: Ken Howard

The Plough and the Stars, with Siobhan McKenna and Cyril Cusack. For reasons Lichtenstein cannot quite explain, BAM never presented a production directed by Trevor Nunn, then the artistic director of the Royal Shakespeare Company.

The Bicentennial also brought a collaboration with the Kennedy Center in Washington, DC, on three American plays: Tennessee Williams's *Sweet Bird of Youth*, with Irene Worth and Christopher Walken; George S. Kaufman and Edna Ferber's *The Royal Family*, which moved to Broadway, with Eva Le Gallienne, Rosemary Harris, George Grizzard, and Sam Levine; and Eugene O'Neill's *Long Day's Journey into Night*, with Jason Robards Jr., Zoe Caldwell, Michael Moriarty, and Kevin Conway.

Lichtenstein's fondest memory of the first British season is the *Shrew*, with Dale walking to the edge of the stage and hurling his insults for Kate at

fractious bands of feminists, happily booing away. The American season triggers another favorite memory: "I became good friends with Irene Worth. I took her to lunch once at a restaurant on the East Side, like on 50th Street and First Avenue. And she said, 'Oh yeah,' she said, 'I used to come here a lot,' she said, 'with Johnny G.' And I said, 'Who?' She said, 'Johnny G. You know, John Gielgud.'"

The success of these British and American seasons inspired Lichtenstein to venture down a brave but dangerous path. Ever since his first encounter with the Royal Shakespeare Company, he had dreamed of founding a true American repertory ensemble at BAM. He began in the fall of 1976 with a company under Frank Dunlop's direction. It wasn't a true repertory company, in that each production played separately and the core group of actors was augmented for each show. Dunlop initiated the BAM Theater

Laurie Kennedy in *He and She,*
Rachel Crothers / BAM Theater Company,
1980. Photo: Ken Howard

The critics were tepid, the audience dwindled, and Lichtenstein had to shut down Dunlop's company after the spring of 1978.

What happened? Lichtenstein, for one, is bitter about the critics. "*Joseph,*" he insists, "was a terrific production, absolutely terrific. It should have been a great Christmas show, and it just got slaughtered by the critics. I was just absolutely knocked flat by those reviews. Just killed me." The reviews were not Lichtenstein's only problem. Dunlop was chronically late in deciding on his repertory and casting, "so that when we tried to publicize this thing and sell it as a subscription, we would have no time. He just drove me up the wall. And so at the end of the second season, which I thought had fallen down in quality, I approached Frank and said, 'Frank, I think this thing is really not going to work.'"

Lichtenstein was not done yet. After a season's hiatus, he was back with a second iteration of the BAM Theater Company, less starry but a real repertory ensemble led by David Jones—though this time, Lichtenstein says, with more direct involvement from himself. Jones led off with *The Winter's Tale*—BAM has had a curious fixation on this late Shakespeare masterpiece, presenting numerous productions of it—and followed it with a mix of classics and revivals, some of them worthy but long-forgotten plays: Charles MacArthur's *Johnny on a Spot,* Gorky's *Barbarians,* Rachel Crothers's *He and She,* and a double bill of Brecht's *The Wedding* and Georges Feydeau's *The Purging,* their titles most curiously coupled as *The Marriage Dance*—performed by an ensemble that included Gary Bayer, Christine Estabrook, Boyd Gaines, Roxanne Hart, Cherry Jones, Laurie Kennedy, Frank Maraden, Bill Moor, and Brian Murray. The second Jones season had Shakespeare, Farquhar, Ibsen, Brecht, and Sophocles.

This time, initial interest rose in terms of advance ticket sales, but again the critics were not as kind or supportive or enthusiastic as Lichtenstein had hoped. It all started with that first *Winter's Tale.* As Lichtenstein (a most impartial observer) tells it: "It was a terrific production. Whenever that final scene took place, where the statue of his long-dead wife is brought to life, and I saw it almost every night, I would be in tears. Every night. It was amazing. Walter Kerr was then the theater critic for the *New York Times.* I won't characterize him. But anyway, he came, and the son of a gun fell asleep during the goddamn production and gave it a very mediocre bad review. Much of it, he didn't even see because he was asleep. And he can't contradict me now because he's dead. But it was devastating. We'd raised almost a million dollars to start this thing, and it was a terrific production. It was a terrific production. And it got killed by the *New York Times.*"

Some of the later reviews were kinder, especially outside the *Times,* but Lichtenstein remains convinced that Kerr's opening salvo killed his beloved repertory

Company in December with the first New York performances of Andrew Lloyd Webber and Tim Rice's *Joseph and the Amazing Technicolor Dreamcoat,* an early work from Lloyd Webber's rock opera phase. Lichtenstein hoped that it would become a modern-day *Nutcracker.* But it was savaged by the New York critics, who are at least consistent in their disdain for Lloyd Webber. Lichtenstein tried to bring it back the next season, this time deferentially restaged by Graciela Daniele, but had to cut the run short by a week due to poor ticket sales. The other two productions that first season directed by Dunlop were of Langdon Mitchell's *The New York Idea* and Chekhov's *Three Sisters.* The second season offered Shaw, Molnár, Shakespeare, and Beckett. The actors, some at the outset of their distinguished careers, included Rene Auberjonois, Ellen Burstyn, Blythe Danner, Richard Dreyfuss, Denholm Elliott, Tovah Feldshuh, Margaret Hamilton, Rosemary Harris, Barnard Hughes, Austin Pendleton, George Rose, Chris Sarandon, Carole Shelley, and Sam Waterston.

dream. "It should have been given a kind of support to give it an opportunity to grow. Attendance followed pretty much what happened in the press. BAM was having a hard time attracting an audience in any case. So it went down the drain." There was a second season, partly encouraged by positive words from Frank Rich, who was critic in waiting at the *Times* during the first season. But after Rich ascended to the top job, he "killed us, killed us," Lichtenstein lamented. For that second season, the production budget had been cut back and Lichtenstein concedes that things did look a little sparse. So the BAM Theater Company died a second and final death, followed by a couple of seasons with no theater at all. Lichtenstein was deeply depressed: "It was a huge blow to me, to a vision I had of building a really important theater company based on Shakespeare and American plays rediscovered. It was something I was deeply committed to, and we just got kicked in the stomach. That was really a terrific, terrific blow."

Lichtenstein managed to keep himself and hence BAM in the public eye with some strategically chosen engagements, and by taking a more active role in local and national cultural politics at the height of the so-called culture wars, serving on National Endowment for the Arts committees and such. But the failure of the theater companies forced a severe cutback; the budget fell from $5 million to $3 million. Once again, Lichtenstein "was meeting payroll by the skin of my teeth every week, getting two hours of sleep a night." In addition, the AIDS epidemic was taking its toll on the BAM staff and several of the artists BAM favored. Finally, BAM managed a half-million-dollar loan from a consortium of eight banks, and the city chipped in another $300,000. "We cut everything to the bone. But what was extraordinary about that, in the very next year, the revival began." The surrounding neighborhood began to perk up, the result of serious urban renewal efforts by the city and local corporations, this time led by BAM itself. And

Christine Estabrook and Frank Maraden in *The Wedding*, Bertolt Brecht/ BAM Theater Company, 1980. Photo: Ken Howard

Alvin Ailey. Photo (detail).
Courtesy of Eva F. Maze / International
Artists Productions

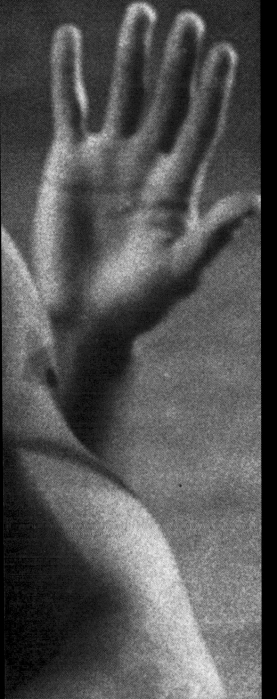

the following year, he created his first works, which included *According to St. Francis* and *Morning Mourning*. Ailey left the company in 1954, when he and de Lavallade joined the cast of the Broadway-bound musical *House of Flowers*. However, once in New York, Ailey chose to study modern dance rather than pursue a Broadway career. In his autobiography he wrote, "The concert dance scene was basically closed to black dancers. . . . I very much wanted to be a choreographer . . . and the time had come for me to make my own decisions."

In 1958, Ailey formed the Alvin Ailey American Dance Theater, which performed for the first time at the 92nd Street Y in New York, where in 1960 he debuted his classic masterpiece *Revelations*. Starting in 1968, the troupe performed regularly at BAM for several seasons. The company returned to the BAM Howard Gilman Opera House in 2008 for the jubilant occasion of its 50th anniversary.

Ailey's work was framed by the Horton technique, but it was fed by the African American experience—be it the blues, church, or juke joints. The company, which was made up of his peers, became a platform for telling their life stories. His dancers would in turn form their own companies to that end. When Ailey died in 1989, he left behind his American Dance Theater and a second company, Ailey II; a school that preserves the Ailey tradition; and myriad works of lasting importance. Ailey is best known for making works that represented the black tradition in America, which he called "blood memories." He often said that "dance came from the people and that it should always be delivered back to the people."

then came Glass's *Satyagraha* and the first two seasons of the Next Wave series, which preceded the festival proper in 1983. "Somehow," says Lichtenstein," we were able to turn a losing situation into the beginning of a winning situation."

The strategically placed engagements that allowed BAM to keep its head above water in the down years included a dance series called Ballet America in 1980–81, with companies from San Francisco, Los Angeles, Cleveland, Akron, Houston, and Philadelphia—the ever faithful Pennsylvania Ballet. That was followed in 1982–83 by Ballet International, another of Lichtenstein's slightly quixotic efforts to convince a Balanchine-devoted dance public of the virtues of European choreographers; companies included the Norwegian National Ballet, the Cullberg Ballet Company, the Dutch National Ballet, the Basel Ballet, the Hamburg Ballet, and the London Contemporary Dance Theatre.

By now, though, all attention within BAM was focused on the idea of Next Wave performances, first bruited as a concept by consultants Anne Livet and Steve Reichard, with the name coming out of the BAM press department. The festival and its name—along with the Majestic/Harvey Theater— came to define the second half of Lichtenstein's BAM tenure. The idea of grouping a string of vanguard events into a fall season, of reemphasizing BAM's commitment to the avant-garde by engendering new productions but also capitalizing on the smaller-scaled lower Manhattan successes of the potent New York performing arts scene of the 1970s, came just at the right time, for BAM and the scene. Some complained that Lichtenstein was exploiting the innovations of others. But BAM chose its artists wisely and well, and offered them a platform that could lead to national and international success. In truth, the innovations spread over the entire season, which, even with the introduction of air-conditioning in 1978, did not include the summer, and it was not always clear why one production appeared under the Next Wave banner and another did not. Gradually, theater and opera came to dominate the winter and spring. And although the term *Next Wave* was a play on the French New Wave film movement, Lichtenstein says there was no conscious attempt to emulate European festivals such as the Festival d'Automne in Paris, which in any case is a citywide affair organized very differently from BAM's. Lichtenstein and his staff and board, even with Hopkins firmly in place in the development department, were hesitant about committing to a full-scale fall festival. So a two-year trial run, the Next Wave series, with four or five productions per season, was floated before the big commitment to a festival came in time for the fall 1983 season.

Tympani, Laura Dean Dancers and Musicians, 1981.
Photo: Lois Greenfield

The Tempest, Norwegian National Ballet, 1982. Photo: Karsten Bundgaard

The first Next Wave series opened in October 1981 with the Trisha Brown Dance Company, followed by Laura Dean Dancers and Musicians. Then came one of the signature events in BAM's history, the American premiere of Philip Glass's first "real" opera, meaning one with opera singers and an orchestra, as opposed to the more idiosyncratic forces that peopled *Einstein on the Beach*, even if it, too, was called an opera. *Satyagraha*, which has just now reached the mainstream in a successful production at the Metropolitan Opera, is a strange, powerful, haunting meditation on the life of the young Mahatma Gandhi, and the staging of the European production by David Pountney and Douglas Perry's performance as Gandhi won over the public and those members of the music press attuned to such new work, if not the mainstream press, including Donal Henahan, then the chief critic of the *New York Times*.

Satyagraha was followed that first season by the Lucinda Childs Dance Company in collaboration with Robert Wilson and the composer Jon Gibson. The second Next Wave series in the fall of 1982 and winter of 1983 was highlighted by Laurie Anderson's *United States: Parts I–IV*, an epic panoply of America that put her on the map as a leading force in contemporary music, hovering between classical and rock.

That series also included Steve Reich, the Flying Karamazov Brothers, the always colorful composer Glenn Branca (who laid siege to Lichtenstein in his office, which the trapped impresario did not find amusing), and dance from Dana Reitz and from Bill T. Jones/Arnie Zane, with music by Max Roach and Connie Crothers and decor by Robert Longo.

The BAM lobby as a milling swarm of black-clad hipsters was born then, and it redefined BAM's image forevermore. But it is instructive to remember, on the eve of the Next Wave Festival, how much trial and error preceded the crystallization of BAM's image and its success in subsequent years. For Lichtenstein, BAM was a long, thrilling, sometimes painful education. He sought for 15 years to find a focus, an identity for the place that would attract audiences and critical attention. After Anderson's *United States*, he was finally confident enough to commit to a full-scale fall Next Wave Festival. Joseph V. Melillo was hired to produce it, and the future of BAM began.

Above: Lepercq Space. Photo courtesy
of BAM Hamm Archives Center

Right: *Quarry*, Meredith Monk, 1976.
Photo: Lauretta Harris

by Meredith Monk

I am thinking about the first time I walked into the Lepercq Space. It was on a sunny Saturday afternoon sometime in 1974. I remember what I was wearing—my overalls and black high-top sneakers—but I can't recall why I was there. My first impression of the enormous, clear, open space with tan walls, a high ceiling, a parquet floor, and exposed pipes was that it had the quality of both an industrial space and a ballroom. There was a balcony running along one long wall and huge windows along the other.

I knew from that first time that the Lepercq Space was ideal for my work. I had always preferred an audience looking down at the landscape of a piece and in a sense being part of it rather than watching events through a picture frame. The Lepercq Space offered the possibility of tactility: a combination of intimacy and epic scale, close-up and long shot simultaneously. At that time, I was interested in breaking down conventional notions of the audience–performer relationship. When I entered the space, I immediately began visualizing a variety of performance configurations and situations.

I presented two works at the Lepercq Space in the 1970s: *Quarry*, a large-scale music-theater work in three movements about World War II, in 1976 and a revival of my opera *Education of the Girlchild* in 1979.

In *Quarry*, I placed the audience on bleachers down the two long sides of the space. Visually, the mass of audience members on the other side of the space became the set. I was thinking of the huge meeting halls where the Nazis organized rallies before and during World War II. The overall visual scheme of the opera was a giant mandala, with a pallet bed on the floor in the middle of the space; the four corners around the bed comprised four different environments or worlds, each with one, two, or three performers. During the first movement, "Lullaby," the audience could choose what to look at since the activities in the four corners and the bed happened simultaneously. The size and scale of the Lepercq Space offered perfect yet differing vantage points so that each audience member had a unique experience. There were 42 performers in the piece, and I especially remember our Christmas and New Year's Eve performances, when there were approximately as many people in the audience as in the piece—a one-to-one relationship.

Education of the Girlchild was designed as a site-specific piece that would change in relation to the particular performance space. I would go into a space and sit there for many hours listening for what it seemed to want, having a silent dialogue with it. I ended up playing with the extreme depth and layering that was intrinsic to the Lepercq Space. I seated the audience on one end of the space looking down the long, tunnel-like room. The depth of space became a metaphor for the passage of time, one of the main themes of *Education of the Girlchild*.

What I always loved about the Lepercq Space was its versatility, spaciousness, and scope, which inspired the mind to be lucid, the imagination to fly. Anything could happen there. And then, of course, there was Harvey standing on the balcony during rehearsals as he looked down like a beautiful and fierce eagle, not letting anything escape his gaze.

Above, left: Julian Beck (featured) in
Paradise Now, Living Theatre, 1968.
Photo: Kenneth L. McLaren

Above, right: Carl Einhorn and Karen
Weiss in *Paradise Now*, Living Theatre,
1968. Photo: Kenneth L. McLaren

Opposite: Miguel Godreau and
Judith Jamison in *The Prodigal Prince*,
Alvin Ailey American Dance Theater,
1970. Photo: Sigrid Estrada

Opposite: Eliot Feld in
At Midnight, American Ballet Company,
1970. Photo: Pino Abbrescia

Above: *Tread*, Merce Cunningham
Dance Company, 1970.
Photo: James Klosty

Statement, Jeff Duncan Dance
Company, 1970. Photo: V. Sladon

Violostries, Ballet Theatre Contemporain, 1972. Photo courtesy of BAM Hamm Archives Center

Top: *Candide*, Leonard Bernstein and
Hugh Wheeler/Chelsea Theater Center,
1974. Photo: Martha Swope

Bottom, left: Christopher Lloyd in
Kaspar, Peter Handke/Chelsea
Theater Center, 1973.
Photo: Amnon Ben Nomis

Bottom, right: Frank Langella in
The Prince of Homburg,
Heinrich von Kleist/Chelsea Theater
Center, 1977.
Photo: Martha Swope

Opposite: Grayson Hall in
The Screens, Jean Genet/
Chelsea Theater Center, 1971.
Photo: Alan B. Tepper

Opposite: *Yerma*, Nuria Espert
Company, 1972.
Photo: Juan Gyenes

Top: Raymond Andrews in
Deafman Glance, Robert Wilson, 1971.
Photo: Ed Grazda

Bottom: Robert Wilson (featured) in
his *Deafman Glance*, 1971.
Photo: Pietro Privitera

Top: *Angels of the Inmost Heaven*,
Erick Hawkins Dance Company, 1974.
Photo: Kenn Duncan

Bottom: Cindy Lubar and George
Ashley in *The Life and Times of
Joseph Stalin*, Robert Wilson, 1973.
Photo: Kazuko Oshima

Opposite: Jeremy James-Taylor,
Jim Dale, and Ian Charleson in
Scapino, Young Vic Company, 1974.
Photo: Reg Wilson

Left: Michael Moriarty and
Jason Robards Jr. in *Long Day's
Journey into Night*, Eugene O'Neill/
American Theatre Season, 1976.
Photo: Richard Braaten

Right: Rosemary Harris in *The Royal
Family*, George S. Kaufman and
Edna Ferber/American Theatre Season,
1975. Photo: Cliff Moore

Left: Eva Le Gallienne in *The Royal Family*, George S. Kaufman and Edna Ferber/American Theatre Season, 1975. Photo: Cliff Moore

Right: George Grizzard in *The Royal Family*, George S. Kaufman and Edna Ferber/American Theatre Season, 1975. Photo: Cliff Moore

Go for Barocco, Les Ballets Trockadero
de Monte Carlo, 1976. Photo courtesy
of BAM Hamm Archives Center

Messiah, Lar Lubovitch Dance
Company, 1976. Photo: Milton Oleaga

Above: Alan Howard in *Henry V*,
Royal Shakespeare Company, 1976.
Photo: Nobby Clark

Opposite: David-James Carroll in
*Joseph and the Amazing Technicolor
Dreamcoat*, Tim Rice and Andrew
Lloyd Webber, 1976. Photo: Ken Howard

Top: Ruth Andrien (featured) in *Images*,
Paul Taylor Dance Company, 1977.
Photo: Costas

Bottom: Ruth Maleczech, David
Warrilow, and JoAnne Akalaitis in
The Red Horse, Mabou Mines, 1976.
Photo: Richard Landry

Top: *Good Lads at Heart*, National
Youth Theatre of Great Britain, 1979.
Photo: Nobby Clark

Bottom: *Songs of Mahler*,
San Francisco Ballet, 1978.
Photo: Arne Folkedal

121

Opposite: Richard Dreyfuss and Rene Auberjonois in *Julius Caesar*, BAM Theater Company, 1978. Photo: Martha Swope

Top: Edward Zang and Blythe Danner (featured) in *The New York Idea*, Langdon Mitchell/BAM Theater Company, 1977. Photo: Martha Swope

Bottom: Rene Auberjonois and Carole Shelley in *The Play's the Thing*, Ferenc Molnár/BAM Theater Company, 1978. Photo: Frederic Ohringer

Opposite: William Whitener in *Baker's Dozen*, Twyla Tharp and Dancers, 1979. Photo (detail): Paul Kolnik

Above: Tom Rawe, Twyla Tharp, Rose Marie Wright, and Kenneth Rinker in *Sue's Leg*, Twyla Tharp and Dancers, 1976. Photo: Tom Berthiaume

A Flea in Her Ear, Georges Feydeau/
Comédie-Française, 1979.
Photo: Agence de Presse Bernand

Joan of Arc, Bread and Puppet Theater,
1979. Photo: Paul Kolnik

Left: Boyd Gaines and Christine
Estabrook in *The Winter's Tale*,
BAM Theater Company, 1980.
Photo: Ken Howard

Middle: Sheila Allen and
Gerry Bamman in *A Midsummer
Night's Dream*, BAM Theater Company,
1981. Photo: Ken Howard

Right: Brian Murray in *The Winter's
Tale*, BAM Theater Company, 1980.
Photo: Ken Howard

Left: Richard Jamieson and Joe Morton
in *Oedipus the King*, BAM Theater
Company, 1981. Photo: Ken Howard

Right: Seth Allen in *Jungle of Cities*,
Bertolt Brecht/BAM Theater Company,
1981. Photo: Ken Howard

Top: Christopher Gillis and
Monica Morris in *Private Domain*,
Paul Taylor Dance Company, 1981.
Photo: Jack Vartoogian

Bottom: Lila York in *Diggity*, Paul Taylor
Dance Company, 1981.
Photo: Jack Vartoogian

Opposite: Edward Myers, Sylviane
Bayard, and Mark Trares (featured) in
Swan Lake, Pennsylvania Ballet, 1981.
Photo: Adam Laipson

Opposite: International Afrikan
American Ballet, *DanceAfrica*, 1983.
Photo: Tom Caravaglia

Above: Lisa Kraus and Vicky Shick in
Glacial Decoy, Trisha Brown Company,
1981. Photo: Babette Mangolte

Ivan Liska (featured) in *Mahler's Third
Symphony*, Hamburg Ballet, 1983.
Photo: Joachim Flügel

"For Lichtenstein, BAM was a long, thrilling, sometimes painful education. He sought for 15 years to find a focus, an identity for the place that would attract audiences and critical attention. After Anderson's *United States*, he was finally confident enough to commit to a full-scale fall Next Wave Festival. Joseph V. Melillo was hired to produce it, and the future of BAM began."

Opal Loop/Cloud Installation #72503,
Trisha Brown Company 1981.
Photo (detail): Harry Shunk

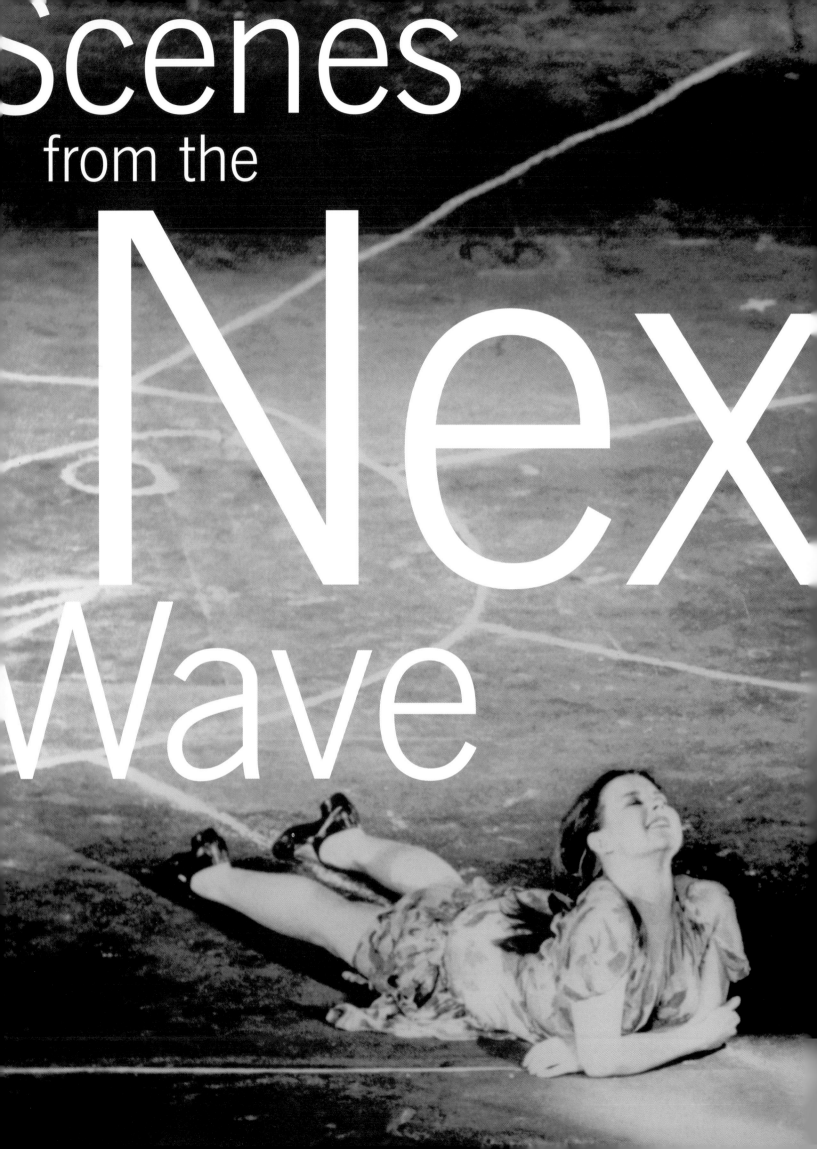

Scenes
from the
Next
Wave

t

Finding the Harvey

by Peter Brook

It has always been impossible for Harvey to give up. Whatever the obstacles, defeat was never an option, only another temporary pause. Nothing shows this more clearly than the story of the Majestic Theater.

By the time the 1960s began to shake up the old patterns of Western culture, our friendship was already deep. My working relationship with Harvey went back to the days when he invited *A Midsummer Night's Dream* to come straight from Broadway to Brooklyn—already an unprecedented event. Together, we took a step that was revolutionary at the time—the cheapest seats were no longer remotely in the gallery. They were those closest to the actors, with cushions on the side of the stage for just one dollar. We knew at once that we spoke the same language with the same aims, so when the first international company was formed, Harvey was a convincing and eloquent fundraiser. After our series of journeys, which led us from Africa to the Campesinos in California, it was natural to do our first open workshops at BAM.

When years later *The Mahabharata* appeared in Avignon and Paris and an English version was made, it was obvious that if this played in New York, it could only be with Harvey. But where? Brooklyn, yes, but BAM had no big space other than the Opera House. Meanwhile, for several years we had broken away from conventional theater buildings—a quarry, a shipyard, an abandoned movie studio, but no conventional theater buildings. In the ruined Bouffes du Nord, we had found the ideal place for our work.

Harvey reluctantly, sadly for us both, accepted the inevitable, no New York for *The Mahabharata*. Then suddenly an excited phone call: "This is Harvey. I've found it! Today I was walking to the theater and as always I passed a derelict facade just opposite BAM. This time I paused to ask myself what is this place? I spoke to our technical director, he answered it was an old movie house, the Majestic, that had been closed for years. Immediately, we got a ladder, took a flashlight, broke a first-floor window and—Peter! You must come over at once! It's a second Bouffes du Nord!"

And so it came about. Now the practical difficulties began—to put it into working order a huge budget was needed, so Harvey called on all his powers of persuasion to convince the Brooklyn borough president, the New York City Council, and the New York City Department of Cultural Affairs. I was asked to fly over from Paris to explain. I tried to be as persuasive as possible while telling no lies. There was one argument I used again and again that I know was true. A theater city like New York could no longer be locked into its old buildings. New theater demanded new spaces and no longer in the center of the city, where theater was supposed to take place. The Majestic would not be just for us—it would be for the whole theater community.

Of course, Harvey succeeded, the funds were raised, our technical director Jean-Guy Lecat was mobilized, and our designer Chloe Obolensky created a team to treat the walls like she had done at the Bouffes, so that they retained all that age and time had printed on them. We could now bring *The Mahabharata*—and again Harvey had won against all odds.

He had proved that New York was no longer just Manhattan—those in search of adventure began to know that BAM was the place to go. We could come again and again—we created *The Cherry Orchard*, then *The Man Who*, and *Hamlet*—and now, who knows.

Today, the building vibrates with so much vital work, recharged and reinspired in Harvey's tradition by Karen Brooks Hopkins and Joe Melillo. And it has a new name, the only name that covers all aspects of past, present, and future. Today, the Majestic has rightly become "The Harvey."

Previous page: Josephine Ann Endicott and Ann Höling in *The Seven Deadly Sins*, Tanztheater Wuppertal Pina Bausch, 1985. Photo: Ulli Weiss

Opposite: The Majestic Theater, 1987. Photo: Robert Davis

by Jayme Koszyn

The BAM era from 1981 to 1999 was framed by two monumental occasions: the inception of the Next Wave Festival and the retirement of Harvey Lichtenstein, president and executive producer. In between these milestones, BAM transformed into an institution in the most positive sense of the word. Fueled by a successful fundraising machine created by Karen Brooks Hopkins and galvanized by both Lichtenstein and his creative partner Joseph V. Melillo, BAM's programming took off within the contexts of the Next Wave Festival; the development of spring seasons in opera, theater, and dance; and the refashioning of its facilities. During this era, the BAM aesthetic became deeply defined through the Next Wave and its expansion of year-round programming, impacting the surrounding Brooklyn community, New York City at large, and the international cultural scene with a boomerang effect of nurturing and presenting both homegrown and international artists.

The Next Wave Series

As outlined in the previous chapter, in 1979 Lichtenstein reestablished the BAM Theater Company under the direction of David Jones, the second attempt by Lichtenstein to create a purely American repertory company that he believed had enormous potential for BAM both as a presenter and a producer. Yet by 1981 the company had failed after only two seasons, hemorrhaging money. BAM was about to go under, with a deficit of nearly $2 million. To keep the institution alive, not to mention sustainable, Lichtenstein conceived an artistically driven series that would be an extension of BAM's programming philosophy while simultaneously generating extraordinary visibility and creativity. As Hopkins recalls, BAM had to spend less and stage fewer performances, yet somehow get more firepower into the bargain.

In the fall of 1981, a marketing challenge fused with Lichtenstein's creative vision of cross-disciplinary programming helped jump-start the Next Wave series, the forerunner of the Next Wave Festival. The BAM staff strategized about how to promote three contemporary dance companies: Trisha Brown, Laura Dean, and Lucinda Childs. BAM was mostly programmed along disciplinary lines—theater, opera, chamber music, and so on—and here were three dance companies that could be marketed together. But, according to then press director Ellen Lampert-Gréaux, there was the Philip Glass opera *Satyagraha* "sticking out like a sore thumb."

This dilemma, accentuated by Lichtenstein's artistic vision, became the catalyst for the Next Wave series. *Satyagraha* would be packaged with the dance works during a tightly scheduled period from October

Douglas Perry (featured) in
Satyagraha, Philip Glass, 1981.
Photo (detail): Jaap Pieper

Lucinda Childs (featured) in *Available Light*, Lucinda Childs Dance Company, 1983. Photo: Johan Elbers/ Beatriz Schiller

to December. By fusing these performances into a series, critical mass would be achieved. Now they needed a name. French cinema's New Wave had been floating around in the collective consciousness for some time; the BAM staff brainstormed—New Wave, Next Wave!— and the idea of the Next Wave series took hold.

Satyagraha was hugely successful, selling out and receiving extraordinary reviews, while the dance companies attracted unprecedented numbers from the entire metropolitan area. The inaugural season of the series—followed by a second season in 1982–83, which presented Steve Reich and Musicians, the Flying Karamazov Brothers, Glenn Branca, Laurie Anderson, Dana Reitz and Dancers, and Bill T. Jones / Arnie Zane with musicians Max Roach and Connie Crothers—had all of the elements of what would come to define the Next Wave Festival: controversy, wild success, sold-out houses, walkouts, and an unorthodox mix of the new and the known. These first two seasons were, in retrospect, the true beginning of the Next Wave Festival.

Redefining the Next Wave

The success of the Next Wave series inspired Lichtenstein to expand the artistic venture into a festival. With audiences connecting emotionally to the series, he was encouraged to create a multi-disciplinary festival, structured within one intense, focused period of time and featuring a diverse range of artists and programming. Influenced by the power of consolidated presenting, Lichtenstein perceived the Next Wave as an innovative showcase for the experimental performing arts that would promote important contemporary artists and introduce little-known, younger artists to a wide audience. He wanted to create something new, something that would define BAM as an institution.

In keeping with BAM's knack for renewable reinvention, if not resurrection—from fire, flood, and financial ruin—the Next Wave Festival was launched in the fall of 1983, when BAM presented a season of 11 productions by some of the most innovative performing artists of the time, including Glass, Brown, and Childs from the first season of the series, along with George Coates, Lee Breuer and Bob Telson, Carolyn Carlson, Molissa Fenley, Rina Schenfeld, Mikhail Matiushin and Robert Benedetti, and Nina Wiener. All three BAM venues were utilized: the 2,100-seat Opera House, the 1,000-seat Carey Playhouse (now the BAM Rose Cinemas), and the flexible, 300-seat Lepercq Space.

The festival would commission, develop, produce, and present new work in the performing arts from around the world in all disciplines. It would ultimately become the nation's most significant presenter of contemporary and experimental performance. Over the next 15 years of Lichtenstein's tenure, artists would be discovered as well as nurtured,

The Way of How, George Coates
Performance Works, 1983.
Photo: Debra Heimerdinger

Philip Glass. Photo (detail): Isabelle
Carlota Rodriguez

later attended Juilliard in New York City, then as now the most important music conservatory in America.

During the summer of 1960, Glass worked with the distinguished composer Darius Milhaud. Thanks to a Fulbright Scholarship, he went to Paris in 1964, where he studied for two years with Nadia Boulanger, a legendary music pedagogue who had also taught Aaron Copland, among many other prominent American and international musicians. Though Glass's compositions have been controversial as well as innovative, they nonetheless reflect a very sophisticated preparation.

Returning to New York in 1967 and joining the downtown art world, he forged parallel careers in experimental theater, as a founding member of Mabou Mines (which performed at BAM in 1976), and music composition. Unable to get others to play his scores, Glass formed in the mid-1960s an eponymous ensemble that still exists with some of its original personnel; he even self-published some recordings of his music. Within only a few years, miraculously it now seems, he became a celebrity within this aesthetically fertile yet discriminating community. By the late 1970s, Glass had established himself as a prolific and influential composer known to a much wider audience less for his chamber-sized works than for musical theater, operas, and film soundtracks. *Satyagraha*, his opera based on Mahatma Gandhi's work as a young activist in South Africa, was performed at BAM in 1981 in the initial season of the Next Wave series. Since then, BAM has presented numerous Glass works, including the 1984 revival of *Einstein on the Beach*, his collaboration with Robert Wilson, and 25 years later the American premiere of his opera *Kepler*.

Characterized as "minimalist" because his music was less elaborate than traditional classical music, his early compositions are more accurately described as modular, dependent upon musical motifs that were repeated and elaborated. The culmination of this style, *Music in Twelve Parts*, composed between 1971 and 1974, is among his masterpieces. While some recent compositions for small ensembles echo his earlier style, most of his later music, especially for film, is more accessible. Indeed, like no one else of his generation, Glass has succeeded with elite composition and popular music.

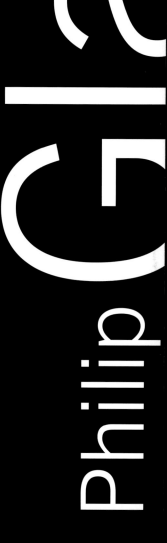

Philip Gla

while most, already established through performances in lofts and studios, were provided with larger stages and monumentally bigger budgets. Major American creators, like Robert Wilson and Philip Glass, came home to BAM after having spent years presenting work primarily in Europe.

"Basically, the work that encompassed the Next Wave series was a continuation of work we'd been doing for many years. But it seemed to give coherence to the idea that there was a relationship between what these dancers were doing and what these composers were doing, and so on," said Lichtenstein to Amy Virshup in her 1987 *New York* magazine cover story, "BAM Goes Boom." As the culmination of Lichtenstein's interests and his artistic focus, and the fulfillment of his fierce ambition to release BAM's fullest potential, the festival came to define him as an impresario. Through an organic process, beginning in 1967 with his arrival at the building whose performance spaces were shared with a boys' prep school and judo academy, the Next Wave Festival gave Lichtenstein the one elusive, and virtually indestructible, element of his artistic vision—BAM's niche.

With the Next Wave's developing aesthetic and the organization's mission entwined, BAM's vision became clearer; the festival was both institutional crucible and burnisher. Such refinement strengthened BAM's core purpose. Even in the festival's earliest days, fundraising became more focused and successful in support of the Next Wave's intensity and cohesion. From the festival's launch in 1983 to Lichtenstein's retirement in 1999, BAM grew exponentially as an institution.

Under the leadership of now-president Karen Brooks Hopkins, who had arrived just two years before the Next Wave series, the fundraising and development program established itself internally as BAM's vital organs and externally as a nonprofit model, with its diversified donor mixes and fundable layers of support. The Lafayette Avenue building and the various performing venues underwent extraordinary transformation, with the Lepercq Space, the Carey Playhouse, and Fulton Street's Majestic Theater all being reconfigured, developed, or renovated with significant help from New York City.

To help broaden the scope of programming, Joseph V. Melillo was brought on prior to the launch of the festival as producing director. The then 36-year-old marketing specialist, trained stage director, and arts administrator worked intimately with Lichtenstein to facilitate the artworks that comprised the Next Wave, finding artists, forging interdisciplinary partnerships, and commissioning and producing the work. Melillo was essentially the third point in a leadership triangle headed by Lichtenstein that defined the aesthetic synonymous with the festival—an aesthetic that still defines BAM, almost 30 years after the Next Wave began.

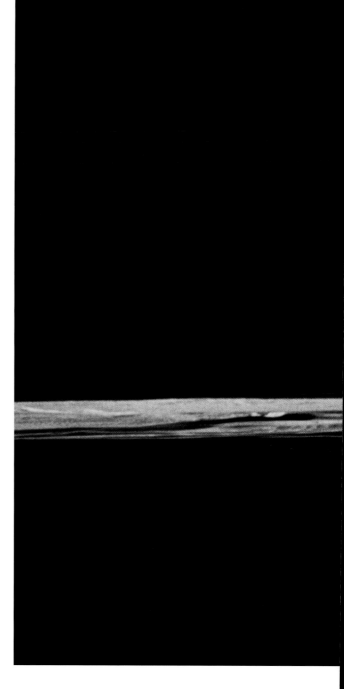

The Next Wave Aesthetic

In inimitable BAM fashion, need and desperation gave rise to glorious innovation. The productions presented during the Next Wave series had all the creative ingredients that would become the festival's signature, since they mixed the completely new and contemporary with reinventions of the canonical. Eclecticism characterized by extraordinary artistic quality would be the values driving what BAM chose to present, commission, and produce under the festival's umbrella. The festival would not be about minimalism, or expressionism, or any one movement. This was the defining paradox for the festival: BAM's aesthetic was anti-aesthetic.

"The Next Wave Festival is a crapshoot; that's what it was chartered to be," observes Melillo. Yet if its mandate was to be a crapshoot—already an ironic

Susanne Linke in her *Solos*, 1985.
Photo: Beatriz Schiller

practice in itself—it was a crapshoot with a mission. The Next Wave would come to be far from random in its artistic sensibilities and structure. "Being taught to follow the artist was one of Harvey's great life lessons," says Melillo. "And that is what drove us in all of our decisions—to follow the artist, but also to use our own curatorial judgment required to find in the universe which artist we should choose. What makes us choose this artist, or that production, over another? There are life experiences, there's education, research—our individual selection and choices mattered, so that it really came together as a festival that shaped and prodded and challenged audiences each year."

John Cage, another Next Wave artist, said once that art is "simply a way of waking up to the very life we're living." There was no better audience wake-up call than the Next Wave, since BAM chose artists and productions that incensed, provoked, and astonished.

And the chemistry between BAM and those artists, conjoined within a fast and furious two- to three-month season, caused a combustion—with audiences, critics, donors, and, of course, the artists themselves.

The Next Wave quickly became a magnet for all types of contemporary issues, social movements, and intellectual dialogue. Its anti-aesthetic developed along with American as well as world history. "You have to set the stage for when the Next Wave Festival was launched," Hopkins says. "Ronald Reagan was in the White House. AIDS was a mystery disease, poised to become a tragic signature for the decade, and prickly navigations of race, class, and gender were coalescing, all fertile issues debated on Next Wave stages."

Both globalization and multiculturalism, terms now entrenched in our vocabulary but barely established during the 1980s, had been BAM's focus

since its resurgence under Lichtenstein. By placing international companies side by side on BAM stages, the Next Wave Festival enabled audiences to learn about work from around the globe. Artists cross-referenced their work, breaking down boundaries and creating, as Peter Brook writes, "a space where we can encounter each other."

The Next Wave was not merely artistically prescient, it was politically prescient. While "globalization" was coined early in the 1940s as a corporate or sociological concept, it wasn't commonly discussed within an economic context until the publication of Theodore Levitt's article "The Globalization of Markets" in 1983, coincidentally the first year of the Next Wave Festival. The "culture wars" as a common trope, adopted in the mid-1980s during the Reagan administration and snowballing to its climax in the father-and-son Bush era, was only beginning to be defined when the festival began.

The festival's productive clash of cultures—productive in the sense that artists drew on the energy, the pain and struggle, and the emotions released by those clashes—was doubly layered because of those culture wars, the phrase used to describe the tension between Reagan-era conservatives and artists who felt that their range of free expression should encompass what their detractors viewed as indecent or obscene. From many vantage points, Next Wave artists during the Lichtenstein era told stories of globalization and the so-called shrinking of the world (underscoring our commonality as well as our disconnection), notably Anne Teresa De Keersmaeker, with *Rosas Danst Rosas* (1986); John Adams/Alice Goodman, with *Nixon in China* (1987); Bill T. Jones/Arnie Zane, with *Last Supper at Uncle Tom's Cabin/The Promised Land* (1990); Robert Lepage, with *Needles and Opium* (1992); Pina Bausch, with *Two Cigarettes in the Dark* (1994); and Lin Hwai-min, with *Nine Songs* (1995).

BAM's artistic leadership combed the world for work that had the Next Wave Festival vibe. "We were part of the global community," says Melillo, "so we were seeing work in international locations, primarily urban centers. Harvey and I knew that because of the industrial-strength travel we were doing, we had a responsibility to get that work to New York City. We wanted BAM to be a global center." That responsibility was to the local New York audiences, or as Melillo describes, "It was a service we were rendering to the civilian culture buyer and those who traveled to New York City to learn   we were displaying ideas and practices, new non-narratives, and new visual presentations."

As a result of Lichtenstein and Melillo's peregrinations, the Next Wave presented during its first 15 years more than 200 productions with numerous artists and companies from around the world. The developing aesthetic of the festival was overwhelmingly influenced by the crosswinds of international artists

Robert Lepage in his *Needles and Opium*, 1992.
Photo (detail): Alastair Muir

by Susan Yung

Steve Reich's body of work reflects an imagination both profoundly curious and disciplined, ranging from studies that use the body as an instrument to large-scale compositions concerning philosophical issues. Born in New York City, Reich received a philosophy degree at Cornell. At Mills College, in Oakland, California, he studied composition with Luciano Berio and Darius Milhaud, earning an MA in music. In his early compositions, Reich experimented with tape loops, text, and shifting phrasing, notably in *Piano Phase* (1967). From 1974 to 1976, he composed *Music for 18 Musicians*, a hypnotic performance in which percussionists move between instruments, creating an invisible web of movement. "I think it's effective because it's coming out of necessity," Reich said. "It's not choreography—it's simply watching a task being done."

This concept was central to the Judson Church movement, whose performances Reich attended. Around the same time, he also saw Balanchine's ballets set to music by Stravinsky. "I've always been interested in dance and in the relationship between music and dance. I've also always felt that what I do is danceable because sometimes while composing, I dance while I'm doing it," Reich noted. A rich emotional soundscape arises out of his music's complex, shifting sections, graduated dynamics and volume that shape phrases, and words that dart between meaning and aural pattern. His rigorous compositions have been favored by choreographers who have frequented BAM, particularly Anne Teresa De Keersmaeker, who has employed Reich's work in numerous productions, beginning with *Fase, four movements to the music of Steve Reich* (1982), which Reich calls a masterpiece. Other choreographers who have set dance to Reich's music include Jerome Robbins, Laura Dean, and Doug Varone.

Reich's history at BAM is extensive. In 1971, Reich and his group performed *Drumming*, and in 1982 he was first presented under the Next Wave rubric. In 2002, with his wife, video artist Beryl Korot, he created *Three Tales*, a documentary digital video opera about the Hindenburg, the atomic bomb, and cloning. With other large venues, BAM hosted a major element of *Steve Reich @ 70* (2006)—a two-part evening with choreography by De Keersmaeker and Akram Khan. Reich—who has garnered a Pulitzer Prize, received Grammy and Bessie Awards, and been honored by the American Academy of Arts and Letters and awarded the Ordre des Arts et Lettres—might be forgiven if he sported a laurel wreath rather than the baseball cap he favors in performance.

getting to know one another, and audiences getting to know them. And within performances, particularly of American-based work, gone were the single or representative ethnicities, body and beauty types, or any form of monolithism—except where such choices served the artistic purpose.

The (Non-Traditional) Tradition

All the elements that comprised the Next Wave aesthetic were—in keeping with the self-contradiction that defined the festival—anything but new. The festival began as an extension of a tradition that reached back to the Dadaists and their founding performance site, Zurich's Cabaret Voltaire, an almost violently mixed bag of poets and other writers, performers, sculptors, painters, and composers. Most uncannily similar was the preponderance of tide-changing visual artists who took part in the cabaret's anarchic shenanigans, including Jean Arp, Wassily Kandinsky, Paul Klee, Giorgio de Chirico, and Max Ernst. Set that list against the Next Wave's visual artist collaborators—among them Robert Rauschenberg, Donald Judd, Sol LeWitt, Roy Lichtenstein, Marisol, Francesco Clemente, Keith Haring, Adrianne Lobel, and Anish Kapoor—and the avant-garde tradition of unleashing visual artists into the performance space emerges.

Lichtenstein himself could draw a symbolic dotted line from the festival he created to the Dada movement. When a cousin of his married the expressionist artist Jack Tworkov, he began an early education in visual abstraction. As a student at Brooklyn College, he developed an interest in dance and spent a memorable summer at Black Mountain College in North Carolina, where he met Rauschenberg, Charles Olson, Franz Kline, and Merce Cunningham, who would later perform regularly at BAM, while commissioning scores by John Cage and sets by Rauschenberg, Jasper Johns, and Andy Warhol. Having trained in Martha Graham technique (Graham herself collaborated with sculptor Isamu Noguchi), Lichtenstein performed with modern dance companies, including those of Sophie Maslow and Pearl Lang. "For me," observed Lichtenstein, "the worlds of painting, dance, and poetry opened almost all at once. In those days, Abstract Expressionism and dance were the most cutting edge of the arts in America. I think we've begun to see music, theater, and performance come to the fore in works like *Satyagraha*, *Einstein on the Beach*, and *Gospel at Colonus*."

Lichtenstein's personal aesthetic—in part forged by these experiences—found its full actualization in the Next Wave's collaborative, visual artist–friendly, cross-disciplinary embracing of creators from all worlds. Next Wave presentations were rarely the work of one artist in a single discipline. From the festival's inception, artists collaborated across fields. The festival's first season was emblematic of the cross-pollination that would characterize the next 30 years. It opened with *The Photographer / Far from the Truth*, conceived by Dutch visual artist Rob Malasch and composer Philip Glass, directed by JoAnne Akalaitis, and designed by Santo Loquasto, with a book by Robert Coe,

Callas, Tanztheater Bremen, 1985.
Photo: Johan Elbers

Trudy Ellen Craney (featured) in
Nixon in China, John Adams and
Alice Goodman, 1987.
Photo: Martha Swope

155

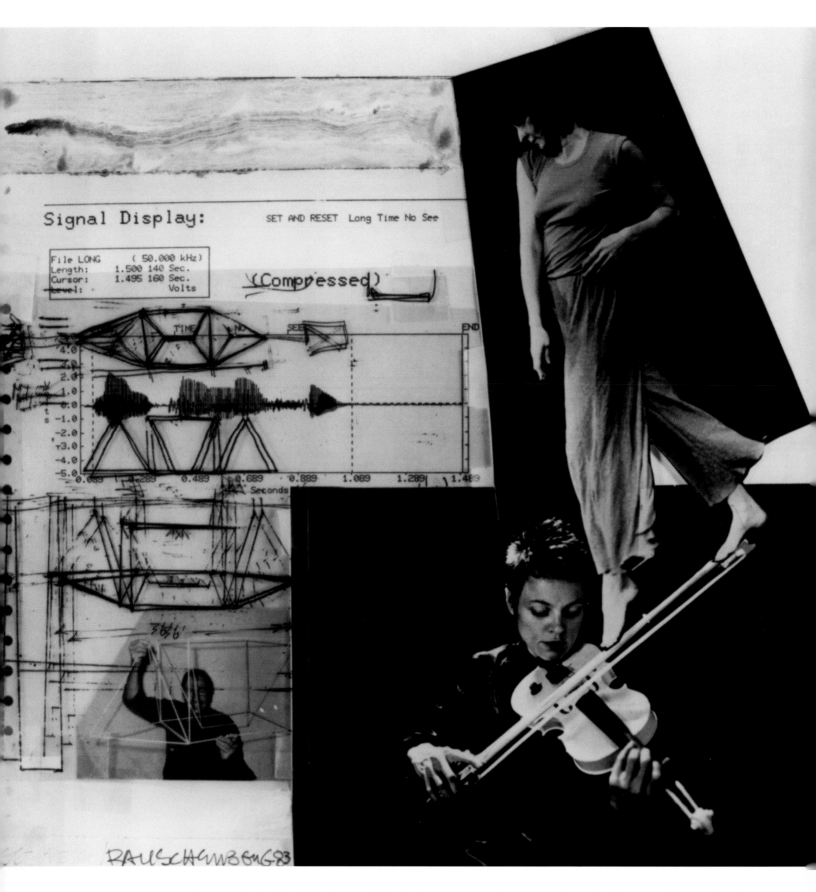

Signal Display: SET AND RESET Long Time No See

File LONG   (50.000 kHz)
Length: 1.500 140 Sec.
Cursor: 1.495 160 Sec.
Level: Volts

(Compressed)

RAUSCHENBERG83

Set and Reset, Trisha Brown Company,
1983. Collage: Robert Rauschenberg.
Photos: Johan Elbers (Trisha Brown)
and Paula Court (Laurie Anderson)

choreography by David Gordon, and lighting by
Jennifer Tipton. In that same season, choreographer
Trisha Brown collaborated with composer-
performer Laurie Anderson and visual artist Robert
Rauschenberg, who designed a set he characterized
as "a mix to provide a hovering environment for
the dance"; Lucinda Childs collaborated with
composer John Adams and architect Frank Gehry;

and choreographer Nina Wiener collaborated with
composer Sergio Cervetti and sculptor Judy Pfaff.

The interdisciplinary eclecticism would continue
through the years. "What BAM did more than anyone
else was take the natural phenomenon of collaboration
and put it in a greenhouse," said then BAM consultant
Tim Carr in 1987. The collaborations were not
exclusively organic, with teams of artists from different

worlds approaching BAM as one; indeed, eventually Lichtenstein would send lists of artists to performers he wanted to present at the Next Wave as a gentle nudge toward collaboration, a kind of "Just in case you're interested, we're interested" prod to cross creative boundaries. Of course, not all the collaborations were heavenly. Several—including the infamous partnership for *The Birth of the Poet* (1985) among director Richard Foreman, writer Kathy Acker, painter David Salle, and composer Peter Gordon— were more in keeping with John Adams's observation about such endeavors: "It has occurred to me," he writes on creative collaboration, "that, next to double murder-suicide, it might be the most painful thing two people can do together."

In order to facilitate the crossing of these boundaries, many Next Wave artists brought technology to an entirely new status on the stage, such as Merce Cunningham's groundbreaking multimedia collaborations with Elliot Caplan. Laurie Anderson's *United States: Parts I–IV* (1983), featured during the second season of the Next Wave series, used electronic keyboards, violin, highly technical sound

effects, and an unceasing roundelay of slides and film images. Robert Wilson's precision-based lighting cues and technical rehearsals, along with his gigantic representations of Abraham Lincoln and cinematographic trains from the epic production of *the CIVIL warS* (1986), with music by Philip Glass, made his Next Wave productions among the most technically advanced on the live stage.

These productions represented an aspect of the festival's aesthetic that developed alongside technology. Director Peter Sellars observed in 1987, the year *Nixon in China* was presented at the Next Wave, "Technology has finally made it possible for artists to put dance, song, spoken words, music, visual art, text and poetry together. For the first time, it is now possible to realize Wagner's ideal of the *Gesamtkuntswerk*, in which the arts merge into something larger than any one of them could be by itself."

Mostly, the Next Wave was an emotional experience. Next Wave audiences alternately felt and expressed rage, fear, ecstasy, heartbreak, euphoria, hunger (during nine-hour "sleeping bag" performances), seductiveness, abject disappointment, and

The Photographer/Far from the Truth, Philip Glass and Robert Coe, 1983. Photo: Johan Elbers

Mark Morris. Photo (detail): Peter Hujar

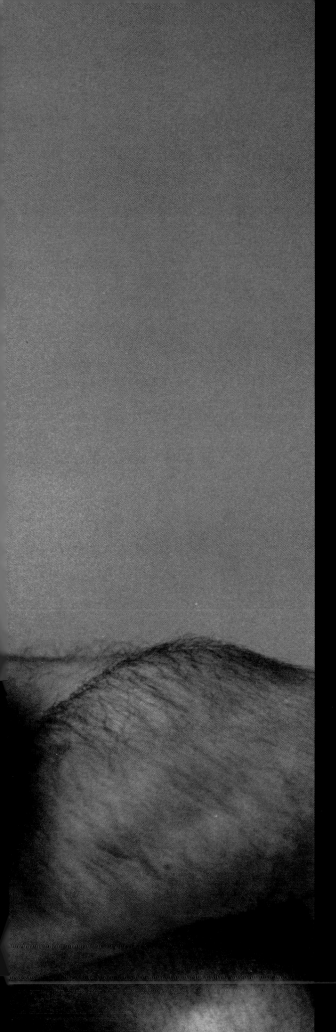

by Joan Acocella

Mark Morris was the most promising choreographer to come up in the 1980s. After the conceptual dances of the sixties and seventies, and the highly political dance-theater of the seventies and eighties, many people were looking to see again some classic modern dance, with its weightiness and naturalness and corresponding idealism. But they didn't want it too earnest. At that point Morris arrived, with old-fashioned humanism, but also a new, scorching quality—dark, strange, extreme. He was also funny.

The crucial concert came in 1984 at BAM: *Gloria*, *O Rangasayee*, and *Championship Wrestling after Roland Barthes*. That show, with its huge range of tone and reference, made Morris famous. It also, in some quarters, made him unpopular, and not just with people who didn't get his jokes but also with those who disliked a smart aleck, which he was in those years. Of course, this complaint made him more beloved by his fans. Six years later, at BAM, he unveiled his *L'Allegro, il Penseroso ed il Moderato* and *Dido and Aeneas*, and the controversy, to the grief of some, was over. Since that time, he has taken certain new paths—he has worked more intensively in opera and ballet than he did before—but he is still making what, in most years, are America's most profound and beautiful new modern dance works, the most recent being his *Socrates*, which premiered at BAM in the 2010 Spring Season.

The Mark Morris Dance Group has changed. It has survived Morris's retirement from the stage—a considerable loss. He was a very strong and charismatic dancer. The ensemble has become a sharper instrument, more exact, more unified, than the happy gang he started with. And Morris's choreography has become more sophisticated, more severe—more adult, you could say. He is no longer promising. He is simply one of America's foremost artists.

Mark Morris

The Gospel at Colonus, Lee Breuer
and Bob Telson, 1983.
Photo: Tom Caravaglia

epiphany (religious, intellectual—and otherwise). Next Wave performances explored the subconscious, enabling audiences to dream with their eyes open; they were experimental, with Ovidian transformations, and intense.

Anne Teresa De Keersmaeker, the Belgian choreographer whose work was first presented at the Next Wave in 1986, once said, "I want to tell stories without telling them." Many of the Next Wave's stories were told in this contradictory way; they were nonlinear and impressionistic, characteristics already associated with the type of avant-garde work that BAM had been presenting since the late 1960s. Most rejected conventional plotting to unfold tales using the language of image and sound, often as a replacement for language. Robert Wilson urged his audiences to make of the work what they would: "I feel my responsibility as an artist is not to say what something is, but to ask what it is."

Nonrational imagery, abstraction, intuitiveness—all reflected the time of great flux out of which the Next Wave was born. Its artists provoked,

Richard Bernstein, "A lot of the art that resulted from government subsidies is pretty establishment. But a lot of it throws mud in the face of the establishment. It deals with issues of the day, such as gay rights and women's rights."

"We are a lab," Bill T. Jones explained. "What are the toughest questions we can ask ourselves and answer?" In 1994, the festival would ratchet up its controversy quota with his production of *Still/Here* and would be both lambasted and apotheosized for doing so. The work was a choreographic petri dish encircling the profound and wrenching musings, confessions, and images of individuals living with terminal illness. With the infamous "victim art" debate, set off by Arlene Croce's *New Yorker* "review" (she refused to attend any performances, claiming that work about the terminally ill and other "victims" was an unfair critical trap), the Next Wave reached a new level of political and cultural embroilment not confined to the aesthetic.

Even from the festival's beginnings, controversy was the main onstage force, whether the context was content, structure, or aesthetics. Milestone productions like Lee Breuer and Bob Telson's *The Gospel at Colonus* (1983), with Clarence Fountain and the Five Blind Boys of Alabama portraying Oedipus, and the highly acclaimed production of *Nixon in China* challenged audience perception of ancient Greek tragedy and opera, respectively. Similarly, Mark Morris's *L'Allegro, il Penseroso ed il Moderato* (1990) as well as *The Hard Nut*, an arrant rethinking of the standard annual holiday classic *The Nutcracker* first performed at BAM in 1992, redefined the conventional notion of story ballet and dance-theater. And *Zingaro*, the French equestrian theater troupe led by the charismatic Bartabas and a glamorous black stallion, brought BAM to Battery Park City in lower Manhattan for two buzz-worthy big top productions—*Chimère* (1996) and *Eclipse* (1998).

The Artists and Their Work

Between 1981 and 1999, the Next Wave presented a wide range of artists in varying stages of their careers. Artists like Steve Reich, Trisha Brown, Meredith Monk, Peter Brook, and Robert Wilson were nurtured prior to the establishment of the festival. Others were introduced to New York audiences on a large stage for the first time during the series, like Laurie Anderson and Bill T. Jones/Arnie Zane. And still others debuted as the festival began to have more international focus, like Reinhild Hoffmann, Seburo Teshigawara, Lin Hwai-min, Robert Lepage, and Lev Dodin. The well-established artist long considered avant-garde—and living the dichotomy of aging experimentalist—found a home in the festival, with Monk, Wilson, and Glass sharing seasons with emerging and developing artists like Mark Morris, Peter Sellars,

educated, inspired, failed, and triumphed. Stirring the pot was part of it. It was all about controversy, observed Lichtenstein, "people reaching for more than they can grasp." By the mid-late 1980s and early 1990s, the Next Wave, with its diversified and established base of corporate, individual, foundation, and even government funding, had become a haven for the exploration of provocative issues and probing in-your-face attacks on staid sensibilities.

In a *New York Times* preview of the upcoming 1990 Next Wave Festival, Lichtenstein told writer

William Forsythe, and Declan Donnellan. Many of these artists marked turning points, defined eras, or, through their sheer longevity with BAM and the festival, came to be defined as "Next Wave artists." While other presenters and producers worked with these innovators, their recurring artistic journeys within BAM's focused fall seasons came to be part of the festival's very DNA, and vice versa. The festival unfolded parallel to their individual development in a mutual contract between BAM and the artists called the Next Wave.

For many, the Next Wave was an opportunity to move from small spaces to large, technically equipped stages—the Next Wave stretched its artists and gave them support to graduate to a different creative universe. "I performed *The Games* in the Opera House with Ping Chong in 1984," remembers Monk, "and it was the first time I could work with production values and on such a huge scale. It was a whole new dimension for me." As a composer, singer, director, choreographer, filmmaker, and pioneer in extended vocal technique and interdisciplinary performance,

Monk was the quintessential Next Wave artist— before there was a Next Wave. She first performed at BAM in the 1970s, with *Quarry* (1976) and *Education of a Girlchild* (1979), then went on to appear regularly in the Next Wave. Monk's roots in BAM are deep— her grandfather, a bass baritone, performed at the first Brooklyn Academy of Music on Montague Street at the turn of the 20th century.

Monk's Next Wave performance of *The Politics of Quiet* (1996) was the last live theater to be performed in the Carey Playhouse before it was renovated into the BAM Rose Cinemas. She had been with BAM from its early days and now was signaling one of its many transformations: "I think the idea for the Next Wave was to just open up possibilities, and that's what art is about. BAM was a venue that was willing to take chances and wanted to open up people's perceptions. My work was and is about combining and weaving different aspects of perceptions, and the Next Wave had the same philosophy."

Most important to Monk, who is frequently referred to as a choreographer, was that the festival

Meredith Monk in her *Meredith Monk, an Artist and Her Music*, 1987.
Photo: Peter Moore

recognized—indeed, celebrated—the multiplicities of her artistic identity. In the late 1980s, for example, Melillo invited her vocal ensemble to perform with Bobby McFerrin, and the crossover aspects—aligning Monk's identities as choreographer and concert artist, pairing the downtown performance artist with the popular singer—were emblematic of Next Wave division bending. For the self-proclaimed "vocal archaeologist," the offer was irresistible.

Monk was also impressed by the de-emphasizing of the flashy, hypermarketed world premiere, an intensely sought-after commodity for presenters. The pressure a premiere put on the artist could be overwhelming, and having to perfect a work by its first run was both daunting and diminishing. "The beauty of live performances is that sometimes it doesn't work out well the first time round," says Monk. Lichtenstein and Melillo often saw initial performances at a European festival, or in a downtown loft, or even another American venue. Then kinks were ironed out, artists learned from their audiences, and by the time the work came to BAM, the presentation had been marinated in time and public repetition.

Laurie Anderson's *United States: Parts I–IV* was another Next Wave production that was developed over several years before it premiered in full at BAM, during the second season of the Next Wave series.

Taking on issues of patriotism, class, and the politics of nuclear warfare over the course of eight hours—it was controversial in both form and content—the production was indicative of the blending of performance elements, audiences, and disciplines that would become a Next Wave signature. And because of the technical and technological advances that characterized the performance—with its electrified acoustic instruments, slides, synthesizers, and film sequences—for years to come both Anderson and *United States: Parts I–IV* would help to define the Next Wave as high-tech.

With her crossover appeal to the young and hip who bought her *Big Science* album, which included the worldwide hit "O Superman," Anderson embodied the "high art"–meets–"low art" persona. As Don Shewey wrote in a *New York Times* feature on Anderson, "When a major [pop record] label and a high culture musical institution join forces to endorse an experimental artist, it strongly suggests that performance art has infiltrated the mainstream after a decade or more of appealing mainly to the arty SoHo crowd in the lofts and basements of lower Manhattan." That "arty SoHo crowd," eager to see high meet low onstage, combined with the very young Anderson fans and the more central and upper Manhattanites slowly but surely finding their way to Brooklyn—the Next Wave audience, as early as 1983, was beginning to take shape.

Laurie Anderson in her
United States: Parts I–IV, 1983.
Photo: Allan Tannenbaum

Laurie Anderson in her
United States: Parts I–IV, 1983.
Photo (detail): Allan Tannenbaum

by Don Shewey

Anytime someone in contemporary culture wants to peer into the future, they usually try to engage Laurie Anderson to serve as consciousness scout. She's a visionary who can be relied upon to bring curiosity, humor, and intelligence to the question "What's next?" whether the subject is art, media, technology, spirituality, outer space, the political climate, or the new millennium. She's a dauntless pioneer who surfs the edge between the known and unknown with a visual artist's eye, a linguist's ear, and a storyteller's tongue, wearing her signature spiky haircut and soft, spangly slippers. She has put a friendly face on the sometimes-forbidding phenomenon we call avant-garde art.

A university-trained sculptor and art historian from a large, affluent suburban Chicago family, Anderson emerged from the fertile, cross-pollinated art garden that was 1970s SoHo to become the world's first performance-artist-as-pop-star, thanks to "O Superman," the unlikely hit song from her 1980 performance *United States Part II*. Its "ha-ha-ha-ha" sampled-voice tape-loop has joined the pop pantheon of famous riffs alongside the buzzing guitar of "(I Can't Get No) Satisfaction" or the opening notes of "Billie Jean." And the accompanying video, album, and concert tours—including the complete four-part *United States*, unveiled at BAM in 1983 in the second season of the Next Wave series, the first of Anderson's many appearances at BAM—created a new form of pop-performance collage in which DIY graphics, images, electronic sounds, movement, and spoken word could be infinitely re-combined, paving the way for innovative art-music-video prac-titioners from the early days of MTV to innovative contemporary rock-theatrical performers such as Björk and Lady Gaga.

In addition to producing a dozen major-label albums, one film, and several books on her own, Anderson has assumed a kind of cultural ambassadorship that transcends her output as an individual artist. Besides collaborating with an array of filmmakers, choreographers, and musicians, including her mate, legendary rocker Lou Reed, she took part in the first Internet community (Stewart Brand's The WELL), brainstormed with Peter Gabriel and Brian Eno on a millennial theme park, and served as NASA's first artist in residence. The permanent collection of the Guggenheim Museum includes an eight-inch-high holographic representation of Laurie Anderson. Doing what? Sitting in a corner telling a quirky story.

Anderson, who brought a range of works to the Next Wave, also set the tone for the festival's visual arts through line. As a sculptor, object maker, and photographer, she integrated her visual creations into her performances. She was the quintessential cross-disciplinary artist who created the type of multifarious work, with its collage-based elements, that could be launched—like the nightmare-inducing nuclear missiles depicted in United States—to more expanded audiences, both in Brooklyn and around the world. Following the BAM performance, Anderson took *United States* on tour in Europe and the United States, beginning a tradition for Next Wave works that would help the festival become an international establishment, with its productions serving as living, global "visibility raisers."

Along with Anderson, Robert Wilson was an artistic hybrid, a theater and opera maker who was also a visual artist. He trained a stone's throw from BAM, at Brooklyn's Pratt Institute, and eventually his drawings, objects, furniture designs, and other works

would be exhibited worldwide. BAM showed his work early in his career—in December 1969 and again in May 1970, the then-unknown Wilson presented *The Life and Times of Sigmund Freud* to a sparse audience. Three more Wilson productions appeared at BAM during the 1970s, but his work was expensive and challenging to produce and was presented almost exclusively in Europe. With the 1984 Next Wave revival of *Einstein on the Beach*, BAM brought him back home, and New York audiences had a place to go to see work that Europeans had been wildly praising for almost a decade.

Lucinda Childs was commissioned to choreograph the work, and her dancers performed it. The *Wall Street Journal* critic Dale Harris observed that all the elements—musical composition, direction, and choreography—were now on equal terms. The vastness of such artistry required a huge stage, more than adequate financial resources, and a commitment to "betting the ranch," as Hopkins often described BAM's risk taking. But if almost a decade before

Robert Wilson

by Jonah Bokaer

During a recent viewing of *KOOL: Dancing in My Mind*, a 2009 production by Robert Wilson in homage to his longtime movement collaborator Suzushi Hanayagi, I realized that Wilson is my favorite choreographer. Although renowned as a theater artist, and described by the *New York Times* as "a towering figure in the world of experimental theater," Wilson orchestrates the movement of people, objects, narration, scenography, and light, composing total works of live performance with immense physical clarity.

Choreography on Wilson's stages is an expanded field where production elements move, reconfigure, and interact in new combinations. Fundamental to this approach, beyond his stunning command of technical theater—often in fullest realization on BAM's stages, where his work has been performed since the 1969–70 production of *The Life and Times of Sigmund Freud*—is Wilson's understanding of movement, stillness, and their interpenetration. "Movement is sculpture," he once told me, while critiquing a passage of choreography for Gounod's *Faust* at Teatr Wielki, Warsaw, in 2008. Two years after this statement, void of metaphor or simile, his words remain in memory. To Wilson, movement is sculpture, and vice versa.

Probably less familiar to public spectators of Wilson's performance works is his receipt of the Golden Lion for Sculpture at the Venice Biennale in 1993 for the installation *Memory/Loss*. Such works invoke movement, from inanimate objects, while also inviting stillness in the busy mind of the viewer. By colliding motion with stillness, Wilson creates vast spaces of reflection, which are often choreographed.

Few artists have been as voraciously interdisciplinary in their approach, while also inviting comparisons to great masters across many media. One frequently reads commentary on Wilson's "painterly approach" to the stage. Not so: he is restlessly kinetic, onstage and off, and feels dramatic action in his body as instinctually as any dancer. He cites artists including George Balanchine, Mikhail Baryshnikov, Merce Cunningham, Sylvie Guillem, and Rudolf Nureyev as influences to his movements onstage. "Attack your way through this aria, like a dancer," he once directed Italian opera icon Giovanna Casolla at the Teatro dell'Opera di Roma while restaging Verdi's *Aida* in 2009. And no other theater artist knows better than Wilson what that direction means.

Wilson's work had faced a near-empty theater, now it was one of the most sought-after tickets in town. "The greatest audience reaction I can remember," recalls Melillo, "was the extraordinary avalanche of response to *Einstein on the Beach*." With his frequent appearances at the Next Wave—including *the CIVIL warS*; *The Forest* (1988), with David Byrne; *The Black Rider* (1993), with Tom Waits and William Burroughs; and *Time Rocker* (1997), with Lou Reed—Wilson made a monumental contribution to the festival and to New York City at large, whose audiences were able to witness at BAM what was truly a reinvention of opera and music-theater.

Wholehearted support for artists' work was one thing; building a theater tailor-made for an artist's vision, as BAM did for acclaimed British director Peter Brook's *The Mahabharata*, broke the barrier even for BAM—and, indeed, New York City. Brook, whose provocative production of *A Midsummer Night's Dream* had appeared at BAM in 1971, called Lichtenstein in 1986 to inquire about a theater for his nine-hour epic production of the ancient Sanskrit text. Lichtenstein eventually thought of a boarded-up vaudeville-turned-movie theater a few blocks away on Fulton Street. By October 1987, with help from architect Hugh Hardy and the city of New York (mainly the Brooklyn borough president's office and the New York City Department of Cultural Affairs), a restored yet ripped-apart venue called the Majestic Theater hosted what to date would be the single largest, most ambitious production in BAM's history. *The Mahabharata* cost BAM $2.2 million, in addition to the $4 million needed in capital funds to renovate the New York City–owned building into an 875-seat, open-proscenium performance space.

The production was three plays in one, featuring 24 actors (including 11 children), 6 musicians, and a backstage crew from 20 countries. It broke the usual pattern of the Next Wave, running for nearly three months, and redefined the term "a night at the theater." Audiences could experience it in three versions: a nine-hour marathon with meal breaks; three consecutive weekday nights; or one weeknight for three weeks. *The Mahabharata* exponentially multiplied every characteristic that defined BAM's signature work. It had the perfect BAM balance of humanist depth and literary gravity. It was ferociously cross-disciplinary, with dance, drumming, and live music, theatrical storytelling, and an almost sculptural elemental set comprising 20,000 pounds of dirt covering a concrete riverbed—with a river running through it. It had nudity. It even had a program guide providing context and recommendations for long-term sitting on hard surfaces. This was all overseen by a world-renowned avant-garde theater master.

The Mahabharata was a monumental success. It played to near-capacity audiences for its entire run, with box office receipts of $1.5 million. Even more

Richard Fallon, Georges Corraface, and Jeffrey Kissoon (featured) in *The Mahabharata*, Peter Brook and Jean-Claude Carrière, 1987. Photo: Martha Swope

Left: Mallika Sarabhai in
The Mahabharata, Peter Brook
and Jean-Claude Carrière, 1987.
Photo (detail): Gilles Abegg

Right: *The Mahabharata*, Peter Brook
and Jean-Claude Carrière, 1987.
Photo (detail): Gilles Abegg

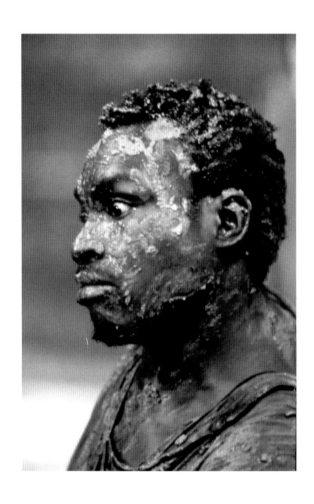

Left: Mamadou Dioume in
The Mahabharata, Peter Brook
and Jean-Claude Carrière, 1987.
Photo (detail): Gilles Abegg

Right: Tam-Sir in *The Mahabharata*,
Peter Brook and Jean-Claude Carrière,
1987. Photo (detail): Gilles Abegg

175

significant was that New York had a new theater that would become host to myriad productions—epic and intimate, by the famous and not-so-famous, in every single performance discipline—for many years to come.

Makers of Contemporary Dance

Carnations. Cigarettes. Sheep. Schoolgirls in ripped tights perching on custom-made cane chairs. Gritted, bared teeth. And . . . a hippopotamus. Pina Bausch, the choreographer-dancer from Wuppertal, Germany, first performed at BAM in the 1984 Spring Season with a program that included *The Rite of Spring, 1980, Café Müller,* and *Bluebeard.* Bausch's work—visual anarchy, structured iconoclasm—stretched received notions of what dance should be by portraying human nature in its widest realm of emotions, from primitive to skillful and sophisticated, violent to the utmost tender, dyspeptic to the deliriously hopeful. It challenged entrenched belief systems. And as Next Wave audiences saw in productions during Lichtenstein's tenure, such as *Two Cigarettes in the Dark* as well as *Arien* (1985), *Palermo Palermo* (1991), and *Der Fensterputzer* (1997),

Bausch broadened the definition of dance to embrace what she called the "theater of experience."

While her work was not lighthearted—although it often mined humor from the bleakest situations— nothing was better for the Next Wave's developing treasure trove of backstage lore than a work by Bausch. One of the more memorable moments in BAM's chronicles came on the opening night of *Arien,* which required dancers to move slowly through an onstage pool filled with 10,000 gallons of water. The stage had to be flooded, recalled Melillo. "We set up a pool underneath, and the water had to be heated to a certain temperature so the dancers wouldn't get cramps. But there was a drought in New York City, so we had to buy water from New Jersey." However, when the delivery truck arrived, the crew learned that the water was toxic after a stagehand tested the water with an industrial thermometer that literally melted. Another shipment had to be delivered, then heated to dancer-friendly temperature. It was a gala night performance, so the stakes were even higher to bring audiences a great show. Fortunately, the evening was salvaged because Rémy Martin was the gala sponsor, and BAM's always nimble staff served the audience

Opposite: Akram Khan (featured) in *The Mahabharata,* Peter Brook and Jean-Claude Carrière, 1987. Photo: Gilles Abegg

Below: Beatrice Libonati and Lutz Förster in *Arien,* Tanztheater Wuppertal Pina Bausch, 1985. Photo: Ulli Weiss

Pina Bausch.
Photo (detail): Jeffrey Henson Scales/
HSP Archive

by Susan Yung

Was Pina Bausch a romantic? No, judging by the numerous gritty
dance-theater works that were routinely tagged as sadistic and
nightmarish, and in which she rendered the darkly imagined
real—a flooded stage, a toppling cinder block wall, a dirt pit.
Or yes, definitely, based on a number of the pieces she created
over her last two decades. In these, she incorporated enduring
memories from locales—Mumbai, Hong Kong, Buenos Aires.
She combined lasting imagery, rituals, music, and costumes
bound together with theatrical panache and her expressionistic
dancing. In any case, she was a visionary who captured in a
completely distinctive voice the totality of the human condition,
the harmony and tension between the sexes, life's absurdity
and humor.

Her dancers—the men often formally attired, the women in
stilettos and satin evening gowns that would become shredded
or filthy—perform with a fearless abandon, a life-or-death commitment. Her *Tanztheater* forged a genre that exploded dance's
possibilities, transporting her influence to other milieus such as
film. Her working process involved exploring funny or poignant
personal anecdotes by her dancers that would be integrated
into the larger piece. She confronted audiences with depictions
of psychological trauma or sybaritic pleasures, but also with
verbal banter, or waiter service, conducted from the stage apron
or aisle. Intermission was announced with a wink by a smoky-
voiced dancer or on a sign carried dramatically across the stage.
Remarkably, BAM was the only New York City venue where
Bausch's company performed before her unexpected death in
2009. The BAM audience's devotion to the group's numerous
regular visits was evident in ticket waitlist lines snaking
throughout the lobby.

Bausch was born in Solingen, Germany, and studied dance at
the Folkwang School in Essen with Kurt Jooss. She attended
Juilliard in New York City and danced at the Metropolitan Opera.
She returned to Essen, performing with Jooss's Folkwang
Tanzstudio and assisting with choreography. Bausch became
head of the Wuppertal Ballet in 1973, soon renaming it
Tanztheater Wuppertal. Early on, she created interpretations
of operas and began using popular and folk music, which she
would combine to craft multi-scene pieces of over shifting
moods and dynamics. In her later work, edges softened, visu-
als were often projected, and lush dance segments became
more prominent. Bausch the visionary, the romantic, had come
full circle, tapping myriad human emotions en route.

champagne to take the edge off as they waited out a 90-minute delay. As noted by Hopkins, "By the time the performance started, most of the audience was tipsy and ready for anything." Another story from *Arien*: Upon learning that there was a hippopotamus onstage, an ASPCA staff member called BAM inquiring about the "care and feeding of the animal." BAM's Ellen Lampert-Gréaux assured the caller, "Yes, the two dancers playing the hippopotamus are being fed and cared for very well, thank you."

The Next Wave came to be a place where you suspended your disbelief the moment the usher took your ticket. Openness was key to the experience, and simply by abandoning yourself to a production's visual and aural language, you were guaranteed an unforgettable experience. Bausch, both icon—at the time of her premature death in 2009, she was considered one of the most important modern dance choreographers—and iconoclast, created work that required such openness.

One of the stalwart early BAM and Next Wave artists, Trisha Brown is another icon—considered one of the leaders of postmodern choreography—who has questioned every given, even the force of gravity, the very foundation of dance and the human form. Notably, she incorporated dancers in flight into her 1999 Spring Season production of Monteverdi's *L'Orfeo* and utilized aerial choreography in several of her other BAM productions. Brown first performed with her company at BAM in 1976, and then during the first season of the Next Wave series. Along with other choreographers, composers, and theater makers who began their careers in places like the Franklin Furnace, P.S. 122, The Kitchen, and Dance Theater Workshop as well as venues like the Mudd Club and Danceteria, Brown was stamped in the downtown world of cross-pollinators, beginning with her work with the Judson Dance Theater in the 1960s. With *Set and Reset*, which premiered during the first season of the Next Wave Festival, she helped to establish the festival's multidisciplinary through line with an innovative collaboration with Laurie Anderson and Robert Rauschenberg.

Because it brought together three great artists who were each major innovators in their fields, *Set and Reset* came to be viewed as one of the Next Wave's characterizing milestones. In her 1983 *New York Times* review, Anna Kisselgoff wrote that the work "fits snugly into the theme of collaborative endeavors in this year's experimental 'Next Wave' series at the Brooklyn Academy of Music, and there is no denying that the socialites, art dealers, collectors and art-rock fans in the house at Thursday night's world premiere of *Set and Reset* were attracted by something beyond a dance performance. This is by no means a reflection on Miss Brown, who has long been part of the Minimal and Conceptual art scene even before its painters became famous, and who certainly has her own

following." Brown remains an influence cited by artists from many disciplines, including the visual arts, film, and traditional ballet.

As early as the festival's first season, critics and cultural commentators were taking note of the collaborative work as well as the "collaborative audience," the latter to become part of the controversy. For the production of *Secret Pastures*, Bill T. Jones observed that the audience was both critical and criticized: "In 1984, our hair and makeup person insisted that the

cast have outrageous cuts. The show had a transgressive pop attitude that people never forgave us for because it was *trendy*. Like it was all about style. Those were the characteristics of what people at that time were calling, derisively, 'BAM-itis.'"

In 1982, Jones cofounded his own company with his partner, Arnie Zane, which first appeared in the Next Wave series in 1983 and then in the festival the following year with *Secret Pastures*, a collaboration with music by Peter Gordon, sets by visual artist Keith

Haring, and costumes by fashion designer Willi Smith. Jones would become an established Next Wave artist and a performer familiar with criticism and controversy. One milestone was his Next Wave showing of *Last Supper at Uncle Tom's Cabin / The Promised Land*, a fearless exploration of class, race, and sexuality through an imagistic and fabulist unfurling of ideas and concepts, marrying content—confusing, disorienting, and disturbing—to unfettered form. The dancers themselves, African American and

Marion Cito and Jan Minarik in *Bluebeard*, Tanztheater Wuppertal Pina Bausch, 1984. Photo: Ulli Weiss

Bill T. Jones (featured) in *Last Supper at Uncle Tom's Cabin / The Promised Land*, Bill T. Jones / Arnie Zane & Company., 1990. Photo: Jeff Day

white, Latino and Asian, slim and portly, tall and small, showed what a dance company could and should look like in the eighties and nineties, revealing that America's multiculturalism, within one society internally, was a prodding statement in itself. An exclamation point came in the finale, when 70 naked performers who were residents of Brooklyn appeared onstage, stretching the scope of individualism.

Jones linked BAM's commitment to inviting him and other choreographers to create work for the large proscenium stage of the Opera House with, in turn, encouragement for them to think big, not just in artistic but in philosophical terms. "What has that stage meant to my generation?" he asked in a *New York Times* feature in 1992 by Jennifer Dunning. "The hallmark of a lot of contemporary dance is introspection. It's small-scale. Suddenly, that's got to be translated for the larger stage. A lot of us are looking to fashion, the art world, the classics and theatrical devices. Large stages ask for large statements and I think that's a good exercise for my generation."

Notes dance writer and BAM historian Susan Yung, "As an impresario, Harvey Lichtenstein is renowned for bringing to fruition his passion for a multitude of performing arts. But bolstered with a background in dance that surely honed his curatorial hawkeye, his tenure at BAM made an extraordinary imprint on the history of dance in New York City, and by extension, the U.S. Contemporary dance was strongly represented in the early years of the Next Wave, illustrated most emphatically in the 1985 festival that included Pina Bausch's Tanztheater Wuppertal, Laura Dean Dancers, and six more dance companies (remarkably, all led by women), followed in the next year with the Merce Cunningham, Michael Clark, Anne Teresa De Keersmaeker, Molissa Fenley, Mark Morris, Eiko & Koma, David Gordon, and Bill T. Jones / Arnie Zane companies. Perhaps the only thing more impressive than the roundly superb quality of these companies is the range of styles— essentially a core sample of the world's dance, as well as predictions of many who have since become icons of dance. Perhaps no other American curator cultivated the genre of dance, and its audiences, as propitiously as Lichtenstein while he was at BAM."

Mixing and Music

On those large stages, Next Wave presentations mediated between combative content and controversial artistic forms. Composer-performer Steve

The Cave, Steve Reich and Beryl Korot, 1993. Photo: Stephanie Berger

Bill T. Jones and Arnie Zane in their
Secret Pastures, 1984.
Photo (detail): Tom Caravaglia

by Susan Yung

Many artists succeed by finding a niche and pursuing it with a single-minded focus. Others, such as Bill T. Jones, experiment in many forms within a broad genre such as dance-theater, and have the rare ability to move between strongly voiced narratives, kinetic poetry, and pure entertainment. It doesn't hurt to be a charismatic performer seemingly chiseled from Apollonian marble. He founded Bill T. Jones / Arnie Zane & Company (later Bill T. Jones / Arnie Zane Dance Company) with his late partner, Arnie Zane, in 1982, after studying dance at SUNY–Binghamton. For all their experimentation with accumulation, contact improvisation, and formalism, basic identifying facts about Jones and Zane (who died of AIDS in 1988)—black, white, tall, short, velvety, precise—provided immediate contextualization, whether desired or not. Their company members also became noted for their widely varying body types and distinct personalities.

Jones once said, "Arnie and I used to feel if you want to be in the avant-garde, really be a provocateur, you take your ideas from the preserved domain and carry them into the mainstream." Even though Jones later said he had come to favor the preserved domain, his statement certainly resonates in his work's broad reach. The pair incorporated social issues and narrative threads, collaborating with visual artists and musicians to add even more intriguing layers. One example, *Secret Pastures*, performed at BAM in 1984, featured sets by Keith Haring, costumes by Willi Smith, and music by Peter Gordon, encapsulating the BAM Next Wave Festival's spirit of collaboration.

Jones has choreographed dances dense with formal experimentation and lyricism, from poignant solos to the rich group passages at which he so excels. Yet in the context of dance-theater, he is even better known for topical works addressing race, AIDS, cancer, murder, family bonds, and historical figures. One such work, *Still/Here*, which premiered at BAM in 1994, became notorious for provoking critic Arlene Croce to write about it despite refusing to see it, declaiming it as "victim art" and "unreviewable." These productions show his skill at storytelling, dynamics, pacing, using space and movement—essentially, understanding what really works in a theater. And capping the pop culture / narrative thread of his career are highly acclaimed Broadway productions—he choreographed *Spring Awakening* and directed and choreographed *Fela!* One unerring consistency through this artist's complex and varied output is his selection over the decades of remarkable performers. Many of his company's dancers have become successful choreographers, developing their own style and extending a legacy of diversity and experimentation in form and content.

Princess Diana and Harvey Lichtenstein
at the Royal Gala performance of
Falstaff, Welsh National Opera, 1989.
Linda Alaniz / Martha Swope Associates

Building the Institution

The growth of BAM as an institution, one wielding huge impact and influence in the cultural world and for millions of audience members, evolved organically during the period between the Next Wave's formal inception and Lichtenstein's retirement. Through the festival and spring productions as well as programs for young people, which evolved into the education and humanities department, and community engagement initiatives, BAM was acquiring institutional flesh and muscle.

During those years, according to Hopkins, "BAM found its greatest coming together of itself. It was a time of incredible creativity and mission commitment. It was an amazing period." Building BAM was a team effort under the leadership of Lichtenstein, Hopkins, and Melillo. Hopkins was the designated master of the money, raising it; Melillo the master of the revels, spending the money and, in turn, presenting the work that would bring in the earned income. They also were known to swap responsibilities—Lichtenstein and Melillo fundraised and Hopkins conceived fundable ancillary programs.

While painters, sculptors, filmmakers, and videographers displayed their REM-cycle-induced imagery on the Next Wave's stages and program covers, visual artists created BAM's unmistakable brand identity. Lichtenstein had already enlivened the somnambulant "Brooklyn Academy of Music" moniker so that its spunky youthful offspring "BAM" would pop off pages and explode in the mouths of the culturally aware. During this period of intense BAM branding, Tambra Dillon, then vice president for marketing and promotion, hired Michael Bierut and the innovative design firm Pentagram in 1995 to stamp BAM into the brainpans of every New Yorker and global citizen possible.

With the intense focus on the festival in the fall—BAM's brand-within-a-brand—the challenge was to ensure that "BAM was not just the Next Wave," says Melillo, and to galvanize and inspire potent year-round programming. As Melillo recalls, "The ship was listing a bit too much toward the Next Wave. The festival offerings became the signifiers of the spring to come. We had to grow the festival so that BAM overall could be truly year-round and have an artistic identity from January to September."

Anchored by the Next Wave, the institution produced and presented from the winter to the early fall some of its most extraordinary and lasting work. The BAM Spring Seasons brought several of the most prominent international companies to New York City, including the Hamburg Ballet, Les Arts Florissants, the Central Ballet of China, Cheek by Jowl, and the Kirov Opera, as well as initiatives like the Spoleto Comes to BAM series. There was more work from extraordinary homegrown artists like

Equidistant between Adams's two Next Wave outings, BAM's *Night of a Thousand Bands* (1989)—a blowout, all-night, no-holds-barred celebration of New Music America's 10th anniversary—was the first all-building, all-city BAM event. Supported by a group of corporations, foundations, and record label executives, *Night of a Thousand Bands* turned the entire BAM facility into a bricks-and-mortar nickelodeon, with audience members brandishing admission bracelets that allowed free-flowing access to bands ranging from the Butthole Surfers to the Cambodian pop Thoeung Son-Chlangden Band. It wouldn't be the first time BAM focused all its ambitious energies on one driving concept, partnering with other New York organizations—the Ingmar Bergman Festival, Shakespeare at BAM, and other events would be produced in the 1990s—but *Night of a Thousand Bands* put BAM on another cultural map, that of centers for musical adventure. This status would be achieved even more fully with the opening in 1999 of the live-music venue BAMcafé.

Twyla Tharp and Merce Cunningham, and BAM introduced Mark Morris as a young choreographer in both the festival and during its spring dance seasons. BAM also provided an American home for international theater companies and artists rarely seen in New York City, including the Royal Shakespeare Company, the Comédie-Française, the Market Theatre of Johannesburg, and the Royal Dramatic Theatre of Sweden. The Rustaveli Theatre Company of Tbilisi, in then-Soviet Georgia, presented *King Lear* in 1990; in that same year, BAM presented a Japanese-language *Macbeth*, directed by Yukio Ninagawa. In 1996, the Paris-based butoh troupe Sankai Juku, founded by Ushio Amagatsu, made its first appearance at BAM with *Yuragi: In a Space of Perpetual Motion*. It was with these and other non-English-speaking companies that BAM broke new ground.

The BAM Spring Season introduced artists not presented in the Next Wave as well as festivals in their own right, such as Sweet Saturday Night, an overview of "black street and social dance" that influenced American popular culture—presented in both 1984 and 1985—and international programs of Japanese and Israeli performance in 1989 and 1992, respectively.

In 1989, BAM launched the spring opera season with the goal of presenting a diverse repertoire in both the Opera House and the newly renovated Majestic Theater. The season opened with Peter Stein's extraordinary Welsh National Opera production of Verdi's *Falstaff*. The company's debut was elevated—and graced—by the "Royal Visit": Princess Diana—Her Royal Highness the Princess of Wales—on her first official visit to the United States (which required more security detail than BAM had experienced in its history), along with a gala evening at the Winter Garden in the World Financial Center that was covered by the international press. "The opera was a huge success," recalls Hopkins. "The champagne intermissions flew. Her Highness met and greeted all who were presented to her (you don't introduce people to a princess, you present them). At the gala, with Harvey on one arm and Brian McMaster, then

Donald Maxwell in *Falstaff*,
Welsh National Opera, 1989.
Photo: Zoë Dominic

189

Ingmar Bergman and Bjorn Granath
in rehearsal, *A Doll's House*, Royal
Dramatic Theatre of Sweden, 1991.
Photo (detail): Bengt Wanselius

by Gordon Rogoff

He called his autobiography *The Magic Lantern*, as if his life's work could be defined by film alone, yet the title was his way of momentarily hiding the news that life really began when Ingmar Bergman, 10 years old, did his first plays in his puppet theater called "Magic Lantern." More than 40 films, and three times that number of stage productions, later, Bergman was—as always—playing with interior conflicts, setting soul against soul, even as he refused to settle the argument between film's durable images and the stage's ephemeral solidities. His theatrical gods always included Shakespeare, Schiller, Ibsen, and even Eugene O'Neill, but their volcanic eruptions were nothing compared to Strindberg's, his favorite playwright, master of the intimate chamber theatricality that was Bergman's signature in both movies and plays.

He liked to say that he "was very much aware of my own double self," one "very under control," the other "in touch with the child . . . responsible for all the creative work." Perhaps it was the child who also liked to see "cinema as an exciting mistress" while giving sway to the theater, his "faithful wife," as he put it. His open secret, however, was that his most lasting romance was with the mighty centerpieces of all his work—the actors. In his last years, playing recluse on the stark Swedish island of Faro, he held almost daily telephone conversations with Erland Josephson, faithful to the end as one of his favorite actors, notably in *Fanny and Alexander*, *Scenes from a Marriage*, and *Saraband*, but no more important than so many others, such as Max von Sydow and Gunner Björnstrand, and most of all the women—Bibi Andersson, Harriet Andersson, Liv Ullmann—and notably at BAM Peter Stormare and Lena Olin in Strindberg's *Miss Julie* (1991), and in Schiller's *Maria Stuart* (2002) Pernilla August, Lena Endre, and, in one of those small roles that mark Bergman's essentially pointillistic art, Erland Josephson again. In 1995, BAM joined with six cultural partners to produce the citywide Ingmar Bergman Festival in which the Royal Dramatic Theatre of Sweden returned to BAM with Bergman directing Shakespeare's *The Winter's Tale* and Yukio Mishima's *Madame de Sade*.

If it is the actors who finally defined his life, it's because he could write his story on their bodies, their open wounds, even their shadows. He had long left puppetry behind, choosing to give space and time to all his sensual muses, those magical figures who couldn't keep away from his relentless intensities.

managing director of the Welsh National Opera, on the other, down the steps she came wearing white in a sea of black (you know, New York). Squadrons of cameras flashed. It was the entrance of the decade."

But BAM would be no traditionalist when it came to presenting an art form so knee-jerkingly associated with the then-traditional repertoire and proscenium-bound presentations of the Metropolitan and New York City Operas. BAM being BAM, opera was yet another sacred cow to topple, and experimentalists like Stein and Sellars were commissioned to reinvent the form. William Christie, a repatriated American who lived and worked in France, brought the works of the French Baroque, performed by his extraordinary ensemble Les Arts Florissants, and in 1997, Jonathan Miller would stage Bach's *St. Matthew Passion* in a stripped-down operatic concert at the Majestic, which thereafter would continue to return to BAM in selective seasons.

Throughout the years, the spring opera season would become a superlative alternative to standard opera fare, presenting both reenvisioned versions of traditional work as well as bringing to surface rarely performed repertoire, such as the Brussels-based Théâtre Royal de la Monnaie's production of Mozart's *La Finta Giardiniera* (1990); *Orpheus und Eurydike*

(1991) by the Komische Oper, appearing at BAM from the former East Berlin shortly after the fall of the Berlin Wall and German reunification; Monteverdi's *L'Incoronazione di Poppea* (1996) with the Glimmerglass Opera; William Christie's production of Handel's *Orlando* (1996); and Mark Morris's staging of Purcell's *Dido and Aeneas* (1998), among many others, thus laying the groundwork for BAM to be a significant contributor to the international development of the art form in the late 20th century.

Season-related events, like the Ingmar Bergman Festival, also presented a little friendly competition for the Next Wave, which was absolutely what BAM's spring and summer needed. Hopkins, in one of her functions as creator-of-product-that-will-help-raise-money, produced the citywide festival, which ran from May to September 1995. Coordinated by BAM and powered by Bergman's quadruple-threat artistic persona—in theater, opera, film, and television—it was the most comprehensive presentation of Bergman's work ever produced in the United States. The festival was another 360-degree BAM experience: Bergman directed the Royal Dramatic Theatre of Sweden in Shakespeare's *The Winter's Tale* and Yukio Mishima's *Madame de Sade* at BAM; Bergman films were screened at the Film Society of Lincoln Center,

Woud, Anne Teresa De Keersmaeker/ Rosas, 1997.
Photo: Herman Sorgeloos

one of BAM's six cultural partners, and featured in a PBS series; and various events, talks, and exhibitions illustrated Bergman's artistic legacy.

In 1988, Mikki Shepard and Leonard Goines formed 651 (later 651 ARTS), a not-for-profit organization focused on establishing relationships with African American and other minority artists, both local and international. The 651/Kings Majestic Corporation was launched in the following year as an independent multicultural arts program then associated with BAM, presenting artists from all performing disciplines like Billy Eckstine, Betty Carter, Tito Puente, Ruth Brown, Donald Byrd, and Anna Deavere Smith. One of its transformative presentations, in 1992, was the 100 Years of Jazz and Blues festival, which supplemented its presentations with symposia, master classes, and visual arts exhibitions. In addition to programming by 651, the renowned work of Chuck Davis, founder and artistic director of the African American Dance Ensemble, was to become a Memorial Day tradition, cohering under the sparkling umbrella of DanceAfrica. Along with a street bazaar featuring local vendors, an

education program, and an African sculpture garden, this became the single largest homage to African dance in New York. During this period, BAM also expanded and upgraded its onstage performances for young audiences, enlarged its adult education offerings, and established community engagement initiatives with schools and community groups, such as the Bedford Stuyvesant Restoration Corporation.

Although the fall season at BAM is driven mainly by the Next Wave, there were periodic presentations during the Lichtenstein era that were not formally part of the Next Wave, such as the Festival of Indonesia in Performance in 1990; the John Adams / Alice Goodman collaboration *The Death of Klinghoffer*, with the Mark Morris Dance Group, in 1991; and most notably the production in 1992 of *Les Atrides*, backstage, a four-part, 10-hour marathon created by Ariane Mnouchkine and her company, Théâtre du Soleil, which was so vast in scope that it had to be presented in the Park Slope Armory in Brooklyn and which earned critical accolades but forced BAM to begin its next season with a significant deficit.

Stina Ekblad and Anita Björk in *Madame de Sade*, Ingmar Bergman/ Royal Dramatic Theatre of Sweden, 1993. Photo: Bengt Wanselius

193

Les Atrides, backstage viewing area,
Ariane Mnouchkine / Théâtre du Soleil,
1992. Photo courtesy of BAM
Hamm Archives Center

That undertaking inspired one of Lichtenstein's more pungent observations about a project, one that was very much in keeping with BAM's indefatigable and unending drive to challenge itself: "The whole thing has been difficult as hell. Everyone knows that BAM is crazy and we go out on a limb. So here we are out on a limb again."

Fundraising

As illustrated by the production of Les Atrides, fundraising became increasingly crucial both to support risky experimentation as well as to bolster BAM's extraordinary growth. It was with the Next Wave that Hopkins was able to create the financial model that

would serve BAM in all other areas—that of a flexible, varied consortium of public and private funding, with backing both institutional (foundations and corporations) and individual (board and nonboard, high-volume lower-level gifts and major contributions). "Most important for fundraising," says Hopkins, was that with the Next Wave "the whole institution spoke in one voice; the marketing and fundraising looked like the programming and that made it clear."

A pioneer in cultural fundraising, Hopkins coined some of the most memorable tropes of the profession: "Delayed gratification is the fundraiser's creed" being just one of them. Beginning with the Next Wave series, she and her staff embarked on the most exciting, complicated, and diversified campaign

Time Warner Inc., AT&T, the Ford Foundation, and the Howard Gilman Foundation all had representatives there. Hopkins knew that with the total of $1 million generated for the festival, they had raised the bar for BAM. And the initial success of Hopkins's approach enabled Lichtenstein to make an important hire, bringing on Melillo to produce the festival.

The early Next Wave development strategy had all the ingredients of the BAM fundraising platform that evolved over the years. First, BAM created a Producers Council, an idea put forward by Steve Reichard of Livet Reichard, an event and art consulting firm that BAM enlisted to tap into the downtown visual arts community and its hip residents, art buyers, and art makers. The Producers Council consisted of patrons inclined toward the new and incorporated the notion of a certain donor persona: younger, more adventurous than the usual funders' group but, most important, reflective of the idea of the festival and its audience.

The National Endowment for the Arts, headed by Frank Hodsoll from 1981 to 1989 during the Reagan administration, also provided a challenge grant. Hopkins recalls, "The agency was looking for significant programs to define their administration. It was amazing that an avant-garde festival in Brooklyn was something they hooked into and connected with. It was a little out of their zone, and that made it interesting for them." Since a major touring component was part of the package, bringing great artists home from the state-sponsored European theaters became an almost jingoistic cultural goal.

There would also be partnerships with other cultural institutions to help foot the bills for large-scale work—six partners, mostly European, were brought on for both *Nixon in China* and *The Death of Klinghoffer* alone. Then came the corporate sponsorships, most significantly Philip Morris Companies Inc., whose philanthropic mission was to fund programs that honored individuality and innovation. From an initial contribution of $50 from its future CEO Hamish Maxwell, who lived in Brooklyn, Philip Morris (and later Altria Group, Inc.) would become the Next Wave Festival's lead sponsor for the next 30 years. "It was a very important partnership," says Stephanie French, former vice president for corporate contributions and cultural programs for much of Philip Morris's sponsorship tenure. French felt that through joint advertising and marketing, the festival could impart the idea that being new and different and innovative was a crucial aspect of Philip Morris's corporate character. Hopkins has said, "I firmly believe that without the ongoing support of Philip Morris the Next Wave would never have become the major success it is today. Even its survival without their support would have been questionable."

"In an interesting way, the fundraising for the festival was a festival in itself," Hopkins says.

BAM had ever embraced, one that gave shape to the institution's ongoing fundraising endeavors.

Lichtenstein and Hopkins approached the Rockefeller Foundation about the idea of the festival—when the BAM Theater Company had failed and BAM itself was struggling to survive—as a program that would redefine the institution. "We had Howard Klein and Alberta Arthurs at Rockefeller, old friends and supporters of Harvey's and true visionaries, who developed philanthropic programs focused on supporting unique, creative ideas," Hopkins recalls. At one pivotal meeting in a dusty Rockefeller Foundation boardroom, the foundation started off saying, "'We will commit x amount of dollars to the Next Wave Festival,' and then other people saying, 'We will match the Rockefeller Foundation!' It was great."

BAM Harvey Theater, 2003.
Photo: Ned Witrogen

by Akram Khan

Winter, 22 years ago, I entered through the front door of the Majestic Theater—re-named the Harvey in 1999 in honor of Harvey Lichtenstein—then a young actor in Peter Brook's production of *The Mahabharata*. I was 14 years old and immediately quite disorientated by the unfinished demeanor of the building. Of course, my naiveté lead me to believe that maybe the builders, decorators, and electricians had not finished refurbishing the interior and exterior for our big opening night. But then I asked one of the actors, who impatiently told me: "This is it." From then on, I decided to make the place my friend. If I was going to spend three months here, then I would make it my home. So all throughout the rehearsal period, I started to explore every corner, passageway, closet, and even the overhead walkways, which had access to the lighting rig high above the stage. I probably knew the layout better than the care-takers. And for the next few months, this place became my imagined, magical world.

However, I would like to confess now that during my stay at BAM, at the end of one particular show, when the audience had left and the stage crew was preparing to leave, and the actors were still in the dressing rooms taking off their costumes and makeup, I took it upon myself to chip away a bit of the infamous stone wall that created the backdrop of the show using one of the props from the production, and kept it for personal memory. It was a terrible thing to do, I know, but at the time, I wanted to hold on to some essence of my magical time at the Harvey. I knew I might never come back there, in the same way, ever again.

Autumn, 22 years later, I entered through the front door of the Harvey, this time as a choreographer/dancer of the Akram Khan Company. I was now 34 years of age, and immediately quite disorientated by the still unfinished demeanor of the building. What struck me was that the theater I remembered as a child had been some-how preserved or frozen in time. Some people say that theater work has the ability to transport you to the past or to the future, well, it was no work of theater, but the theater itself, that instantly transformed me back into the child I was two decades before. And as I was now given a tour around the theater, my right hand was in my jacket pocket, stroking the very piece of evidence that I stole as a memory. And I was smiling—not sure why, but I knew I had to return the small part of the theater I had sliced off 22 years before. I had to empty the burden I had carried with me for so many years. It is now a great relief to say that I returned the chipped stone to its origin and left it somewhere in the corner of the stage, close to the infamous wall I had illegally tortured.

Writing this now, I realize that the reason I decided to return the chipped stone was because as a child I thought the memory was hidden within the object, but now I realize that the memory was actually stored somewhere in my body. I didn't need another object to hold it for me. I didn't realize or trust that knowledge as a child. But this understanding that my body is the closest object I could possess, which would store all my secret adventures, scars, hopes, and desires, was one of the most important lessons in my career. How blessed we are to be given a body that witnesses and absorbs all our secrets from the moment we are born.

Theater

Harvey

BAM

And during this period, private donors, staff representatives, leaders of foundations and corporations, and government officials—all commingled at what Hopkins describes as "the wackiest and most innovative fundraising parties and galas the city had ever seen."

On the Eve of Transformation

Fueled for over three decades with Lichtenstein's personal fire, vision, tenacity, and resilience, BAM had undergone the essential transformation for survival; the institution had become one with Lichtenstein's artistic values. The generational transfer could now take place.

Throughout all the strategies, donors, dollars, parties, and mutually beneficial relationships, Hopkins had learned how to lead the institution into the next century, as Melillo had honed his curatorial, producing, and presenting gifts through his work on the Next Wave Festival and year-round BAM programming. So when Lichtenstein hurled his Prospero's wand into the Atlantic in 1999, his two chosen successors were ready for the transformation. "We needed a different model—BAM was too big at that point to be the vision of one man," Melillo says. "And we still had the artists. The artists taught me, and I'm still being taught." When speaking about BAM's future upon Lichtenstein's retirement in 1999, Melillo told the *New York Times*, "Harvey delivered a performing arts center and opened the cinemas. [Karen and I are] going to create a performing, cinema and media arts center for the 21st century." This was accomplished by the extraordinary "marriage of true minds" in the partnership between Hopkins and Melillo.

Having undergone an intense and thorough strategic planning process in 1999—the first in its history—BAM emerged with a new concept, one that would support the transition in leadership. "Destination BAM" would become the fresh idea, embracing all the transformations of BAM's spaces— the Opera House, the renovated rehearsal studios, the BAM Rose Cinemas (formerly the Carey Playhouse), and the BAMcafé in the Lepercq Space, the latter two venues greatly expanding BAM's mission as a cultural and community institution.

The Majestic, meanwhile, was renamed the BAM Harvey Theater upon Lichtenstein's retirement, and an eerily precise photo-based Chuck Close portrait of the theater's namesake was prominently displayed in the lobby. For all time, Harvey Lichtenstein would beam that piercing yet avuncular gaze from under those proscenium-arch eyebrows in a temple for the great impresario's grandeur, generosity, ambition, and quintessential (never-take-no-for-an-answer-and-when-you-do-get-no-turn-it-into-a-yes) chutzpah

The Most Dangerous Room in the House, Susan Marshall & Company, 1998. Photo (detail): Stephanie Berger

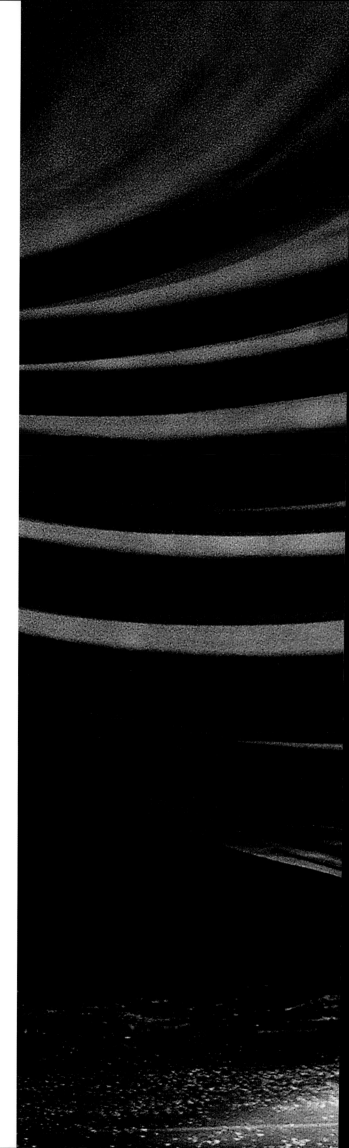

by Joseph V. Melillo

Once upon a time, Harvey Lichtenstein conceptualized a festival dedicated to the contemporary performing arts, and by some extraordinary stroke of luck his secretary, Ruth Nolan, called me to arrange a meeting. It was scheduled late on a Friday afternoon, and I found out that I was one of three candidates for the newly created position of producer of the inaugural Next Wave Festival. The year was 1983. At the time, I had a job accompanying a dozen or so international theater professionals across the United States for the State Department, and I was going to Washington, DC, the next day to begin my orientation. I was in Louisville, Kentucky, attending the Humana Festival of New Plays produced by the Actors Theatre of Louisville, when I arrived back at my hotel to discover a telephone message from Harvey. He offered me the job and approximately three weeks later I entered the front door of 30 Lafayette Avenue, and my life was inextricably altered from that precise moment.

My first management assignment was to take the single piece of paper containing the names of individual artists and productions that Harvey wanted me to either produce or present within the inaugural festival and make a manila file for each name. I proceeded to do my work without an office or telephone. Eventually, a former costume dressing room across from Harvey's office was transformed into my space, and it was to be shared with Roger Oliver, the humanities director of the Next Wave Festival—"Dr. Next Wave," as we affectionately referred to him.

I had met Karen Brooks Hopkins many years before when she was working at the New Playwrights' Theatre in Washington, DC. She attended a workshop at the O'Neill Theater Center at a conference convened by my then-employer Fred Vogel, the founder and executive director of the Foundation for the Extension and Development of the American Professional Theatre. Our colleague William Stewart, the managing director of the Hartford Stage Company and codirector of the weeklong program, remarked after Karen made her initial presentation on the first day at this workshop, "She's a star!" How true that observation would prove to be in our lives together here at BAM.

There was a sense of terror on my part—and I am not being theatrical here—that this "new" artistic initiative was a Harvey folly. Harvey's directive for me was to integrate the festival into the life of BAM, not to create an alternative unit separate from the daily life of his organization. I first produced *The Photographer/Far from the Truth*, a Philip Glass/Robert Coe triptych performance work with a play, multimedia section, and finally a movement/dance section. It was 90 minutes in the Opera House with JoAnne Akalaitis directing, Wendall K. Harrington doing the media, Jennifer Tipton the lighting, Santo Loquasto the sets and costumes, and David Gordon the choreography. It proved to be the controversial hit that the Next Wave Festival needed for its launch. New York City had not seen a professionally produced performance work on that scale—which had migrated from the Canal Street studios to the Beaux Arts glory of BAM's 2,100-seat Opera House. The second music-theater work I produced was the legendary *The Gospel at Colonus*, a collaboration between Lee Breuer and composer Bob Telson. A classical play updated and situated within an African American Pentecostal church, it had Clarence Fountain and the Five Blind Boys of Alabama playing the role of Oedipus, a relatively unknown actor named Morgan Freeman as the minister and narrator, and, among many other singers, the Institutional

Radio Choir of Brooklyn onstage. This was all produced within the Carey Playhouse, now the location of the BAM Rose Cinemas, which was really a recital hall in the original plans for BAM. I called the play the Brooklyn phenomenon—an immensely successful hybrid art form that finally made it to Broadway five years after BAM produced it and continues to tour the world today.

Harvey, Karen, and I forged a special relationship. We diligently worked to position the Next Wave Festival within every conceivable venue in both Manhattan and Brooklyn where individuals who were interested in contemporary art could be found. It was at once immensely challenging and in equal measure thrilling to be part of something bold and innovative. The place was redolent with energy, everything was new, and ideas flowed from Steve Reichard and Anne Livet, who were consulting on the festival. I was deeply involved with Harvey in making the art happen but also in planning for the future. One of the productions on his list for the inaugural festival was the Robert Wilson and Philip Glass collaboration *Einstein on the Beach*. As I did my research, it was absolutely clear that it would be impossible to revitalize that operatic work for 1983, but I guaranteed that we could deliver it in the following year. I remember working with the Wilson and Glass teams to reconstruct the work. They had decided that the work needed new choreography, and so Lucinda Childs was commissioned to create the dances while also performing her original role with Sheryl Sutton in the "Knee Plays," duet interludes linking the acts of the opera. All the rehearsals were held at BAM, and in December 1984 BAM presented the full work for the first time since its presentation in 1976 at the Met. It was an artistic eruption throughout New York City. The fact is that we were able to do it a second time in 1992, and at the time of this writing there are plans to present it a third time in 2012—in a word: historic.

This gift that has been given to me, courtesy of Harvey, that finds me as Karen Brooks Hopkins's professional partner, continues to humble me. As the executive producer, I have been able to advance the annual Next Wave Festival into the 21st century. I have learned many, many lessons. I was not formally mentored by Harvey, but I learned about artists and art from him. Karen has taught me how to be more responsive to our immediate Brooklyn community, among many other insights into how to work with a board of directors and build an institution. I have also had the good fortune in actualizing my artistic vision with the extraordinary assistance of Alice Bernstein, executive vice president, who possesses the creative skill and talent for quantifying what creates art and making magic with production budgets. She has made a very important contribution to BAM. And I have the board leadership of Alan Fishman, Bill Campbell, and Adam Max to thank for their support of my endeavor to move BAM forward into a unique, hybrid presenting and producing organization with both a local and global agenda.

BAM is special. It distinguishes itself by the art that is presented on its stages or in its cinemas for greater New York City, while balancing the international distribution of American art that it generates or curates. In my earlier life, I studied theater and wanted to make art happen. Who knew in 1983 that I was going to look back more than 25 years later and find that my contribution and destiny were in Brooklyn? I say it again: it's a gift. I was taught to be polite, so—thank you.

Opposite: Robert Wilson in *Einstein on the Beach*, Philip Glass and Robert Wilson, 1984. Photo courtesy of BAM Hamm Archives Center

Above: Morgan Freeman in *The Gospel at Colonus*, Lee Breuer and Bob Telson, 1983. Photo: Johan Elbers

Above: Michael Clark (featured) in
No Fire Escape in Hell, Michael Clark &
Company, 1986. Photo: Tom Brazil

Opposite: Ian Leslie Harding in
The Birth of the Poet, Kathy Acker
and Peter Gordon, 1985.
Photo: Beatriz Schiller

Opposite: *Elegy*, Eiko & Koma, 1986
Photo: Beatriz Schiller

Above: Zhang Dan Dan and Zhang Ruo
Fei in *Giselle*, Central Ballet of China,
1986. Photo courtesy of BAM Hamm
Archives Center

Top: *Carnations*, Tanztheater Wuppertal
Pina Bausch, 1988. Photo: Ulli Weiss

Bottom: *The Forest*, Robert Wilson
and David Byrne, 1988.
Photo: Gerhard Kassner

Opposite: Börje Ahlstedt, Pierre Wilkner,
and Peter Stormare in *Hamlet*,
Ingmar Bergman / Royal Dramatic
Theatre of Sweden, 1988.
Photo: Bengt Wanselius

Can We Dance a Landscape?,
Min Tanaka and Karel Appel, 1989.
Photo: Nico Koster

Guillermo Resto and Mark Morris
(featured) in *Dido and Aeneas*,
Mark Morris Dance Group, 1990.
Photo: Tom Brazil

Opposite: Olivia Maridjan-Koop,
Rob Besserer, and Mikhail Baryshnikov
in *Wonderland*, Mark Morris/
Monnaie Dance Group, 1990.
Photo: Martha Swope

Above: Michael J. Anderson (featured)
in *Endangered Species*, Martha Clarke,
1990. Photo: Martha Swope

215

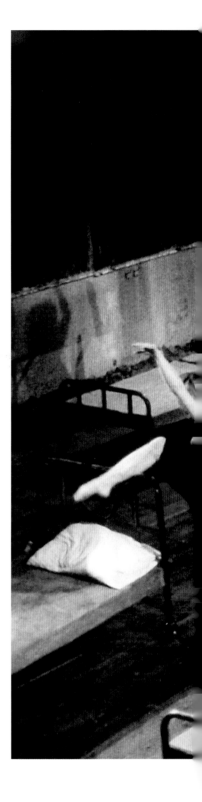

Opposite, top: Mireille Leblanc and
Alain Gaumond in *Don Quichotte*,
O Vertigo Danse, 1990.
Photo: Ormsby K. Ford

Opposite, bottom: Masane Tsukayama
in *Ninagawa Macbeth*, Ninagawa
Company, 1990. Photo courtesy of
BAM Hamm Archives Center

Above: *Le Dortoir*, Carbone 14, 1990.
Photo: Yves Dubé

Top: Dominique Mercy and Mariko
Aoyama in *Palermo Palermo*,
Tanztheater Wuppertal Pina Bausch,
1991. Photo: Ulli Weiss

Bottom: Jan Minarik in *Palermo
Palermo*, Tanztheater Wuppertal
Pina Bausch, 1991. Photo: Ulli Weiss

Opposite: Peter Stormare and Lena Olin
in *Miss Julie*, Ingmar Bergman/
Royal Dramatic Theatre of Sweden,
1991. Photo: Bengt Wanselius

Achterland, Anne Teresa
De Keersmaeker / Rosas, 1992.
Photo: Herman Sorgeloos

Praise House, Urban Bush Women,
1991. Photo: Cylla von Tiedemann

221

Top: *The Hard Nut*, Mark Morris
Dance Group, 1992.
Photo: Catherine Ashmore

Bottom: Scott Handy and Adrian Lester
(featured) in *As You Like It*, Cheek by
Jowl, 1994. Photo: Dan Rest

Opposite: John Kelly in *Light Shall
Lift Them*, John Kelly and Company,
1993. Photo: Paula Court

Above: Steven Berkoff and Zigi Ellison
(featured) in *Salome*, Oscar Wilde,
1995. Photo: Dan Rest

Opposite, top: *Gaudeamus*, Maly Drama
Theatre of St. Petersburg, 1994.
Photo courtesy of BAM Hamm
Archives Center

Opposite, bottom: Gary Chryst in
Susto, Nederlands Dans Theater 3,
1994. Photo: Hans Gerritsen

Left: *Rites of Passage: Celebrating Women of the African Diaspora*, *DanceAfrica*, 1996. Photo: Dan Rest

Middle: Rennie Harris PureMovement in *Rites of Passage: Celebrating Women of the African Diaspora*, *DanceAfrica*, 1996. Photo: Dan Rest

Right: Women of the Calabash in *Rites of Passage: Celebrating Women of the African Diaspora*, *DanceAfrica*, 1996. Photo: Dan Rest

Top: Trisha Brown and Mikhail Baryshnikov in *You can see us*, included in *Trisha Brown at 25: Post Modern and Beyond*, 1996. Photo: Dan Rest

Bottom: Thomas Jay Ryan (featured) in *The Predators' Ball: Hucksters of the Soul*, Karole Armitage, 1996. Photo: Dan Rest

Opposite: *Chimère*, Equestrian Theater by Zingaro, 1996. Photo: Marc Enguerand

The Seven Streams of the
River Ota, Robert Lepage, 1996.
Photo: Dan Rest

Yuragi: In a Space of Perpetual Motion,
Sankai Juku, 1996. Photo: Dan Rest

Left: Annette Paulmann (featured)
in *Time Rocker*, Robert Wilson,
Lou Reed, and Darryl Pinckney/Thalia
Theater, 1997. Photo: Hermann
and Clärchen Baus

Middle: Annette Paulmann and
Stefan Kurt in *Time Rocker*, Robert
Wilson, Lou Reed, and Darryl Pinckney/
Thalia Theater, 1997. Photo: Dan Rest

Right: Hannes Hellmann and
Stephan Benson (featured) in *Time
Rocker*, Robert Wilson, Lou Reed, and
Darryl Pinckney/Thalia Theater, 1997.
Photo: Hermann and Clärchen Baus

Vera Sotnikova, Polina Medvedeva, and
Olga Barnet in *Three Sisters*, Moscow
Art Theater, 1998. Photo: Dan Rest

Sarita Choudhury in *Much Ado*
About Nothing, Cheek by Jowl, 1998.
Photo: John Haynes

Above: *EIDOS:TELOS*, William Forsythe/
Ballett Frankfurt, 1998.
Photo (detail): Dominik Mentzos

Opposite: Joseph Mydell in *Everyman*,
Royal Shakespeare Company, 1998.
Photo: Dan Rest

Hindenburg, Steve Reich and
Beryl Korot, 1998. Photo: Dan Rest

L'Orfeo, Concerto Vocale, Collegium Vocale, and Trisha Brown Company, 1999. Photo: Johan Jacobs

Regina Advento and Jan Minarik in
Der Fensterputzer, Tanztheater
Wuppertal Pina Bausch, 1997.
Photo: Ulli Weiss

"BAM emerged with a new concept, one that would support the transition in leadership. 'Destination BAM' would become the fresh idea, embracing all the transformations of BAM's spaces—the Opera House, renovated rehearsal studios, the BAM Rose Cinemas (formerly the Carey Playhouse), and the BAMcafé in the Lepercq Space, the latter two venues greatly expanding BAM's mission as a cultural and community institution."

Adolfo Vargas in *Hey, What's All This to Me!?*, Compagnie Maguy Marin, 1989.
Photo: Gilles Abegg

A Center of Warmth

by Lin Hwai-min

One summer afternoon in 1991, I met Joe Melillo in Ubud, Bali. We were introduced by Rachel Cooper, a mutual colleague and currently the curator of performing arts at the Asia Society in New York. I did not know much about the Next Wave Festival and Joe was unaware of the existence, or more accurately the nonexistence, of Cloud Gate Dance Theatre of Taiwan, which I was forced to disband in 1988 for financial reasons. It was hot in Ubud, and Joe was unaccustomed to the heat; his T-shirt and the waistline of his sarong were soaked. However, he was kind and patient and asked me lots of questions about my work. In the end, he told me that I should invite him to a premiere if I ever revived Cloud Gate.

Later, when the company made a comeback and *Nine Songs* was due to premiere, I remembered Joe; I thought his remark in Bali might have just been politeness, but I invited him anyway. And he came. After seeing *Nine Songs* at the National Theater in Taipei, Joe invited the company to make its Next Wave Festival debut, which we did in 1995 to great success.

Leaving the National Theater that night, Joe surprised me with a request to go to a bar where a younger crowd hung out. I managed to find one. The bar was bright and vibrant, and Joe was pleased because he always wants to know the society and the people from which individual works originate. That is his style. Joe would never choose a program for the Next Wave just by seeing a DVD. He has to feel it with an audience. It's even better when he can see it with an audience in the artist's home country, so he can try to appreciate the performance through the eyes of the locals as well as from a New Yorker's point of view. Through the years, he has made long journeys to see *Songs of the Wanderers* in Los Angeles, *Moon Water* in Taipei, and *Wild Cursive* in Hong Kong—all of which he has presented in the Next Wave.

Despite his busy schedule and globe-trotting, Joe always replies to letters immediately. Whenever we have run into each other around the world, Joe has invited me to dinner. Over a bottle of wine, we chat about our work and private lives, and he has never hesitated to answer my endless questions about the latest developments in dance and theater. When a fire destroyed Cloud Gate's studio complex in February 2008, Joe was one of the first people outside Taiwan to send his condolences.

In attending symposia and conferences in Asia, Joe has always been gracious and generous in sharing both his professional experience and personal wisdom, assisting Asian artists in widening their horizons and preparing them to reach larger audiences around the world. Whenever Cloud Gate has performed at BAM, he and Karen Brooks Hopkins have always made time to spend with us, talking with the dancers.

Touring the world is exciting. Sometimes, however, solitude sets in. Cities and theaters come and go and are quickly forgotten as one blurs into the next. Brooklyn in late autumn can be freezing and wet, especially in comparison to Taipei, but to all of us in Cloud Gate—BAM is a center of warmth.

Who could have guessed that a chance meeting in Bali would lead to a lifelong connection? To me, Joe Melillo is a dear friend, a mentor, an inspiration. To Cloud Gate, the Next Wave is the bridge connecting East and West—uniting the far corners of the world.

by Tina Silverman

For the last 40 years, audiences and artists have treasured BAM as the rare venue where they can experience the pioneering, the challenging, the outrageous and risky in the performing arts on a scale that few other cultural institutions could or would present. One of New York City's foremost impresarios, Harvey Lichtenstein not only created a home address for avant-garde performing artists, he established BAM as a partner in their creative journeys. He could look back on his tenure at BAM as one of enormous artistic achievement. This was the world that Lichtenstein created, and the two key people who supported and helped him to move that vision forward were Karen Brooks Hopkins and Joseph V. Melillo.

In 1999, Lichtenstein's mantle was passed on to his chosen successors and inheritors of his legacy—protégés with visions of their own. Hopkins and Melillo were ready to take BAM into the new millennium with a bold, more expansive programming mission, one that would position BAM as a premier arts institution like no other on the world cultural map. Passing the baton to Hopkins and Melillo needed to be a seamless, organic process. The management and renovation of the buildings, the staff, the fundraising, and the artistic activity within the performing venues had to keep running smoothly as Hopkins and Melillo found their way into their new leadership positions. The question was how to turn what had been a one-man show into a dual partnership. A major shift in leadership needed to appear as a tiny blip on the screen.

Melillo remembers that when it became clear that Lichtenstein was going to retire, he and Hopkins looked at each other and said, "Okay, the buck stops here, what do we do?" Yet the two of them knew they had a shared vision for BAM. They both wanted to move more deeply into their Brooklyn community, while simultaneously advancing the organization's global identity. For Hopkins and Melillo, this is a passion, not an agenda—a passion that defines their artistic sensibilities.

Hopkins explains that they didn't want to lose anything they had learned from Lichtenstein. The idea was not to distance themselves from the past. They were part of the past. They had helped build it. Hopkins points out that if you look at BAM today, you'll see that the relationships from the Lichtenstein era that they wanted to continue were never interrupted. Robert Lepage returns regularly with new productions, as do Trisha Brown, Meredith Monk, William Christie, Steve Reich, Philip Glass, Robert Wilson, Peter Brook, Ralph Lemon, Laurie Anderson, Chuck Davis, and numerous others. The only time they didn't maintain a relationship was when they regrettably could not justify the expense.

With the change of leadership came a new mission statement that clearly defined what Hopkins,

Variété de Variété, included in *Parcours*, Lucinda Childs Dance Company, 2000. Photo (detail): Stephanie Berger

Melillo, and the board of trustees wanted for the institution. The BAM mission was to be "the preeminent, progressive performing and cinema arts center of the 21st century, engaging both global and local communities. BAM strives to create a distinctive environment for an inspirational and transformative aesthetic experience."

Hopkins and Melillo met in 1978, when Hopkins was invited to a workshop at the O'Neill Theater Center conducted by the Foundation for the Extension and Development of the American Professional Theatre (FEDAPT). Melillo was serving as the deputy director under Fred Vogel, the founder and executive director of the foundation. At the time, Hopkins had been recently hired as the director of development at the New Playwrights' Theatre in Washington, DC, a struggling 125-seat theater with a 16-square-foot stage that only presented new plays. As she readily admits, "I had no idea what I was supposed to be doing." Luckily, she got a spot at the last minute for the one-week learning experience that changed her life and career. The FEDAPT workshop was designed to assist arts administrators across the country to successfully manage the business side of theater. In those days, the regional theater movement was in its prime, and FEDAPT was a very effective service organization whose purpose was to help young new theaters create boards, set up fundraising, and move forward toward their respective goals.

For Hopkins, the training program was revelatory. She was exposed to the various ways that an arts organization could work if one had the right resources and the right artistic product. As a result, Hopkins's focus turned not just to fundraising but to institution building. She began to make sense of a development system that in a few years she would perfect into a successful strategy for fundraising in the arts and beyond.

After a year at the New Playwrights' Theatre, and having had the FEDAPT experience, Hopkins wanted to take her concepts and her ambition to her spiritual home, New York City. She had the training, she had the contacts from the workshop, now all she needed was a job. She'd heard that there was an opening in development at the Brooklyn Academy of Music. With a recommendation from Fred Vogel, she was invited to interview for a position in the newly revamped development department. Hopkins had been to Manhattan often but had never been to Brooklyn. After the initial shock of stepping out of the subway into the heart of teeming downtown Brooklyn, she walked into Lichtenstein's office. Not one to waste time, he made an offer, and just as quickly she accepted. She was in the right place at the right time.

Three years later, Melillo got a phone call to interview for a job working for Lichtenstein to help turn the Next Wave from a series into a festival, and, like Hopkins, acknowledges the moment as a turning point in his life. He joined Hopkins, remembering her from her stellar participation at the FEDAPT workshop, and he is still impressed. "Karen is a brilliant talent. She's unparalleled in fundraising, plus she has a broad, open perception of the institution, the services of the institution, and the vibrancy of the institution."

Hopkins went straight to work fundraising. She was writing grants and running special events in what was then a small department, with just five people on the team. Today, BAM's development staff numbers more than 30, as BAM now needs to raise close to 10 times the amount of funds to support its programming and facilities. In 1981, the then vice president for planning left BAM at the end of the fiscal year. Lichtenstein had to hire someone he could trust, who would work hard, and someone he could get cheap. He was completely broke with the demise of the BAM Theater Company. Hopkins applied for the job and got it. It was big. In two years, she went from being a development officer to a very young vice president.

Melillo began his tenure working furiously with Lichtenstein on the Next Wave Festival. Their first production together, *The Photographer / Far from the Truth* (1983), a Philip Glass / Robert Coe triptych performance work, proved to be the contentious hit that the festival needed to wake up audiences in New York to the fact that there was something happening in Brooklyn that wasn't happening anywhere else in the city.

Hopkins will never forget the opening night of *The Photographer / Far from the Truth*. Steve Reichard and Anne Livet, who were consultants to the Next Wave Festival, were very connected to the visual artists and to the whole young, hip downtown scene. Reichard and Livet were helping build a persona for the Next Wave Festival by throwing big BAM parties

Mikel Murfi in *The Whiteheaded Boy*, Lennox Robinson / Barabbas . . . the company, 1999. Photo: Kevin McFeely

at the city's trendier nightclubs, like Danceteria and Area, where artists mixed with donors, celebrities, BAM aficionados, and a colorful array of spectators. At the opening, Hopkins was standing at the back of the Opera House, watching the audience arrive, when Judy Daykin, who was then executive vice president and general manager at BAM, came up to her and said, "I've never seen a more unattractive group of people attend a theatrical event in my entire life!" People had green hair; it was a whole different crowd.

She walked away, and then Reichard ran up and put his arms around Hopkins and said, "Have you ever seen a more fabulous looking group of people attend a theatrical event in the history of New York City?" Hopkins remembers thinking, *This is going to be great, because everybody has an opinion and is talking about it. They're even talking about the audience.*

The buzz around BAM's programming was getting louder, and early into her tenure at BAM, Hopkins was asked by FEDAPT, as one of the

OPERATION : ORFEO, John Cage, Bo Holten, and Christoph Willibald Gluck / Hotel Pro Forma, 1999. Photo: Roberto Fortuna

William Christie.
Photo (detail): Michel Szabo

by Edward Rothstein

There aren't many times when a seismic shift can be felt in musical perception, unveiling an alternate mode of thinking and feeling. But that was the effect William Christie had at BAM in 1989, when he led Les Arts Florissants in Jean-Baptiste Lully's opera *Atys*. I recall the music as unearthly yet thoroughly sensuous, scrupulous yet supple and free, alien yet intimately affecting. Christie's affinity for the neglected music of the French Baroque had been evident in recordings, but the opera went far beyond expectations. Since then, Christie has become a more familiar part of New York's musical life, but his early performances in Brooklyn did more than bring Lully, Charpentier, and Rameau to our attention.

Christie's approach grew out of what was once called the "authenticity" movement, which reinterpreted pre-19th-century music by embracing historical performance practice. Authenticity was once a charged, polemical term, but Christie simply took it for granted. It was not his point; it was his starting point. He argued that the repertoire's stylistic rules were based on 17th-century pronunciation of French; language determined the music's phrasing, its emphases, its pulse. "There is a box, an enclosure," Christie said of the constraints—a rectangle resembling Leonardo's Vitruvian man circumscribing the music. "That is a magic square. Our playing has to fill that space but not go beyond it." But within that space the music is in play.

This makes Christie's performances both rigorous and improvisatory. Many liberties are taken, and they can be startling. *Atys*, for example, might seem a quaint drama replete with nymphs, spirits, and woodland deities. But Jean-Marie Villégier's staging stripped away the natural world and set the drama as if it took place at the court of Versailles. And, indeed, that was how it was originally perceived. So when characters worry over their feelings, over how much to show and how much to conceal, our attention is drawn to similar musical tensions. We hear not formulas of pastoral myth, but a supple, courtly drama of understated expressions and cloaked passions.

This is far different from mainstream 19th-century repertoire. Grand opera pits the private passions of the individual against the state and its institutions. Christie's *Atys*, along with his other performances at BAM, revealed another way to see the world, turning an antique musical language into a still-living force.

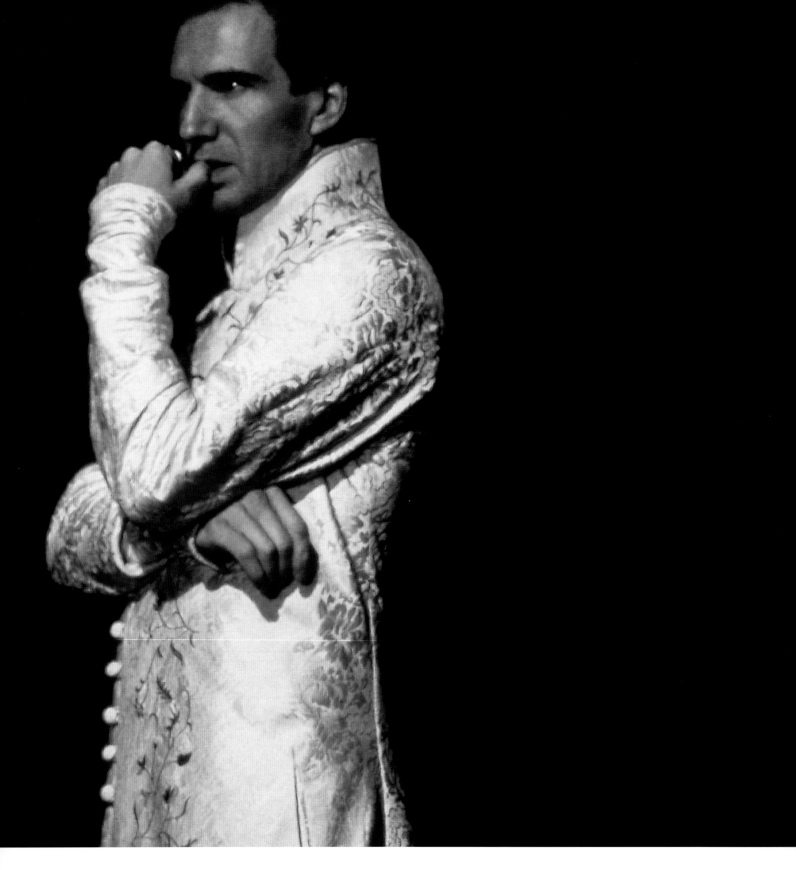

Ralph Fiennes in *Richard II*,
Almeida Theatre Company, 2000.
Photo: Ivan Kyncl

program's successful graduates, to give a speech at its annual conference in New York. "I wrote down all of the thoughts I had put together from that one week," she says, "and how, having the actual experience of working at BAM, I was using what I'd learned. I remember that the speech locked in my ideas. I committed to paper a system of how to successfully do this work." That speech turned into a book she wrote with Carolyn Stolper Friedman,

Successful Fundraising for Arts and Cultural Organizations, now in its second edition and third printing.

Lichtenstein and Hopkins turned out to be a brilliant team, but they also fought and their relationship could sometimes be tumultuous. The arguments were usually about Hopkins being very conservative about spending and not wanting to take risks with substantial amounts of money. Lichtenstein was all about risk. He would always go forward if he thought something was worth it. Hopkins understood that Lichtenstein's major attribute was also his biggest liability. Money was tight and the stakes were high but, as Hopkins recalls, "When an idea worked our world changed for the good, and when it didn't the world at BAM collapsed."

One of their most heated disputes was over the Ariane Mnouchkine production of *Les Atrides* (1992), the four-play cycle of Greek tragedies that required a special venue and was staged in the cavernous Park Slope Armory in Brooklyn. Hopkins knew that the cost of building a theatrical space in the armory was way beyond what their budget could tolerate—nonetheless, it was a towering artistic achievement. But in 1998, when Lichtenstein presented the French equestrian theater troupe Zingaro for the second time—the company's initial appearance two years earlier had been a great success—BAM lost a million dollars in a very short time, and it was contentious. When a production failed, it cost a fortune, and Hopkins understood what it took to raise those funds. However, Lichtenstein made some great bets: among them, Peter Brook's *The Mahabharata* (1987), off the charts; Ingmar Bergman's *Hamlet* (1988) in Swedish; William Christie's *Atys* (1989); bringing *Einstein on the Beach* back for a second round in 1992; the Cheek by Jowl production of *As You Like It* (1994); Robert Lepage's *The Seven Streams of the River Ota* (1996); Jonathan Miller's *St. Matthew Passion* (1997).

The Next Wave series had evolved out of Lichtenstein's interest in new work and in bringing artists to BAM who had formerly had to do their large scale work in Europe because there was no home for it in the United States. He wanted to be a champion for these artists. And he understood that being in Brooklyn would create a niche that Lincoln Center wasn't going to touch, that nobody was going to touch. In 1981, BAM evolved the Next Wave series, which after two seasons, with Melillo joining the institution in 1983, morphed into the Next Wave Festival. As quickly as the BAM Theater Company had failed, the Next Wave succeeded. Lichtenstein presented innovative programming that immediately put the Next Wave on the map and galvanized people to come to BAM, especially young people eager to engage in the BAM experience.

The branding of BAM began in the mid-1970s with Charles Ziff, then vice president for promotion, who coined the Brooklyn Academy of Music as BAM. He created marketing strategies that began to give BAM a cool edge, and Hopkins, Melillo, and the marketing team at BAM later pushed it to the next level. They understood that the strength in the BAM brand lay in a consistently sophisticated look that was instantly recognizable as BAM, from the signage in the building to the marketing and fundraising collateral. Hopkins says, "As in all things BAM, our work really starts with the artist. We find the best way to feature their work and make sure that the marketing and the fundraising reflect their artistic identity. Everything comes back to this very deep connection between the artist and the institution. It's no longer just the Next Wave. The Next Wave gave BAM a certain persona and everything else has evolved from that." BAM became an institution both artistically and administratively that spoke in one voice, no matter what the program or initiative.

Collaborative Partnership: Redefining the Institution

In 1999, when Hopkins and Melillo succeeded Lichtenstein, Brooklyn was changing rapidly and BAM was a huge part of that change. The Mark Morris

Anja Silja in *The Makropulos Case*, Glyndebourne Festival Opera, 2001. Photo: Michael Le Poer Trench

Dance Center had broken ground across the street. BAMcafé opened in the Lepercq Space, and the transformation of the Carey Playhouse into the BAM Rose Cinemas had been completed. The rest of the neighborhood was also transforming, and Lichtenstein was at the center of much of the change. Upon retiring, he immersed himself in the BAM Local Development Corporation (now part of the Downtown Brooklyn Partnership) with the purpose to create a 14-square-block cultural district that had BAM at its center. The BAM Local Development Corporation was conceived as an independent nonprofit organization, whose mission was to create a vibrant, mixed-use multicultural arts district in downtown Brooklyn. As a result, the vision for the BAM cultural district is distinguished by its diverse arts programming, its well-designed and accommodating public space, and its innovative, world-class architecture. It continues to evolve as a resource for the arts, the local community, the borough of Brooklyn, and the city as a whole.

Fiona Shaw in *Medea*, Abbey Theatre, 2002. Photo: Stephanie Berger

No matter where one stands on the topic of real estate development, Brooklyn has been going through a massive renewal; local developers, along with a supportive City Hall, are changing the architectural face of the borough. Abandoned buildings and decaying waterfronts are being transformed into attractive residential units, trendy shops, a riverside park, and top-rated restaurants. Brooklynites have a lot to be smug about. From Red Hook to Williamsburg, Brooklyn has heated up. With real estate across the bridge unaffordable for artists, Brooklyn is now overflowing with edgy talent that can find a collaborative partner in BAM. There are presently more artists living and working in Brooklyn than in Manhattan or in fact anywhere in the United States. The difference between BAM and many other established cultural institutions is that change is part of its DNA. Another difference is that a critical part of the institution's mission is to promote inclusiveness that translates into collaboration.

A crucial component in establishing BAM as a cultural destination is an involved board of trustees that works with Hopkins and Melillo as they move the institution forward. According to board chairman Alan H. Fishman, "The partnership between Karen and Joe continued the ascendance that Harvey had established. They took what they were given by Harvey to a new level, flawlessly, complemented by the incredible talents of the institution's staff." A combination of personal style and personality brought a new spirit of collaboration with the board, with the community, and with global artists. Although the board's responsibilities haven't changed since Lichtenstein's tenure, Hopkins, very much aware of financial realities given her professional background and character, has brought the board much closer to the whole process of running the institution. She depends on their combined professional and leadership skills to help fulfill the artistic and financial initiatives that she and Melillo have planned. Fishman notes, "We are very much part of the game plan. We're part of the whole experience, which is a very dramatic shift under their leadership. The budget has more than quadrupled in Karen and Joe's tenure, from $10 to $40 million."

Through strategic nurturing, the board has grown in size, in involvement, and in stature. The trustees understand the unique position of being a cultural leader in Brooklyn, and that understanding is a major part of BAM's mission and success. The board has mirrored the changes Hopkins and Melillo made and continue to make. There have been, during Hopkins's tenure alone, more than 100 trustees, yet the institution tries to make sure that each trustee is an intimate part of the institution. Fishman contends that the personal involvement is part of BAM's success and charm. Audiences and artists, too, feel attached to BAM personally—a pervasive attitude that starts from

the top. "I'm sure I speak for the entire board leadership, the vice chairs, Bill Campbell and Adam Max, the three of us have really had a ball doing this," says Fishman. "There hasn't been one tough day doing this. Not one. That's because of Karen and Joe."

Early in their tenure, Hopkins and Melillo began to investigate how to reach out and make BAM work more effectively in the community. The Rockefeller Foundation gave BAM a grant to conduct a large-scale community engagement survey. BAM wanted to understand what kind of services local residents and artists really needed and wanted, and how they felt about BAM. The survey found that people not only wanted more diverse programming and more education programs, but they also wanted more access to BAM itself. However, with the cost of running the existing facilities, BAM couldn't always provide space to satisfy those needs. "In 2004, five years into our tenure," says Melillo, "Karen and I were at an executive committee meeting when Alan Fishman turned to me and said, 'Okay, you guys are a success.' What he meant was that the artistic programs were successful and the management of the institution had stabilized."

Melillo took that success as an indication that it was time for the next step. He felt that the institution needed a smaller, completely flexible theater as a venue for the contemporary artist. He knew there was work being done on a small scale that was not getting to

New York from the global marketplace. He also knew there were artists in the local community who could not work in the Howard Gilman Opera House or the Harvey Theater because the scale was too big. In effect, Melillo wanted to incorporate the transition of the borough with the artistic responsibility of the institution. "It's only going to mutate, continue to evolve," Melillo told Fishman. "This borough is robust with young talent."

"We had to find ways with integrity, with honesty, to welcome this burgeoning artistic community," says Melillo. "While maintaining artistic quality and our competitive edge, we needed to address diversity with more intensity, not only in our performing venues, cinemas, and the BAMcafé Live series. We were trying to find a way that BAM could provide more access to the institution for the community at large."

The change in the immediate Fort Greene neighborhood is readily apparent, propelled to a large extent by artists. Melillo explains, "Brooklyn is a very complex borough, the largest in New York City. It's racially and ethnically diverse, it's ever changing and growing, so the worst thing that could happen would be to remain static. Karen and I had this mantra 'Destination BAM' and this kind of 'Experience BAM.' We had a shared vision of creating multiple opportunities for the community to access BAM. We wanted BAM to be the destination for audiences

Mikhail Baryshnikov (featured) in *See Through Knot*, White Oak Dance Project, 2000. Photo: Stephanie Berger

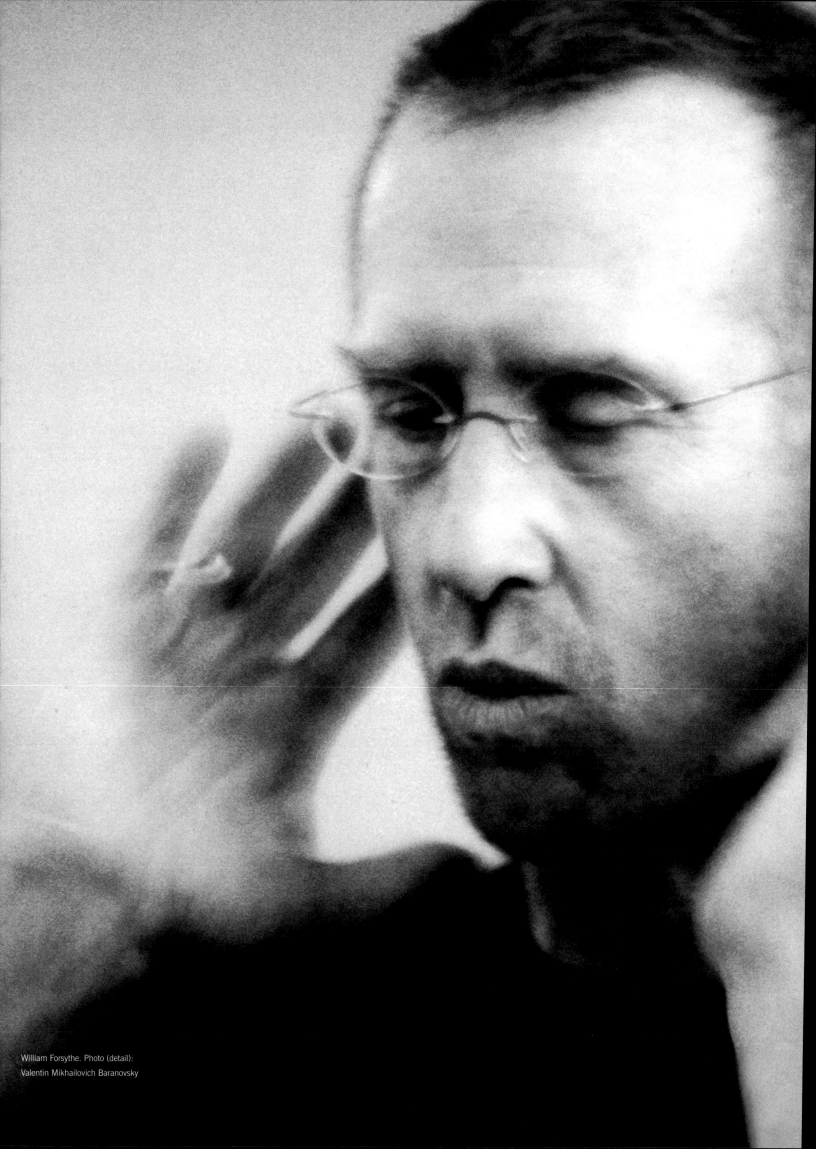

William Forsythe. Photo (detail):
Valentin Mikhailovich Baranovsky

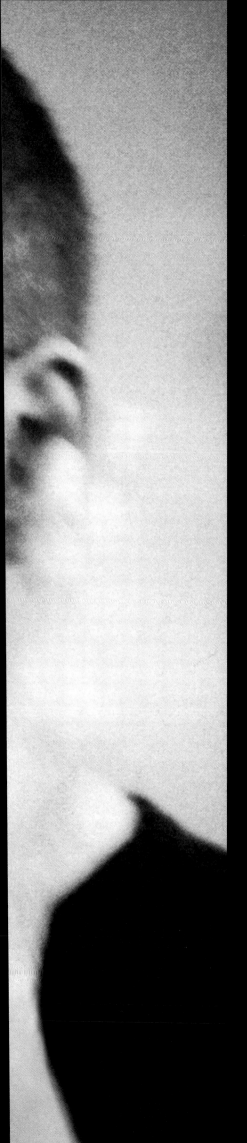

by Roslyn Sulcas

Over the last three decades, William Forsythe has fundamentally changed the way we look at, and think about, classical dance. That revolution in perception was quickly apparent in Europe, where Forsythe first began to choreograph, soon after the New York–born dancer joined the Stuttgart Ballet. It has taken longer for his influence to percolate to the United States, but it's likely that there is no one in the ballet world today who is unaware of his importance and influence. BAM presented *EIDOS:TELOS* in 1998 and since then has brought five of Forsythe's works to the Howard Gilman Opera House.

Like George Balanchine, Forsythe has enlarged the physical possibilities of ballet. He has investigated the limits of balance and flexibility, changed the practices of partnering by demonstrating its dynamics, removed the imperatives of a vertical torso and effortless appearance, and instigated movement from every part of the body while retaining ballet's lines and sophisticated vocabulary. Early in his work, Forsythe introduced a contemporary theatricality to his ballets that was more often found in the theater or film of that era. The works sometimes—although not always—included speech, film, highly innovative lighting that he designed, improvisation, electronic music and soundscapes, nonlinear narrative, and surprising visual and theatrical effects that frequently shocked as much as they delighted audiences.

Although a fervent musical comedy fan who was "always dancing around," Forsythe didn't study dance formally until he discovered Christa Long's ballet classes at Jacksonville University in Florida. A year later, he was offered a scholarship to the Joffrey Ballet School, where he was exposed to the Joffrey's eclectic, innovative repertoire. He joined the Stuttgart Ballet in 1973 at age 23, and in 1976 he created his first work, the pas de deux *Urlicht*. Forsythe became Stuttgart's resident choreographer, creating nine more ballets for the company before embarking in 1980 on a freelance career.

In 1984, he became the artistic director of the Ballett Frankfurt, and over the next two decades he created a body of work for that company, as well as many works for others, that established him as the most important voice to emerge in the post-Balanchine era. In 2004, amid huge public outcry, Forsythe was forced to disband the company, eventually forming a smaller ensemble based in both Frankfurt and Dresden. This change has marked a new choreographic stage in Forsythe's work, with a greater concentration on installation and non-proscenium pieces and a movement vocabulary that is less dependent upon ballet as its generative basis. His influence, however, is greater than ever as the innovations of his ballets of the 1980s and 1990s are absorbed and reiterated by a younger generation. Never predictable, it remains to see what he'll do next.

William Forsythe

a desperately needed 250-seat black box theater, comprised of the Samuel H. Scripps Stage in the Judith R. and Alan H. Fishman Space, there will be the Peter Jay Sharp Lobby, a 1,400-square-foot rehearsal studio (the Rita K. Hillman Studio), a green-design rooftop for special events (including the Geraldine Stutz Gardens), and a multimedia classroom/workshop space (the Max Leavitt Theater Workshop). BAM will be able to provide subsidized space for community and education programs, as well as professional development for smaller organizations. "We'll not only be a better neighbor, but a more grassroots partner to local groups," Hopkins says. The Fisher Building will also allow BAM to ramp up its education initiative with a summer camp, after-school programs, and projects that cannot be realized in the other buildings.

The Next Wave and the Global Stage

The artistic vision shared by the BAM leadership, staff, and entire board is informed by their commitment to engage both local and global communities in the BAM experience. Programming for the BAM stages often requires years of negotiation and planning, and Hopkins and Melillo have developed an expertise in successfully managing the inventory of a comprehensive performing and cinema arts center. "Our idea," states Hopkins, "is to present an event that is only at BAM for this many nights, right here, right now, and nowhere else." As a result, having a limited number of tickets for a BAM performance not only generates fundraising from its membership but also creates a buzz, which is another way of pushing the brand. As a global presenter and partner, BAM has established a reputation of expectation and excellence, especially as a showcase for artists of international stature: Pina Bausch, Robert Lepage, Ushio Amagatsu, Bibi Andersson and Erland Josephson, Ralph Fiennes, Fiona Shaw, John Kani and Winston Ntshona, Vanessa and Lynn Redgrave, Lena Olin, Cate Blanchett, Isabelle Huppert, Ian McKellen, Patrick Stewart, Juliette Binoche and Akram Khan, James Thiérrée, Alan Rickman, Geoffrey Rush, and Derek Jacobi.

Throughout the Hopkins and Melillo era, the core of BAM programming has remained the Next Wave Festival, setting the tone for most of what audiences see at BAM in the fall seasons. Melillo says, "Because major advancements in technology have influenced the visual material in performance, new narratives are surfacing. The Next Wave serves audiences and artists by introducing both new productions and new art forms." In order for BAM to stay vital, he has to find a balance between embracing the advancements in the international scene and remaining true to legacy artists like Pina Bausch's company or Philip Glass or Laurie Anderson. And, of course, there are discoveries right here in Brooklyn and

Above: Simon Russell Beale in *Twelfth Night*, Sam Mendes/Donmar Warehouse, 2003. Photo: Stephanie Berger

Opposite: Mark Strong and Emily Watson, *Twelfth Night*, Sam Mendes/Donmar Warehouse, 2003. Photo: Manuel Harlan

interested in experiencing every aspect of the arts. Whether you are interested in theater, dance, music, visual arts, literature, or film, our vision was to offer a complete immersion into what we were producing or presenting."

Within a few weeks of the executive committee meeting, Hopkins and Melillo learned that the Salvation Army building next door was for sale, and with help on the acquisition from Two Trees Management and funding from the city of New York and BAM donors, the Richard B. Fisher Building is now under way. "The Fisher Building, built with fantastic public and private sector support, will be a dream come true for BAM," says Hopkins. Besides

New York City. There are generally 16 to 18 Next Wave productions from September to December that all the other departments within BAM find their paths into as well. For example, the BAMcinématek creates complementary programming; likewise, the BAM education and humanities department presents schooltime performances, artist talks, and post-performance discussions between the cast or the performers and the audiences.

While it is impossible to adequately do justice to the expanse of BAM programming during Hopkins and Melillo's tenure, several groundbreaking productions deserve special attention. As a precursor to the

Bridge Project, in the 2003 Spring Season Melillo brought Sam Mendes and the Donmar Warehouse's brilliant interpretations of *Twelfth Night* and *Uncle Vanya* to the Harvey Theater, bringing back to BAM perhaps the greatest stage actor of his generation, Simon Russell Beale.

From the 2003 Next Wave Festival, the celebration of Merce Cunningham's 50th anniversary season was a highlight and pure Next Wave. BAM audiences saw the world premiere of *Split Sides*, with music performed live by Radiohead and Sigur Rós, and had the opportunity to enter Cunningham's world of art according to the *I Ching* and his "chance

in the 2004 Spring Season, director Edward Hall's all-male company, Propeller, wowed audiences and reviewers alike with a touching and contemporary *The Winter's Tale*. In 2006, along with Lincoln Center and Carnegie Hall, BAM paid tribute to Steve Reich on his 70th birthday by presenting the U.S. premiere of Akram Khan's dance *Variations for Vibes, Pianos and Strings* with a commissioned score by Reich. Anne Teresa De Keersmaeker, a choreographer with a long association with both BAM and Reich, performed her classic work *Fase, four movements to the music of Steve Reich*. An artistic colleague of BAM's for more than four decades, Reich has been hailed as one of "just a handful of living composers who can legitimately claim to have altered the direction of musical history."

In 2007, the Next Wave Festival celebrated its 25th anniversary. As confirmation of its artistic mission, the festival opened with Lin Hwai-min's *Wild Cursive*, performed by Cloud Gate Dance Theatre of Taiwan, and included local artists Charles Mee, John Jasperse, and Sufjan Stevens; Tan Dun conducting the Brooklyn Philharmonic; and international companies such as TR Warszawa from Poland performing *Krum*, the Tero Saarinen Company from Finland with *Borrowed Light*, Israel's Batsheva Dance Company with *Three*, the Thalia Theater from Germany with *Lulu*, the Japanese dance-theater company Pappa Tarahumara with *Ship in a View*, and Swiss-born James Thiérrée's La Compagnie du Hanneton production of *Au Revoir Parapluie*. In honor of the occasion, BAM commissioned New York–based sculptor Leo Villareal to transform and illuminate the exterior of the Peter Jay Sharp Building with a site-specific LED artwork installed in the distinctive arched windows and designed to resonate with the structure— a beacon of light for the BAM audience.

Finding productions that are right for BAM isn't easy. Lichtenstein and Melillo traveled together across the pond and from sea to shining sea looking for shows that no one else in New York City was willing to present. When Lichtenstein retired, Melillo was on his own and thinking about not only how to bring the work to Brooklyn but also, with an increasingly large global goal in mind, which institutions BAM could partner with to further broaden its artistic vision. During the Lichtenstein era, there were plenty of international companies that brought established pieces and premieres to BAM, and under Hopkins and Melillo the ratio has remained fairly constant. The difference is that BAM was now expanding, building series, adjunct events, and complementary programs around both the foreign and domestic performance works.

Traveling to various continents had to be factored into Melillo's life. He travels, at the minimum, three or four months out of the year on behalf of BAM. He looks for a qualitative line, the most basic

operations." "We are here to cast the dice," said Cunningham as selected audience members tossed dice to determine the order of the evening's program. That same season also found the radical interpreter of contemporary ballet, choreographer William Forsythe, back at BAM for his third appearance at the helm of Ballett Frankfurt with a program that included *The Room as it Was, Duo, (N.N.N.N.)*, and *One Flat Thing, reproduced*. Tables scraped, screeched, and bounced onstage as adrenaline-rushed dancers performed with unbelievable flexibility and speed.

Returning to BAM in the 2005 Next Wave, after a triumphant run of *A Midsummer Night's Dream*

Ralph Lemon in his *Tree*, 2000.
Photo: T Charles Erickson

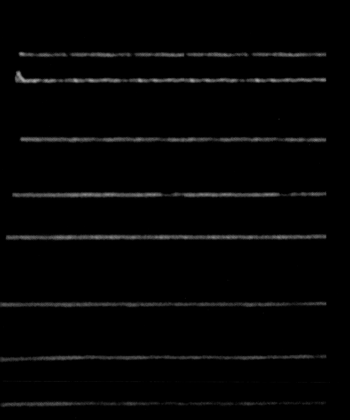

by Deborah Jowitt

Ralph Lemon's muse is risk. He has an appetite for experiences that knock his choreographic vision off balance in unforeseen ways. Born in Cincinnati in 1952, a graduate of the University of Minnesota, he studied with Nancy Hauser and became a member of her company before he dived into New York's post-modern dance scene. In his *Wanda in the Awkward Age*, a 1982 solo piece expressing the ungainliness and warring emotions of adolescence, he performed in a little cotton dress.

In 1985, Lemon assembled a brilliant group in what could be construed as a daring move: the dancers were almost all white, which earned their African American director the disapproval of some members of the black dance community. His dances—full of sensuous, fluid, careering movement, brainy juxta-positions, and startling images—often seemed to be about societies that couldn't cohere and stories that ate their own plots. In *Happy Trails* (1988), a man periodically rocked on a saddle set on the floor—a cowboy with no herd but his own galloping frustrations.

After 10 years, Lemon dissolved his company. For its last New York season, he collaborated on a duet with his mentor, former Cunningham dancer Viola Farber, who was 64 at the time, and shortly thereafter he embarked on an immense, profoundly challeng-ing project. A trip to Côte d'Ivoire inaugurated actual and artistic journeys and yielded a dance trilogy that crossed cultural boundaries and tracked diasporic change. *Geography* (1997) was developed with dancers and drummers brought from West Africa; *Tree* (2000) bravely juxtaposed and mingled Asian cultures and performers; and *Come home Charley Patton* (2004) traveled into the dark past of the American South—all three were presented at BAM and known collectively as the *Geography Trilogy*. Lemon's books, *Geography: Art/Race/Exile* (2000) and *Tree: Belief/Culture/Balance* (2004) vividly reveal—in journal entries, rehearsal notes, drawings, and photographs—the inspired reawakening of this fearlessly innovative artist.

Ralph Lemon

being production values and prowess in techniques and discipline. The core is communication. Is the artist communicating his or her ideas eloquently? He is quick to add, "Now, that doesn't eliminate challenging, aggressive work. I don't seek out ambiguity. I seek out clarity. I always have my antennae up for innovative and progressive ideas, so I'm not intimidated by something I've never seen before." He's looking to see if the work is well crafted and articulated. These days, there are a lot more opportunities for major artists to be programmed by BAM's competitors, which is why Melillo travels as often as he does. "I try to run faster," he explains, "and make strategic decisions about

Aissawa Ensemble in *Sufi Music Ensembles*, included in *Muslim Voices: Arts & Ideas*, 2009.
Photo: Jack Vartoogian

where I go. Wherever I go, I always take the BAM audience with me, because I am the BAM audience."

Each year brings new work to the adventurous BAM audience, and, fast-forwarding to 2010, choreographer Ralph Lemon presented the New York premiere of his emotionally turbulent, multimedia dance work, *How Can You Stay in the House All Day and Not Go Anywhere?* In this moving and challenging (for the audiences and performers) piece, Lemon combined dance, film, and spoken word to explore, as *New York Times* reviewer Claudia La Rocco noted, the sad but positive truth that "Life and art go on, until they don't."

Beyond the borders of Brooklyn and Next Wave programming, another way that BAM is reaching out globally is through the ambitious DanceMotion USA project for the U.S. State Department. In 2008, the department issued a request for proposals to send American dance companies to three different regions of the world rarely visited by American artists: South America, Southeast Asia, and Africa. The BAM staff put together the strategy that won the competition. The logistics were amazingly complicated, and the results were far beyond anyone's expectations. From January through March 2010, 33 dancers from three dance companies, ODC/Dance, Evidence, and Urban Bush Women, acted as artist-diplomats and traveled to nine countries, involving 12 U.S. embassies and consulates in 16 cities. They put on 21 public and student performances and participated in more than 100 exchange and educational activities, and BAM distributed close to 600 books and DVDs from America's finest dance companies to 27 libraries in the host cities. The inaugural program was so successful that BAM was selected to lead the initiative for another exchange in the following year.

Perhaps BAM's most ambitious and challenging foray into content-driven, international producing was *Muslim Voices: Arts & Ideas*, a multi-venue celebration of Islamic cultures that addressed a current and pressing global issue. In September 2005, a Danish daily newspaper published a series of 12 cartoons containing unflattering images of the Prophet Muhammad as an attempt to debate the issues surrounding Islamic terrorism as well as criticism of Islam and self-censorship in the press. As a result, Muslims around the world took to the streets in protest after the images went viral and were reprinted in newspapers in more than 50 countries. Against this background of global distrust and violence between Islam and the West, Hopkins was invited by Mustapha Tlili, founder and director of New York University's Center for Dialogues, a think tank based on Muslim and Western relations, to participate in an international conference in Kuala Lumpur called "Who Speaks for Islam? Who Speaks for the West?"

During the conference, Hopkins was shocked at the level of tension and rage among participants and

Youssou N'Dour in *Muslim Voices: Arts & Ideas,* 2009.
Photo: Jack Vartoogian

discussed with Stephen Heintz, the president of the Rockefeller Brothers Fund, the conference's funder, what role BAM could play in fostering a healthy dialogue between such contentious players. "There was a sense of urgency surrounding the complete misunderstanding between the Muslim world and the West," says Hopkins. "Stephen, Mustapha, and I weren't arrogant enough to think we could solve the problems, but it seemed worthwhile to offer the arts as a way of simply learning more about Muslim culture and fostering mutual respect without all the hostility."

Hopkins returned to BAM with the idea of a citywide festival of art, music, theater, cinema, and talks that would entertain, educate, and expose audiences to the cultural world of Islam. Melillo recalls, "*Muslim Voices* was another historic moment for BAM. We created, in the most positive way, a festival featuring individual performers and companies with artistic merit and ideas that are progressive and innovative, within and outside of their traditions." BAM and its partners presented more than 300 artists, performers, policy makers, and scholars from as far away as Asia, Africa, and the Middle East as well as artists from Brooklyn, home to over 100,000 Muslims. Audiences experienced evenings of traditional Sufi devotional music

and Arabic hip-hop. Alongside the artistic programming, the festival included a companion conference on issues of political policy, cultural exchange, and East/West values. BAM joined forces with other supporting and media partners, including the Asia Society and New York University's Center for Dialogues, in presenting the first festival of its kind in the United States. At BAM, Melillo came up with the idea of headlining a show with Youssou N'Dour, the renowned Senegalese Muslim musician and singer. In addition, there were electrifying nights of musical contrasts and collaborations like gospel singer Craig Adams from New Orleans and Faiz Ali Faiz from Pakistan performing together. An outdoor mini-souk packed with artisans and merchants energized the block surrounding BAM.

Muslim Voices took more than three years to mount and a tremendous amount of money. Every aspect of producing the festival proved to be a challenge. The principal funding came from the Rockefeller Brothers Fund, the Rockefeller Foundation, the Doris Duke Foundation for Islamic Art, and the Robert Sterling Clark Foundation. Hopkins says that fundraising for *Muslim Voices* was incredibly hard, much harder than she thought it was going to be. Everything about the festival was difficult: obtaining visas, the subject matter—even the press was complicated. "But *Muslim Voices* reflected the kind of issue-based work we were interested in presenting," she says, and adds that she is very proud of it.

Beyond the Next Wave

From January to June, Melillo finds individual productions that are each unique cultural events for the city of New York. His artistic focus is to create a balance between the progressive and innovative of the Next Wave Festival and the identity, visibility, stature, and rigor of the theater, dance, and opera programming in the spring. For example, in the 2010 Next Wave Festival, BAM presented the American premiere of *Gezeiten*, directed and choreographed by

music in the streets, and a large African bazaar in the parking lots. As noted by Melillo, "The ultimate objective for both the Next Wave and Spring Season is to have a holistic mainstage artistic program."

The initial years with Hopkins and Melillo at the helm saw plenty of outstanding and diverse performances, from Laurie Anderson's *Songs and Stories from Moby Dick* and Pina Bausch's *Danzón* at the 1999 Next Wave to Mikhail Baryshnikov in 2000 dancing with the White Oak Dance Project, and in 2001, the Anne Teresa De Keersmaeker/Steve Reich collaboration *Drumming*, the Robert Wilson/Lou Reed production of *POEtry*, and the American premiere of *Cloudstreet*—part of the Next Wave Down Under program within the Next Wave Festival that included over 100 Australian artists—plus the launch of BAMcafé Live. But Hopkins and Melillo really began to strut their stuff in the 2002 Spring Season

Left: Olga Pitarch and Cyril Auvity in *Il Ritorno d'Ulisse in Patria*, William Christie/Les Art Florissants/Aix-en-Provence European Academy of Music, 2002.
Photo: Stephanie Berger

Middle: *L'incoronazione di Poppea*, Dutch National Opera, 2002.
Photo: Stephanie Berger

Right: Andrew Funk and Jacqueline Wall in *Orfeo*, Chicago Opera Theater, 2002.
Photo: Stephanie Berger

Sasha Waltz, a devastating look at human helplessness in the face of disaster. In a wonderful contrast to *Gezeiten*, the 2011 Spring Season featured the upbeat, vibrant Ballet Nacional de Cuba performing *La Magia de la Danza*, choreographed by its legendary general director Alicia Alonso, which was part of the *¡Sí Cuba!* Festival, a citywide artistic and cultural celebration of Cuban arts. The company rarely performs in New York, so this was an opportunity for BAM audiences to see scenes from Alonso's most celebrated pieces. In addition, spring programming includes Chuck Davis's annual DanceAfrica festival, a BAM production and Memorial Day weekend tradition—shows in the Howard Gilman Opera House, dancing and

with the mounting of all three of Monteverdi's operas. Melillo had the idea of giving New York an opera experience beyond what was regularly presented at the Metropolitan and New York City Operas when he put together the Monteverdis with the distinctive BAM twist. Both Hopkins and Melillo think that the Monteverdi cycle changed the way the arts community saw BAM, and its success motivated them to use the same model for more productions.

Melillo says, "We try to stand shoulder to shoulder with the Metropolitan Opera. I take the same philosophy programming opera as in other disciplines: How can we give New York City what it doesn't have?" Since no other venue or presenter had offered the three extant Monteverdi operas in the same program, Melillo selected three different opera productions from three different places in the world. BAM split the performances between the Howard Gilman Opera House and the Harvey Theater, so there was spectacle, epic opera, and intimate opera. BAM not only presented the operas, it wrapped the performances with discussions about Monteverdi and demonstrations about the musical style. In essence, BAM contextualized the program. "It was the beginning of what we envisioned BAM to be," Melillo continues, "a total, in-depth artistic experience. You come to 'Experience BAM.' We program events that are unique in New York City, which is difficult to do in an over-saturated cultural marketplace."

Opera was a challenge for BAM because of the expense. Early on, it had become clear that what BAM did would have to be very specific, very

providing the funds to enable Christie's revival of Jean-Baptiste Lully's legendary *Atys* in 2011, selected as the opening production of BAM's 150th season. With American Express and the Florence Gould Foundation adding their support, BAM's opera agenda was able to move forward with in-depth programming.

Whether in dance, opera, music, or theater, strong presenting is a given, but it is Hopkins and Melillo's focus on producing that is catapulting BAM onto the global stage while raising the artistic bar for the performing arts in New York City. Hopkins, Melillo, and the board had been discussing the move to producing for a long time. The perfect opportunity to find out if it was a viable option for BAM came when Melillo started having an extensive conversation with director Sam Mendes about classical theater and the relationship between American and British

limited. The trick would be to find a niche that was either traditional opera with a twist that fit the BAM persona or rarely seen productions that had not come to New York. The Baroque opera genre, especially as interpreted by gifted conductors like William Christie, became a way for BAM to add to the New York City lexicon. When the BAM leadership planned the Monteverdi cycle, the development staff started raising money almost two years before it opened. The new opera festival initiated in 2010, which showcased a variety of full-length works and ancillary concerts, talks, and films, was underwritten by the Andrew W. Mellon Foundation, with major support from Ronald P. Stanton, who also played an instrumental role in

actors. Melillo says, "I felt that we could demonstrate that they are equal, by putting them together in classical material under Sam's direction."

After the success in the 2003 Spring Season of *Twelfth Night* and *Uncle Vanya*, the final productions under Mendes's artistic direction of the Donmar Warehouse in London, Melillo and Mendes initiated the Bridge Project, which is equally American and British, not only in terms of its actors but among its creative personnel. "Sam has an affinity with the Harvey Theater," says Melillo, "so the topic of producing surfaced." Melillo and Mendes invited the participation of Kevin Spacey, the artistic director of the Old Vic. It became clear that Melillo, Mendes,

by Roger Oliver

Propeller describes itself as "an all-male Shakespeare company which seeks to find a more engaging way of expressing Shakespeare and to more completely explore the relationship between text and performance." For Edward Hall, founder and artistic director of Propeller, performing the plays with all-male casts, as they were done by Shakespeare's own company, not only revives a long-abandoned tradition but enables both actors and audience to envision the plays in new ways. Established in 1997 at the Watermill Theatre, one of England's premier regional theaters, Propeller performs regularly in London and tours extensively in the United Kingdom and internationally throughout Europe, Asia, and North America.

Major productions directed by Hall for his Propeller ensemble company include *Henry V*; *A Midsummer Night's Dream*, which in 2004 introduced BAM audiences to the company's energetic and entrancing performance style; *The Winter's Tale*, *The Taming of the Shrew*, *Twelfth Night*, *The Merchant of Venice*, and *The Comedy of Errors*—all of which were presented at BAM—as well as the critically acclaimed *Rose Rage*, his two-part adaptation with Roger Warren of the *Henry VI* trilogy that tells the story of the collapse of Henry V's empire and the chaos of the Wars of the Roses, and *Richard III*, which brings the cycle of history plays to a close in what the company describes as "bloody fashion."

In 2010, Propeller launched a new education program, Pocket Propeller, aimed at providing a "first class" theatrical experience to a young audience based on a condensed version of a Propeller production, initiated with *Pocket Dream*, based on Hall's production of *A Midsummer Night's Dream*. One of the leading theater practitioners of his generation, in addition to his duties as artistic director of Propeller, Hall—the son of famed stage director Sir Peter Hall—is also an associate director of the Watermill, National, and Old Vic Theatres. In January 2010, he was also named artistic director of the Hampstead Theatre, known for its commitment to emerging and developing writers and innovative contemporary drama.

Propeller

and Spacey could work together and that they had similar interests and needs. "It just took on a life of its own," Melillo says. Not that he can be cavalier about any of these projects. He has to keep in mind that what works creatively must also work financially. "With the Bridge Project, we felt blessed that this was the right risk for the institution," he explains. "Three years of intense work and now, we have far more invitations from around the world than we can possibly honor."

Partnering with the Old Vic and Mendes's Neal Street Productions, coordinating international tours, building sets, and having rehearsals every day was a little off-center from BAM's usual role of presenting. Melillo, being a theater person to his core, felt that this was another issue-based opportunity for BAM to make an impact in the theater world as a whole. The combination of Americans and Brits, the producing and touring, and giving a director like Mendes the opportunity to put a body of work forward is another example of BAM going deep as opposed to a one-off. This has become a major attribute of the way Hopkins and Melillo have looked at fulfilling BAM's institutional mission. "Given its scope," Hopkins says, "the Bridge Project worked because Bank of America came in with three years of leadership support." This project is another illustration of how BAM has evolved since the Lichtenstein years: producing theater that is financially successful and critically acclaimed.

The Bridge Project partnership was launched in 2009 with the production of a new translation of Chekhov's *The Cherry Orchard* by Tom Stoppard, followed by Shakespeare's *The Winter's Tale*. After opening at BAM, the productions then embarked on an international tour that included a two-month run at the Old Vic. Born in Brooklyn, the Bridge Project's first tour ended on the very stage where modern theater began—the ancient amphitheater in Epidaurus, Greece.

The artistic reach and range of work presented to New York audiences during the BAM Spring Seasons is mind-boggling. Among the many extraordinary evenings in the theater was the 2003 revival of *The Island*, created by actors John Kani and Winston Ntshona in collaboration with playwright Athol Fugard and presented at BAM by South Africa's Market Theatre. Melillo had seen a performance on Broadway in the 1970s, and 30 years later, with the same actors, BAM audiences saw the touching humanity of two black South African prisoners living in a tiny cell during the apartheid years. In that same season, audiences saw Ingmar Bergman's production of the Ibsen classic *Ghosts*, which exposed the hypocrisy of 19th-century morality. Productions in 2004 included Tony Kushner's revised geopolitical drama *Homebody/Kabul* with Linda Emond and Maggie Gyllenhaal, and the world-renowned

Comédie-Française's rollicking production of Molière's *The Imaginary Invalid*. Together with Molière, director Claude Stratz skewered the 17th-century medical establishment with a cautionary tale about the effects of terminal foolishness. In 2005, Melillo brought two classic works to BAM presented by two outstanding British companies: Theatre Royal Bath in director Peter Hall's superb production of *As You Like It*, of which Ben Brantley of the *New York Times* wrote, "I have never seen a production of *As You Like It* that so insists on keeping in mind how harsh and capricious the world can be. . . . It's as if the whole spectrum of human nature had been crammed into a fast-footed three hours," and the Royal Shakespeare

Company's production of Euripides' tragic *Hecuba* that featured the legendary Vanessa Redgrave as the tortured, vengeful, dethroned queen of Troy. The Sydney Theatre Company's production in 2006 of Ibsen's *Hedda Gabler* was Cate Blanchett's first stage performance in the United States. Blanchett returned to BAM three years later to perform her shattering interpretation of Blanche DuBois in Tennessee Williams's *A Streetcar Named Desire*, directed by Liv Ullmann. The 2006 season also included two companies that have made regular Spring Season (and Next Wave) appearances, the Mark Morris Dance Group, presenting the "Month of Mark," with immersive programming choreographed by Morris,

and the newly formed Forsythe Company, with the riveting *Kammer/Kammer*. Edward Hall's all-male troupe, Propeller, returned to BAM in 2007 with two rambunctious, highly inventive productions of Shakespeare's *Taming of the Shrew* and *Twelfth Night*. More Shakespeare in that same year, this time a Cheek by Jowl production of *Cymbeline* directed by Declan Donnellan, made one of the Bard's more difficult plays to stage look surprisingly simple.

The 2008 Spring Season was magical for BAM, staging two Beckett masterpieces: *Happy Days* with Fiona Shaw and *Endgame* with John Turturro, Max Casella, Alvin Epstein, and Elaine Stritch. There was also Patrick Stewart in the Chichester Festival

Winston Ntshona and John Kani in *The Island*, Athol Fugard, John Kani, and Winston Ntshona / Royal National Theatre / Market Theatre of Johannesburg, 2003.
Photo: Ruphin Coudyzer

men honorably not only gave us profit participation in the Broadway run, but they gave us equal billing with them above the title. I was like, 'Wow! BAM's on Broadway!'"

That same season also included a triumphant presentation of composer-performer Paul Simon's work at BAM. Because Simon had a relationship with a member of the board of trustees, Dan Klores, Melillo and Hopkins gradually got to know him over a conversation that went on for nearly a decade. Simon first performed at BAM for the benefit that was Lichtenstein's retirement party. "From the moment he stepped on our stage, we knew he was a BAM artist," Melillo says, "courageous, pioneering, and deeply heartfelt, with a massive creative output incorporating an extraordinary variety of musical styles and influences." Simon's performance established a mutual connection, which is essential to artistic programming of this magnitude at BAM. Simon would have lunch with Hopkins and Melillo, and they would end up at his home, listening to him perform a song he had just written. Melillo says, "The right moment surfaced in his life to make a commitment to us, and we agreed to present a range of concerts representing in essence the 'body' of his work through a month-long, in-depth engagement." He adds, "I felt like the exorcist: We knew that Paul had to confront his failed Broadway musical of *The Capeman*. He faced his demons and delivered a kick-ass concert of that wonderful music." It achieved exactly what the institution hoped it would, which was a reimaging, a repositioning, and a rediscovery of the music.

The Simon concerts were another example of how BAM continues to bring an extensive view to producing and staging work. This wasn't about a one-night tribute to a popular music icon. Hopkins and Melillo wanted to present a full portrait of an artist during an extended residency, giving BAM audiences a chance to immerse themselves in Simon's music. Hopkins says, "Our goal was to find a way to liberate the music of *The Capeman*, which we thought was brilliant, from the Broadway show that had gotten such terrible reviews and had so many problems." BAM presented Simon in three different programs: *Songs from The Capeman*, *Under African Skies*, and *American Tunes*.

In effect, Hopkins and Melillo found the key to moving past Simon's crushing Broadway experience. The more they talked, the clearer it became that they needed to make the project larger by putting *The Capeman* in the context of Simon's enormous 50-year history of great music making and songwriting. Not only could they create a place for *The Capeman*, where the music could rise without the chatter, but they could also showcase Simon's spectacular career. Hopkins continues, "It was such a BAM way of going deep. He agreed to do it and worked incredibly hard. I have never seen anyone put that kind of attention and focus

Theatre presentation of *Macbeth*, directed by Rupert Goold. "I went and saw it when it played in the West End," Melillo says. "The young, firebrand director, Rupert Goold, had masterfully taken this play and set it in the most incredible environment. It was revelatory. Patrick was divine, and the rest was history." By the third week into the run at BAM, the play was sold out, and the producers, Duncan C. Weldon and Paul Elliott, decided to move the show to Broadway. They asked for BAM's help, and BAM gave it. BAM worked in conjunction with the American commercial producer Emanuel Azenberg to facilitate the transfer of the production from the Harvey Theater to the Lyceum Theater. Melillo explains, "Those two

on every song." They ended up with a month of concerts—six *Capemans*; five *African Skies*, which showcased his world music; and five *American Tunes*, which was about the New York/American experience. "It was just magnificent," Hopkins declares, "and what made it even more wonderful was that many members of the audience came to all three shows, just like the Monteverdi program."

Engaging the Community

In keeping with the effort to be more involved with the local Brooklyn scene, BAM's community outreach initiatives are serving local residents across the scope of its programming and services. Besides DanceAfrica, there are other annual series of note: free outdoor concerts at the BAM Rhythm & Blues Festival at MetroTech and the BAMboo! Halloween extravaganza. In the cinemas, BAMcinématek has presented a broad spectrum of film programming that has included innovative community-based series such as ActNow: New Voices in Black Cinema, the Brooklyn Jewish Film Festival, Senior Cinema, the Afro-Punk Festival, Cinema Tropical, and the New York Korean Film Festival. In addition, BAM hosts the annual Brooklyn Tribute to Dr. Martin Luther King Jr., in cooperation with the office of the Brooklyn borough president and Medgar Evers

College and sponsored by Target. Easy, affordable access to the creative programming of BAM's education and humanities department, the BAM Rose Cinemas, BAMcafé Live, the Eat, Drink & Be Literary series, and the new BAM Hamm Archives Center combine to enlighten, serve, and challenge the cultural lives of local residents as well as all New Yorkers. As Hopkins states, "We don't want ticket prices to be an obstacle to visit our campus. BAM always offers budget priced tickets and student rush and provides hundreds of free tickets for festival productions to Brooklyn groups through our Ticket Assistance Program and community affairs department, enabling audiences to attend performances regardless of their ability to pay." Hopkins adds, "Keeping community in the heart of BAM has absolutely made us a stronger institution, makes the community stronger, and makes the city stronger."

At the center of BAM's community-based initiatives is its education and humanities department. In 1997, the BAM leadership was looking for ways to expand the scope of BAM's programming and align it more closely with the values and mission of the institution. Fueled by world-class stage productions, the idea was to put the "academy" back into BAM. And the result was twofold: first, innovative and dynamic programming that presents a high level of arts education to underserved children and young adults, which strengthens outreach to the local

Fiona Shaw in *Happy Days*, Samuel Beckett/National Theatre of Great Britain, 2008.
Photo: Richard Termine

by Susan Yung

James Thiérrée seems to lack both fear and bones. His theater works defy categorization and are largely absent of language but for some of its cadences. They combine elements of mime, puppetry, sleight of hand, acro- and aerobatics, and old-fashioned slapstick. He charges headlong into sequences, tumbling head over heels and bouncing to his feet like an inflatable punching clown. His kinetic genius transforms even the simplest task—reading the newspaper, for example—into a giddy adrenaline rush. While philosophical or existential ideas emerge as his pieces unfold, it is amply rewarding to simply experience them, absorbing scene after scene as he taps the gamut of human emotions. These can ping-pong between childlike wonder, humor, sympathy, terror, exhilaration, and sadness in the span of moments.

Thiérrée's performances revolve around his everyman persona, navigating banal chores, or tumultuous land- or seascapes wondrously jerry-rigged from parachute silk and ropes, oftentimes populated with whimsical characters or creatures. In *Raoul*, presented at BAM in 2010, he grapples with a split personality, picking a convincing fistfight with himself. The episodic structure at times follows that of a circus—his work is often dubbed *cirque nouveau*—although the structure can resemble musical theater, with physical routines in place of songs. Add feats of gymnastic audacity on a workaday prop (a sofa or an iron gate) or a stunning apparatus (a giant cascade of woman-eating ropes, a crow's nest pendulum)—and you have the makings of thrilling theater accessible to all, regardless of age or language.

Tangential but relevant is Thiérrée's heritage. At four, he traveled with his parents, actor Jean-Baptiste Thiérrée and dancer Victoria Chaplin, appearing in their troupe, Cirque Imaginaire (later Cirque Invisible), as a piece of luggage that sprouted legs and ambled around the stage. He went on to perform higher-profile (and higher, period) routines, which led to a number of film roles, and formed La Compagnie du Hanneton in 1998. He is the grandson of Charlie Chaplin; they share a physical brilliance, characterized by quicksilver reflexes, rock-steady balance, a melodic play of subtle and bold slapstick, and open, rubbery faces that flick between innocence and world-weariness. Thiérrée's mother has been a frequent collaborator, creating his magical critter companions in *Raoul*. Thiérrée acknowledges his forebears, but there is the sense that his art has—luckily for us—chosen him as much as he has chosen it.

community while developing new audiences; and, second, opportunities to enrich the experience of BAM productions, through the Artist Talks series, where audiences listen to and engage in discussions with Next Wave and Spring Season artists, and to invite audiences to Eat, Drink & Be Literary as the literary arts were added to BAM's repertoire.

Everyone connected to BAM understands that as BAM's role as a cultural leader in Brooklyn grows, and with the decline of arts education in the public schools, it has become even more important that the institution step in and serve the schools and families of the borough. BAM developed free after-school programs such as Young Critics and Young Film Critics, where high school students discuss and write about the performances and films they see at the Howard Gilman Opera House, the Harvey Theater, and the BAM Rose Cinemas; the Arts & Justice program that focuses on theater and visual arts with a concentration on social issues relevant to young people; and Dancing into the Future, a choreography lab, which offers master classes with professionals in the field. Programs with schools include the presentation of student matinees of mainstage productions. Students have the opportunity to see world-class artists in extraordinary and often challenging productions. BAM also presents performances designed exclusively

for student audiences. An annual highlight is Poetry: Expression in the Right Direction, a cross-generational and interdisciplinary performance program featuring diverse and groundbreaking professional poets along with musicians who demonstrate the vitality of the spoken word. A film literacy series introduces students to classic films of contemporary importance, and post-screening guests include filmmakers or others who have expertise related to the film's theme. Several in-school artist-in-residency programs like AfricanDanceBeat, AfricanMusicBeat, and Shakespeare Teaches Students provide young audiences with in-depth engagement in the performing arts.

Each class that attends a performance or film program receives an in-school, pre-show preparation workshop from a BAM teaching artist and engages in post-performance discussions. Teachers also receive extensive customized study guides. To support the integration of the arts into the school curriculum, BAM offers professional development workshops for teachers and administrators, including the Shakespeare Teaches Teachers series. BAM also presents programs for families such as the BAMkids Film Festival, a marathon weekend of international films for families, as well as periodic concerts and children's book author events. Community collaborations include a partnership with the Bedford Stuyvesant Restoration

Ballet Folclorico Cutumba in *Gaga*,
included in *25 Years of DanceAfrica*,
2002. Photo: Richard Termine

Corporation in which students perform side-by-side
on the BAM stage with visiting dance ensembles
at DanceAfrica. BAM also provides a humanities
curriculum around the culture of the visiting company
from Africa or the African diaspora to provide the
students with an in-depth educational and artistic
experience. In addition, through a grant from the
SHS Foundation, BAM offers annual college scholar-
ships to students participating in various BAM
education programs.

Suzanne Youngerman, director of the
department, believes that the scope of programming
has grown tremendously over the last decade. "We
serve about 200 schools a year, involving approximately
25,000 students, teachers, and parents in schooltime
or family programs." The Artist Talks series enriches
an audience's experience of the performances and
offers insights into the creative process of the artists
featured at BAM: Peter Brook, Robert Wilson,
Cate Blanchett, Sam Mendes, Paul Simon, Laurie
Anderson, Meredith Monk, Alan Rickman, William
Christie, and Jonathan Miller, among numerous
others. Programs have included interviews, conversations between artists or between artists and cultural

artistic repertoire has created opportunities for the cross-pollination of art forms and generated revenue. However, from its inception, Lichtenstein took heat for it. Even the board feared he had gone too far since no performing arts organization had ever attempted to build a multiplex within the confines of an arts center. It was a completely different business from presenting live work onstage. The four-screen complex, named for BAM trustee Jonathan Rose and his wife, Diana, began showing films in 1998, offering Brooklyn residents both alternative, independent films that were not being shown elsewhere in the borough and curated programs on one screen presented as a "cinématek." When Lichtenstein retired, Hopkins and Melillo inherited the movie business. They focused on expanding the scope of the cinemas in the same way that they had approached the rest of the programming.

"We created a wonderful paradigm for the so-called BAMing of our cinemas," says Hopkins. Three screens show first-run independent films and specialty releases, while BAMcinématek features foreign films, retrospectives, and festivals—the entire operation sponsored by the *Wall Street Journal*. Adrienne Mancia, who was instrumental in building the MoMA film department, served initially as a freelance consultant, helping to devise BAMcinématek programming. She was succeeded by full-time curators Florence Almozini and Jake Perlin. But the early days were dicey: no one was coming to the screenings, and, even more problematic, BAM struggled to get first-run films. Ultimately, however, with good programming, efficient theater management and procurement, and focused promotional efforts by the BAM marketing and communications staff, the cinemas became a seamless part of BAM's daily operation.

Besides the artistic and educational programming opportunities, the cinemas draw a continuous stream of people into the Peter Jay Sharp Building 365 days a year. Hopkins is surprised that more performing arts centers haven't jumped into this sector: "The cinemas have been a great aesthetic companion to what we do onstage. Plus, it's a great audience builder. Once people are inside the facility for the movies, it is possible to market everything else we do and convert them into BAM mainstage patrons as well." However, it was the partnership with the Sundance Film Festival that gave BAMcinématek programming the street credentials it needed to become a player. "Sundance was very important because it gave us stature," says Melillo. "It gave us visibility and an identity among a broad-based constituency of filmmaking and cinema industries."

Through a number of trustee relationships, particularly Jeanne Donovan Fisher, who was a member of the Sundance Institute's board, Hopkins and Melillo approached Sundance founder Robert Redford about partnering, and he turned out to be

commentators, panel discussions, and lecture demonstrations. As BAM extends its mission into the neighboring Richard B. Fisher Building, with support from a variety of donors including trustee Brigitte Vosse, Goldman Sachs Gives (through the guidance of BAM trustee Donald R. Mullen), and the Leona M. & Harry B. Helmsley Charitable Trust, the education and humanities programming will continue to engage and enrich the community.

In retrospect, Lichtenstein's decision to build the BAM Rose Cinemas is seen as a stroke of genius at every level. The inclusion of film into the BAM

Ann Hamilton in *mercy*,
Meredith Monk and Ann Hamilton,
2002. Photo: Jack Vartoogian

a huge fan of Brooklyn and BAM. Together they forged a three-year partnership in which BAM would screen films directly from the most recent Sundance Festival. In 2006, the first Sundance Institute at BAM series energized the BAM cinemas and positioned the institution as a major player in the film festival world. In true BAM fashion, the screenings were only part of the programming, which featured more than 40 events, including talks with independent film-makers, screenwriters, and actors, and an evening of music that featured participating songwriters and lyricists. Bringing Sundance to BAM was a fantastic "up" move for the cinemas, again drawing attention and visibility to the institution while aligning itself with certainly the most important film festival in the United States and perhaps in the world. In 2009, after the three-year partnership concluded, Redford returned to BAM for a retrospective of his work in which, for one event of the program, he joined Bob Woodward and Carl Bernstein in a memorable dialogue following the screening of Alan J. Pakula's *All the President's Men*, exemplifying the historic programming for which BAMcinématek is known.

Other BAMcinématek programs of note included the From Hanoi to Hollywood series in 2002, in which BAM screened films dealing with the Vietnam War. When Oliver Stone came to BAM for a screening of *Platoon*, 50 Vietnam veterans arrived dressed in their full army uniforms. There was an emotional outpouring from those men that reached into the hearts and minds of the audience and created

an amazing connection between the director, the film, the vets, and the audience members—men and women who lived through one of America's more tumultuous and violent historical moments. At another screening in the series, the former 1960s antiwar activist and Jesuit priest Daniel Berrigan came to BAM. He walked onto the stage to greet the audience with his arm raised, fist clenched, and declared, "Unrepentant, unchanged." The entire audience was on their feet. Similarly, when BAMcinématek showed *Serpico*, curators invited the Frank Serpico to the screening. Hopkins stood before the audience and announced, "Ladies and gentlemen, please welcome retired police lieutenant Frank Serpico," and the whole place gave him a stand-ing ovation. Hopkins notes, "The cinemas aren't just about movie going. Our curators craft programming that is about movie going in a profound and personal way. We have several special events each month, including silent movies with live music. Our program has real personality and attracts young audiences."

However difficult the early years were in building the cinema programs, BAM is now a performing *and* cinema arts center. The number of filmmakers living in Brooklyn is exceptionally large, and BAM wants to be a participant in their creative lives. Melillo nurtures local talent to present projects that are unique and distinct. The cinemas are also a component in BAM's education and humanities programming supported by the greater New York City school system, using Hollywood and independent films as a teaching supplement.

Beyond the mainstages, creating a venue for aspiring musicians and spoken word artists to join the BAM universe was another Lichtenstein initiative that blossomed under Hopkins and Melillo's tenure. If BAM is a petri dish for fresh ideas in the performing arts, then BAMcafé Live is one of the indisputable leaders in its lab. Until Lichtenstein initiated BAMcafé, there were few venues in the borough for artists and audiences to hear the gifted, up-and-coming, hungry artists in the new music scene in Brooklyn. Limor Tomer, an unsung hero of BAM's producing history, was BAMcafé's first music curator.

BAMcafé Live started to present acts sporadically in 1997, with an eye on generating new audiences. Then, in 1999, after a total and lengthy renovation that included new floors, kitchen facilities, sound systems, and refitting all the lighting, the Lepercq Space was turned into an inviting, beautifully appointed, huge open area that could accommodate galas, dinner parties, literary evenings, a bar/restaurant, and a live music venue that would present close to 70 acts during the fall and spring seasons.

Brooklyn now had a magically sophisticated space for groups that had usually performed in small clubs or funky music venues. Renowned artists like Don Byron and experimental guitar guru Gary Lucas gigged at BAM, as did the incomparable jazz trumpeter Graham Haynes and drummer-turned-crooner Grady Tate. For performers like ETHEL, Stew, Eisa Davis, and Sekou Sundiata, the venue helped serve as a launchpad for their careers. BAMcafé Live ramps up the amps and packs the house—a unique space with a definite focus on presenting local Brooklyn artists. Listeners are sitting at tables, leaning against the walls, and crowding around the bar. BAM has become the place to kick off a Friday or Saturday night, before heading out for late-night revelry—and it's free. Artists are very aware that performing at BAM is good for their résumés. "I played at BAM" means something in the broader context, especially as the indie music scene is highly competitive. Performing at BAMcafé Live carries weight, and audiences come because they themselves are artist driven. BAMcafé Live is part of BAM's history as an avant-garde epicenter.

Like Melillo, Hopkins reads every piece of communication that arrives on her doorstep, desk, or computer. Ideas are everywhere, and you never know, perhaps a line item in the *Chronicle of*

One Flat Thing, reproduced, William Forsythe/Ballett Frankfurt, 2003. Photo: Jack Vartoogian

Philanthropy or an unsolicited brochure might spark a new concept for an artistic or fundraising opportunity. The enormously successful Eat, Drink & Be Literary series began with Hopkins going through her mail and finding an annual report from the National Book Foundation. It was 2005, and Oprah's Book Club was in full force; all over the country, people who loved to read were meeting in their homes and libraries to discuss literature. It was time for literature to join the BAM calendar of cultural programming.

With Brooklyn historically being home to so many of America's greatest authors, adding the literary arts to BAM programming seemed like a "Why didn't I think of that before?" moment and Hopkins was inspired. Here was an opportunity to start an über–book club and bring literature into the fold of BAM. The National Book Foundation seemed to be the perfect partner, one that understood the world of literature and had contacts with great authors. With support from Bloomberg, the founding sponsor of the series, the BAM leadership saw an opportunity to create a community around literature, the same way they had done around music, theater, opera, and film. Why not transform the Lepercq Space into a literary salon? Literary soirees would begin with an informal buffet dinner party with great wine donated by longtime BAM patrons and winery owners Joseph and Diane Steinberg, then the audience would settle in for an evening of readings by the author, an intelligent discussion with a moderator, and an audience Q&A, followed by a book signing. Melillo named it Eat, Drink & Be Literary; then he began to hammer out a format to make it work.

The first year attracted spectacular authors: Rick Moody, Paul Auster, Walter Mosley, Jhumpa Lahiri, Joyce Carol Oates, and Edward P. Jones. Since then, the series has been a blockbuster success with most nights sold out well in advance; entire book clubs reserve tables for these intimate evenings with writers they love. The BAM series also capitalized on a Brooklyn literary scene that was just exploding. The borough continues to be a fertile resource to recruit for the series as writers like Jonathan Safran Foer, Nicole Krauss, and Jonathan Lethem live in the neighborhood. Brooklyn playwright Lynn Nottage, a MacArthur Fellow and Pulitzer Prize winner, read in 2010; in 2011, Edward Albee joined the roster of writers who have generously allowed readers a brief look into their creative process. Eat, Drink & Be Literary embraces the idea of the institution as a forum for ideas. This platform, like many others, has helped to lay the groundwork for BAM's renewed sense of mission, which perfectly describes what BAM delivers: a home for adventurous artists, audiences, and ideas.

Below: *Kagemi: Beyond the Metaphors of Mirrors*, Sankai Juku, 2006. Photo: Jack Vartoogian

Opposite: Yolanda Martín in *White Darkness*, Compañía Nacional de Danza, 2007. Photo: Jack Vartoogian

Ushio Amagatsu in *Hibiki*,
Sankai Juku, 2002.
Photo (detail): Jack Vartoogian

Sankai Juku

by Yoko Shioya

Tatsumi Hijikata's *Kinjiki*, which was performed in Tokyo in 1959, is regarded as the birth of butoh. From this starting point, Hijikata, along with Kazuo Ohno—another "founder" of butoh—and other experimental dancers in the 1960s began to explore this new style of dance. As the "first generation of butoh," they addressed their art in an abstract language, resulting in the lack of a codified definition of butoh. Even with this absence of definition, in the early days it was still easy to recognize butoh through its apparent common elements: chalk-white painted bodies, distorted joints, exaggerated facial expressions, and extremely slow movements. However, today, with the emergence of later generations of butoh dancers, whose work involved quick turns and straight limbs without white paint, butoh has evolved as a far more complex art form.

Ushio Amagatsu, who founded Sankai Juku in 1975, belongs to the second generation. Following the success of the group's legendary full-evening piece *Kinkan Shonen* in 1978 in Tokyo, Amagatsu took his company to France in 1980, where they first performed in front of a Western audience. Since the invitation from the Théâtre de la Ville in Paris the following year, 12 works have been coproduced with the theater, and the company has performed in more than 40 countries and 700 cities, with regular stops at the Howard Gilman Opera House beginning with the group's BAM debut in 1996 with *Yuragi: In a Space of Perpetual Motion*. Sankai Juku, translated as "Studio of Mountain and Ocean," remains faithful to the original elements of butoh but at the same time has incorporated elaborate stage sets, props, costumes, and lighting in a stylish way that no other butoh company has done. For example, in his works Amagatsu never leaves the stage surface with flat, simple Marley dance flooring, but rather covers it with white sand, creates the illusion of waves, or places a type of textured board in the center. These treatments generate a poetic beauty, which is further amplified by a delicate lighting design.

Although the extreme slowness of butoh used to be quite a challenge for the general audience, Sankai Juku's spectacle has become admirably sophisticated over the years and obtained the power to communicate to a wider audience. Amagatsu, unlike the first generation, explains in simple words that butoh is a "dialogue with gravity." Since all humans begin to learn about gravity through their body from the moment of birth through standing and walking, the dialogue he has sought and presents on the stage can provoke the common memory of a universal audience.

Another addition to the cultural and physical impact that BAM is having on its immediate neighborhood is the Hamm Archives Center. Hopkins says, "I've been an advocate for establishing a BAM archives that will serve the world community of artists, patrons, and anyone else who wants to find out about our historic presence in the city." The need for the archives arose when, in the early stages of the endowment campaign—established in 1992 in honor of Lichtenstein's 25th anniversary with major support from the Wallace and Ford Foundations—the BAM leadership set out to gather as much historical material as possible to launch the effort. They discovered that no one knew how to access much of the precious archival material. What they found was in garbage bags, moldy boxes scattered all over the building, and files shoved into corners. Even when they thought they'd found it all, every renovation uncovered more material. Hopkins was determined to sort out the mess. BAM negotiated office space on the 16th floor of what was then the Williamsburg Bank Building around the corner, which became the first home of the archives. Hopkins then focused on how to make the archives part of the BAM campus. In response, board member Charles J. Hamm and his wife, Irene, gave BAM a generous gift that allowed the organization to acquire a 3,800-square-foot space adjacent to the Harvey Theater—the new home of the Hamm Archives Center. From BAM's very beginnings in the mid-19th century, the institution had a purpose that went beyond filling its seats. The founders of the Brooklyn Academy of Music saw themselves as having a larger mission of service.

Sharon Lehner, the director of the archives, has taken on the task of managing a mountain of material with typical BAM passion. Lehner believes that the performing and cinema arts have a unique way of documenting what's happening in the world, and the center will be an active place to explore the collection or visit the new gallery space before a show or movie. The street-level space with a glass facade invites passersby into an architecturally compelling interior of compact-shelving units with oversized cranks that move the stacks; in addition, video research stations and exhibitions of archival materials and visual art further enhance the goal to engage the BAM community. For researchers, BAM audiences, or artists and companies that have performed at BAM, the archives will be an invaluable resource, presenting a little piece of every player in BAM's rich history of artistic programming.

Visual artists have always felt close to BAM and have added yet another layer to the artistic experience of BAM, while also creating a wonderful means of generating resources for the institution. To further support BAM programming, donated artworks in all disciplines are available for purchase, and exhibition space seems to appear everywhere, with plans for more galleries as the campus expands. BAMart, as it is known today, began in its most rudimentary form with the inaugural season of the Next Wave Festival, when visual artist Roy Lichtenstein was invited to create an image for the festival that became its poster and the cover of the first *Next Wave Journal*. Visual arts became a permanent component of the Next Wave in 2002, for the 20th anniversary of the festival, which was followed by an ongoing program of exhibitions. Melillo brought the celebrated art curator Dan Cameron on board to oversee the initiative, while BAM trustee David L. Ramsay secured artists for the BAMbill covers. BAMart was such a success with Brooklyn artists that BAM has extended its program significantly. Now there are BAMart rotating exhibitions all year long in both theater lobbies, the Diker Gallery Café in the Lepercq Space, and the Leonard Natman Room in the Peter Jay Sharp Building. BAM also coordinates shows with local arts organizations and community groups. Hopkins says, "Looking over the list of some of the artists who've contributed to BAM is a humbling experience; you'll see Louise Bourgeois, Willem de Kooning, Robert Rauschenberg, Chuck Close, William Wegman, Alex Katz, and William Kentridge, among many others."

In 2005, the annual BAMart Silent Auction was added to the program, an event that features multiple visual artists and designers, established and emerging. In all types of mediums and price ranges. All the bidding is done online, and more than 200 new works are contributed and sold—and the BAM lobby looks incredibly festive overflowing with art. Between the BAMbill covers, the exhibitions, the portfolios and the auction, the photo and print editions, BAM is continually coming up with ideas to expand the program. Hopkins notes, "With the addition of the new Rudin Family Gallery in the Hamm Archives Center, we further the idea that from the moment you come into any of BAM's buildings you are in a place where art lives and where art is made." She and Melillo have made this an objective of their leadership.

Fundraising and the Future

Without a fierce and savvy development department, a not-for-profit cannot stay alive, much less thrive. Hopkins likes to say that you build a campaign dollar by dollar. When a corporate sponsor steps up and

gives, it becomes a collaborator in the artistic process. When one sponsor or individual donor ends the relationship, another has to step in. The aim is to keep the BAM campus vital.

Hopkins always believed that the fundamental principle of successful fundraising is to take programs and initiatives and create fundraising layers and levels. "We raise money for BAM the institution, then we raise money for the Next Wave Festival, BAM opera, and BAM theater, and so on. The next layer is to find funding for each production under those initiatives; then we might raise money for all international productions across initiatives; then for all dance, theater, and other productions," explains Hopkins. "The idea is to keep taking the same product and cutting it into packages that could be owned by a sponsor 20 different ways." Hopkins excels at devising how to create the packages and matching them to the right donor, and the talented BAM fundraising staff is perennially focused on maximizing this process.

In 1992, the BAM board leadership launched the endowment campaign, a big step forward for the institution. The goal was to build a powerful endowment, one that would ensure the institution's stability

The BQE, Sufjan Stevens, 2007. Photo: Rahav Segev

in perpetuity. Getting things on very strong financial footing, building a strong endowment, and creating cash reserves in order not to deal with endless cash flow problems were the things the BAM leadership was concerned with at the basic financial level. Lichtenstein had gone international with mostly European offerings, and Melillo wanted to go global— and that took money. At the same time, because Lincoln Center was moving into some of BAM's territory by programming more experimental work, BAM had to further extend itself. Melillo had to step up an already aggressive travel schedule.

Nevertheless, once Lincoln Center established its annual summer festival, BAM took aim at an even younger audience, focused on becoming more global, and began to make its theaters more active in the spring and summer. Hopkins and Melillo knew that there was going to be more competition with BAM for certain shows and that other institutions possessed more resources. "We needed the artists who were loyal to us to remain loyal," Hopkins says. Melillo had an extensive artistic agenda of projects he wanted to launch, and Hopkins had a financial and administrative agenda focused on solving institutional problems. They also wanted to complete renovations on the buildings and to upgrade the facilities. Therefore, the

strategic plan they formed at the beginning of their tenure covered every aspect of the operation.

In 1999, Bruce Ratner, who had been a superb board chair since 1992, decided that after Hopkins and Melillo succeeded Lichtenstein, he wanted to step down as chair but stay on the board. Hopkins asked if he would remain chair for one more year to help them through the transition, which he agreed to do. When Ratner retired as chair in December 2001, Alan H. Fishman, the vice chair, succeeded him. The change in leadership of the board was critical because it paved the way for the next stage of fundraising and for the business accomplishments of the Hopkins and Melillo era. The team of Fishman and vice chairs William I. Campbell, who had also been on the board for many years, and Adam E. Max became a powerful triumvirate of leadership for the board. At the same time, as BAM's reputation grew, it became easier to attract high-quality board members who could make a financial commitment and who wanted to be involved with the institution. The idea was that business strategies would continue to grow, improve, and have specific fundraising objectives, while the programming also flourished.

There were also key grants that provided critical institutional support. The Peter Jay Sharp

Nína Dögg Filippusdóttir and Ingvar E. Sigurdsson in *Woyzeck*, Georg Büchner/Vesturport and Reykjavik City Theatre, 2008. Photo: Richard Termine

Norman Hacker and Fritzi Haberlandt
in *Lulu*, Thalia Theater, 2007.
Photo: Richard Termine

Foundation made a huge difference with an initial grant of $8 million, which was transformational for the theater and opera endowment. Norman Peck, the president of the foundation, also joined the BAM Endowment Trust as vice chair, introduced by Peter Jay Sharp's sister, Mary Sharp Cronson, a great friend and member of the arts community both as a producer of Works & Process at the Guggenheim and a philanthropist in her own right. The gift was a major breakthrough. To have that kind of money was game-changing for BAM.

The most significant moment with the Peter Jay Sharp Foundation came in 2004 when BAM was renovating the facade of its historic building at 30 Lafayette Avenue. The project was an enormous undertaking: the building was filthy, the cornice had been ripped off years before, and the decorative cherubs on the facade had broken noses and fingers. In short, the building was a mess. The renovation was slow, complicated, and expensive. For one year of the process, the entire building was completely covered in scaffolding and tarpaulin. The visual artist Vik Muniz, who thought the building resembled a cake, created a huge *CandyBAM* painting on the covering, making it look festive while the work was taking place.

As construction continued, the wrapper was finally removed, leaving scaffolding for the workers to stand on while making repairs. During this time, Hopkins called Peck and asked him to come visit and

see how the renovations were evolving. As a Brooklyn native and an "old real estate nick" (as he often calls himself), Peck couldn't resist a climb on the facade. Hopkins, petrified of heights but a loyal fundraiser and leader of BAM, offered to take him on a tour up the scaffold. Before long, he was jumping and climbing while she was turning green, too scared to move. With the scaffold swaying, Peck practically had to carry Hopkins back down to the street. "It was embarrassing (to say the least), but when Norman called to say that the foundation's trustees wanted to give $20 million to name the building for Peter Jay Sharp, I knew my misery had not been in vain." This gift was and still remains the largest single donation in BAM's history.

After the death in 1998 of Howard Gilman, a strong and early supporter of BAM, the board of his foundation, which included his longtime professional colleague Natalie Moody, decided to make a $5 million grant to name the Opera House, followed several years later by a second $5 million grant to support programming in that venue. In addition, Richard B. Fisher, who was the first chairman of the BAM Endowment Trust and did so much for the institution, gave millions of dollars over many years. Ultimately, after Fisher's untimely death in 2004, Hopkins and Melillo believed that they could enhance BAM's agenda if they had a new, smaller building dedicated to presenting more intimate work as well as to expanding the education, humanities, and community-based programs. Jeanne

293

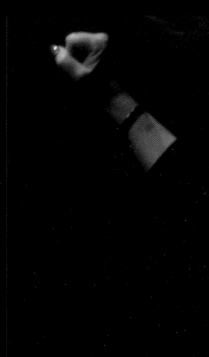

Left, top: Liv Ullmann, 2009.
Photo: Troy Dandro

Left, middle: Jim Jarmusch, 2000.
Photo courtesy of BAMcinématek

Left, bottom: Robert Redford, 2009.
Photo: Jonathan Barth

Above, top: Bill Murray, 2004.
Photo: Jonathan Barth

Above, bottom: Gena Rowlands, 2005.
Photo: Jonathan Barth

by Nathan Gelgud

BAM had been an established performing arts venue for more than three decades around the time that cinema was born in 1895, but it took another full century for the institution to begin showing films. Judging from the density, quality, and imagination of its film programming, BAM has made up for lost time. In 1998, the four-screen BAM Rose Cinemas opened to present first-run independent and specialty releases, making BAM both a premier performing *and* cinema arts center; in the next year, BAMcinématek was born—one screen of the cinemas devoted to retrospective, festival, and art-house fare—beginning what has been more than a decade of thoughtfully curated and innovative programming.

The series and retrospectives at BAMcinématek host screenings of cinematic gems unified by highly relevant, unique, and sometimes humorous themes. Explorations of film's relationship to politics, as in From Hanoi to Hollywood: The Vietnam War on Film, might alternate with fare lighter of heart, such as Shelley Winters vs. The Water.

Giving voice to multiple perspectives and worldviews, BAMcinématek often plays host to other festivals, as when it screens the best films from NewFest (New York City's leading festival for LGBT cinema) or the New York Korean Film Festival. It also copresents new films with other organizations like the Czech Center New York, while teaming up for past series with Cinema Tropical and the African Film Festival. For three years it presented Sundance Institute at BAM and then created its own festival, BAMcinemaFEST, inaugurated in 2009 and fast becoming a prime venue to discover new American filmmakers.

Regularly hosting intimate Q&A sessions as a means of personalizing the cinema experience for the audience, with luminaries like Gena Rowlands, Robert Redford, Manoel de Oliveira, Bill Murray, Arnaud Desplechin, Liv Ullmann, Jim Jarmusch, and Catherine Deneuve, BAMcinématek also draws on the heavy presence of local talent: Brooklyn's own Steve Buscemi, John Turturro, and Darren Aronofsky have all introduced their films. One of the most intriguing aspects of BAMcinématek is its guest-curated series, wherein up-and-comers like Josh and Benny Safdie could choose to screen Wim Wenders's masterpiece *Alice in the Cities*, while French master Olivier Assayas curated a series of films based on their soundtracks.

This spirit of playful carte blanche intermingling with a serious consideration of movies of every vintage is what emblemizes BAMcinématek. Its programming is surprising and inventive, dense without a trace of filler: nostalgic completists should look elsewhere. Throughout the history of film, alarmists have regularly decreed the medium dead, but that's inconceivable as long as places like BAMcinématek are here to keep it alive.

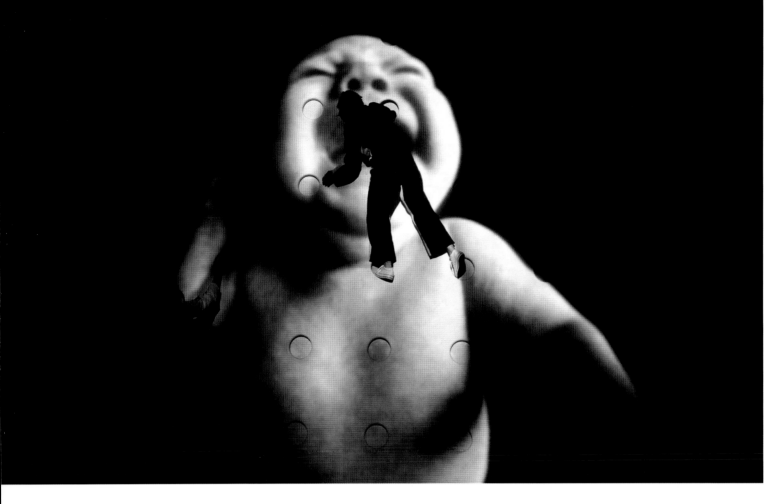

Donovan Fisher came forward to make a $10 million grant to name the building in her late husband's honor. The Fisher Center at Bard College was already a spectacular cultural building, and BAM and Bard were two things Fisher was very connected to during his life. Hopkins says, "Jeanne believed that having signature spaces at each institution would truly honor his legacy."

Meanwhile, Juilliard board chair Bruce Kovner, who developed an appreciation for BAM, was approached about becoming a major supporter. "I will give you $5 million over four years," he said. "But I want you to be a better organization at the end of the grant process. Give me a business plan explaining how you're going to build endowment and get rid of all this deficit by the end of the four-year period." Lynn M. Stirrup, former vice president for planning and development, worked with Hopkins and created many of the pillars of the plan Kovner accepted, and over time the problems were solved. BAM's long-term financial issues were cleared up by 2008, right before the recession hit. "This was a major accomplishment," Hopkins says, "and it meant that during the recession we were able to focus on the present. No creditors meant no deficits were going to bog us down." In effect, Kovner's grant allowed BAM to operate through 2010 with less pain.

There was also very significant support from Fishman, Campbell, and Max. Fishman named the theater in the new building, and many other board members stepped up. There was also Rita K. Hillman. An early and loyal fan of Lichtenstein, Hillman had

been a board member of BAM for some 30 years, and when she passed away, the family foundation made contributions to name the rehearsal studios in both the Peter Jay Sharp Building and, later, the Fisher Building. "What I'm saying," noted Hopkins, "is our whole family of supporters, old and new, got involved and helped the institution move to the next level. That kind of firepower in fundraising gave us the ability to be a serious player in New York City and the world."

All these grants allowed BAM to be very expansive with programming. Fishman, Campbell, and Max were focused on building the board and laying the groundwork for the next major fundraising initiative to follow the initial launch in 1992 of the BAM endowment campaign. In an audacious move in light of the recession, BAM announced the Next Stage Campaign in early 2009. Hopkins says, "In a way we couldn't wait, despite the economy; we had planned it for so long. At the time of the announcement, we had put together, out of a $300 million goal, about $150 million." Intense fundraising was going on, and all of this helped create a buzz about the institution's future.

Sometimes a major funder moves on and Hopkins needs to find supporters to fill the void. Philip Morris Companies, which morphed into Altria, had been the sponsors of the Next Wave Festival for 25 years. Hopkins says that without their support and commitment to the artistic vision, there simply wouldn't have been a festival. When the company moved out of New York City, it signified the end of their sponsorship; however, BAM was to some extent prepared for the transition because Altria was thoughtful about the wind down: "They brought BAM in two years ahead of time and told us how the transition was going to work." Nevertheless, you are never really ready for such a loss until you've gotten the next sponsor. Luckily for BAM, Time Warner stepped in. They were already an enthusiastic sponsor of BAM through the Diverse Voices at BAM initiative, and picking up the Next Wave just as the recession was coming on saved the day. After their two-year commitment to the festival ended, American Express became the new Next Wave sponsor. The bottom line on institutional success is that the staff, the board, and the sponsors have to be able to work together.

Another important area of funding for BAM has been the generous contributions of charitable foundations. Some foundations just give, while others guide, then give. For example, not only has the Ford Foundation made ongoing transformative grants to BAM but it also "audited" the institution to offer assistance where there was the greatest need. Ford gave grants for both the cash reserve and the development of giving programs focused on raising funds from individual donors. As a result, cash flow is no longer a problem at BAM. Individual giving has evolved to become the largest part of BAM's fund-raising effort. Because of the increasing stature of the institution, BAM can now attract wealthy patrons.

"But we wouldn't have evolved," Hopkins states, "had Ford not seen what we needed and helped us achieve these goals."

The BAM staff has also grown organically over the years. For example, when the movie business was added, it became necessary to add curators, managers, people who could pop the popcorn and take the tickets. The same thing happened when the archives became a formal space: it created a need for archivists. Each new program has increased the staff, expanding BAM's role as a major employer in Brooklyn. The staff has grown to meet the needs of the institution, as Hopkins points out, "not only because of the amount of money we have to raise, but because of the level of service we provide to our patrons. Once you support BAM, we want you to continue to give, and we want you to be satisfied with the experience. Service is part of our focus."

Winning Hearts and Minds

Because BAM was not in Manhattan competing for funds or productions with other large arts organizations, many people in the arts community never believed that BAM could become a major force in the cultural marketplace. Everyone's low expectations meant that BAM had the freedom to do whatever it

Mortal Engine, Gideon Obarzanek/ Chunky Move, 2009. Photo: Julieta Cervantes

wanted artistically. However, there was the considerable challenge of bringing people across the bridges to Brooklyn to see the work as well as upgrading the facilities. In addition, Melillo had to entice artists of the highest quality to be featured at BAM versus anywhere else. "Now," says Hopkins, "everyone wants to come to Brooklyn to check out the scene."

Hopkins, Melillo, and the board are very grateful to the city of New York for its invaluable support of culture. BAM's buildings are owned by the city, and that has fortunately translated into substantial capital budget funding. Over the years, the city has been a critical component of BAM's survival, largely due to the efforts of mayors like Abraham Beame, Ed

Koch, Rudy Giuliani, and now Michael Bloomberg as well as Brooklyn borough presidents, notably Howard Golden and Marty Markowitz. Right after Bloomberg was elected, he came to BAM for *The Hard Nut*, the outrageous Mark Morris version of *The Nutcracker*. Hopkins stood up in front of a packed Opera House to greet everyone and said, "Tonight is a special night because the landlord is in the house," and out came the new mayor and everybody cheered.

Sharing the leadership of BAM was not only a smart, practical move, it was one that allowed Hopkins and Melillo to shine professionally. With BAM as "the boss," their roles intertwine, but they manage to remain faithful to their personal missions

Hopkins and Melillo have created a great partnership over the years, one that works because of their mutual respect for each other's unique talents. They trust each other. Melillo says of Hopkins, "One of Karen's great virtues is her loyalty. Decade after decade, I have benefited from her loyalty. Along the way, some bridge was crossed. It's not something you plan. It's not something consciously managed, it's something that evolves and surfaces out of life experiences." They have no ambiguity when the tough decisions have to be made. When one or the other needs to compromise, the end result is based on serving the interests of the institution. Melillo notes, "I've learned that from Karen."

Hopkins describes their professional success together in no-nonsense terms. "I have the most profound regard for Joe's fortitude and commitment to BAM's artistic presentations that cover so many disciplines and venues. We also have an understanding that when we disagree, we put it on the table, close the door, and battle it out privately. The bottom line is that I don't want Joe's job and he doesn't want mine. We are both for BAM, and we put that ahead of anything. Sometimes he will prevail and sometimes I will prevail, but we're not in a power struggle. That has worked for us." Having both worked for Lichtenstein all of those years and then sharing the leadership of BAM, they found that they're very closely aligned in their perception of what the institution should be, what its values should be, what its governance should be, how it should feel, and how it should look. "We're also not interested in every decision being a fight to the death, there's give and take," says Hopkins. "We had to break the job in two because BAM became so big. Its business and artistic missions require 24/7 governance." Both Hopkins and Melillo think that the dual leadership arrangement is a good model—that is, if you can get the right pair as well as the right staff and the right board to deliver the vision.

"Whatever else is written about this period," observes board chair Alan H. Fishman, "what is more important than anything else is that Hopkins and Melillo are geniuses, and their records speak for themselves." Fishman's view is that the unbelievable relationship that exists between the two of them will never be replicated. "You cannot control the future, you cannot control the past, and you can only control the present to some extent. However, if your goal is always grounded in mission and bringing great work to the audience and having an institution as a forum for ideas, a place where people can learn, where they can connect, where they can feel they are in the presence of art and culture and that it's a good place to be, then you can do many great things."

without getting in each other's way. Because of their unique partnership, BAM the institution has become a beacon in the arts community, a light that is widening and getting brighter with each new initiative. As noted by Hopkins, "We are particularly fortunate that our top-tier colleagues—Alice Bernstein, executive vice president and Joe's deputy in getting all the productions on and off the BAM stages; Keith Stubblefield, our brilliant CFO and vice president of finance and administration; Lisa Mallory, our gifted, creative vice president of marketing and communications; and Matthew Bregman, our resourceful vice president for development—are all equally committed to BAM's success."

BAM Howard Gilman Opera House,
2010. Photo: Elliott Kaufman

by William Christie

One of the great impresarios of the 20th century, Harvey Lichtenstein, former president and executive producer of BAM, traveled the globe to listen to people he liked and discover people he didn't know. We were first introduced when he came to our performance of Lully's *Atys* at the Opéra Royal of Versailles; he was absolutely bowled over by the piece and wanted to bring it to BAM. Working with Peter Brook, Pina Bausch, or Robert Wilson, and now taking on a 17th-century French Baroque opera, was risk-taking, but Harvey knew his public and he knew about creating an audience for what he liked. So we met and became friends, and decided to work together. "Look," Harvey said, "we can't provide an orchestra, and we don't have a standing choir. What we can provide is intelligence, creative programming, we can provide an audience, and we can provide a venue." And that was the beginning of a BAM career for me and for my ensemble, Les Arts Florissants.

It was the spring of 1989 when we finally brought *Atys* to BAM. Coming from Europe, where opera houses and civic theaters are generally in the plushest parts of town, when I arrived at BAM it looked as if I had entered a war zone. Here was this incredible building, this great white elephant, surrounded by little more than parking lots. Once inside, of course, it was heaven. First of all, you have a staff that is one of the best in the world, not only the people up top but the people in and around the stage who actually work with you. It's a truly wonderful team. And the hall itself is brilliant, with marvelous visibility and acoustics, and the people who go to the opera, who want to see things as well as hear things, are virtually guaranteed a visual experience as exciting as the musical experience.

Every opera house has its own personality, some are opulent and grand, some intimate and elegant, others have an extraordinary sense of history. The Howard Gilman Opera House at BAM is nothing less than magnificent, with very savvy people coming in to hear its productions. It caters to the connoisseur, which I mean as a compliment to the BAM audience, and offers a different repertoire than other lyric houses in New York. The reputation it has in Europe, under Harvey and now under Karen Brooks Hopkins and Joe Melillo, is that the cutting edge of things has found a way first to BAM, in terms of theater, music, and dance, for the past 25 to 30 years. Cutting edge I define as simply a repertoire, a way of performing and dealing with the public where there are new things to be said and new things to be received and new things to be understood.

The Howard Gilman Opera House is clearly a house that we love, and Karen and Joe are people we admire greatly. There's no compromise about certain things that I find important. For me, opera is essentially enjoyment, and I've had as much enjoyment doing period pieces as I have with performances that you might call contemporary or even postmodernist. The awful reality is that it's not the same world as it was when we started. There is a world crisis, economically speaking, and it obviously affects us terribly, but Karen and Joe are very clever people who have the ability to face this reality, and it seems that over the years we've never lost touch with BAM. As for what comes next for us at BAM—as much as BAM can give us.

Inside Perspective

by Karen Brooks Hopkins

With a recommendation from Fred Vogel, founder and executive director of the Foundation for the Extension and Development of the American Professional Theatre, I was invited to interview for a position in the newly revamped development department at the Brooklyn Academy of Music. I had never been to Brooklyn in my life. So armed with optimism and determination, I took the subway from Manhattan to Atlantic Avenue, which to me at that time was like arriving on a different planet. Thousands of people rushing, moving, reading, talking, laughing, running—it was crazy!

My next stop was a brisk walk to the world-famous Junior's, where I was interviewed by my mentor-to-be, BAM board member and head of the finance committee, I. Stanley Kriegel. Stanley was Brooklyn-born and -bred, and we immediately connected. Years later, at board functions on my 5th, 10th, 15th, 20th, 25th, and 30th BAM anniversaries, he would make a speech saying that on the day I was hired, he told me they'd give me a shot on a trial basis: "We'll see how it goes." Most recently, at a board dinner celebrating his 99th birthday, Stanley declared, "We decided you're not on trial anymore!"

To return to the original story of my interview, I was politely questioned by the former vice president for planning, Philip Jessup, who then sent me on to meet Harvey—the impresario himself, Harvey Lichtenstein, president and executive producer of BAM. Sitting behind a massive desk in his corner office, Harvey seemed huge to me. And he turned and said, "I need someone who can work like hell." I replied, "I'm your gal," and that was it. We shook hands, and voilà—the adventure began.

It was 1979 when I arrived at BAM, and minimalist music was just beginning to attract a large audience. And without knowing exactly how or why—there I was, front and center. My introduction to BAM: a performance piece titled *Dance*, with music by Philip Glass, choreography by Lucinda Childs, and scenic elements by the artist Sol LeWitt. I was just a new kid on the block and didn't quite know what to expect, but I certainly wasn't prepared for opening night, when there was sheer hysteria in the audience at the end of the show. Half the crowd stood and cheered while the other half threw tomatoes—they actually *threw* tomatoes! It was intense—like nothing I had ever seen—but I was thrilled to see an audience respond so passionately. And I knew then and there that BAM was my kind of place.

And the adventure continued—I remained a loyal BAM employee for the next 20 years, and in 1999, when Harvey announced his retirement, I was named president by the board of trustees. So I already knew pretty much everything about BAM anyone in the world could possibly know—or so I thought. Now, however, the stakes were completely different; with my colleague Joe Melillo as the new executive producer, I would have an opportunity to lead the institution and set a course for its future. Joe and I had both been thoroughly trained and indoctrinated by Harvey in the "BAM culture," and we certainly understood the magnitude of the challenges before us. It was the beginning of a new chapter—for me, for Joe, and for BAM.

During his tenure, Harvey had transformed BAM from a teetering ruin on the verge of extinction to a performing arts center of international importance, but there was still work to be done to move BAM forward as an institution. We had significant financial problems to overcome, as the needs of the institution were constantly outstripping its resources. We needed to clear up the deficit, build an endowment, upgrade the technical capacities and audience amenities for the theaters, and build the board of trustees into a powerful, focused governing body that could strengthen the organization administratively. We were also launching a new cinema business, and we had to learn how to manage and select films while integrating the cinema space into a complex known strictly for live performing arts. All of these goals had to be achieved while maintaining the quality of the work onstage.

And so it began—we meticulously chipped away at the deficit and doubled the size of the board, thus boosting our fundraising capacity. The amazing Alan Fishman took over as chairman from Bruce Ratner, who had loyally and dynamically served for 10 years. Alan recruited two spectacular and energetic vice chairs—Bill Campbell and Adam Max—and they recharged the board by creating new committees, enhanced governance, oversight procedures, and new rules of engagement for members. I focused on fundraising and development, while Joe traveled the globe in order to make the art happen by identifying new artists to bring to BAM while continuing to nurture the established BAM artists in their creative endeavors.

Together we focused on building connections to a young, hip audience that had no qualms about coming out to Brooklyn for new experiences, a demographic that was already beginning to populate the area in record numbers. We reached out to the local community in new and unexpected ways through programming, education, and service initiatives as well as grassroots outreach to bring our neighbors closer to BAM. We launched new artistic initiatives and mounted specially themed cultural festivals that drew large crowds and created even larger buzz. We partnered with world-renowned institutions like the Sundance Institute, the Old Vic Theatre, the Asia Society, New York University, and the National Book Foundation.

We wanted to create diverse entry points so that everyone would have access to BAM through a familiar port, often using every one of our venues to organize interdisciplinary programs that enabled the audience to experience an idea or issue through theater, film, music, dance, visual art, and the humanities all working together. Our young, adventurous audiences never disappointed us with their enthusiasm, and in fact their support for BAM events encouraged us to go further in taking on new and ever more challenging programs.

Working at BAM is always a high-stakes game. The theaters are large and located away from midtown Manhattan. The works presented are often little known and sometimes controversial. BAM is expensive to operate, and it needs major support to be successful. BAM is constantly consumed with raising the necessary funds to support its work. The organization as a whole requires financial support, as does every separate initiative, individual production, opening night, building repair, new staff position, and new program.

Every day at BAM is a wild ride—including the one from Harlem to Brooklyn organized by artistic director Chuck Davis to celebrate the DanceAfrica festival and comprised of a flag-waving motorcycle for each African nation. Something you don't see every day, but then again, that's life at BAM. We're fortunate to work with a dedicated BAM staff, especially our incredible vice presidents, and we—myself, Joe, and the board—are proud of what has been accomplished over the last decade: the deficits have been eliminated, endowment has grown, and attendance is at an all-time high. Throughout the years, Joe's artistic work on behalf of BAM has simply been exemplary. I am proud to be his partner. And, as always, we look forward to the next adventure. BAM might be 150 years old, but every day begins with something new. As I always say, "BAM is not a job, but a crusade."

Top: *Uttar-Priyadarshi*, Ratan Thiyam's
Chorus Repertory Theatre of Manipur,
2000. Photo: Ratan Thiyam

Bottom: *Four Saints in Three Acts*,
Mark Morris Dance Group, 2001.
Photo: Susana Millman

Opposite: Wang Wei-ming in
Songs of the Wanderers, Cloud Gate
Dance Theatre of Taiwan, 2000.
Photo: YU Hui-hung

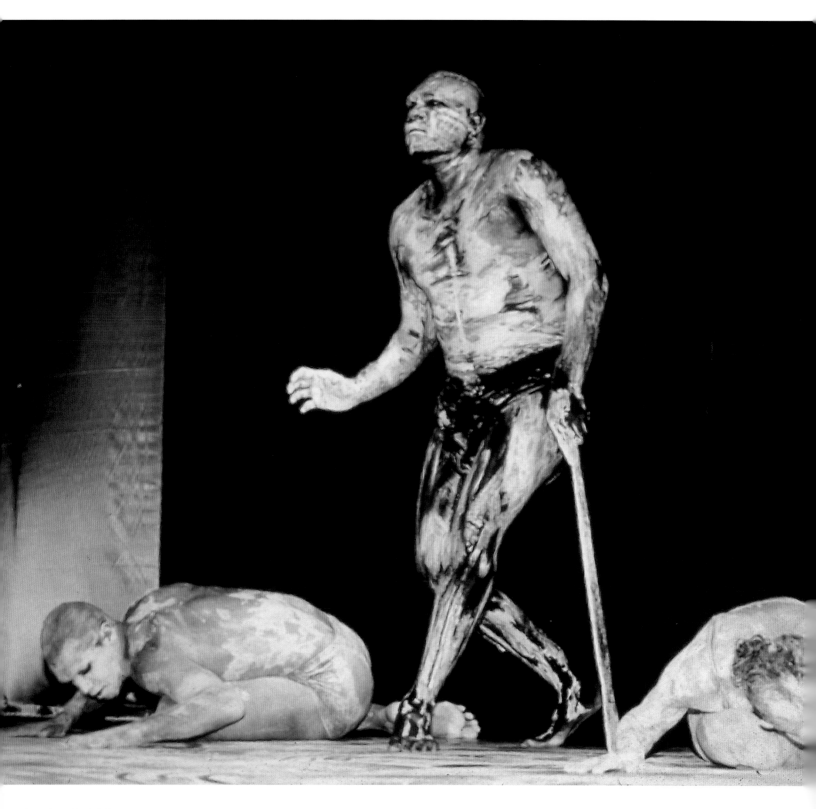

Above: Victor Bramich, Djakapurra
Munyarryun, and Frances Rings in
Corroboree, Bangarra Dance Theatre,
2001. Photo courtesy of Bangarra
Dance Theatre

Opposite: Christopher Pitman and
Daniel Wylie in *Cloudstreet*, Company
B Belvoir / Black Swan Theatre, 2001.
Photo: Heidrun Lohr

Opposite, top: *Masurca Fogo*,
Tanztheater Wuppertal Pina Bausch,
2001. Photo: Michael Rayner

Opposite, bottom: Mark Rylance,
Abigail Thaw, and Jane Arnfield in
Cymbeline, Shakespeare's Globe
Theatre, 2002. Photo: Richard Termine

Above: Aimée Guillot (featured) in
Big Love, Charles Mee/Goodman
Theatre, 2001. Photo: Richard Trigg

Above: *Rite of Spring*, Ballet Preljocaj,
2002. Photo: Régine Will

Opposite, top: *Naharin's Virus*,
Ohad Naharin / Batsheva Dance
Company, 2002. Photo: Gadi Dagon

Opposite, bottom: John Duykers in
Galileo Galilei, Philip Glass,
Mary Zimmerman, and Arnold Weinstein /
Goodman Theatre / Eos Orchestra,
2002. Photo: Liz Lauren

Top: *O Corpo*, Grupo Corpo, 2002.
Photo: Richard Termine

Bottom: Toshiaki Karasawa in
Macbeth, Ninagawa Company, 2002.
Photo: Richard Termine

Opposite: *Körper*, Sasha Waltz/
Schaubühne am Lehniner Platz Berlin/
Théâtre de la Ville, 2002.
Photo: Richard Termine

Opposite: Bernice Coppieters in
Cinderella, Les Ballets de Monte-Carlo,
2003. Photo: Hans Gerritsen

Top: *Les Boréades*, William Christie/
Les Arts Florissants/Paris National
Opera, 2003. Photo: Jack Vartoogian

Bottom: *Les Boréades*, William
Christie/Les Arts Florissants/Paris
National Opera, 2003.
Photo: Jack Vartoogian

Rain, Anne Teresa De Keersmaeker/
Rosas/Steve Reich, 2003.
Photo: Herman Sorgeloos

Moon Water, Cloud Gate Dance
Theatre of Taiwan, 2003.
Photo: Jack Vartoogian

Maarten Seghers and Viviane
De Muynck in *Isabella's Room*,
Jan Lauwers/Needcompany, 2004.
Photo: Richard Termine

Top: *Near Life Experience*,
Ballet Preljocaj, 2004
Photo: Jack Vartoogian

Bottom: Carl Hancock Rux and
Helga Davis in *The Temptation of
St. Anthony*, Robert Wilson and
Bernice Johnson Reagon, 2004.
Photo: Stephanie Berger

Reading, Mercy and The Artificial Nigger, included in *The Phantom Project—The 20th Season*, Bill T. Jones/Arnie Zane Dance Company, 2004. Photo: Jack Vartoogian

Left: Nancy Euverink and Stefan
Zeromski in *Claude Pascal*,
Nederlands Dans Theater, 2004.
Photo: Stephanie Berger

Right: Amandine François in *Tricodex*,
Lyon Opera Ballet, 2004.
Photo: Jack Vartoogian

Violet Cavern, Mark Morris Dance
Group, 2004. Photo: Stephanie Berger

Alain Pralon (featured) in *The
Imaginary Invalid*, Comédie-Française,
2004. Photo: Stephanie Berger

Top: Nonso Anozie and Caroline Martin
in *Othello*, Cheek by Jowl, 2004.
Photo: Richard Termine

Bottom: Isabelle Huppert in
4.48 Psychose, Sarah Kane, 2005.
Photo: Richard Termine

Top: Ingo Hülsmann and Henning Vogt in *Emilia Galotti*, Deutsches Theater Berlin, 2005. Photo: Richard Termine

Bottom: Maggie Gyllenhaal in *Homebody/Kabul*, Tony Kushner, 2004. Photo: Stephanie Berger

Top: *Tall Horse*, Handspring &
Sogolon Puppet Companies, 2005.
Photo: Richard Termine

Bottom: Simon Scardifield and
Vince Leigh (featured) in
The Winter's Tale, Watermill Theatre
(UK)/Propeller, 2005.
Photo: Richard Termine

Opposite: *Bright Abyss*,
James Thiérrée/La Compagnie
du Hanneton, 2005.
Photo: Richard Haughton

Vanessa Redgrave (featured) in
Hecuba, Tony Harrison / Royal
Shakespeare Company, 2005.
Photo: Richard Termine

Patti Smith, *Horses*, 2005.
Photo: Rahav Segev

Above: Rebecca Hall in *As You
Like It*, Theatre Royal Bath, 2005.
Photo: Jack Vartoogian

Opposite: Hugo Weaving and
Cate Blanchett in *Hedda Gabler*,
Andrew Upton / Sydney Theatre
Company, 2006.
Photo: Richard Termine

Top: *Nine Hills One Valley*, Ratan
Thiyam's Chorus Repertory Theatre of
Manipur, 2006. Photo: Jack Vartoogian

Bottom: Anne Teresa De Keersmaeker
and Tale Dolven in *Fase, four movements
to the music of Steve Reich*, included
in *Steve Reich @ 70*, Anne Teresa
De Keersmaeker / Rosas / Steve Reich,
2006. Photo: Stephanie Berger

Opposite: Sekou Sundiata in his
the 51st (dream) state, 2006.
Photo: Stephanie Berger

Dana Caspersen in *Kammer / Kammer*,
William Forsythe / The Forsythe Company,
2006. Photo: Julieta Cervantes

Top: Ingela Bohlin in *Hercules*, William Christie/Les Arts Florissants. 2006. Photo: Jack Vartoogian

Bottom: Christopher Schaldenbrand in *Don Juan in Prague*, Prague National Theatre, 2006. Photo: Jack Vartoogian

Left: Lynn Redgrave in *The Importance of Being Earnest*, Theatre Royal Bath / Peter Hall Company, 2006.
Photo: Richard Termine

Right: Chou Chang-ning in *Wild Cursive*, Cloud Gate Dance Theatre of Taiwan, 2007.
Photo: Jack Vartoogian

Left: Ian McKellen in *King Lear*,
Royal Shakespeare Company, 2007.
Photo: Stephanie Berger

Right: Daniel Bernard Roumain in
his *Une Loss Plus*, 2007.
Photo: Stephanie Berger

Hotel Cassiopeia, Charles Mee/
SITI Company, 2007.
Photo: Richard Termine

Kronos Quartet: More Than Four,
2007. Photo: Julieta Cervantes

Opposite: Paul Simon in *Under African
Skies*, included in *Love in Hard Times:
The Music of Paul Simon*, 2008.
Photo: Jack Vartoogian

Above: Winston Ntshona in *Sizwe Banzi
Is Dead*, Athol Fugard, John Kani, and
Winston Ntshona / Baxter Theatre Centre,
2008. Photo: Richard Termine

Above: *Misuse liable to prosecution*,
John Jasperse Company, 2007.
Photo: Julieta Cervantes

Opposite: *The Gate*, Tan Dun/
Brooklyn Philharmonic, 2007.
Photo: Stephanie Berger

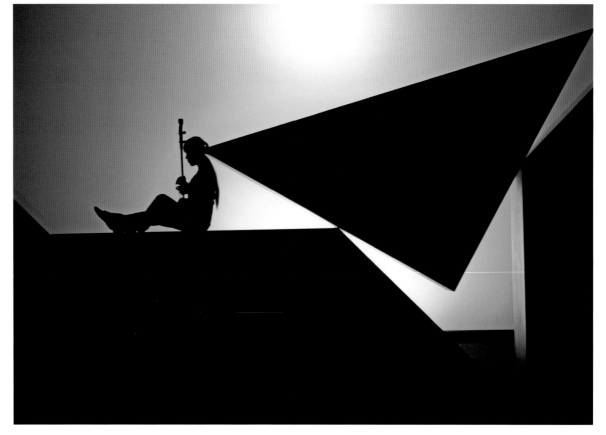

Top: Erick Montes, Peter Chamberlin,
and Tracy Ann Johnson in
A Quarreling Pair, Bill T. Jones/
Arnie Zane Dance Company, 2008.
Photo: Stephanie Berger

Bottom: *Les sept planches de la ruse,*
Aurélien Bory/Compagnie 111 and
Scènes de la Terre, 2008. Photo:
Richard Termine

Top: Moya Michael (featured) in
Eight Lines, included in *Steve Reich
Evening*, Anne Teresa De Keersmaeker/
Rosas/Steve Reich/Ictus, 2008.
Photo: Jack Vartoogian

Bottom: *Continuous City*,
The Builders Association, 2008.
Photo: Richard Termine

Left: Hadewych Minis and Oscar van
Rompay in *Opening Night*, Toneelgroep
Amsterdam/NTGent, 2008.
Photo: Richard Termine

Middle: Elsie de Brauw (featured)
in *Opening Night*, Ioneelgroep
Amsterdam/NTGent, 2008.
Photo: Richard Termine

Right: Chris Nietvelt and Elsie de
Brauw in *Opening Night*, Toneelgroep
Amsterdam/NTGent, 2008.
Photo: Richard Jermine

Opposite: *Max*, Ohad Naharin/
Batsheva Dance Company, 2009.
Photo: Julieta Cervantes

Top: Zach Condon of Beirut,
Sounds Like Brooklyn Music Festival,
2009. Photo: Rahav Segev

Bottom: *Nearly Ninety*, Merce
Cunningham Dance Company, 2009.
Photo: Stephanie Berger

Top: Meredith Monk (featured) in
Songs of Ascension, Meredith Monk
and Ann Hamilton, 2009.
Photo: Stephanie Berger

Middle: Isabelle Huppert in *Quartett*,
Robert Wilson / Michael Galasso, 2009.
Photo: Stephanie Berger

Bottom: Juliette Binoche and
Akram Khan in their *In-I*, 2009.
Photo: Jack Vartoogian

Opposite: Anna Chancellor in *Creditors*,
August Strindberg / Alan Rickman /
Donmar Warehouse, 2010.
Photo: Hugo Glendinning

Opposite: *Gezeiten*, Sasha Waltz &
Guests, 2010. Photo: Richard Termine

Top: Alan Rickman, Lindsay Duncan,
and Fiona Shaw in *John Gabriel
Borkman*, Henrik Ibsen/
Frank McGuinness/Abbey Theatre,
2011. Photo: Richard Termine

Bottom: Derek Jacobi in *King Lear*,
Michael Grandage/Donmar Warehouse,
2011. Photo: Johan Persson

James Thiérrée in his *Raoul*,
La Compagnie du Hanneton, 2010.
Photo: Richard Haughton

". . . if your goal is always grounded in mission and bringing great work to the audience and having an institution as a forum for ideas, a place where people can learn, where they can connect, where they can feel they are in the presence of art and culture and that it's a good place to be, then you can do many great things."

Geoffrey Rush in *The Diary of a Madman*, Nikolai Gogol / Belvoir, 2011.
Photo: Stephanie Berger

1823   Augustus Graham and a group of prominent citizens establish an Apprentices' Library in the village of Brooklyn.

1843   The Apprentices' Library renews its charter, changing its name to the Brooklyn Institute and vowing to continue its policy of providing education for adults.

1858   The Philharmonic Society of Brooklyn proposes building a cultural center for all of Brooklyn; the leaders of Brooklyn society and business assemble at the Polytechnic Institute and plan for an "academy" of music.

1859   The Brooklyn Academy of Music is incorporated "for the purpose of encouraging and cultivating a taste for music, literature and the arts."

1861   Designed by Leopold Eidlitz, the first Academy of Music on Montague Street in Brooklyn Heights is inaugurated on January 15 with an elaborate program including Mozart, Donizetti, Verdi, and Friedrich von Flotow; Mercadante's *Il Giuramento*, the Academy's first opera performance, appears one week later with the First Lady, Mary Todd Lincoln, in attendance.

1862   Immense public gathering endorses President Abraham Lincoln's emancipation policy.

1863   John Wilkes Booth performs in Shakespeare's *Richard III* and Charles Selby's *The Marble Heart*.

1864   During the Civil War, the Brooklyn and Long Island Sanitary Fair is held to raise money for the U.S. Sanitary Commission, which aided sick and wounded Union soldiers.

STAGE. **Memorial Service** Commemorative of the late **GEN'L ULYSSES S. GRANT,** —AT THE— Brooklyn Academy of Music, —ON— **Tuesday Evening, Sept. 29th, 1885,** At Eight o'clock.	**1864** Prominent Brooklyn preacher Henry Ward Beecher speaks out against slavery. **1880** D'Oyly Carte Opera Company presents Gilbert & Sullivan's *The Pirates of Penzance*. **1883** Celebration for the opening of the Brooklyn Bridge on May 24 with President Chester A. Arthur and Grover Cleveland, then governor of New York, culminates with a reception at the Academy of Music. **1884** Mark Twain and George W. Cable entertain with readings and storytelling.

1885   **Memorial services held for former president Ulysses S. Grant.**

1887   The recently established Boston Symphony Orchestra, under the auspices of the Philharmonic Society of Brooklyn, begins an annual residency that will continue for 75 years.

1890   The Brooklyn Institute is reincorporated as the Brooklyn Institute of Arts and Sciences.

1891   **Edwin Booth gives his last public appearance on April 4 in the title role of Shakespeare's *Hamlet*.**

       Booker T. Washington delivers a speech on full emancipation.

WELCOME MY FAIR GUESTS! ONCE MORE I SHOWER A WELCOME ON YOU! *Henry VIII.*

1896   Eleonora Duse and her company appear in *Camille*.

1903   The first Academy of Music burns to the ground on the morning of November 30.

1904   Martin W. Littleton, Brooklyn borough president, names a Citizens' Committee of 100 with the purpose to build a new Academy of Music.

1904   From 1904 to 1908, Academy of Music concerts, recitals, and lectures take place in substitute Brooklyn locations.

1905   The site for the new Academy is selected on Lafayette Avenue in Fort Greene; Henry B. Herts and Hugh Tallant are named as architects.

1908   The Academy of Music opens in its new home with a song recital by Madame Ernestine Schumann-Heink and an inaugural gala featuring the Metropolitan Opera with Geraldine Farrar and Enrico Caruso in Gounod's *Faust*.

       Isadora Duncan dances three movements from Beethoven's Symphony No. 7 with Walter Damrosch conducting the New York Symphony Orchestra.

1909   Gustav Mahler conducts the Philharmonic Society of New York.

1910   Arturo Toscanini conducts the Metropolitan Opera Company in *Aida* with Emmy Destinn.

       Anna Pavlova makes her Academy debut with dance partner Mikhail Mordkin.

1911   Jacob Riis lectures on "America's Most Useful Citizen."

       Ruth St. Denis dances with her all-female company.

1913   Helen Keller and Anne Sullivan discuss their work together in "The Heart and the Hand."

1915 Former president William Howard Taft speaks on "Our World Relationships."

1917 Sarah Bernhardt gives six performances in three days at the age of 73, all despite an amputated leg.

1919 Sergei Rachmaninoff gives his first recital at the Academy.

1920 Caruso falls ill when he begins to sing in *L'Elisir d'Amore* on December 20.

William Butler Yeats delivers an address on "A Theatre of the People."

1931 Paul Robeson gives a song recital.

1933 Martha Graham performs with her company.

1935 Ted Shawn and His Men Dancers explore shamanistic dance.

1936 The Brooklyn Institute of Arts and Sciences merges with the Brooklyn Academy of Music.

1938 Marian Anderson sings at the Academy.

1939 Thomas Mann, having fled Germany, speaks on "Democracy."

1940 President Franklin D. Roosevelt appears to packed crowds, with 2,200 seated in the Opera House, 700 jamming the stage, and another 6,000 outside in the street.

1941 The Brooklyn Symphony Orchestra has its inaugural concert, but despite illustrious conductors, such as Sir Thomas Beecham, it does not survive the war.

1948 Pearl Primus and Company dances her experiences of Africa.

1952 Robert E. Blum, president of the Brooklyn Institute of Arts and Sciences, announces the plan to save the Academy of Music by the conveyance of the building to the city of New York at a nominal rent of $1 per year for a term of 100 years.

Physical deterioration and fundraising challenges necessitate the removal of the cornice at 30 Lafayette Avenue.

Theater for Dance combines the talents of Merce Cunningham, Jean Erdman, Erick Hawkins, and Donald McKayle.

1954 Agnes de Mille Dance Theatre performs.

1955 The Brooklyn Philharmonia debuts with Siegfried Landau conducting.

1956 Pearl Lang and Company performs.

1957 Jazz concert series features musicians such as Duke Ellington, Benny Goodman, Louis Armstrong, and Count Basie.

1958 The Brooklyn Opera Company brings repertory opera and local singers to the Opera House.

1960 The Academy begins performing arts programming for young people.

1962 Rudolf Nureyev makes his American debut with the Chicago Opera Ballet shortly after defecting from the Soviet Union.

1964 Paul Taylor Dance Company performs.

1967 Harvey Lichtenstein is appointed president of the Academy; "Overnight," says the *New Yorker*, "the somnolent Academy became the country's leading dance center."

Sarah Caldwell's American National Opera Company opens with *Lulu*, *Falstaff*, and *Tosca*.

1968 Merce Cunningham Dance Company performs its first extended New York season.

The Living Theatre, under the direction of Julian Beck and Judith Malina, returns from exile in Europe to perform *Mysteries and Smaller Pieces*, *Antigone*, *Paradise Now*, and *Frankenstein* in repertory.

The Chelsea Theater Center of Robert Kalfin and Michael David opens its first Brooklyn season.

American Ballet Theatre performs with guest artists Carla Fracci and Erik Bruhn.

Alvin Ailey American Dance Theater performs.

1969 Twyla Tharp performs *Group Activities*, which places the audience onstage with the dancers.

The Polish Laboratory Theatre, directed by Jerzy Grotowski, performs *The Constant Prince*, *Acropolis*, and *Apocalypsis Cum Figuris*; produced under the auspices of the Academy, off-site performances are held at the Washington Square Methodist Church in Manhattan.

Robert Wilson makes his Academy debut with *The Life and Times of Sigmund Freud*.

1971 The St. Felix Street Corporation is created and the Academy of Music declares its independence from the Brooklyn Institute of Arts and Sciences.

The Royal Shakespeare Company makes its Academy debut with *A Midsummer Night's Dream*, directed by Peter Brook.

The first Afro-Asian Festival includes performances from Cambodia, Senegal, Morocco, Iran, India, and Sierra Leone.

Steve Reich and Musicians perform.

Lukas Foss follows Siegfried Landau as conductor of the Brooklyn Philharmonia.

1973 The acronym BAM is introduced in place of the Brooklyn Academy of Music.

BAM's newly renovated ballroom is formally dedicated as the Lepercq Space, named after Paul Lepercq, chairman of the board.

The Chelsea Theater Center revives Leonard Bernstein's *Candide* in a production directed by Hal Prince that following its BAM run moves to Broadway.

1974 BAM presents a four-month British Theater Season with productions from the Royal Shakespeare Company, the Actors Company, and the Young Vic.

The Tashi Quartet inaugurates the Chamber Music Series, produced by Scott Nickrenz.

1977 The BAM Theater Company presents its first production, Langdon Mitchell's *The New York Idea*, featuring Rene Auberjonois, Blythe Danner, Denholm Elliott, Margaret Hamilton, and Rosemary Harris.

1977 A month before the fall season opens, a 30-inch city water main under Ashland Place bursts, causing severe flooding; legendary actress Helen Hayes heads an emergency campaign to raise funds for the "big mop-up."

BAM presents the inaugural DanceAfrica, the country's largest celebration of African American dance, created by Chuck Davis.

1978 The BAM Theater Company performs Samuel Beckett's *Waiting for Godot* with Michael Egan, Milo O'Shea, Austin Pendleton, and Sam Waterston, its final production under the direction of Frank Dunlop.

Four members of the Chelsea Theater Center remain at BAM and form the Dodger Theater, launching their season with Barrie Keeffe's *Gimme Shelter*, directed by Des McAnuff.

1979 The Comédie-Française performs Molière's *The Misanthrope* and Feydeau's *A Flea in Her Ear.*

Karen Brooks Hopkins joins the BAM staff as development officer in the planning department.

1980 The BAM Theater Company is reestablished with an ambitious repertory season under the direction of Royal Shakespeare Company veteran David Jones.

1981 The Next Wave series debuts with the Trisha Brown, Laura Dean, and Lucinda Childs dance companies and Philip Glass's opera *Satyagraha.*

1982 The Brooklyn Philharmonia is renamed the Brooklyn Philharmonic.

1983 Laurie Anderson makes her BAM debut with *United States: Parts I–IV* in the second season of the Next Wave series.

The Next Wave series is expanded as the Next Wave Festival; Joseph V. Melillo joins BAM as producing director of the festival.

The Next Wave Festival is launched with *The Photographer / Far from the Truth*, a Philip Glass, Robert Coe, JoAnne Akalaitis, David Gordon, Jennifer Tipton, and Santo Loquasto collaboration.

Above: The flooded Carey Playhouse (now the BAM Rose Cinemas), 1977. Photo courtesy of BAM Hamm Archives Center. Opposite: Next Wave poster by Roy Lichtenstein, 1983

1983   BAMart begins with the inaugural season of the Next Wave Festival; visual artist Roy Lichtenstein is commissioned to create an image for the festival poster and journal.

The Gospel at Colonus, Lee Breuer and Bob Telson's synthesis of Sophocles and soul, opens at BAM and later wins an OBIE Award.

1984   Pina Bausch's Tanztheater Wuppertal makes its BAM debut with a program comprised of *The Rite of Spring*, *1980*, *Café Müller*, and *Bluebeard*.

Bill T. Jones/Arnie Zane & Company performs *Secret Pastures*, an interdisciplinary work created with composer Peter Gordon, visual artist Keith Haring, and fashion designer Willi Smith.

BAM revives Philip Glass and Robert Wilson's *Einstein on the Beach* during the second season of the Next Wave Festival.

1985   Tanztheater Wuppertal Pina Bausch returns in a Next Wave engagement with a program that includes *Arien*, *Kontakthof*, and *The Seven Deadly Sins*.

1986   Central Ballet of China performs in its first American tour.

Anne Teresa De Keersmaeker makes her BAM debut with *Rosas Danst Rosas*.

Kronos Quartet makes its first BAM appearance as part of the Next Wave.

Robert Wilson's *the CIVIL warS: a tree is best measured when it is down: Act V—the Rome Section*, with music by Philip Glass, has its American premiere.

1987   BAM produces its first Martin Luther King Jr. tribute in collaboration with the office of the Brooklyn borough president.

Twyla Tharp Dance presents a monthlong program of performances.

The BAM Majestic Theater is inaugurated with the English-language version of Peter Brook's *The Mahabharata*, which runs nine hours in length.

John Adams, Alice Goodman, Peter Sellars, and Mark Morris collaborate on *Nixon in China*, which makes its New York debut in a BAM co-commission with the Houston Grand Opera and the John F. Kennedy Center for the Performing Arts.

1988   Harvey Lichtenstein accepts a special Tony Award presented to BAM.

Ingmar Bergman, with the Royal Dramatic Theatre of Sweden, makes his American stage debut with a production of Shakespeare's *Hamlet*; performances are in Swedish with no translation.

Eiko & Koma perform *Thirst*, *Tree*.

1989   The Welsh National Opera makes its American debut with Peter Stein's production of *Falstaff*, inaugurating BAM Opera; Princess Diana—Her Royal Highness the Princess of Wales—attends the opening night performance and gala reception.

651 (later 651 ARTS), taking its name from the Fulton Street address of the BAM Majestic Theater, is launched to present events reflecting the cultural diversity of Brooklyn while creating a broader market for its artists.

The American premiere of Jean-Baptiste Lully's *Atys*, in association with the Théâtre National de l'Opéra de Paris, features the BAM debut of William Christie and Les Arts Florissants.

The Next Wave celebrates and produces the 10th anniversary of New Music America, featuring concerts by more than 100 composers at 23 venues throughout New York City.

1990   BAM's Performing Arts Program for Young People begins its 30th season of dance, music, and theater for New York City's school children.

The Festival of Indonesia features dance, shadow puppetry, and gamelans.

Mark Morris Dance Group performs *L'Allegro, il Penseroso ed il Moderato*.

NEXT WAVE FESTIVAL

4 October–4 December 1983

BROOKLYN ACADEMY OF MUSIC

1990 Robert Lepage makes his BAM debut with *Polygraph*, a theatrical adaptation of a true crime and its aftermath told through a series of interconnected stories created with Marie Brassard.

1991 The Royal Dramatic Theatre of Sweden returns with three Bergman productions: *Miss Julie*, *Long Day's Journey into Night*, and *A Doll's House*; performers include Pernilla August, Bibi Andersson, Erland Josephson, Lena Olin, and Peter Stormare.

BAM Opera presents the American premiere of *The Death of Klinghoffer*, a second collaboration by John Adams, Alice Goodman, Peter Sellars, and Mark Morris.

The Brooklyn Philharmonic Orchestra opens its season with Dennis Russell Davies as its principal conductor; Lukas Foss is named conductor laureate.

1992 Ian McKellen performs in Shakespeare's *Richard III* with the Royal National Theatre of Great Britain.

BAM presents the New York debut of Ariane Mnouchkine with *Les Atrides* at the Park Slope Armory in Brooklyn.

American debut of *The Hard Nut*, the Mark Morris version of *The Nutcracker*.

1992 At a celebratory event marking Harvey Lichtenstein's 25th season, the Campaign for BAM is introduced with $10.5 million pledged toward the institution's first endowment fund; Richard B. Fisher serves as the fund's inaugural chair.

1993 Philip Glass's presentation of *Orphée* begins a trilogy of music-theater pieces exploring Jean Cocteau's work.

American premiere of *The Black Rider* from Robert Wilson, Tom Waits, and William S. Burroughs.

1994 Next Wave opens with *Radical Graham*, a retrospective look at the work of Martha Graham on the 100th anniversary of her birth.

The Nederlands Dans Theater presents a program with three separate companies.

The Maly Drama Theatre of St. Petersburg makes its BAM debut with *Gaudeamus*.

Tanztheater Wuppertal Pina Bausch performs *Two Cigarettes in the Dark*.

The renamed Bill. T. Jones / Arnie Zane Dance Company performs *Still/Here*, which deals with terminal illness, and sets off a vigorous international debate about so-called victim art.

1995 The Kirov Opera performs *The Legend of the Invisible City of Kitezh*, featuring the BAM debut of Valery Gergiev.

The Royal Dramatic Theatre of Sweden returns as part of a citywide Ingmar Bergman Festival with more than 350 events; Karen Brooks Hopkins acts as executive producer.

1996 Robert Spano joins the Brooklyn Philharmonic as music director.

BAM pitches its tent in Battery Park City and presents the French equestrian theater troupe Zingaro—with its 26-horse ensemble—in *Chimère*.

Trisha Brown dances in *Post Modern and Beyond*, a retrospective of her career.

Sankai Juku makes its BAM debut with *Yuragi: In a Space of Perpetual Motion*.

Robert Lepage returns to BAM with *The Seven Streams of the River Ota*.

BAM presents *The Harlem Nutcracker*, with music by Tchaikovsky as arranged by Duke Ellington and Billy Strayhorn, with David Berger, and choreography by Donald Byrd.

1997   BAMcafé opens in the Lepercq Space.

DanceAfrica celebrates its 20th anniversary and launches the DanceAfrica Education Program in partnership with the Bedford Stuyvesant Restoration Corporation.

Jonathan Miller directs Bach's *St. Matthew Passion*.

1998   BAM completes the conversion of the Carey Playhouse to the BAM Rose Cinemas, opening the country's first multiplex cinema in a performing arts center.

The Moscow Art Theater performs Chekhov's *The Three Sisters*.

The Royal Shakespeare Company in its first American residency presents five productions in repertory.

William Forsythe and Ballett Frankfurt present the American premiere of *EIDOS:TELOS*.

1999   The Almeida Theatre Company performs Racine's *Phédre* and *Britannicus* in repertory, featuring Diana Rigg.

Harvey Lichtenstein retires and is succeeded by Karen Brooks Hopkins as president and Joseph V. Melillo as executive producer.

The BAM Majestic Theater is renamed the BAM Harvey Theater in honor of Harvey Lichtenstein and in conjunction with an endowment gift from the Doris Duke Charitable Foundation.

Laurie Anderson opens the Next Wave with her performance of *Songs and Stories from Moby Dick*.

BAMcafé Live is launched in the Lepercq Space, programming live music and spoken word.

2000   Ralph Fiennes is featured in the Almeida Theatre Company productions of Shakespeare's *Richard II* and *Coriolanus*.

Ratan Thiyam's Chorus Repertory Theatre of Manipur performs *Uttar-Priyadarshi*.

2001   BAM presents two productions of *Hamlet* in the same season: one adapted and directed by Peter Brook, the other by the Royal National Theatre, directed by John Caird.

White Oak Dance Project performs in Past*Forward*, a program by pioneering Judson Church choreographers featuring Mikhail Baryshnikov.

Company B Belvoir performs *Cloudstreet* as part of Next Wave Down Under, a mini-festival of Australian performance including over 100 artists; all performances go forward despite the 9/11 attack on the World Trade Center.

Rosas performs *Drumming*, with music by Steve Reich and choreography by Anne Teresa De Keersmaeker.

2002   Restoration of BAM's facade at 30 Lafayette Avenue begins; *CandyBAM*, visual artist Vik Muniz's gingerbread house, wraps the building.

Israel's Batsheva Dance Company performs Ohad Naharin's *Naharin's Virus*.

BAM Opera presents all three Monteverdi operas with each production by a different ensemble: Les Arts Florissants and the Aix-en-Provence European Academy of Music, the Dutch National Opera and Les Talens Lyriques, and the Chicago Opera Theater.

Fiona Shaw plays the title role of Euripides' *Medea*, directed by Deborah Warner; following its BAM run, the Abbey Theatre production moves to Broadway.

2003 The Royal National Theatre/Market Theatre of Johannesburg production of *The Island*, originally directed by Athol Fugard, features John Kani and Winston Ntshona.

William Christie conducts Les Arts Florissants in the Paris National Opera production of Rameau's *Les Boréades*, directed by Robert Carsen.

Merce Cunningham Dance Company performs the world premiere of *Split Sides* to live music performed by Radiohead and Sigur Rós.

2004 Propeller's first appearance at BAM with an all-male production of *A Midsummer Night's Dream*, directed by Edward Hall.

Tony Kushner's *Homebody/Kabul*, featuring Maggie Gyllenhaal and Linda Emond, fills the Harvey Theater for three weeks.

Ralph Lemon performs *Come home Charley Patton*, the final part of his *Geography Trilogy*.

2005 BAM completes renovations on the facade of its 30 Lafayette Avenue building and names the facility in honor of philanthropist Peter Jay Sharp, recognizing a $20 million gift from the Peter Jay Sharp Foundation.

Eat, Drink & Be Literary begins its first season in partnership with the National Book Foundation in BAMcafé.

Vanessa Redgrave plays the title role in the Royal Shakespeare Company production of Euripides' *Hecuba*.

BAM president Karen Brooks Hopkins celebrates 25 years of service to the institution.

Isabelle Huppert performs in Sarah Kane's *4.48 Psychose*.

James Thiérrée, with La Compagnie du Hanneton, makes his BAM debut with *Bright Abyss*.

2006 BAM presents two radically different productions of *Hedda Gabler*: one by the Sydney Theatre Company with Cate Blanchett, directed by Robyn Nevin, and one by the Schaubühne am Lehniner Platz Berlin, directed by Thomas Ostermeier.

Robert Redford inaugurates Sundance Institute at BAM, a new partnership featuring cutting-edge independent films, readings, concerts, and talks.

BAM celebrates *Steve Reich @ 70*, which includes choreography by Anne Teresa De Keersmaeker and Akram Khan.

BAM presents *the 51st (dream) state*, a soul-searching investigation of post–9/11 America, created by poet Sekou Sundiata.

2007 Metropolitan Opera: Live in HD begins screening high-definition live satellite feeds of Met Opera performances in BAM Rose Cinemas with Gounod's *Roméo et Juliette*.

Visual artist William Kentridge directs his interpretation of Mozart's *The Magic Flute*.

DanceAfrica celebrates its 30th anniversary.

The Royal Shakespeare Company returns with Ian McKellen in Shakespeare's *King Lear* and Chekhov's *The Seagull*.

The 25th Next Wave Festival opens with *Wild Cursive*, choreographed by Lin Hwai-min and performed by Cloud Gate Dance Theatre of Taiwan.

The BAM Endowment reaches $72 million.

2008 BAM presents the National Theatre of Great Britain's production of Samuel Beckett's *Happy Days* with Fiona Shaw.

BAMkids Film Festival celebrates its 10th anniversary.

Patrick Stewart plays the title role of Shakespeare's *Macbeth* in a Chichester Festival Theatre production directed by Rupert Goold; following its BAM run, the production moves to Broadway.

Paul Simon performs in three BAM-produced concert engagements in a monthlong residency billed as *Love in Hard Times: The Music of Paul Simon*.

2008 Alvin Ailey American Dance Theater returns to BAM with programs of new and classic works celebrating its 50th anniversary.

2009 BAM launches the Bridge Project, a transatlantic partnership with the Old Vic Theatre and London's Neal Street Productions; the Bridge Project opens at BAM with productions of Chekhov's *The Cherry Orchard* and Shakespeare's *The Winter's Tale*, directed by Sam Mendes, before touring venues around the globe.

BAM celebrates Merce Cunningham's 90th birthday with *Nearly Ninety*, performed by the Merce Cuningham Dance Company.

BAM presents *Muslim Voices: Arts & Ideas* with the Asia Society, New York University's Center for Dialogues, and other supporting and media partners, highlighting the rich diversity of the Islamic world through performances and events throughout New York City, featuring artists like Youssou N'Dour and Sulayman Al-Bassam.

Cate Blanchett defines the role of Blanche DuBois in the Sydney Theatre Company's production of Tennessee Williams's *A Streetcar Named Desire*, directed by Liv Ullmann.

BAM celebrates executive producer Joseph V. Melillo's 25 years of service to artists and audiences.

2010 BAM breaks ground on the BAM Richard B. Fisher Building, named in his honor by his widow, Jeanne Donovan Fisher, with substantial support from New York City; the arts and community center is the first addition to the BAM campus since the Majestic Theater (now the BAM Harvey Theater).

The inaugural BAM Opera Festival explores the work and milieu of composer Henry Purcell in a program of operas, concerts, and other events selected by guest curator William Christie.

Alexei Ratmansky creates a new version of *The Nutcracker* for American Ballet Theatre's five-year seasonal residency at BAM.

DanceMotion USA, a program of the Bureau of Educational and Cultural Affairs of the U.S. Department of State produced by BAM, showcases contemporary American dance abroad; the first tours feature Evidence, ODC/Dance, and Urban Bush Women.

BAM begins development of the Hamm Archives Center in a new facility adjacent to the Harvey Theater, providing a permanent home for its archival collection.

2011 The Spring Season includes six U.S. premieres with performances by Lindsay Duncan, Derek Jacobi, Alan Rickman, Geoffrey Rush, and Fiona Shaw.

Alicia Alonso's Ballet Nacional de Cuba performs *La Magia de la Danza* as part of the citywide *¡Sí Cuba!* Festival.

BAM's 150th Anniversary celebration begins with the restaging of the land-mark production of Jean-Baptiste Lully's *Atys*, conducted by William Christie.

Top: BAM Peter Jay Sharp Building. Photo: Peter Mauss

Bottom, left: Architectural rendering of the BAM Richard B. Fisher Building
Courtesy of H3 Hardy Collaboration Architecture LLC

Bottom, right: BAM Harvey Theater. Photo: Elena Olivo

Opposite, top to bottom (interiors): BAM Harvey Theater, 2003.
Photo: Ned Witrogen; BAM Howard Gilman Opera House, 2010.
Photo: Elliott Kaufman; BAM Rose Cinemas, 1998. Photo: Toby Wales;
BAMcafé, 1998. Photo: Toby Wales

BAM Campus

Joan Acocella is the dance critic for the *New Yorker*. She is the author of the critical biography *Mark Morris*, among other books.

Jonah Bokaer is an international choreographer, media artist, and social entrepreneur. His work integrates choreography with digital media, resulting from cross-disciplinary collaborations with artists and architects. Bokaer has created four works with Robert Wilson, in addition to touring his own productions.

Peter Brook was born in London in 1925. He directed his first play in 1943 and since then has directed over 70 productions in London, Paris, and New York. His work with the Royal Shakespeare Company includes *Measure for Measure*, *King Lear*, *Marat/Sade*, and *A Midsummer Night's Dream* (BAM 1971). In 1970, he moved to Paris, where he founded the International Centre for Theatre Research, which in 1974 opened its permanent base in the Bouffes du Nord theater. His productions at BAM include *Conference of the Birds* (1973), *The Mahabharata* (1987), *The Cherry Orchard* (1988), *The Man Who* (1995), and *The Tragedy of Hamlet* (2001). He has also directed opera at Covent Garden, the Metropolitan Opera House, and for the Aix en Provence Festival. His films include *Moderato Cantabile*, *Lord of the Flies*, *Marat/Sade*, *King Lear,* and *Meetings with Remarkable Men*. Brook's autobiography, *Threads of Time*, was published in 1998 and joins other titles including *The Empty Space*, translated into more than 15 languages, *The Shifting Point*, *There Are No Secrets*, and *Evoking (and Forgetting) Shakespeare*.

William Christie, harpsichordist, conductor, musicologist, and teacher, is the inspiration behind one of the most exciting musical adventures of the last 30 years. His pioneering work has led to a renewed appreciation of 17th- and 18th-century French repertoire. Born in Buffalo, New York, Christie studied at Harvard and Yale universities and has lived in France since 1971. In 1979, he founded Les Arts Florissants. As director of this vocal and instrumental ensemble, Christie brings new interpretations of largely neglected or forgotten repertoire to fruition. Major public recognition came in 1987 with the production of *Atys* at the Opéra Comique in Paris. Christie has since collaborated with renowned theater and opera directors and has created a discography spanning more than 100 recordings. Since 2002, he has appeared regularly as a guest conductor with the Berlin Philharmonic. In November 2008, Christie was elected to the Académie des Beaux-Arts.

Nancy Dalva is the producer/writer of the Web series "Mondays with Merce" and a widely published critic. Her Web site at nancydalva.com has an archive of her work and her current musings as "the informal formalist." In the last two years of his life, Merce Cunningham sat for 19 filmed interviews with her.

Nathan Gelgud is an artist and writer. He lives in Brooklyn, New York.

Deborah Jowitt has written about dance for the *Village Voice* since 1967. Her books include *Dance Beat*, *The Dance in Mind*, *Time and the Dancing Image*, and *Jerome Robbins: His Life, His Theater, His Dance*. She teaches at New York University's Tisch School of the Arts.

British-born choreographer **Akram Khan** is celebrated internationally for the vitality he brings to cross-cultural, cross-disciplinary expression. His dance language is rooted in his classical Kathak and modern dance training and continually evolves to communicate ideas that are intelligent, courageous, and new. Khan performs his own solos and collaborative works with other artists and presents ensemble works through the Akram Khan Company.

Individual entries on **Richard Kostelanetz's** work in several domains appear in various editions of *A Reader's Guide to Twentieth-Century Writers*, *Merriam-Webster's Encyclopedia of Literature*, *Contemporary Poets*, *Contemporary Novelists*, *Webster's Dictionary of American Writers*, *HarperCollins Reader's Encyclopedia of American Literature*, *Baker's Biographical Dictionary of Musicians*, *Directory of American Scholars*, *Who's Who in American Art*, NNDB.com, Wikipedia.com, and Britannica.com, among other distinguished directories.

Jayme Koszyn is president and founder of Koszyn & Company, a fundraising, strategic planning, and development firm based in New York City. As a Princeton graduate and former Boston College/Boston University faculty member, Koszyn is extensively published on the topic of dramaturgy. She was BAM's first director for education and humanities.

Lin Hwai-min, choreographer and artistic director of Cloud Gate Dance Theatre of Taiwan, studied Chinese opera movement in his native Taiwan, modern dance in New York, and classical court dance in Japan and Korea. In 1973, Lin founded the first contemporary dance company in any Chinese-speaking region. He is heralded as "the most important choreographer in Asia" by *Berliner Morgenpost* and was made a Chevalier de l'Ordre des Arts et des Lettres. He is the recipient of a Lifetime Achievement Award from the International Movimentos Dance Prize. In 2005, he was celebrated by *Time* magazine as one of "Asia's Heroes."

Phillip Lopate is the author of a dozen books, including *Waterfront, Portrait of My Body*, *Notes on Sontag*, *Getting Personal*, and *Being with Children*. He is a professor at Columbia University and lives with his wife and daughter in Brooklyn. He has won Guggenheim, New York Public Library, and National Endowment for the Arts fellowships, and is a member of the American Academy of Arts and Sciences.

Charles Mee has written *Big Love* (BAM 2001), *True Love, First Love*, *bobrauschenbergamerica* (BAM 2003), *Hotel Cassiopeia* (BAM 2007), *Orestes 2.0*, *Trojan Women: A Love Story*, *Summertime*, and *Wintertime*, among other plays. Honored with a full season of his plays at the Signature Theatre in New York, he is the recipient of the gold medal for lifetime achievement in drama from the American Academy of Arts and Letters and of the Richard B. Fisher Award. He is also the author of a number of books of history, and the former editor in chief of Horizon, a magazine of history, art, literature, and the fine arts. His work is made possible by the support of Richard B. Fisher and Jeanne Donovan Fisher.

Sam Mendes began his theater career as assistant director at the Chichester Festival Theatre and was the first artistic director of the Minerva in 1989. In 1992, he founded the Donmar Warehouse in London, where he was the artistic director until 2002, directing award-winning productions of *Assassins*, *The Glass Menagerie*, and *Company*, as well as *Uncle Vanya* and *Twelfth Night*, both at BAM in 2003. Other stage productions include *The Plough and the Stars*, *London Assurance*, and *Oliver!* in the West End; *Troilus and Cressida*, *The Tempest*, *Richard III*, and *Othello* for the Royal Shakespeare Company; and *The Blue Room*, *Gypsy*, *The Vertical Hour*, and *Cabaret* on Broadway. His film credits include *American Beauty* (Academy Award), *Road to Perdition*, *Jarhead*, *Revolutionary Road*, and *Away We Go*. Mendes has been the recipient of the Directors Guild of Great Britain Lifetime Achievement Award and the Olivier Award for outstanding achievement in the theater, and in 2000 was made a Commander of the Order of the British Empire. In 2009, he launched the initial season of the Bridge Project, a transatlantic collaboration between Neal Street Productions, BAM, and London's Old Vic.

Meredith Monk is a composer, singer, director/choreographer, and creator of new opera, music-theater, films, and installations. During a career spanning more than 45 years, she has been acclaimed by audiences and critics as a major creative force in the performing arts. Monk has received many distinguished awards including the prestigious MacArthur "Genius" Award in 1995. In 2006, she was inducted into the American Academy of Arts and Sciences and named a U.S. Artists Fellow. Her music has been performed by numerous soloists and groups, including the Chorus of the San Francisco Symphony, Musica Sacra, the Pacific Mozart Ensemble, Double Edge, Björk, and the Bang on a Can All-Stars, among others.

Roger Oliver created and directed humanities programs for the BAM Theater Company and the Next Wave Festival and coordinated humanities activities for the 1995 citywide Ingmar Bergman Festival, for which he edited the book *Ingmar Bergman: An Artist's Journey*. He is a professor at the Juilliard School and New York University.

John Rockwell is a freelance writer. A longtime classical music, rock music, and dance critic for the *New York Times*, as well as an arts editor and foreign cultural correspondent, he has been actively involved in the "downtown" New York arts scene for nearly 40 years. He was the founding director of the Lincoln Center Festival and has published four books. He also participated in an extensive series of recorded conversations with Harvey Lichtenstein about his tenure at BAM for the Harvey Lichtenstein Oral History Project for the BAM Hamm Archives Center.

Gordon Rogoff is a professor of dramaturgy and dramatic criticism at the Yale School of Drama. His books include *Theatre Is Not Safe* and *Vanishing Acts*; his work-in-progress is *Sunset Over Ice: Late Works of Verdi, Ibsen, Richard Strauss, Ingmar Bergman, and Matisse*. In 1986, he received the George Jean Nathan Award and in 1991 the Morton Dauwen Zabel Award for Criticism by the American Academy of Arts and Letters.

Edward Rothstein is cultural critic at large for the *New York Times*, where he has also served as chief music critic. He is the author of *Emblems of Mind: The Inner Life of Music and Mathematics* and coauthor of *Visions of Utopia*.

Don Shewey is a journalist and critic in New York City who maintains a blog called AnotherEyeOpens.com. His articles for the *New York Times*, *Esquire*, *Rolling Stone*, and other publications are archived at donshewey.com, and he has published three books about theater.

Yoko Shioya has been responsible for the year-round performing arts program of the Japan Society in New York City since 2003. She has increased the number of North American tours of Japanese artists and expanded commission opportunities for American artists on Japan-related subjects. A published author, she holds BA degrees in musicology and dance history from Tokyo National University of Fine Arts and Music.

Tina Silverman is a writer and visual artist. She had her own graphic design studio in Boston before moving to Israel, where she was the art director and a contributing writer to the *Jerusalem Report Magazine* for 15 years. Presently working on a collection of short stories, she is the art director for Dance Place in Washington, DC.

Rachel Straus is the dance critic for MusicalAmerica.com, a history columnist at *Dance Teacher* magazine, and a scholar-in-residence at Jacob's Pillow Dance Festival. She has lectured at London's Roehampton University and the Juilliard School. She holds master's degrees from Purchase College's Conservatory of Dance and Columbia University's School of Journalism.

Roslyn Sulcas is writing a book about William Forsythe's work. She is a dance critic at the *New York Times*.

Charmaine Patricia Warren, PhD, is a faculty member at Alvin Ailey/Fordham University. She teaches dance history, theory, and movement nationally and internationally. After performing with major New York dance companies, she joined david rousseve/REALITY. She writes for *Dance Magazine*, the *Amsterdam News*, and others; sits on various dance committees; and is a freelance consultant.

Robert Wilson is among the world's foremost theater and visual artists. His works for the stage integrate a wide variety of artistic media, including dance, movement, lighting, sculpture, music, and text. Together with composer Philip Glass, he created the seminal opera *Einstein on the Beach* (BAM 1984). With productions such as *The Life and Times of Sigmund Freud* (BAM 1969), *Deafman Glance* (BAM 1971), *KA MOUNTAIN AND GUARDenia TERRACE*, the *CIVIL warS* (BAM 1986), *Death, Destruction and Detroit*, and *A Letter for Queen Victoria*, he redefined and expanded theater. Wilson's collaborators include diverse writers and musicians such as Susan Sontag, Lou Reed, Heiner Müller, Jessye Norman, David Byrne, Tom Waits, and Rufus Wainwright. Wilson has also left his imprint on masterworks such as *The Magic Flute*, Wagner's *Ring* cycle, *The Threepenny Opera*, Shakespeare's *Sonnets*, and *Krapp's Last Tape*. The recipient of numerous international awards, Wilson was elected to the American Academy of Arts and Letters in 2000, and in 2002 was made a Commandeur de l'Ordre des Arts et des Lettres.

John Yohalem, editor of *Enchanté: The Journal for the Urbane Pagan*, is a native and connoisseur of New York and an alumnus of the Metropolitan Opera Archives. He has attended performances of more than 500 different operas, some of the best of them at BAM.

Susan Yung has overseen BAM's publications for more than a decade, in addition to writing freelance about dance, visual art, and performance.

Index

Above: Merce Cunningham,
Joseph V. Melillo, and Mark Morris,
1999. Photo courtesy of BAM
Hamm Archives Center

Page numbers in italics
refer to illustrations.

Karen Brooks Hopkins, Cate
Blanchett, and Joseph V. Melillo
(featured), 2006. Photo courtesy
of BAM Hamm Archives Center

Hillary Rodham Clinton and Karen Brooks Hopkins, 2000. Photo courtesy of the BAM Hamm Archives Center

Credits

Clara Cornelius, Designer
Susan Yung, Associate Editor
Violaine Huisman, Managing Editor
Sharon Lehner, Archivist

BAM Hamm Archives Center:

Karyn Anonia
Jan Carr
Kate Ehrenberg
Louie Fleck
Anita Goss
June Reich

Copyright © 2011 BAM: The Brooklyn Academy of Music

Manufacturing by South China Printing Co. Ltd

All rights reserved
Printed in China
First Edition

Library of Congress Cataloging-in-Publication Data
BAM : the complete works / edited by Steven Serafin. —1st ed.
    p. cm.
ISBN 978-1-59372-046-9
1. Brooklyn Academy of Music. 2. Centers for the performing arts—New York (State)—New York.
3. Performing arts—New York (State)—New York. I. Serafin, Steven. II. Title: Brooklyn Academy of Music.

PN1588.N5B35 2011
711'.558--dc22

2011008502

Credits and copyright notices for the photographs reproduced in this book can be found on page 380,
which constitutes a continuation of this page.

The Quantuck Lane Press
New York
www.quantucklanepress.com

Distributed by: W.W. Norton & Company, 500 Fifth Avenue, New York, NY 10110
www.wwnorton.com
W.W. Norton & Company Ltd., Castle House, 75/76 Wells Street, London, WIT 3QT

1 2 3 4 5 6 7 8 9 0

Endpapers, front: Merce Cunningham and John Cage in *How to Pass, Kick, Fall and Run*, Merce Cunningham Dance Company, 1970.
Photo: James Klosty; back: *A Dream Play*, Robert Wilson / Stockholm's Stadsteater, 2000. Photo: Lesley Leslie-Spinks